Business Ethics from Antiquity to the 19th Century

David George Surdam

Business Ethics from Antiquity to the 19th Century

An Economist's View

Stan:
thanks for
reviewing the material
on labor and slavery.
as always, I appreciate
your help and encouragement.
Dave Surdam

palgrave
macmillan

David George Surdam
Department of Economics
University of Northern Iowa
Cedar Falls, IA, USA

ISBN 978-3-030-37164-7 ISBN 978-3-030-37165-4 (eBook)
https://doi.org/10.1007/978-3-030-37165-4

This Palgrave Macmillan imprint is published by the registered company Springer Nature Switzerland AG.
The registered company address is: Gewerbestrasse 11, 6330 Cham, Switzerland

Acknowledgments

This book had its origins in conversations with my late dissertation advisor, Nobel Prize winner in Economics Robert W. Fogel. For years after I graduated from the University of Chicago, Bob (as he insisted his graduated students call him) would graciously take time from a busy schedule to discuss my latest work. He encouraged me to investigate topics in business ethics, and I attended his class on the subject at the Graduate School of Business at Chicago. He emphasized the historical phenomenon of changing views of what was ethical in business.

I later taught courses in business ethics at Loyola University of Chicago and the Graduate School of Business, University of Chicago. Many of the ideas for this book emanated from these courses.

As with most authors, many people helped me along the way. The following paragraphs are among the most pleasurable ones for me to write.

I thank graduate assistants Caroline Mutonyi, Madiha Ahsan, and Shanaya Alvares at the University of Northern Iowa, for processing thousands of the note cards and looking up articles and books. Undergraduate Kobe Diers provided help with a particularly tedious task (deleting 2102 superscripts representing endnotes). Matt Goodwin helped compile the citations and the bibliography.

There are plenty of friends in academia to thank. David Galenson, sole surviving member of my dissertation committee, has continued to support and encourage my endeavors; Louis Cain encouraged me to teach a course on the ethics of economic activities at Loyola University of Chicago. Years ago, the late Max Hartwell sparked an interest in Great Britain's industrial transformation. He also gave a struggling graduate student much-needed and appreciated encouragement.

Tim Fuerst, formerly of Notre Dame University and a dear friend and colleague, read the early chapters and provided sagacious comments, even as he battled cancer. He is sorely missed. Walter Grinder suggested Jane Jacobs' and Peter Brown's books; these were valuable additions to my reading list. Kenneth Atkinson of the University of Northern Iowa read chapters on Ancient Near East, Greeks, Romans, and Jewish and Christian Attitudes. James Kegel reviewed chapters on Ancient Near East and Jewish/Christian Attitudes. Richard Lindholm suggested valuable books on the medieval era while reading the chapters on medieval and early modern Europe, as well as the birth of a consumer society chapter. Stanley Engerman reviewed some of the material in the chapters on labor and slavery.

I thank the two anonymous reviewers for their useful comments, especially the reviewer who urged me to include descriptions of basic approaches to business ethics.

Librarians at the University of Chicago, Northwestern University, Notre Dame University, Chicago Public Library, the University of Oregon, and the University of Northern Iowa helped me locate manuscripts. The staff at the University of Northern Iowa inter-library loan department were unstinting in obtaining books from around the country.

I also thank Farzad Moussavi and Leslie Wilson, former and current Dean, respectively, of the College of Business Administration of the University of Northern Iowa, who offered encouragement and support—both moral and financial (for research trips). Fred Abraham, Head of the Economics Department at the University of Northern Iowa, has long been a supporter of my work.

I appreciate Elizabeth Graber, Commissioning Editor for Palgrave Macmillan, for her interest in my work. Her encouragement and quick responses made my experiences with Palgrave Macmillan pleasant and enjoyable. Editorial Assistant Sophia Siegler and Project Coordinator Tikoji Rao were enthusiastic and gracious throughout the preparation of the manuscript for publication. Anish Divya thoroughly copy edited the manuscript and corrected several errors.

Contents

CHAPTER 1

You Can't Live (Well) Without Business Ethics

You can't live (well) without business ethics. Business ethics matter greatly and affect our lives on a daily basis. Without reasonably high business ethics throughout the marketplace, people throughout the world would not enjoy high standards of material well-being. The necessity for businesspeople and consumers to interact in ethical fashion has drawn the attention of a wide variety of thinkers, including Athenian Greek philosophers, Islamic and medieval theologians, secular scholars, businesspeople, consumers, and legislators. What people considered ethical differed across times and societies. The evolution and development of business ethics across societies and through the ages are fascinating topics.

Some people have told me that a book on business ethics throughout history would be the "world's shortest book." The assumption underlying the witticisms is that business ethics are completely lacking. One need not make much effort to find examples of unethical behavior by businesspeople, as major ethical lapses attract much attention. The nightly news frequently publicizes the really spectacular lapses, such as Bernard Madoff's Ponzi scheme or the sub-prime housing loan debacle.

The nightly news is not the only forum highlighting lapses in business ethics. With the fall of the Soviet Empire, Hollywood has had to cast for new stock villains, and businesspeople fill the niche. Motion pictures and television shows depict businesspeople as being beyond rapacity and duplicity, such as that 1980s' icon, J.R. Ewing, of *Dallas.* Apparently, J.R.'s chief negotiating tactic was to bellow, "I'll pay you any amount of

D. G. Surdam, *Business Ethics from Antiquity to the 19th Century*,
https://doi.org/10.1007/978-3-030-37165-4_1

money," for something he wanted; he must have failed "Negotiating 101." Children's cartoons and movies rely upon businesspeople for stock villains (right up there with evil scientists), especially businesspeople engaged in despoiling the environment.[1]

In the world of literature, the lack of ethics in business is a common plot device. Mario Puzo's epigraph to his *The Godfather* reads: "Behind every great fortune there is a crime."[2] The Corleone family ran a business of sorts, but few would laud or emulate their tactics. Arthur Miller's *Death of a Salesman* and *All My Sons* famously depicted businesspeople in an unfavorable light, with the recurring theme of an erring father committing suicide upon realization of his perfidy (Puzo [1969] 1978; Miller 1947, 1998).

The purveyors of fictitious depictions of businesspeople used crude caricatures. As economist Ludwig von Mises wrote in the 1950s, Hollywood's depiction of duplicitous businessperson portrayed, "all other Americans as perfect idiots whom every rascal can easily dupe. The [trick of feeding cattle salt and letting them drink water before marketing them] …is the most primitive and oldest method of swindling. It is hardly to be believed that there are in any part of the world cattle buyers stupid enough to be hoodwinked by it" (Von Mises [1956] 1972, 71–72).

The media's spotlight, though, may create a distorted view of business ethics in general. There is an asymmetry operating. Colorful tales of business corruption are attention grabbing. Many tales of business corruption are later debunked, but by then, the stories have assumed legendary status and the corrections are of interest only to a few academics and apologists. The media rarely report on the rather humdrum activity of millions of businesspeople earning dollars honorably and quietly satisfying customers by providing goods and services at reasonable prices and who treat their workers fairly.

Certainly the perceptions of business ethics, as measured by trustworthiness, appear dismal. The Gallup poll conducts periodical surveys, asking: "Please tell me how you would rate the honesty and ethical standards of people in these different fields—very high, high, average, low, or very low?" Nurses received the highest combined percentages (85%) of very high or high ratings. Pharmacists and medical doctors ranked second and third in the professions listed. Among the business professionals, funeral directors ranked highest with 44%. Accountants had 39% very high or high ratings. Bankers and building contractors each received 25% very high/high ratings, just between journalists (27%) and lawyers (21%). Real estate agents (20%), business executives (17%), stockbrokers (13%), advertising practitioners (10%), car salespeople (8%), and telemarketers (8%) ranked above or at par with members of Congress (8%) and lobbyists (7%). The *Economist* reported a poll after the Enron scandal, with its unethical accounting tricks, that showed that a majority of Americans who responded trusted accountants. Some three-quarters trusted people running small businesses (www.gallup.com/poll/1654/honesty-ethics-professions.aspx, viewed January 3, 2016, 1:20 pm. *Economist*, October 25, 2003, 3–4 and 7).[3]

A moment's reflection, however, should demonstrate that the vast majority of business transactions are conducted without complaint. You may be reading this book—that you perhaps purchased at an airport bookstore—as you hurl through the air at 550 mph in a metal object. You need hardly worry about the object crashing to the ground. You have faith in the airline's safety. Your employer sends thousands of your dollars each year to a group of financial experts to manage on your behalf. You have never met these experts (nor, for that matter, have you ever met the pilot of the jet plane); yet you entrust your life and retirement hopes to them. You go to an espresso kiosk and quaff some beverage. You don't think about the possibility that you might be drinking adulterated coffee. How often during the year does a typical American file a complaint regarding unscrupulous business behavior? Market forces, consumer and government vigilance, and the businessperson's own sense of honor and ethical standards usually induce ethical behavior. Social commentator Jane Jacobs describes our modern world as, "a great web of trust in the honesty of business…how much that we take for granted in business transactions suspends from that gossamer web" (Jacobs 1992, 5).

A World Without Ethical Business Behavior

Why do businesspeople's ethics matter? Aside from generating outrage and providing politicians ammunition for mobilizing public crusades, business practices, ethical or unethical, affect all of us. The American economy is, for instance, incredibly complex, and all of us rely upon our fellow residents to enable us to survive with a modicum of comfort and decorum. Life in America, for the most part, does not reflect Thomas Hobbes' characterization: "solitary, poor, nasty, short and brutish" (Hobbes, 95–96).

Ethical business behavior provides benefits beyond the direct exchange of goods and services. Commerce was beneficial in myriad ways. Peaceful trade enlarged acquaintance with people from other countries; widened people's mental vistas and dampened prejudice; and intertwined people. Others disagree, with philosopher Robert Goodin reflecting that the growing industrialization and complexities created new vulnerabilities in relations between people, such as customers and retailers or workers and employers. Over a century ago, Edward Ross, a sociology professor, described modern people's vulnerabilities: "The sinful heart is ever the same, but sin changes its quality as society develops. Modern sin takes its character from the mutualism of our time. Under our present manner of living, how many of my vital interests I must intrust to other!" The new complexity leaves us vulnerable to the wicked (Ross 1907, 3–4; Weisberg 1986, 57; Goodin 1985, 149–150).

If ethical standards fall low enough, many transactions may cease to be made. Declining trust leads to increased transaction costs of doing business, including the costs of finding someone with whom to conduct a transaction; negotiating a transaction; and monitoring and enforcing transactions. When businesspeople misbehave, they impose direct and indirect costs. Naturally, the defrauded or injured party bears direct costs, but other participants in the economy bear indirect costs. Each act of malfeasance makes other people more cautious, just as each act of honesty and integrity builds (or rebuilds) trust. Law professor Tamar Frankel characterizes this: "Mistrust corrodes the wheels of exchange and commerce and contaminates trusted professional services" (Frankel 2006, 5).

If suspicion of business practices becomes pervasive, transactions become less frequent, commerce is stymied, and economic growth might ultimately come to a standstill. Researchers worry that an absence of economic growth could ignite chronic violence between groups, as occurred throughout much of human history. Do deteriorating economic and social conditions trigger more business malfeasance or vice versa? The International Fraud Report of KPMG cites two major factors "affecting the level of fraud are society's weakening values and economic pressures" (Frankel 2006, 87; see also Porter, December 2, 2015, B1).

Social commentators often claim that unethical behavior by businesspeople may inspire or provide rationales for unethical behavior by non-businesspeople. "Whenever there is an economic dislocation, theft rises. We often fall in love with the little thief if there is a big one at work. The analogs of the robber barons and their rapacious greed are the small-time thieves in the underworld." Even the perception of widespread unethical business behavior molds attitudes. Television's depictions of businesspeople as "unscrupulous creeps," who are rich, affected young people's perceptions of business (Shteir 2011, 64, Shteir interview with Stephen Mihm, January 2008; Lichter et al. 1991, 300).[4]

Business Ethics in a Wider Context

The focus on businesspeople's ethics may be too narrow. Businesspeople operate in a mosh pit of conflicting self-interests—not just their own self-interest but also the self-interests of workers, consumers, reporters, and government officials. In addition, authorities—both religious and secular—and the general populace are often hostile to businesspeople and their activities, regardless of whether such activities are deleterious or beneficial. Businesspeople's activities are often misunderstood, but misunderstandings are sufficient to make them suspect in many people's eyes.

Workers want the most compensation under the best working conditions possible, including minimizing effort, tedium, and discomfort. Employee embezzlement, theft, and shirking are not uncommon. According to an AOL and Salary.com survey, employees wasted just over two hours per eight-hour day by surfing the Internet, socializing, conducting personal business, and other activities. Of course, salaried workers can argue that doing personal business during working hours isn't really stealing from their employers, as long as they complete their work.

Prospective employees sometimes embellish their resumes or leave out relevant but unflattering information about themselves. A slight majority of reference checks revealed discrepancies, whether through carelessness or premeditation, between what prospective employees and their references stated; some 10% of these were "serious" discrepancies. Prospective employees gamble that employers will not spend the time and effort needed to ferret out fictitious alma mater Obscure U. Firms have to expend more resources due to the mistrust of applicants; honest applicants bear some of the costs. Job applicants often omit or lie about drug rehabilitation, incarceration, or illness (Conner, January 17, 2012, no page numbers; Frankel 2006, 15).

Employee theft drained American companies of some $652 billion in 2003, or about 5% of corporate revenues and a much higher proportion of corporate profits (and, hence, shareholder wealth). One study concluded that "a key factor in the rationalization and incentive components of the fraud triangle: whether an employee is disgruntled with his or her employer….Rationalization is the process of aligning an act of fraud with one's personal code of ethics." One way to combat such behavior is to scrutinize employee's e-mail messages, as employee comments that blame executives, demonstrate excessive anger, or are threatening are predictors of criminal action. Because many employee criminal acts involve collusion, monitoring e-mail and conversational comments can ferret out fraud (Holton 2009, 853–855). On the other hand, companies monitoring e-mail messages raise troubling ethical issues.

Consumers want high-quality products for the least amount of money. They are capable of driving hard bargains and of engaging in chicanery. Customers shoplift, return worn clothes for refunds, fraudulently use credit cards, and fail to pay bills. The National Retail Federation's 2014 Return Fraud Survey suggested that retailers lost over $10 billion due to return fraud. Most shoplifting was of an impulsive nature, and shoplifters favored high value, small bulk electronic devices. A Columbia University study found that shoplifting was more common "among those with higher education and income, suggesting that financial considerations were unlikely to be the main motivation" (Allen, December 29, 2014, no page numbers; Rainey and Hobbs, December 8, 2013, no page numbers; Sennco Admin, April 14, 2014, no page numbers).[5]

Journalists crave dramatic, sensational stories (which are sometimes false or exaggerated) that gain them notoriety and awards. Well-known journalists have been caught in various deceptions. Journalists certainly have their biases and must constantly struggle to maintain sufficient objectivity (Levitt and Dubner 2009, 126).[6] Editors and owners of news media seek profits and may resort to emphasizing sensational stories.

Government officials want to perform public service and to extend their bureaucratic power via larger staffs and budgets; these officials often have an incentive to exaggerate the severity and pervasiveness of perceived ethical "crises" by businesspeople. Politicians use false advertising via cosmetic surgery, Botox, and elevator shoes that enable them to put their "best face forward" or to literally gain physical stature. United States senators and representatives do not like competition for their offices, and they erect effective anti-competitive barriers to entry by third-party candidates. These barriers to entry would inspire the envy of nineteenth-century robber barons. Politicians use seniority, postal franking, gerrymandering, and other tactics to maintain their incumbency. I will often compare government officials' and businesspeople's ethics. There are built-in protections from unethical business practices that are not available in protecting the public from unethical government officials and politicians.

All too often, however, the interaction of government and business created opportunities for large-scale, damaging corruption. In the case of government largesse, where money collects, so will scoundrels; this shibboleth will be demonstrated frequently. Crony capitalism was and remains a longstanding tradition around the globe. The distribution of taxpayer money among interest groups by legislators and government officials has often been tainted by unethical behavior.

Legislators around the world and throughout history found the authority to grant exclusive or other rights lucrative, whether in terms of monetary gains or with regard to influence. Consumers and workers should beware of businesspeople seeking regulation. Businesspeople often complain about regulation, but they often seek self-serving legislation that is anti-competitive, provides subsidies for them, or uses the government as a "stamp of approval." Some businesspeople seem to adhere to the idea that capitalism is good…for the other person.

Many people laud non-profit agencies for their selfless service. Non-profit institutions provide many valuable services. There are, of course, unethical non-profit operators. Potential donors are urged to investigate non-profit entities, before they contribute. Natural disasters spawn non-profit charities, most of which operate to benefit victims. Some companies' officers, however, "may do well by doing good," as the saying goes. How "well" these officers should do can be a vexing question. Watchdog groups collect information on the ratio of spending on overhead (including officers' salaries, fringe benefits, and expense accounts) relative to providing services. A few of the newfound charitable projects are, in fact, fraudulent operations preying on the goodwill of people, with little, if any, of the proceeds reaching the putative beneficiaries. A recent example of allegedly self-serving, non-profit operations is the Wounded Warrior Project. Executives of that organization spent donations on lavish hotels and promotions; roughly 40% of its 2014 donations went for overhead. Other charities employ workers with limitations. The concept of employing people with disadvantages is a noble one, but the execution occasionally raises questions. Goodwill Industries and other non-profit organizations frequently pay their workers, who suffer from limitations, wages far below minimum wage. The organizations' CEOs claim that these workers simply are not productive enough for them to be paid the legal minimum wage. Although the economics of their argument is compelling, in other contexts, many people would consider paying workers less than a state-imposed minimum wage to be unethical (Philipps, January 28, 2016, A1 and A14; WBEZ91.5, May 28, 2013, http://www.wbez.org/print/107389, viewed September 22, 2013).

Changing Nature of Business Ethics

Businesspeople face challenges with regard to ethical standards. Business ethics are not static, nor are they standardized throughout the world at any particular time. What was considered ethical has changed over time. Sometimes opinions regarding mores change quickly. A businessperson may need to be nimble in order to adjust. What was ethical at the beginning of a businessperson's career may later be perceived as unethical at the end of their career. Because ethical standards have changed and because people's opportunities have changed dramatically, we should attempt to view their actions within the context of their times. Even such seemingly obvious strictures against lying, cheating, and stealing in transactions have, at times, been, if not explicitly approved, winked at or even openly boasted of. Imposing twenty-first-century mores upon people from the past would be unwise and unfair.

For example, raiding and piracy were often forms of enrichment; raiders, however, frequently evolved into traders (Jacobs 1992, 32). Piracy continues to infest some waters around the world. For most of history, owning slaves was considered desirable and respectable; only within the past 270 years has a concerted effort been made—primarily by British and American activists—to first repudiate and then to eradicate the institution.

Humanity's changing understanding of the world also affected the ethics of business transactions. Modern people take the germ theory for granted, but 150 years ago, the theory was new and controversial. Once the theory became widely accepted, some longstanding business practices no longer passed ethical muster. Technological progress also created new challenges for ethical behavior.

What to Expect

A business historian laments that "most contemporary writing on business ethics is ahistorical. Aside from the obligatory references to Immanuel Kant and John Stuart Mill, one rarely finds any serious discussion of concepts or ideas that date back more than a few decades. Greek, Jewish, Islamic, Catholic, and Protestant thinkers who devoted considerable thought regarding the ethics of business are rarely cited. One also finds remarkably few references in the contemporary business ethics literature to the works of scholars such as Max Weber, Albert Hirschman, and Michael Walzer—all of whom have written extensively about the historical roots of capitalism as an ethical system" (Vogel 1991, 49; see also Hirschman 1982, 1463–1484).

Business ethics is an ever-changing, vibrant corpus of beliefs, customs, and laws. At any given moment, people across the world hold varying ideas of what is ethical in business, based on their current economic situation, as well as their past. For hunter-gatherer groups worrying about how to obtain their meals, raiding and sharing made sense. For twenty-first-century Americans, stricter definitions of property rights with respect to food are efficient. Historical examples, therefore, illustrate evolving concepts of what is ethical.

These volumes represent a survey of changing business ethics throughout history. What follows is not a comprehensive catalog of infamous business practices through the years. Instead the volumes examine ethical beliefs and behavior—both good and bad—dating back to the so-called primitive people, although there is a marked concentration upon nineteenth- and twentieth-century British and American business practices.

Focusing on ethical flaws may distract us from the overriding ethical behavior that benefited consumers and workers. Along the way, we'll meet such ethical characters as a tenth-century Jewish banker turned Egyptian official—Ya'qub ibn Killis; Quaker merchant John Woolman; master showman Phineas T. Barnum; and twentieth-century retailer Julius Rosenwald. Certainly most businesspeople, as with people in general, have their ethical blemishes. There will also, of course, be many examples of scoundrels, some of whom have their charms.

Although I am not a professional historian, I have studied the history of professional team sports, leisure in America, and the Civil War. There are advantages from using historical examples. Readers are likely to be less passionate about long-dead people, as compared with the latest poster person for business lapses. In addition, the passage of time opens up archival material with which to study business ethics situations.

Economists and business historians have debunked many allegations of harmful or unethical behavior by businessmen; in other cases, they have exposed previously unrealized unethical behavior by businessmen.[7]

Business Ethics as an Academic Discipline

Business ethics has arisen as an academic specialty within the past few decades, although there have been some courses on the subject in business schools since the beginning of the twentieth century. Students learn basic approaches to thinking about ethics, including differences in ethics as applied to business compared with everyday life.

There are three categories of ethical theories. Teleological theories judge actions upon the "amount of good consequences they produce." Setting aside the sometimes contentious debates regarding the meaning of "good," such an approach undergirds Jeremy Bentham's utilitarian theory, among other theories. Deontological theories, such as Immanuel Kant's theories, emphasize duties. Greek thinkers, such as Aristotle, relied upon a concept of virtue in formulating their ideas regarding ethics (Boatright 1993, 32).

These theories, as with almost all theories, have strengths and weaknesses, especially in application. Teleological theories require that an individual be adept at recognizing and weighing the subjective and objective aspects of the benefits and costs of a decision upon themselves and also for third parties or for society. The calculus requires empathy and a clear-headed, unbiased assessment. Teleological theories also ignore duties owed to ourselves and others. Business decision makers must consider fiduciary duties to stockholders, so ethical thinking requires an assessment of the duties owed.

On the other hand, deontological theories have drawbacks. There are difficulties in agreeing upon universally accepted duties. Do such duties vary across time and cultures? Are there times that we should violate duties, such as lying to protect an innocent party (Boatright 1993, 58–60)?

The teleological and deontological theories need not be mutually exclusive; these two theories may reinforce each other with respect to promoting ethical behavior. For instance, if most people honor the duty to be honest, their behavior affects the marginal benefits and costs of decisions for themselves and others. The utilitarian approach may help assess whether fidelity to a duty is worthwhile in terms of costs and benefits. An ethical person should consider the costs their actions, including adhering to their duties, impose upon others.

The inability of any particular theory to satisfactorily cover all ethical situations and honest (and, sometimes, dishonest) disagreement regarding what is and is not ethical creates tension. Decision makers, therefore, may find themselves facing ambiguity regarding the ethical considerations surrounding their decisions. For these reasons, this book emphasizes that what is considered ethical in business differs across time and societies.

An Economist Looks at Business Ethics

I am an economist fascinated by ethics in business. I am not anti-business, but I am a friendly critic of business. I believe the profit-motive can be pursued ethically, although the means employed should be subject to scrutiny.

The fields of economics and ethics need not and, indeed, should not be strangers. Adam Smith, David Hume, and other early economists were keenly interested in morality. An ethical person should be interested in the costs and benefits of their ethical positions, not only upon themselves but upon other parties. Economics can illuminate many aspects of business ethics. Economic theories are useful in making decisions. The concepts of marginal benefit and marginal cost are compatible with both teleological and deontological ethical approaches. Economists weigh the objective and subjective benefits and costs; when the marginal benefits exceed the marginal costs, a decision maker should undertake the decision. Economists also incorporate a form of the now-popular "stakeholder" theory with their concept of externalities. In a simple transaction, such as a customer buying meat from a slaughterhouse, the consumer and producer should consider the marginal benefits and costs affecting third parties. If the producer dumps the meat waste products into a river, such pollution might adversely affect (third-party) resort owners. These theories often presuppose an absence of fraud, dishonesty, and so on. Some critics disdain economic theories, because such theories are said to rest upon prices determined by impersonal forces of supply and demand and not by any intrinsic ethical or moral values. Economists also address other pertinent questions. Why does the market foster or sometimes fail to foster discipline and good behavior? Why are some seemingly unethical situations not as dire as depicted?

I am not a formally trained ethicist, so I will not emphasize modern theoretical business ethics as applied to business practice or delve into the debates surrounding such theories. I am mainly interested in considering business ethics as practiced throughout the ages and across societies, along with contemporary discussion of what constituted unethical and ethical behavior.

Notes

1. Self-avowed American liberals S. Robert and Linda Lichter were skeptical of commentator Ben Stein's criticism of television's anti-business portrayals: "We were once inclined to dismiss [Ben Stein's comment]....No more. No immoral or illegal act seems too vile—or too unlikely—to be perpetrated by a television businessman" (Lichter et al. 1991, 132; see 209–210 for their remarks on J.R. Ewing).
2. Puzo ([1969] 1978, 9); some believe that Honore Balzac coined the phrase, but this appears to be disputed or is mistranslated (http://quoteinvestigator.com/2013/09/09/fortune-crime/, viewed May 8, 2015, 2:25; http://answers.google.com/answers/threadview?id=296588).
3. The findings of 2016 were roughly similar to those of a Gallup poll of "America's Most Trusted" dated January 1, 1997.
4. See the Lichter's amusing example of television business shenanigans—an episode of *Get Christie Love!* The plot line took absurdity to new levels (Lichter et al. 1991, 221).
5. Even Canada, lauded as an exemplary country, lost about 1.5% of the country's gross domestic product in 1997 to theft and fraud (Palango July 28, 1997, 10).
6. Levitt and Dubner described the case of Kitty Genovese in 1964 as an example of journalists letting self-interest get the better of them.
7. Throughout the text, the term businessman will be used instead of the somewhat awkward and less precise businessperson. As the discussion turns to eras where women participated more as business owners, the term businessperson will be used.

Bibliography

Allen, Kathy. "Retailers Estimate Holiday Return Fraud Will Cost Them $3.8 Billion, According to NRF Survey." *Loss Prevention*. December 29, 2014, nrf.com/media/press-releases/retailers-estimate-holiday-return-fraud-will-cost-them-38-billion-according-nrf, viewed March 6, 2015.

Boatright, John. *Ethics and the Conduct of Business* (Englewood Cliffs, NJ: Prentice Hall, 1993).

Conner, Cheryl. "Employees Really Do Waste Time at Work." *Forbes*. July 17, 2012. www.forbes.com/sites/cherylsnappconner/2012/07/17/employees-really-do-waste-time-at-work/, viewed January 9, 2016, 9:00am.

Economist. "Tough at the top: A survey of corporate leadership." October 25, 2003, 3–4 and 7.

Frankel, Tamar. *Trust and Honesty: America's Business Culture at a Crossroad* (Oxford, UK: Oxford University Press, 2006).

Gallup Poll. www.gallup.com/poll/1654/honesty-ethics-professions.aspx, viewed January 3, 2016, 1:20pm.

Goodin, Robert. *Protecting the Vulnerable: A Reanalysis of Our Social Responsibilities* (Chicago, IL: University of Chicago Press, 1985).

Hirschman, Albert. "Rival Interpretations of Market Society: Civilizing, Destructive, or Feeble?" *Journal of Economic Literature* 20(4), December 1982, 1463–1484.

Hobbes, Thomas. *Leviathan*, edited by A.P. Martinich (Peterborough, Ontario, CA: Broadway Literary Texts, 2002).

Holton, Carolyn. "Identifying disgruntled employee systems fraud risk through text mining: A simple solution for a multi-billion dollar problem." *Decision Support Systems* (46), 2009, 853–864.

Jacobs, Jane. *Systems of Survival: A Dialogue on the Moral Foundations of Commerce and Politics* (New York, NY: Random House, 1992).

Levitt, Steven and Stephen Dubner. *Super Freakonomics: Global Cooling, Patriotic Prostitutes, and Why Suicide Bombers Should Buy Life Insurance* (New York, NY: William Morrow, 2009).

Lichter, S. Robert, Linda Lichter, and Stanley Rothman. *Watching America* (New York, Prentice Hall Press, 1991).

Miller, Arthur. *All My Sons: A Play in Three Acts* (New York, NY: Reynal & Hitchcock, 1947).

Miller, Arthur. *Death of a Salesman: certain private conversations in two acts and a requiem* (New York, NY: Penguin, 1998).

Palango, Paul. "Mountie Misery: fighting white-collar crime, the RCMP can no longer get its man." *Maclean's* 110(30), July 28, 1997, 10–14.

Philipps, Dave. "Helping Veterans Recover, Spending Lavishly on Itself." *New York Times*, January 28, 2016, A1 and A14).

Porter, Eduardo. "No Growth, No World? Think About It," *New York Times*, December 2, 2015, B1.

Puzo, Mario. *The Godfather* (New York, NY: Penguin, [1969] 1978).

Rainey, Clint and Allegra Hobbs. "Been Caught Stealing." *New York Magazine*, December 8, 2013, nymag.com/news/intelligencer/topic/shoplifting-2013-12/, viewed December 2, 2014.

Ross, Edward. Sin and Society (Boston, MA: Houghton Mifflin, 1907).

Sennco Admin. "Top 5 Shoplifting Statistics from 2013," *Sennco Solutions*, April 14, 2014, www.sennco.com/top-5-shoplifting-statistics-2013/, viewed December 2, 2014.

Shteir, Rachel. *The Steal: A Cultural History of Shoplifting* (New York, NY: Penguin Press, 2011).

Vogel, David. "Business Ethics Past and Present." *The Public Interest* 102, Winter 1991, 49–64.

Von Mises, Ludwig. *The Anti-Capitalistic Mentality* (South Holland, IL: Libertarian Press, [1956] 1972).

WBEZ91.5. "Labor laws allow workers with disabilities to earn less than minimum wage." May 28, 2013. http://www.wbez.org/print/107389.

Weisberg, Robert. "Commercial Morality, the Merchant Character, and the History of the Voidable Preference." *Stanford Law Review* 39(1), November 1986, 3–138.

CHAPTER 2

Overview of Business Ethics

Ethics is tightly interwoven with empathy: How does the other party feel about or view situations. A good imagination may be useful for business-people in developing ethical positions. Economics and ethics are also intertwined. One author wrote, "Far more than we ordinarily suppose, economic relations rest on moral foundations" (Firth [1951] 1961, 144). In this chapter, I shall define "business" and look at some basic aspects of business ethics.

A good definition of business is: "People do business when they transact, or trade. One engages in trade by alienating some property rights and acquiring other property rights by means of exchange. Business is, at least in part, a transaction-executing practice." Businesspeople often have to seek out transactional opportunities: "Finding transactional opportunities requires alertness to them and imagination about how best to exploit them….One engages in business by seeking to identify and implement profitable sets of transactions—seeking to yield something of value that was not there before the transactions were initiated." Businesspeople need not be motivated solely by profit. "It says only that people pursue their aims through business, rather than through other means, when they attempt to transact in a profit-generating (self-sustaining) way. Business, then, is a self-sustaining, transaction-seeking and transaction-executing practice." To clarify his point, Alexei Marcoux relates how a free clinic is not a business doer, as its transactions "are not intended to be self-

D. G. Surdam, *Business Ethics from Antiquity to the 19th Century*,
https://doi.org/10.1007/978-3-030-37165-4_2

sustaining." The free clinic has to elicit donations. "The sum of its activities may be self-sustaining, but its transactions are not" (Marcoux 2006, 59–60).

A simpler definition comes from Islam. Islamic jurists perceived trade and commerce to entail buying and selling. "Trade is the pursuit of profit by means of selling and buying and not by means of craft or manufacture" (Udovitch 1970, 185).

The Basic Transaction

Envy may be one of the seven deadly sins, but it is well-nigh ubiquitous. Two individuals meet up. Individual A has something Individual B would like to possess. Individual B has some choices: use force to steal or expropriate the item or to use exchange, by offering something that Individual A may wish to possess. A basic precept underlying business ethics—and it is a significant moral advance over using force—is to "shun force." Journalist Jane Jacobs makes this explicit: "When violence or intimidation enters a transaction, it's no longer trade." Under the shun force option, there is a set of choices: be honest or attempt to obtain the item by chicanery. Jacobs adds the corollary that to "be honest…[which] gives substance to voluntary agreement." A key element underlying transactions is trust. What are ways to build trust, especially among commercial people? Jacobs points out that receipts were used very early in the trading process. The receipts signified trust to the extent that they and bills of account were exchanged, based on a presumption of honesty and a view that fraud was disgraceful. Jacobs argues that when trust breaks down in large commercial cites: "Many people flee such places if they can" (Jacobs 1992, 34–36).[1]

With the development of marketplaces and an accompanying likelihood of repeated transactions between a pair of individuals, social scientists Daniel Friedman and Daniel McNeill observe that vendors' self-interest in inducing "complete strangers" to become permanent customers forces them to discover and to cater to customers' desires. Marketplaces become places where people gather to meet to make transactions. Although self-interest often dictated mutually beneficial transactions, in some cases, "bazaars also bred novel forms of cheating" (Friedman and McNeill 2013, 38).[2] Fraudsters, though, cheat not just their victims but also threaten the marketplace itself.

Added Benefits of Trade and Commerce

Companies that do not practice corruption may contribute to non-violence; researchers plotted corruption versus whether disputes were handled violently and found a positive correlation, which they noted was not causation. Companies practicing ethical business contributed to a sense of community (Fort 2008, 120–121).

Economists Daniel Friedman and Daniel McNeill relate how lower homicide rates are associated with more developed economies. Friedman and McNeill cite several factors that make such a case plausible. Wealthier societies have the resources to purchase crime prevention. When the bulk of people are relatively prosperous, the lure of crime is diminished. They also suggest that markets are associated with legal systems that reduce the prevalence of *honore* codes which often led to persistent cycles of violence. "Markets also broaden social webs, strengthen bonds, and foster moral behavior" such as patience and prudence. The American South was known for its feuds and well-developed sensitivity to insults that led to brawls. Friedman and McNeill laud bourgeois values, such as truthfulness, tolerance, willingness to work hard, and adhering to rules. These bourgeois values aid the market system. They describe how Spain was, in a sense, cursed by its New World riches, as it gave the Spanish rulers, "the luxury of retaining an antimarket honor culture, and of financing religious fanatics at home and halfway around the world." They argue that people assumed bourgeois moral codes, because these values "breed wealth and lift living standards." Critics find many faults with bourgeois values. True, the bourgeois values seem rather tame, although there remains a place for courage (Friedman and McNeill 2013, 160–161, 210).[3]

Samuel Johnson quipped that, "There are few ways in which a man can be more innocently employed than in getting money" or, as John Stuart Mill noted, "That the energies of mankind should be kept in employment by the struggle for riches, as they were formerly by the struggle of war, until the better minds succeed in educating the others into better things, is undoubtedly more desirable than that they should rust and stagnate. While minds are coarse, they require coarse stimuli and let them have them." Mill then concludes that commerce induces good behavior and ensures peaceful intercourse and progress instead of recourse to war. Alas, Mill's prediction was too optimistic (Boswell 1832, 323; Mill [1909, 1848] 1987, 581–582, 749).

Economist John Maynard Keynes believed that capitalism was morally objectionable but at least was more efficient at attaining economic ends than alternative systems. He also thought that, "There are valuable human activities which require the motive of money-making and the environment of private wealth-ownership for their fruition. Moreover, dangerous human proclivities can be canalized into comparatively harmless channels by the existence of opportunities for money-making and private wealth.... It is better that a man should tyrannise over his bank balance than over his fellow-citizens" (Keynes 1936, 374).

Inculcating Good Behavior

A simple story of inducing good behavior revolves around the threat of punishment; a promise of reward; or ingrained beliefs. Every civilization has created or used "externalized morals" to maintain acceptable behavior in the marketplace. Although traders might have self-regulated themselves or used peer pressure, often rulers erected a moral infrastructure based upon laws. Members of small groups could monitor each other and report unacceptable behavior. Members had an incentive to do so, as bad behavior threatened the group. The drawback to such peer pressure was that "it's pretty ham-fisted." As trading communities got larger, such as in medieval Europe, a more formal system arose—*lex mercatoria* (law merchant) (Friedman and McNeill 2013, 43–45).[4]

Sometimes people just need simple reminders of what the "right thing" to do is. Americans are pretty scrupulous about paying their income taxes. Researchers found that telling taxpayers that a large majority of citizens fully paid their taxes induced better compliance than a letter stating their tax returns were likely to be audited. "[P]eople will restrain themselves when they see that others do so." Unfortunately, research also suggested that people are willing to countenance terrible behavior on the part of the few, even though they, themselves, do not participate. Psychologists Craig Haney, Curtis Banks, and Philip Zimbardo's experiment, which may have skirted ethical boundaries for research, involved splitting college students into guards and prisoners. A minority of the guards quickly became abusive, while the other designated guards did not but also did nothing to prevent the abusive behavior (Frankel 2006, 82–83; Haney et al. 1973, 69–97).[5]

When confronted with a big insurance company, many Americans succumb to the temptation to "pad" their insurance claim. The Insurance

Research Council found that reminding insureds that padding may lead to higher premiums led people to be less tempted to cheat (Frankel 2006, 13).

People are torn between conflicting motivations. They generally like to see themselves as honorable and honest, but they are tempted to cheat and get more money. The trick to reconciling these motivations is to "cheat by only a little bit, [so] we can benefit from cheating and still view ourselves as marvelous human beings." Social scientist Dan Ariely attributes our ability to hold such conflicting attitudes to "our amazing cognitive flexibility," and he dubs this rationalization as "fudge factor theory." He acknowledges that his theory differs from economist Gary Becker's "Simple Model of Rational Crime," where people considering committing a crime weigh the marginal benefits with the marginal costs of crime.

One way to promote ethical behavior is getting people to try to remember moral edicts. Ariely cites an experiment where even self-declared atheists declined to act dishonestly in a subsequent experimental task after they swore on a Bible. Ariely notes that "people are more apt to be dishonest in the presence of nonmonetary objects—such as pencils and tokens—than actual money." This observation suggests that if society becomes cashless, our ethics may slip, because stealing cash is more tangible than stealing via credit card or internet (Ariely 2013, 27–29, 34, 40; Becker 1974, 2–14).

Businesspeople, as with people in general, may approach ethical issues in three stages. The rudimentary stage is to worry that if I act unethically, I might get in trouble and have to pay a fine, suffer public embarrassment, or go to jail. A somewhat more nuanced reasoning might be: If I act unethically, I may or may not benefit or profit. Finally, a person might reason, if I act unethically, I affect other people in various ways. An example of the rudimentary stage might be the so-called "newspaper test," a form of corporate conscience: "Would a proposed transaction cause you or your company embarrassment when reported in the press? If it would, do not do it." A classic example is the headline, "Did Segal's Firm Cheat Nuns?" (*Chicago Sun-Times*, February 15, 2002, no page numbers). Presumably the public relations officer for that firm had a bad day when that headline appeared.

Tamar Frankel uses the phrase, "trust but verify." She believes there are three barriers to dishonesty: moral behavior (individuals exercise self-control); self-protection (individuals rely upon market sanctions to avoid abuse of trust); and the law ("trust but verify"). "One can trust people who exercise self-control in face of temptations. Self-protection and the markets reflect the 'but verify' component in 'trust but verify.' One must verify the other person's statements and promises. The law reflects and supports both the 'trust' component and the self-protection 'verify' component." These barriers to dishonesty require resources, such as time, police, and courts. For Frankel, people are moral, when they exercise self-control in resisting temptations to abuse the trust others are placing in them. Moral people do not take what is not theirs without asking, especially when there are no police around. Moral people *voluntarily* behave honestly, whereas law may *force* people to behave themselves. Moral people behave because this is the "ultimate power—the power of control: 'No one tells me what to do.'" The reward for moral behavior is the "power of self-control. 'I am the master of myself, and can control my weaknesses in the face of great temptations.'" Rewards and punishment are not the motivating force for moral people, as such would make them susceptible to manipulation by others, who, therefore, would have power to dictate how an individual would act (Frankel 2006, 105–107).

Similar to Frankel, ethicist Timothy Fort defines three categories of reasons to be ethical. "Hard trust" is the minimal stage where business participants act ethically in order to avoid legal trouble and bad publicity. Hard trust is intertwined with coercion and police power. "Real Trust" is based on the pragmatic realization that developing a good reputation and goodwill may be profitable in the long run. Although people are capable of being "notoriously nasty" in Fort's phrase, they also often *want* to do good. "Good Trust" is the trust earned by people who possess a moral sense. "We trust people because their moral behavior is part of their very identity." Fort believes that executives, partly out of a reticence to bring aesthetic and spiritual beliefs into the discussion of business ethics, think of trust in terms of Hard Trust and Real Trust. "[T]hey miss the underlying aesthetic and spiritual motivations that effectuate compliance and strategy and shortchange the possibilities for moral excellence that create even strong forms of trustworthiness. Understanding and integrating all three aspects of trust makes companies stronger and more trustworthy."

Fort raises the question of why we rely upon and trust "faceless, distant companies." We assume they will not harm us, not because of some concern for our well-being, "but because there are checks and balances that make it costly for such companies to take advantage of our vulnerability." Because of the legal apparatus and police powers of coercion, "we can repose some degree of 'trust' or 'reliance'" in company's products and services. Fort worries that the crucial role of laws may induce business-people to compartmentalize their thinking (Fort 2008, 57–60, 78).[6]

Fort cites economist Friedrich von Hayek's observation that markets work better, when the participants trust each other. Fort argues that Real Trust is what the people have in mind, when they think in terms of "trust" with regard to businesses: "people living up to promises they make, being honest, producing products and services that are of sufficient quality to satisfy customers, and rewarding people for doing the things the company says are important." Hayek believes the most efficient way to learn basic moral virtues that assist the economy is through "the teachings of religious and educational institutions that these virtues are intrinsically good" (Fort 2008, 81–82; Hayek 1989, 38–47).

The law may deprive moral people of the full benefit of their morality. A person who acts honestly when there are no police around is likely to be more trustworthy. Having police around may mute the signal from people being honest, as even dishonest people are more likely to behave under such circumstances. The question arises, was an individual behaving honestly voluntarily or by coercion; what holds for individuals holds for companies. Regulations may force all companies to be honest, thereby diminishing the benefits an honest company may have held (assuming people can ascertain that the company is honest). In some cases, where legal violations are not punished, the regulators' inaction "can send a worse signal than no law at all. A 'dead letter' rule promotes disrespect for other legal rules as well. Weak or no enforcement signals to the public that breaking the law is not 'really very wrong.'"

Some people take the pragmatic attitude that although voluntary obedience to moral behavior is wonderful, voluntary obedience to law out of fear of punishment is an acceptable second-best. Frankel laments that there "is little satisfaction in a fear-based behavior" and if some people derive a satisfaction from "getting away" with breaking the law, the law won't be completely effective in stimulating good behavior. Without people's voluntary self-limiting within a culture of honesty, changing the law may lead to disappointing outcomes. Calls to change the culture may also fall short. The law's coercive power is relatively limited. Frankel concedes, "In a conflict between culture on one hand, and law on the other hand, culture is very likely to win" (Frankel 2006, 114–117, 191).

Christianity, Islam, Hinduism, and Buddhism assert what is good behavior, and believers can enhance their self-esteem by emulating these precepts, often for the good of society (Fort 2008, 108–109). Philosopher

Loyal Rue wittily deconstructs the conundrum of religious traditions describing the purpose of religious life. Using Buddhism, he presents the paradox: "How can one expect to achieve nirvana without first wanting to achieve it? But if nirvana is the extinction of desire, then wanting it renders it impossible to achieve" (Rue 2005, 291).[7]

Unlike many of today's young economics graduates with PhDs that are based on complicated mathematical models, many of the most prominent economists used mathematics but returned to ethics in telling their economic stories. Adam Smith, John Stuart Mill, and Karl Marx are three of the famous economists who emphasized ethical questions. Economist Amartya Sen laments that many economists equate self-interest with rationality, but others, such as Gary Becker (his "Rotten Kid" theorem, for instance), have inserted concern for other people's welfare in their models and equations. Many economists view maximizing self-interest as the rational goal, but Sen reminds us that actions based on group welfare or loyalty are still common. In some cases, the ethics involved may require a greater sacrifice on the part of a subset of the group, such as women. Although many people view Adam Smith as a patron saint of self-interest, Sen retorts that Smith did not believe that self-love or prudence alone would be sufficient for a good society. "Indeed, he maintained precisely the opposite. He did not rest economic salvation on some unique motivation" (Sen 1987, 6, 15, 23–24; Becker 1981, 179–191; Smith 1982, 299).

Importance of Being Honest

Sociologist Max Weber discussed the distinction between "being honest" and "appearing to be honest." He described Benjamin Franklin's moral attitudes, which were imbued with utilitarianism. "Honesty is useful, because it assures credit; so are punctuality, industry, frugality, and that is the reason they are virtues. A logical deduction from this would be that where, for instance, the *appearance* of honesty serves the same purpose, that would suffice, and an unnecessary surplus of this virtue would evidently appear to Franklin's eyes as unproductive waste" (Weber [1930] 2001, 17–18).[8]

What are the costs and benefits of ethical and unethical conduct? An economist identified a paradox with regard to honoring one's commitments: the "honor among thieves:" "The more faithful the members of a group of thieves are to their mutual commitments, the more efficient their combined efforts, and the worse for honest men. Obviously, similar problems arise in connection with hired killers, cartel members, and other participants in antisocial agreements." To evade such difficulties, he suggests thinking that the morality of honoring one's commitment fosters *production* and not that it is always conducive to *social welfare*. Parties to a proposed transaction may be wise to assume the other party may or will act unethically, so both parties expend resources to monitor and to enforce the agreement. Such endeavors, of course, raise the opportunity costs of transactions. In the case of a long-term service contract, both parties are often distrustful, so sellers "try to devise warranties that will prove attractive to buyers, yet protect them from being saddled with the cost of offsetting the effect of 'improper' or 'excessive' use." If sellers believed buyers had higher ethics, then "more attractive warranties could be offered at given prices." On the other side of the transaction, buyer wariness may reduce the amount of purchases made (Reder 1979, 136–138).

Three "central modes" of trust production, including process-based, characteristic-based, and institutional-based trust production, were identified by sociologist Lynne Zucker. An example of Zucker's characteristic-based trust is the New York wholesale diamond trade. The trade is unique in its level of trust between diamond merchants. The merchants, mostly Hasidic Jews, seal deals with a handshake and uttering "*mazal u'brache* ('with luck and a blessing')" (Zucker 1986, 53).[9]

Jews from Eastern Europe, who arrived in the United States during the nineteenth and twentieth centuries, exhibited: "the paradigmatic example of a group whose situational solidarity, when confronted with widespread native prejudice, was not limited to an adversarial stance, but went well beyond it by taking advantage of a rich cultural heritage. Jewish-American society developed its own autonomous logic governed not so much by what 'natives were thinking of us' than by concerns and interests springing from the group's distinct religious and cultural traditions." Chinese immigrants to the United States responded in a similar fashion to American hostility, including the creation of a "bachelor society" in San Francisco's Chinatown. These ethnic or religious enclaves created an element of moral obligation based upon the inculcation of agreed-upon values and loyalty toward members of the groups. Jewish and Chinese immigrants created informal lending practices to help members start new businesses using rotating credit associations (Portes and Sensenbrenner 1993, 1329–1333).[10]

Group solidarity can take less beneficial turns. On Bali, successful entrepreneurs found themselves besieged by job- and loan-seeking kinsmen, who exploited a central value of Balinese social life: mutual assistance within the extended family and community. Entrepreneurship is valued but also exploited. "The result is to turn promising enterprises into welfare hotels, checking their economic expansion." In San Francisco's Chinatown, the group solidarity had the drawback of a profound conservatism, as the dominant families restricted members' activities and access to the outside family (Portes and Sensenbrenner 1993, 1338–1341).[11]

By the 1970s, the Soviet economy was a cynic's reality. Instead of mutual trust, people were suspicious of all but relatives and close friends. Opportunistic selfish actions became the norm, "a moral vicious cycle that choked the economy." The Soviet Union lacked markets and a moral infrastructure; the rampant corruption of the post-Soviet era should not have been a surprise. A Russian import–export executive described the corruption: "You rob your workplace. You cut in line. You skip out on contracts if it's convenient. Dishonesty is deep-rooted. When a person in business is honest, it is because he has made a conscious, and usually temporary, decision to be honest. There is not a deep-rooted sense of ethics." The government's great inflation contributed to the general cynicism: "the Great Steal was just business as usual." Lacking trust and a moral infrastructure, the generations raised to view property rights as theft and capitalists as evil parasites and scoundrels had difficulty adjusting to opening the economy, "so when criminals flourished [in post-Soviet Russia] public outrage was muffled" (Friedman and McNeill 2013, 61–62).

Honesty and integrity, therefore, are similar to lubricants in an engine; they lower transaction costs and facilitate transactions. The benefits of honesty are such that it may pay an unscrupulous person to create a reputation for honesty and then, at a particularly opportune moment, to revert to their usual nature (Hausman and McPherson 1993, 686–687).[12]

The Golden Rule

In addition to relying upon honesty, people often resort to reciprocity, as implied by the Golden Rule, as a key element underlying business ethics. A variety of moral teachers and thinkers have espoused the Golden Rule. The Islamic version serves as a representative: "No one of you is a believer until he desires for his brother that which he desires for himself" (Wallechinsky and Wallace 1975, 1314–1315). Authors Jeffrey Barach and John Elstrott consider the "theoretical union" of the Golden Rule and free enterprise: "There is a nobility, a neighborly and brotherly love involved in dealing with others in such a way that oneself and the other are both pleased by that transaction.…I like the notion of having mutually rewarding relationships with other people." They suggest that "very one-sided deals" usually founder, although at times, "aggressive avarice in the context of the free enterprise system can sometimes be productive of the greater social well being. Consumers benefit when manufacturers press for innovations, or sell aggressively on price" (Barach and Elstrott 1988, 549).

The Golden Rule, straightforward as it is, has some interesting aspects. A survey of Israelites had mixed findings. A majority agreed with the statement: "I act according to the golden rule, but others do not." Only a handful agreed with the statement, "I do not act according to the golden rule, but others do" (Maital and Maital 1984, 279). Perhaps Jesus was a keen observer of human self-delusion, when he made the pithy remark in Matthew 7:3, "Why do you see the speck that is in your brother's eye, but do not notice the log that is in your own eye?"

There are limits to the Golden Rule's applicability to business ethics. Sociologist Gabriel Abend chronicles the lengthy history of using the Golden Rule as a guide to business ethics, dating back to at least the seventeenth century; these attempts often reduced the Golden Rule to a cliché without much content. The rule becomes difficult to apply to transactions involving more than two participants. Another difficulty is knowing what the other party's preferences are. One cannot simply assume that the other party would like to be treated the same as oneself. Immanuel Kant claimed the rule was an imperfect derivation of the categorical imperative, because "it does not ground duties to oneself…of beneficence to others…strict duties to others, or duties that permit of no exceptions" (Abend 2014, 301–303; Kant quoted in Gensler n.d., no page numbers; Burton and Goldsby 2005, 375–376).

Applying the Golden Rule to business situations, then, is fraught with pitfalls. If a stakeholder approach is used, balancing stakeholders' conflicting desires and needs becomes a challenge. The rule's applicability also raises questions when dealing with different cultural traditions. Confucian tradition might interpret the rule within a framework of hierarchical duties, while utilitarians would view the rule within the utility framework. Despite the possible drawbacks to applying the Golden Rule to business decisions, many companies have installed the rule as their guidepost. James C. Penney, Lincoln Electric Company, and Worthington Industries are three examples (Burton and Goldsby 2005, 373–377). These companies' websites emphasized their adherence to the Golden Rule. Penney named his first store the "Golden Rule Store" and insisted on treating customers "the way they would want to be treated."[13]

Perceived Fairness

People's notions of fairness and acting fairly are intertwined with their self-esteem. Students participating in the ultimatum game reveal behaviors that go against pure self-interest. In the ultimatum game, one player decides how to split $100; the other player decides whether to accept the split or to reject it, whereby neither player gets any money. People do not play the game as predicted by game theorists and economists. The optimal strategy is to offer the minimum amount of $1, figuring that the other player will accept, since $1 is better than zero dollars. Contrary to game theorists' expectations, most people, though, offered much more than $1, and those people offered very small amounts rejected the offer. People treasured self-esteem and the perception that one "is influential one's own small environment" (Lane 2000, 82; Jolls et al. 1998, 1494).

Economists have become interested in perceptions of fairness between economic participants. The collaboration between economists and psychologists has netted some fruitful discoveries. Economists have investigated norms of fairness. In the workplace, "a fair day's work for a fair day's pay" or an exchange of "gifts"—we pay you more than the market rate and your work effort is more what could be enforced are examples of exchanges both parties consider to be fair (Hausman and McPherson 1993, 684; see also Akerlof 1984, 79–83). People often predicate their actions upon their perceptions of how others act. If people perceive a general norm of trust, they are more likely to act accordingly. Transactors benefit from the widespread trust. In the cod fishing industry, if a fisherman believes others will adhere to agreed-upon limits, he or she will probably obey, too (Friedman and McNeill 2013, 18–19).

How do people view the fairness of an economic transaction? What people consider as a fair price need not coincide with economic efficiency. Economist Daniel Kahneman and his colleagues surveyed people with regard to the perceived fairness or unfairness of various scenarios. They found that, "many actions that are both profitable in the short run and not obviously dishonest are likely to be perceived as unfair exploitations of market power." Kahneman and his co-authors found: "A central concept in analyzing the fairness of actions in which a firm sets the terms of future exchanges is the *reference transaction*, a relevant precedent that is characterized by a reference price or wage, and by a positive reference profit to the firm." For instance, when hurricanes ravage cities, local legislators often push for legislation against price gouging by construction companies. If the original price of a standard roof repair had been $1500, this would have been the reference price; the hurricane-induced demand for roof repair should have dramatically raised the price of repairing roofs to well above $1500. A majority of respondents in Kahneman and his co-authors' survey believed (in responding to a similar scenario) it would have been unfair for the construction companies to have charged more than $1500. The respondents who believed that it was unfair to raise prices apparently did not understand the ramifications of maintaining the original price. Respondents' reasoning might have been that the construction companies did not face any increase in their costs, so they should not reap a literal windfall profit. Raising the price violated the principle of dual entitlement, "which governs community standards of fairness: Transactors have an entitlement to the terms of the reference transaction and firms are entitled to their reference profit. A firm is not allowed to increase its profits by arbitrarily violating the entitlement of its transactors to the reference price, rent or wage" (Kahneman et al. 1986, 729–737).

If politicians adhere to the idea of the reference price concept and squelch price increases in response to demand-side changes, then the market will not be efficient. Of course, in the case of a hurricane, if the market price did not increase, then outside construction companies would not have been encouraged to send crews and materials to the stricken city. People would have had to *wait* to get their roofs repaired. The price control ultimately could boomerang against the homeowners. People would have been waiting in line longer than they did.

People are willing to punish employers and vendors, who they deem acted unfairly. Kahneman cited an example where a merchant reduced the price for an item in a new catalog; customers who had recently purchased the item at the original higher price felt aggrieved. They considered the new lower price as the reference point and considered themselves as having sustained a loss by paying the old higher price. Note that people's perceptions of what is fair do not necessarily correlate with justice. In any event, Kahneman relates, "Unfairly imposing losses on people can be risky if the victims are in a position to retaliate. Furthermore, experiments have shown that strangers who observe unfair behavior often join in the punishment.…It appears that maintaining the social order and the rules of fairness in this fashion is its own reward. Altruistic punishment could well be the glue that holds societies together" (Kahneman [2011] 2013, 308).

Whose Interests Count?

In the 1980s, a new theory of business ethics arose, as philosophers and other thinkers began to consider ethics in a business context. Stakeholder theory asserted that business managers and owners needed to take into account the effects upon other relevant parties when making decisions. A decision to close a plant, for instance, not only affected management and employees, but citizens of the town where the plant was located and suppliers. What duties were owed to outside parties?

R. Edward Freeman was a pioneer formulating the stakeholder theory. He claimed not to "seek the demise" of corporations but, rather, the corporations' "transformation." He argued that managerial capitalism, with its emphasis on the fiduciary duties that managers have to stockholders, is too narrow, and that managers have a fiduciary relationship to stakeholders, who "have a stake in or claim on the firm." He identified suppliers, customers, employees, stockholders, and the local community as stakeholders, whose interests management must consider: "each of these stakeholder groups has a right not to be treated as a means to some end, and therefore must participate in determining the future direction of the firm in which they have a stake."

For Freeman, then, management must strive to balance the relationships among all of the stakeholders, since the firm's survival is jeopardized when the relationships become unbalanced. Instead of the firm's purpose being to maximize the welfare (profits) of stockholders, constrained only by moral, legal, or social constraints, he advocated maximizing the welfare of all the stakeholders (Freeman 2011, 1, 56; Goodpaster 2001, 66–67 and 79).

Freeman reminds his readers of Kant's statement, "Treat persons as ends unto themselves." He wonders why more firms do not follow such behavior, especially since he asserts good treatment of stakeholders benefits the firm. If this is true, the question arises: Why don't firms pursue the stakeholder approach to ethics? Are the owners and management ignorant of their best interests? To create the corporate behavior he desires, Freeman appeals to philosopher John Rawls' idea "that a contract is fair if parties to the contract would agree to it in ignorance of their actual stakes. Thus, a contract is like a fair bet, if each party is willing to turn the tables and accept the other side." This is an interesting and useful way to think about fairness (Freeman 2011, 59–64).[14]

Milton Friedman's Position

Not all academics embrace the stakeholder concept. Milton Friedman disputes whether corporate executives have "social responsibility." He argues that when executives veer from the task of maximizing shareholder values and try to satisfy public clamor to redress social ills: "the corporate executive would be spending someone else's money for a general social interest" by spending shareholders' money via reduced returns; reducing employees' pay through lower wages; and raising prices to customers (Friedman, September 13, 1970, 33).[15]

Friedman seems to, ironically, address the interests of three key stakeholder groups—shareholders, workers, and customers—touted by adherents of stakeholder theory. Friedman's argument rests upon the economic concept of opportunity costs—each action to promote social responsibility carries a potential cost to another party. He reminds us that in a free-enterprise system based on private property, the corporate executive is the agent of the corporate owners (the shareholders). "That responsibility is to conduct the business in accordance with their desires, which generally will be to make as much money as possible while conforming to the basic rules of the society both those embodied in law and those embodied in ethical custom."

Friedman doubts that executives would have any particular expertise in addressing social problems, such as inflation or the hard-core unemployed; he shares Adam Smith's skepticism regarding "those who affected to trade for the public good." Friedman identifies the conundrum of those who would prefer to use coercion of businesses to effect public goods: "What it amounts to is an assertion that those who favor the taxes and expenditures in question have failed to persuade a majority of their majority citizens to be of like mind that they are seeking to attain by undemocratic procedures what they cannot attain by democratic procedures."

Friedman argues that there is a danger involved when business executives engage in social responsibility: Such actions may bolster the perception that profit maximization is "wicked and immoral." In the battle of ideas, the executive's actions may contribute to private enterprises' demise, as government bureaucrats usurp control. He labels the executives' misguided actions as a "suicidal impulse." He argues that the free market and private property exert minimal, if any, coercion, while politics relies upon unanimity, coercion, and conformity (Friedman, September 13, 1970, 33, 123–124).

Economist Donald Hay, among others, disagrees with Friedman's association of freedom with market freedoms. "The outcome may well be freedom for the strong, and a greatly restricted range of options for the weak" (Hay [1989] 2004, 152).[16]

Ronald Coase and His Theorem

Some of the conflicts envisioned by the stakeholder approach to ethical considerations are akin to economic externalities. At times, people may be misled by apparent differences in outcomes predicated upon who has property rights to an asset or to situations where a third party is affected (an externality). The market may provide a solution to the externality problem. Economist Ronald Coase, to employ an overused term, *revolutionized* economic and legal thinking with his 1960 paper, "The Problem of Social Cost." Coase considered the problem and concluded that under certain circumstances, "Regardless of the specific initial assignment of property rights, the final outcome will be efficient provided that the initial legal assignment is *well-defined* and that the parties can *reach and enforce an agreement at zero cost*" (Coase 1960, 19). The certain circumstances, then, rest upon well-defined property rights that are easily defended.

When the property rights are well-defined and defended, the externalities may disappear. Suppose there is a resort along a river and a slaughterhouse that is upstream. The slaughterhouse finds it cheaper to dump its disgusting waste into the river rather than by other means of disposal. Naturally, the waste forces the resort owner to devote resources to cleaning the beach. If the resort had property rights to the river bordering its property, it could seek recourse from the slaughterhouse for the pollution (or the slaughterhouse could offer to pay the resort for the right to pollute). If, instead, the slaughterhouse held the property rights to the river downstream, then the resort owner could pay the slaughterhouse to reduce its pollution. The amounts of pollution and clean beach will be the same regardless of whether the resort owner has the property rights to a clean beach, or the slaughterhouse has the property right to dump waste.

Coase's theorem implies a crucial role for the government. Governmental policy should develop and defend perfectly defined property rights. Indeed, ambiguous definitions of property rights can be worse than no property rights and are certainly worse than well-defined property rights. When the rights are ambiguous, many resources may be devoted to capturing the rights via the adversary proceedings in the legal system. Fans of Western movies are familiar with fights to determine grazing rights—cowboys versus sheep herders—or water rights.

Importance of Information and the Adroit Use of It

We currently live in an information-drenched society. Information, of course, has always been a valuable resource, and there are historical examples of ethical and unethical uses of information. How to make best use of the knowledge is a critical question: "[W]hat is the best way of utilizing knowledge initially dispersed among all the people is at least one of the main problems of economic policy—or of designing an efficient economic system." Ultimately decision makers need the price system: "The mere fact that there is one price for any commodity—or rather that local prices are connected in a manner determined by the cost of transport, etc.—brings about the solution which (it is just conceptually possible) might have been arrived at by one single mind possessing all the information which is in fact dispersed among all the people involved in the process."

Access to information raises ethical issues. Friedrich von Hayek emphasizes the importance of the diffusion of information: "practically every individual has some advantage over all others in that he possesses unique information of which beneficial use might be made, but of which use can be made only if the decisions depending on it are left to him or are made with his active cooperation." He continues by noting a paradox, "To gain an advantage from better knowledge of facilities of communication or transport is sometimes regarded as almost dishonest, although it is quite as important that society make use of the best opportunities in this respect as in using the latest scientific discoveries. This prejudice has in a considerable measure affected the attitude toward commerce in general." People seem to believe "that all such knowledge should as a matter of course be readily at the command of everybody, and the reproach of irrationality leveled against the existing economic order is frequently based on the fact that it is not so available" (Hayek 1945, 520–525).

Closely related to the use of knowledge is the role of entrepreneurs. Economist Frank Knight described successful entrepreneurs/managers as good stewards of factors of production—by either providing existing goods and services more cheaply than rivals; improving product quality (commensurate to the price); or by introducing new products that please consumers. To this end, the successful entrepreneur performs a valuable service to an economy. Knight also points out that entrepreneurs are decision makers. They are also adept at appointing managers or supervisors, who will prove to be good decision makers in their sphere. One way to think about entrepreneurs and managers is to consider a situation where there's some fixed amount of existing inputs—ovens, bakers, flour, shortening, and so on. These inputs are currently being used to manufacture bread. There are several different ways to use these inputs. An entrepreneur or manager might think of a new way to mix these inputs to either make more bread from a given set of inputs or to make a new product—donuts, perhaps—from the inputs; if donuts prove popular, people will quickly vote with their dollars and buy donuts enthusiastically and repeatedly. In the first case, figuring out how to use given resources more efficiently, the entrepreneur or manager benefits society. In the second case, producing something that people enjoy more than the bread is also beneficial (setting aside the possibility that the donuts may have some known or unknown long-term deleterious effect). An entrepreneur or manager who achieves one or the other improvement reaps profits. Successful CEOs, for instance, benefit both shareholders and consumers by "undertaking the overall [successful] orchestrating and team monitoring tasks." Since these skills are rare, successful entrepreneurs will be richly rewarded, not only for their abilities but also for the scarcity of such abilities. "It is unquestionable that the entrepreneur's activities effect an enormous saving to society, vastly increasing the efficiency of economic production." Knight cited how difficult it is to identify, "who is a superior entrepreneur." A number of trials (similar to tossing a coin) would be needed to establish who the best man was, as competent men make errors and not-so-competent men make correct decisions. "It is one of the mysteries of the workings of mind that we are able to form the estimates of 'general ability' which have any value, but the fact that we do is of course indisputable" (Knight 1921, 278–283).[17]

Conclusion

We live in a world based on implicit trust between strangers. The Golden Rule and notions of fairness based on a rough reciprocity facilitate the process of people trading goods and services. A belief in the Golden Rule tempers opportunistic behavior.

These elements of trust and reciprocity afford us the benefits of enjoying a much higher standard of living due to the gains from trade associated with specialization in production. Societies lacking trust and reciprocity tend to become stagnant in terms of civility and economic growth.

Just what duties businesspeople owe employees, suppliers, consumers, and residents remains controversial. Stakeholder concepts clash with Milton Friedman's limited duties to outsiders. Other economists identify misunderstood benefits of entrepreneurs and property rights. Economic thinking undergirds much ethical consideration.

Notes

1. Economist Kenneth Arrow made a similar point: "much of the economic backwardness in the world can be explained by a lack of mutual confidence" (Arrow 1972, 357).
2. Game theory suggests that if there is a known and definite end to a game or relationship, the losses from acting opportunistically fall.
3. Economist Deirdre McCloskey challenged economists' hesitance to acknowledge the role of virtue (McCloskey 2006, 4).
4. Sub-Saharan Africa provided examples of what happens when nations lacked the requisite "moral infrastructure." Equatorial Africa and Botswana present stark contrasts. A dictator in the former country destroyed the economy, while the latter country enjoyed prosperity (Friedman and McNeill 2013, 51).
5. One can read about the "Stanford Prison Experiment" at www.prisonexp.org.
6. Psychologist Lawrence Kohlberg also described moral development within an individual (Kohlberg 1976, 32–36).
7. Loyal Rue's conundrum was similar to George Carlin's Catholic Junior High School boys' question of the priest: "If God is all powerful, can he make a rock that he can't lift?"
8. George Akerlof made similar point (Akerlof 1983, 56–57).
9. See also Starr, March 26, 1984, A18. A variation on the New York diamond trade occurred across the world in Vietnam (McMillan 2002, 58).
10. See also 1334–1335 for Cuban exiles in the early 1906s.
11. Winners of lotteries quickly discover many relatives demand a share, in a perverted form of family and group solidarity.
12. Edward Banfield studied the lack of trust among Italian villagers (Banfield 1958, 10, 18).
13. JCPenney Blog, n.d., no page numbers; *Washington Examiner*, February 1, 2012, no page numbers. For Lincoln Electric Company and Worthington

Industries (Singer 1988, no page numbers; Funding Universe n.d., no page numbers; Worthington Industries n.d., no page numbers.

14. See also Oliver Williamson and R. Edward Freeman and William Evan for nuances in the stakeholder theory (Williamson 1985, 304; Freeman and Evan 1990, 346–349).
15. Donald Frey disputed the Friedmanian emphasis upon profit maximizing and efficiency (Frey 2009, 155–156).
16. In comparison with previous societies, economic freedom would seem to have served the poor better than most other social organizations).
17. N. Scott Arnold summarizes the argument by characterizing the successful entrepreneur as "someone who exploits social ignorance about the malallocation of resources" (Arnold 1987, 389).

Bibliography

Abend, Gabriel. *The Moral Background: An Inquiry into the History of Business Ethics* (Princeton, NJ: Princeton University Press, 2014).

Akerlof, George. "Loyalty Filters." *American Economic Review* 73(1), March 1983, 54–63.

Akerlof, George. "Gift Exchange and Efficiency-Wage Theory: Four Views." *American Economic Review* 74(2), May 1984, 79–83.

Ariely, Dan. *The (Honest) Truth About Dishonesty: How We Lie to Everyone—Especially Ourselves* (New York, NY: HarperCollins, 2013).

Arnold, N. Scott. "Why Profits Are Deserved." *Ethics* 97(2), January 1987, 387–402.

Arrow, Kenneth. "Gifts and Exchanges." *Philosophy & Public Affairs* 1(4), Summer 1972, 343–362.

Banfield, Edward. *The Moral Basis of a Backward Economy* (Glencoe, IL: The Free Press, 1958).

Barach, Jeffrey and John Elstrott. "The Transactional Ethic: The Ethical Foundations of Free Enterprise Reconsidered." *Journal of Business Ethics* 7(7), July 1988, 545–551.

Becker, Gary. "Crime and Punishment: An Economic Approach." *Essays in the Economics of Crime and Punishment,* edited by Gary Becker and William Landes (New York, NY: National Bureau of Economic Research, 1974), 1–54.

Becker, Gary. "Altruism in the Family." *A Treatise on the Family* (Cambridge, MA: Harvard University Press, 1981), 172–201.

Boswell, James. *Life of Samuel Johnson, LL.D.: Including A Journal of a Tour to the Hebrides,* edited by John Croker (Boston, MA: Carter, Hendee, 1832). 2 vols.

Burton, Brian and Michael Goldsby. "The Golden Rule and Business Ethics: an Examination." *Journal of Business Ethics* 56(4), 2005, 371–383.

Chicago Sun-Times. "Did Segal's Firm Cheat Nuns? Court documents allege Near North overcharged them." February 15, 2002, https://www.highbeam.com/doc/1P2-1431399.html, viewed February 4, 2017.

Coase, Ronald. "The Problem of Social Cost." *Journal of Law and Economics* 3(1), October 1960, 1–44.

Firth, Raymond. *Elements of Social Organization* (Boston, MA: Beacon Press, [1951] 1961).

Fort, Timothy. *Prophets, Profits, and Peace: The Positive Role of Business in Promoting Religious Tolerance* (New Haven, CT: Yale University Press, 2008).

Frankel, Tamar. *Trust and Honesty: America's Business Culture at a Crossroad* (Oxford, UK: Oxford University Press, 2006).

Freeman, R. Edward. "A Stakeholder Theory of the Modern Corporation." In *Ethical Theory and Business*, edited by Tom Beauchamp and Norman Bowie (Upper Saddle River, NJ: Prentice Hall, 2011), 56–65. Sixth edition.

Freeman, R. Edward and William Evan. "Corporate Governance: A Stakeholder Interpretation." *Journal of Behavioral Economics* 19(4), Winter 1990, 337–359.

Frey, Donald. *America's Economic Moralists: A History of Rival Ethics and Economics* (Albany, NY: State University of New York Press, 2009).

Friedman, Daniel and Daniel McNeill. *Morals and Markets: The Dangerous Balance* (New York, NY: Palgrave Macmillan, 2013). 2nd edition.

Friedman, Milton. "The Social Responsibility of Business Is to Increase Its Profits." *New York Times Magazine*, September 13, 1970, 32–33, 122–124.

Funding Universe. n.d. "Lincoln Electric Co. History," http://www.fundinguniverse.com/company-histories/lincoln-electric-co-history/, viewed January 23, 2016, 3:15 pm.

Gensler, Harry. n.d. "The Golden Rule," http://www.harryhiker.com/goldrule.htm, viewed 1/23/2016, 2:45pm.

Goodpaster, Kenneth. "Business Ethics and Stakeholder Analysis." *Ethical Theory and Business*, edited by Tom Beauchamp and Norman Bowie. (Upper Saddle River, NJ, 2001). 66–75. Sixth edition.

Haney, Craig, Curtis Banks, and Philip Zimbardo. "Interpersonal Dynamics in a Simulated Prison." *International Journal of Criminology and Penology*, 1(1), February 1973, 69–97.

Hausman, Daniel and Michael McPherson. "Taking Ethics Seriously: Economics and Contemporary Moral Philosophy.' *Journal of Economic Literature* 31(2), June 1993, 671–731.

Hay, Donald. *Economics Today: A Christian Critique* (Vancouver, BC: Regent College Publishing, [1989] 2004).

Hayek, Friedrich. "The Use of Knowledge in Society." *American Economic Review* 35(4), Sept. 1945, 519–530.

Hayek, Friedrich. *Fatal Conceit: The Errors of Socialism* (Chicago, IL: University of Chicago Press, 1989).

Jacobs, Jane. *Systems of Survival: A Dialogue on the Moral Foundations of Commerce and Politics* (New York, NY: Random House, 1992).

JCPenney Blog. n.d. "Defining the Golden Rule." http://blog.jcpenney.com/defining-the-golden-rule/; viewed January 23, 2016.

Jolls, Christine, Cass Sunstein, and Richard Thaler. "A Behavioral Approach to Law and Economics." *Stanford Law Review* 50, May 1998, 1471–1550.

Kahneman, Daniel. *Thinking, Fast and Slow* (New York, NY: Farrar, Straus and Giroux, [2011] 2013).

Kahneman, Daniel, Jack Knetsch, and Richard Thaler. "Fairness as a Constraint on Profit Seeking: Entitlements in the Market." *American Economic Review* 76(4), September 1986, 728–741.

Keynes, John. *The General Theory of Employment, Interest and Money* (New York, NY: Harcourt, Brace, 1936).

Knight, Frank. *Risk, Uncertainty, and Profit* (Boston, MA: Houghton Mifflin, 1921).

Kohlberg, Lawrence. "Moral Stages and Moralization: The Cognitive-Developmental Approach." *Moral Development and Behavior: Theory, Research, and Social Issues*, edited by Thomas Lickona, 31–53 (New York, NY: Holt, Rinehart and Winston, 1976).

Lane, Robert. *The Loss of Happiness in Market Democracies* (New Haven, CT: Yale University Press, 2000).

Maital, Shlomo and Sharone Maital. *Economic Games People Play* (New York, NY: Basic Books, 1984).

Marcoux, Alexei. "The Concept of Business in Business Ethics." *Journal of Private Enterprise* XXI(2), Spring 2006, 50–67.

McCloskey, Deirdre. *The Bourgeois Virtues: Ethics for an Age of Commerce* (Chicago, IL: University of Chicago Press, 2006).

McMillan, John. *Reinventing the Bazaar: A Natural History of Markets* (New York, NY: W.W. Norton & Company, 2002).

Mill, John S. *Principles of Political Economy* (Fairfield, NJ: Augustus M. Kelley, [1909, 1848] 1987). Reprint of new edition.

Portes, Alejandro and Julia Sensenbrenner. "Embeddedness and Immigration: Notes on the Social Determinants of Economic Action." *American Journal of Sociology* 98(6), May 1993, 1320–1350.

Reder, Melvin. "The Place of Ethics in the Theory." *Economics and Human Welfare*, edited by Michael Boskin (New York, NY: Academic Press, 1979), 133–146.

Rue, Loyal. *Religion Is Not About God: How Spiritual Traditions Nurture Our Biological Nature and What to Expect When They Fail* (New Brunswick, NJ: Rutgers University Press, 2005).

Sen, Amartya. *On Ethics & Economics* (Oxford, UK: Basil Blackwell, 1987).

Singer, Andrew. "How a Downturn Put One Rust Belt Company's Principles to the Test." *Ethikos and Corporate Conduct Quarterly*, July/August 1988, http://www.singerpubs.com/ethikos/html/lincolnelectric.html, viewed January 23, 2016.

Smith, Adam. *The Theory of Moral Sentiments*, edited by D.D. Raphael and A.L. Macfie (Indianapolis, IN): Liberty Fund, 1982).

Starr, Roger. "The Editorial Notebook: The Real Treasure of 47th Street." *New York Times*, March 26, 1984, A18.

Udovitch, Abraham. Partnership and Profit in Medieval Islam (Princeton, NJ: Princeton University Press 1970).

Wallechinsky, David and Irving Wallace. *The People's Almanac* (Garden City, NY: Doubleday 1975).

Washington Examiner. "J.C. Penney and the Golden Rule." February 1, 2012. http://www.washingtonexaminer.com/j.c.-penney-and-the-golden-rule/article/213246, viewed January 23, 2016.

Weber, Max. *The Protestant Ethic and the Spirit of Capitalism*, translated by Talcott Parsons (London: Routledge-Classics, [1930] 2001).

Williamson, Oliver. *The Economic Institutions of Capitalism: Firms, Markets, Relational Contracting* (New York, NY: Free Press, 1985).

Worthington Industries. n.d. "Our Philosophy." http://worthingtonindustries.com/Company/about-worthington-industries/Our-Philosophy, viewed January 23, 2016.

Zucker, Lynne. "Production of Trust: Institutional Sources of Economic Structure, 1840–1920." *Research in Organizational Behavior*, Vol. 8, 1986, 53–111.

CHAPTER 3

Primitive Trade

Primitive people began exchanging commodities. They had to overcome shyness, fear, and language barriers in order to make exchanges. The peaceful, voluntary exchanges marked an advance in basic ethics, even if we dispute whether the exchanges were trade or business. We owe our distant ancestors gratitude, for peaceful exchange was a huge step toward our elevated standards of living.

The initial lack of standardized weights and measures often led to misunderstandings or outright deception. Early interactions between groups were fragile, and humans gradually developed means to facilitate simple exchange.

Overview

A key factor contributing to our improved material well-being is trade between people. Economists assert that voluntary trade is mutually beneficial. Adam Smith famously identified the propensity to truck, barter, and exchange as unique to human beings (Smith 1981, 26; Viner 1972, 79). Some anthropologists disagree with this belief. They believe that because no currency or bartering is involved, there is no trade. They talk in terms of gifts, but they admit that reciprocity is implicit in the gift giving.

Friedrich Nietzsche, however, noted that "Setting prices, determining values, contriving equivalencies, exchanging…man designated himself as the creature that measures values, evaluates and measures, as the 'valuating

D. G. Surdam, *Business Ethics from Antiquity to the 19th Century*,
https://doi.org/10.1007/978-3-030-37165-4_3

animal as such.'" He continues: "Buying and selling, together with their psychological appurtenances, are older even than the beginnings of any kind of social forms of organization and alliances: it was rather out of the most rudimentary forms of personal legal rights that the budding sense of exchange, contract, guilt, right, obligation, settlement, first *transferred* itself to the coarsest and more elementary social complexes, together with the custom of comparing, measuring, and calculating power against power…the oldest and naivest moral canon of *justice*" (Nietzsche [1967] 1989, 70–71).

Primitive people exchanged goods. For long-extinct cultures, anthropologists and archaeologists have had to deduce how people acquired non-indigenous goods. Anthropologists have sought clues from the many primitive tribes that existed into the twentieth century. Although these tribes offer insights into how primitive people may have lived, there was always the possibility of cultural contamination or that the observer interpreted the primitive people's activities through modern-day filters. As the old *Far Side* comic went, "The anthropologists are coming!" The mere fact of being observed or interacting with outsiders, thus, may have tainted the evidence.

We can envision prehistoric people meeting other people who possess intriguing stuff. Perhaps a coast-dweller possessing some fish encounters a woodland dweller carrying venison. The coast-dweller wants some venison, while the woodland dweller might crave some fish. If they could satisfy the "double coincidence of wants," they could make a trade. Both parties would be better off from making a voluntary transaction than by not making the transaction.

This is a simple story. The conclusion that each individual feels better off (subjectively, if not objectively) depends on the trade being voluntary. A situation where one of the parties—the woodland dweller perhaps—points a spear or aims an arrow at the coast-dweller or surreptitiously steals the fish negates the mutual benefits from voluntary trade.[1]

The idea that voluntary trade is generally mutually beneficial has enormous ethical implications. Many people believe that what the vendor gains, the consumer loses. This belief implies that trade is a zero-sum game, where one party's gain is commensurate with the other party's loss. In voluntary ethical trade, however, each party to the trade is better off after making the trade (unless there has been an error in judgment). Voluntary trade is essentially a *positive-sum* game. You walk into a convenience store and purchase a gallon of milk for $3.00. If you have small children, you might believe that milk is necessary for strong healthy bodies. For the first gallon per week, you might have been willing to pay up to $12.00, but the store owner only charges $3.00. You prefer the gallon of milk to the $3.00; the store owner prefers the $3.00 to the gallon of milk. The storeowner and you both feel better off after the exchange; you might think to yourself, "I valued the gallon at $12 but paid $3, so I'm $9 better off." It is true that a voluntary cash transaction has aspects of a zero-sum game, but only with regard to the money exchanged. The money exchanged is not the true measure of value, however, as explained above. The consumer's and producer's valuations are what matter.[2]

On the other hand, one party might end up much better off by lying, cheating, or stealing. By resorting to these tactics, the unscrupulous person might get the other person's commodities while retaining most or all of his or her original bundle of goods. If one party or the other exercises fraud or misrepresentation, our general conclusion will not hold. Maybe our hypothetical hunter realizes that his venison has "gone bad," and is in haste to rid himself of it. Our villager may know that the fish being offered tastes terrible. An ethical consideration: What duty does each party have to reveal the defect? There is a built-in protection, though, for the two parties. Whether by fraud, coercion, or other means that negates our "mutually beneficial" aspect, the aggrieved party is unlikely to willingly participate in another trade with the opportunistic participant after such an experience. If both hunter and villager feel confident that they will never see the other party again, the temptation to resort of fraud or force may be high. If, on the other hand, they hope to meet again for exchange, then pragmatism puts a brake upon opportunistic behavior. There's a reason why many of the tricksters of American folklore was transitory characters (think of Professor Harold Hill in *The Music Man*).

Primitive people quickly recognized the potential gains from interacting with people in other groups. The opportunity for repeated exchanges that induced growing trust and institutions, such as potlatch and gift-giving, quickly arose to help foster and to maintain such exchanges. Primitive people had to think abstractly when thinking of the future consequences of their choice to trade voluntarily and peacefully or to lie, cheat, and steal.

Definition of Primitive

Legal scholar Richard Posner defines "primitive" as preliterate. Because these societies lack literacy, as well as developed communications systems, the "costs of obtaining information are higher in primitive than in advanced societies…more inputs of time or other resources are required to obtain the same amount of information…it is also true of information concerning the probability that the other party to a contract will perform or that the quantity delivered in a sale is the quality bargained for." Primitive people also face high transaction costs, due to their high "costs of transportation…language barriers, lack of currency, and lack of contract-enforcement mechanisms." Dealing with strangers was often sporadic if not completely novel, so caveat emptor could lead to ill-will (Posner 1980, 4–5, 9, 36). These limitations affected the scope and extent of mutually advantageous trades.

An anthropologist applies the term "primitive" to "cultures lacking a political state." Marshall Sahlins cautions against applying standard economic analysis to re-distribution of goods between individuals and groups in primitive economies. He discounts the role of supply and demand in determining prices, as there were no explicit prices involved in the typical gift-giving exchange; instead, "a current supply-demand imbalance is resolved by pressure on trade partners rather than exchange rates." In order to maintain harmony within the group, one person who profits from another member is disruptive. Although members of a group might display caveat emptor in dealing with members of another group, within the group, "tribal sociability and homebred morality constitute an unlikely arena for economic infighting—for no man can have honor and profit in his own camp" (Sahlins 1972, 187–188, 297, 311; Finley 1975, 117; Saller 2002, 253–255).

Sahlins' denial of the existence of prices may be erroneous. Prices do not necessarily have to be expressed in monetary units. Prices are in essence ratios. If a person can devote their working hours to growing corn or catching fish, the time spent on growing corn incurs the opportunity cost of fewer fish caught. There is an implicit price or opportunity cost of corn with respect to fish not caught.

Anthropologists argue that trade in primitive societies is not based on economics but voluntary reciprocity. The gifts are only in theory "voluntary, [but] in reality given and returned obligatorily." Based on this observation, economist Paul Seabright states that "prices could be established for transactions just as they are in market societies even if they were not prices expressed in terms of money….Given that gifts entailed reciprocal obligations, it is not obvious how they escaped being considered venal." He concludes, "what makes transactions with explicit prices different from others is not their motivation, not their venality per se, but the lack of subtlety with which that venality is communicated. Selling a good is like giving it to someone and simultaneously reminding them of their debt to you, a debt that (it is implied) sensitive and intelligent individuals ought to have been aware of without a reminder and might resent being brought so vulgarly to their attention" (Seabright 2004, 148–149).

Exchange between primitive groups may have helped satisfy material desires but, more importantly, exchange rather than theft and raiding built trust and promoted peace between individuals and groups. In order to do so, however, requires an "exercise of tact and courtesy." For that reason, no Andaman Islander, for instance, could refuse an offer gift. When groups or individuals met, there was a volatile mixture of fear, envy, hostility, and curiosity. Sahlins observes, "trade between primitive communities or tribes is a most delicate, potentially a most explosive, undertaking." He notes there is the potential of "a transition from trading goods to trading blows" (Sahlins 1972, 302).

In California, the survivors of the Nomlaki culture occupied a central position in a chain of north–south trade in California. People in the foothills exchanged various nuts and animals in return for salmon and river animals from people in the valley. These and other groups used shell money and exchange of other valuables. One survivor recalled, "They don't argue over the price. If a man refuses a cheap offer, he is not well thought of. One can't say no to a trade. This system evens out after a while. Whenever a fellow counts his beads close, they don't like to trade with him and might refuse because it takes too long, even if his stuff is good. You have to sell anything that is wanted that you have brought with you." Given the potential hard feelings, similar to the Berbers in Morocco, people often "came back to the *same person* (italics mine) to trade—they are sort of trading partners" (Goldschmidt 1951, 335–336).[3]

If the host and guests are exchanging similar goods, they can easily gauge who got the better of the exchange. More complicated and very common are situations where like is not exchanged for like. The giver has to consider the recipient's valuation of the gift; in addition, the giver has to consider the labor expended on or value to the giver of a potential gift. Here the normal dynamics of barter arise; the parties make it clear whether they each find the exchange satisfactory. Hence, the repeated observations of recipients making casual or indirect remarks about their preferences may be of utmost importance in helping the host determine the balancing. Sahlins denotes this process as "compensating efforts to the producer and utilities to the receiver, the rates set by tactful diplomacy will express many of the elemental conditions" that are incorporated in modern-day conceptions of supply and demand curves. He concludes, "To be a diplomatically satisfactory 'price' however, the price of peace, the customary exchange ratio of primitive trade should approximate the normal market price. As the mechanisms differ, this correspondence can only be approximate, but the tendency is one." Buso villagers exaggerated the efforts required to make pots; Busama members politely agreed but steered the conversation to the "inferior quality of present-day pots." People are constrained from defaulting or reneging on the reciprocity by fear of being criticized as being "mean" (Sahlins 1972, 303–308; see also Dalton 1977, 205–207; Posner 1980, 8; Radcliffe-Brown 1933, 83–84; Hogbin 1951, 82–94).

The benefits of peaceful exchange, though, are significant. If groups can transcend their mutual suspicion, they can exchange their products to the other group for desirable, often hard-to-obtain, items, leaving both parties better off. But within the mutual benefits from voluntary trade lurks the hope of getting more for less; often, groups will establish some sort of customary exchange ratio to minimize potential for hostility from negotiation (Goldschmidt 1951, 337). Economist Douglass North identifies four variables affecting the costs of exchange. Almost from the inception of trading, people faced the "cost of measure," such as assessing the attributes of the goods and services to be exchanged. "I'll give you a 'whole bunch,'" as the author's junior high math teacher claimed his daughter offered. As childish as "whole bunch" may be, the child was expressing a key aspect of trade. Without standardized weight and measures, among other things, trade becomes cumbersome. Ascertaining how much and what quality incurs costs; in the Coasian world with perfect information, this type of cost would not exist. The second variable is the "nature of the exchange process." There are a wide variety of exchange, from gift exchange, personal exchange within a circle of family and friends, and impersonal modern-day market exchange. The last-named exchange often has the greatest potential benefit, in the sense that strangers from far-away often have desirable exotic items to trade, but also carry considerable risk of opportunistic behavior on the part of one or both parties. The third variable is the enforcement aspect. "In a world of perfect enforcement, opportunism, shirking, and cheating would never pay." Due, in part, to the first variable, the difficulties and costliness of measurement create ambiguity regarding whether agreements have been honored or broken. These three variables affect the costs of exchange; individuals optimize at every margin: "If cheating pays, one cheats; if loafing on the job is possible, one loafs; if one could with impunity burn down a competitor, one would do so. In the neoclassical world, behavior is only constrained by rules and the effectiveness of their enforcement." Since enforcement is never perfect, the standard neoclassical model "is clearly incomplete." With significant costs of measuring performance, "complex social organization would be impossible were everyone to murder, cheat, steal, and shirk whenever he found it profitable. Honesty, integrity, living up to the spirit as well as the letter of the law do matter. But how much?" The fourth variable, then, is the changing ideological attitude toward the rules of the game. "The strength of ideology can be measured by the premium people are willing to incur rather than 'free ride.' Such a premium is the cost of one's convictions. Not only does the premium vary according to one's beliefs about the justice of the rules and the contractual arrangements of the society, but it can be influenced by 'education,' propaganda, and symbols" (North 1984, 257–258).

Ubiquitous Scarcity

We live in a world of scarcity. With all of our productive advantages compared with primitive people, modern people still face scarcity. Primitive people keenly concentrated on procuring food, whether obtained by hunting, gathering, cultivating, trading, or stealing. Modern people in industrialized countries rarely worry about obtaining their daily bread; a stop at a supermarket after work and an exchange of currency for food yields the daily sustenance. Most people throughout history, though, worried about their supply of food. A hunter or a group of hunters fortunate enough to bring down big game with hundreds of pounds of meat might feast and gorge themselves, as the meat quickly spoiled. For cultivators, the vagaries of weather and pestilence created a volatile situation with regard to food. A good harvest might have been offset by a subsequent scant harvest. Preserving and storing food were paramount problems facing primitive man, so primitive societies frequently developed insurance devices.

Not all scholars agree with the economists' assertion of ubiquitous scarcity. Economist George Dalton, for one, disputes the concept of scarcity: "the degree of importance attached to material acquisition is most definitely determined by social institutions and values, then it immediately follows that the presence, absence, or existing degree of 'scarcity' of enabling material means (in any society) also depends upon social, not physical circumstances…'scarcity' does not mean physical shortage, but a condition of insufficiency relative to desire" (Dalton 1961, 4).[4] In a similar vein to Dalton, economist Frank Knight observed, "[I]t is human nature to be more dissatisfied the better off one is." Another economist concluded, "insaturability is something that has been in human nature from its very beginning" (Sedlacek 2011, 218, 223).

Professor of Theology Douglas Meeks emphasizes the biblical tradition that reveals "God the Economist." Meeks believes a recurring motif in both the Old and New Testaments is the superabundance of God's spirit, as witness manna in the desert, the Lord's Supper, and the fishes and loaves stories. Meeks disputes economists' basic conception of scarcity and states, "the righteousness of God destroys artificial scarcity.…The pretense of scarcity is not tolerated as the starting point for economics.…The heart of God's economy is found in God's own self-giving, which produces abundance for life" (Meeks 1989, 175, see also 12).

How Humans Learned to Interact

Primitive people may have approached peaceful trade from a strictly pragmatic motive, as they hoped for future transactions. Moral pragmatism, however, may be a rickety structure upon which to erect long-term relationships. The temptations to lie, cheat, or steal often lurked.

How did primitive and ancient people learn to deal with strangers? Paul Seabright identifies humans' ability for rational calculation with respect to the costs and benefits of cooperation and a tendency toward reciprocity, whereby I treat you as you treat me. Both dispositions have to exist, because calculation without reciprocity would create opportunistic people, whom other people would hesitate to trust. Reciprocity without calculation would leave a person vulnerable to exploitation. People had to develop the ability to balance calculation and reciprocity. Eventually people develop ways to treat strangers as "honorary relatives or friends" by deriving a set of rules covering behavior and incentives. Through education and training, primitive people made their behavior "reliable enough for others to count upon."

One of the difficulties facing early people was how to signal to strangers that "they have the element of reciprocity that makes them trustworthy, and they need to signal it in a way that any purely calculating person could not convincingly mimic." When groups of strangers meet, how do trustworthy people act? Seabright points out that an individual wishing to demonstrate they are open to the stranger and trustworthy will laugh: "almost nobody can fake laughter convincingly," to which another author adds, "This is what Good Trust is about" (Seabright 2004, 27–28, 60; see also Fort 2008, 158).

To cope with risk, primitive people often cluster in groups of relatives. Relatives may be more likely to keep promises to family members and "it matters less if they do not." Hunter-gatherers often faced violence and hostility in encounters with other groups. One anthropologist, Carol Ember, suggests that without institutional restraints, "systematic killing of unrelated individuals is so common among human beings that…it cannot be described as exceptional." The dangers facing itinerate traders making first contracts with an unfamiliar group were so prevalent that Seabright finds it, "astonishing that systematic exchange among nonrelatives should have evolved at all" (Seabright 2004, 48–53; Ember 1978, 443).[5]

People may have taken intermediate steps with regard to learning to trust strangers. They may have begun by trusting familiar nonrelatives. By interacting on a tenuous basis, two groups might have found benefits; if these benefits were sufficient and could be repeated, then two groups may decide that cooperation was better than the short-run strategies of cheat, steal, or kill. Humans had to develop enough intelligence to make reasonably accurate calculations of future benefits and costs; people also needed to be able to recognize if and when the other individual or group cheated. Perhaps, too, there was some sort of selection benefiting people able to engage in reciprocity, whereby they mirrored the treatment they received from the strangers (Seabright 2004, 53–54). Such selection may help explain the near-ubiquity of the Golden Rule across cultures and time.

Nomads and Agriculturalists

Agriculturalists sought out land. Did they peacefully displace hunter-gathers? Evidence suggests that they resorted to violence, killing the males and keeping the women. Slavery was widespread and became more prevalent as societies got wealthier until the eighteenth century.

Doing business with strangers might seem, "sordidly commercial, but it would be a major improvement upon the reaction of many of our forebears. The discovery of people controlling a resource that we value more than they do has led…to their murder or enslavement." The willingness to trade peacefully, though, exists simultaneously with the "temptation to take, bully, and extort." Paul Seabright worries that people do not pay enough attention to "the fragility of the commercial motive in the face of more brutal temptations" (Seabright 2004, 220, 233; see also Nieboer [1910] 1971, 255–256, 286–287; Pinker 2011, 153–158).

Nomadic groups' herds were vulnerable to weather, disease, and predatory animals. The precariousness of pastoralists' existence induced them to raid from other groups, including agriculturalists. Herders obtained headgear made of copper that gave them a decisive edge in the combat; the farmers quickly realized their need to acquire similar headgear and, later, weapons made with metal. In order to obtain such, farmers needed to trade with the producers of weapons. Although peaceful voluntary trade has greatly benefited humanity, there were dark aspects to trade, and the arms race was certainly one of the darkest (O'Connell 2002, 21–23; Bernstein 2008, 20, 25).

Technology affected social organization. Nomadism made accumulating material goods difficult. Although sedentism made it easier to accumulate and to store goods, the rudimentary knowledge of food preservation technique proved a limiting factor. Since most foods could not be stored for any extended length of time, surpluses proved ephemeral. With most foodstuffs subject to deterioration, a current surplus was likely to rot or be consumed by vermin. If food could be stored, then specialists in crafts could emerge. In addition, surpluses in food supplies and accumulated stores required management and distribution. It was better to use the surplus to gain prestige and to create reciprocity. Some observers believe that the exchange of gifts was not "trade," because often the gifts were similar commodities (grain today for grain in the future), unlike trade of different commodities (due to specialization or comparative advantage). However, grain today and grain tomorrow were, in essence, different commodities. Trading the same commodity *simultaneously* defeats the insurance aspect of the gift-giving. Both parties could gain, however, if the commodity exchanged was grain *today* for grain *in the future*. An insurance policy, therefore, was to share with others. An individual or a family group that experienced a big kill or an abundant crop could bestow lavish gifts upon another group. "[It] is scarcity and not sufficiency that makes people generous, since everybody is thereby insured against hunger." Primitive man decided that sharing surpluses not only with family members but even other groups might be politic, as such largesse might not just incite reciprocity but also create prestige as a big man (Posner 1980, 14–16).[6]

Given the fragile nature of interaction between individuals or groups outside kinship relationships, suppression of self-seeking, calculating behavior embedded in such tactics as haggling may be conducive to keeping the peace. Groups recognized the long-term advantage of repeated trade and decided to suppress motives to gain an advantage at the expense of terminating the relationship. People devised ways to promote stability between groups. The idea of unbalanced gift-giving worked because the implicit obligation of the recipient to exceed the giver by giving even more in the next meeting kept the relationship going. To renege by not responding with greater generosity or by not responding at all was tantamount to inciting hostility; in modern video-game parlance, failure to reciprocate was equivalent to "Game Over." If even small imbalances existed, the parties were likely to continue reciprocal giving; after each iteration, the groups began to deepen their trust (Sahlins 1972, 194–195, 201, 222–223).

Ethics and Morality of Intra- and Inter-Group Exchange

Actions that would spark opprobrium within the group might create prestige and honor if done outside of the group, such as stealing goods or women. A working hypothesis then is that the further apart people are in terms of kinship distance, the more likely they will engage in opportunistic behavior. An economist might view this as a pragmatic demonstration of a "repeat game," whereby actors interact frequently; the dynamic of cooperative and opportunistic behavior differs from one-time interactions. In the case of the Siuai, for example, interaction with distant groups is perceived as undesirable, although some of their property or techniques might be useful; one is motivated to acquire the distant people's desirable goods or techniques, but at the least possible cost to oneself, whether by shrewd (even deceitful) bargaining or theft. Many primitive societies advocate honesty within the group but are less scrupulous with regard to strangers. The Kapauku believe that traders are cheats, so they discourage intra-regional trade, but they approve inter-tribal trade that nets profits; the latter traders gain prestige (Sahlins 1972, 191–198; Oliver 1955, 82; Pospisil 1958, 127).

The Siassi of New Guinea practice deception with regard to cooking pots. According to anthropologist Thomas Harding, the Siassi trade their man-made pots to distant groups. Many people in the outlying areas are unaware that pots are man-made and may believe that such items are produced by the sea. The Siassis are more than happy to exploit this ignorance and concoct tales of diving for pot-producing mussels; the mussels provide food and pots. By playing upon their trading partners' credulity, the Siassis may be able to inflate the value of their pots. The Siassis' trading partners are unlikely to venture far and to discover the deception (Harding 1967, 42–44 and 140; Sahlins 1972, 284–285). Although the Siassi may chortle about bamboozling their trading partners (one can imagine them saying, "ho, ho, we got pigs for pots"), it is possible that their trading partners were saying, "ho, ho, we got pots for pigs."

The mutually beneficial aspects of trade can override inter-group hostilities. Markets (*suq*) in the Berber Highlands (circa 1900) were often temporary assemblages that offered an opportunity for various tribes to gather for purpose of trade of critical foodstuffs to sustain life, to exchange information, and occasionally engage in political activities; given these various facets of a *suq*, anthropologist Francisco Benet draws a comparison between *suqs* and Champagne fairs of the medieval period. The *suqs* were neutral grounds; all feuds were set aside during the *suq*. Maintaining the peace was a paramount issue; a perception of neutrality by the market officials was critical. In some cases, reliance upon religious strictures helped keep the peace (Benet 1957, 188–193, 198–202).

In the Berber trading places, strict ethical standards applied. Unlike many marketplaces, where vendors downgrade their rivals' products and services, such behavior was punishable by fines: "he who runs down the merchandise out of malice, or with intent of purchasing himself at a cheaper rate, is fined 5 duros if it turns out that the merchandise did not suffer from the shortcomings he had asserted." Benet admits that there was not sufficient evidence to establish whether the canons of fair bargaining worked well in this culture, but he notes, "there are sufficient indications which point to the fact that these were mostly of the 'free' type, and that spontaneous price fluctuations were a widespread feature." Authorities tried to discourage speculation and sometimes fixed retail prices. If a scarcity arose, the authorities might have imposed rationing. In these trading places, all transactions had to be executed and finished on the same market day; no uncompleted transactions could linger until the next day. People could not leave the trading place owing more than a minimal debt. Draconian penalties for theft included gouging out the thief's eyes. These regulations were meant to maintain a neutrality in the market and presumably to foster peace. The road leading into the market area was blocked, so authorities could control entry.

Methods of maintaining the peace of the market—the peace of the *suq*—do not often work in marketplaces with a volatile mix of hostile tribes. Although the tribes supposedly agree to keep the peace (in order to reap the benefits of trade), sometimes an altercation between hot-headed individuals and small groups can spiral out of control; such outbreaks—*nefra*—generally occur in larger inter-tribal markets, where Benet observes it is easier for the "mass psychology" of a *nefra* to occur. Benet described a brawl where hundreds of people were killed or injured (Benet 1957, 203–210).

Injection of Money

There is a function of money rarely broached: "Money serves a useful purpose in the calculus of the Golden Rule." Scholars Jeffrey Barach and John Elstrott observe that if someone does a favor for you and you wish to reciprocate exactly, money allows you to do so; you can calibrate the payment to the penny. They suggest, "There is a certain majesty in that match; for both of us treat the other as we treat ourselves; each values his side of the transaction. Money enables us to do it rather precisely." Rather than focus on money as the root of evil, "it is also a root of good. It is a mechanism that facilitates observance of the Golden Rule." They acknowledge that their depiction of the benign aspect of money depends on the transaction being "freely joined." In the presence of desperation, a monetary transaction may not follow the Golden Rule. One can think of the famous photos from the stock market crash of 1929 depicting men selling their new cars for the proverbial "song." Presumably, the unfortunate stock traders desperately needed cash to redeem their position in the stock market. The ethical question becomes whether a potential buyer is obliged to negotiate as though the seller of the car was not in dire need of funds, or does the fact that the stockbroker willingly accepts a lower price for his car justify a seller offering a low, low price? This exception aside, Barach and Elstrott conclude, "under conditions of free enterprise, economic transactions can and often do represent a calculus of agape, a way of adjusting the relationship between persons so that reciprocity exists, so that each has the same opportunity assign value to his actions" (Barach and Elstrott 1988, 548).

The introduction of money, although useful as an economic tool, had the drawback of becoming, "an all-powerful instrument of acquisition, control, exploitation, or corruption," according to philosopher Marcel Henaff. He claimed that the, "Goods exchanged on specific occasions—such as celebrations, encounters, or weddings—do not have any economic significance or role; their purpose is to recognize, to honor, and to bring together the parties involved." The occasions are based on graciousness, courtesy, and reciprocity: "They still endure remarkably well in everything that involves what is priceless, such as works of the mind, works of art, or expressions of talent—which are sometimes called 'gifts'—but also in moral gestures such as mutual help, compliments, and renunciation." He wondered whether the priceless endures in our age (Henaff 2010, 14–18).[7]

Echoes of Primitive Trade

Modern-day people make many market exchanges. In this context, personal acquaintance is often immaterial. Gift exchange is a highly personal endeavor. The "price" and the timing of reciprocal are to some degree indeterminate. There are benefits beyond the material aspects of the trade: "Exchange is not only an economic transaction, it is also a good in itself… usually in the form of a *personal* relationship." Such interactions provide much satisfaction and created a wide range of desirable responses, but, in particular, that of *regard*. Adam Smith wrote, "From whence, then, arises that emulation which runs through all the different ranks of men, and what are the advantages which we propose by that great purpose of human life which we call bettering our condition? To be observed, to be attended to, to be taken notice of with sympathy, complacency, and approbation, are all the advantages which we can propose to derive from it" (Offer 1997, 451–452; see also Smith 1982, 50).

People enjoy giving and receiving gifts. Giving money has often been scorned as impersonal and crass, although the popularity of gift cards seems to have softened this. In a business context, customers may perceive the vendor's regard for them as insincere. Gifts are personalized, and even when obtained in a market context, the gift is evidence of "an effort to gratify a particular individual. It conveys a signal that is unique to giver, receiver, or both….A gift without regard would be a bribe."

One can ask how genuine these relationships are, with their holiday greeting cards and superficial questions regarding the family. Then again, one can easily take too cynical a view of the proceedings. Economic historian Avner Offer observes that money may make the relationship suspect, what he terms "pseudo regard." "Rapport with customers is often driven, back at the office, by output quotas as relentless as any in the old Soviet Union. In the web of commerce, every human bond is open to betrayal." Any human relationship, though, is likely to contain traces of self-interested behavior. Purely altruistic relationships may be rare.

Such intra-group reciprocity and trust can be used for nefarious purposes. The Cosa Nostra, Chinese Triads, and Russian Mafia use similar group-trust building tactics to foster their criminal activities. These small groups, with their ultra-loyalties, can collude very effectively. Offer speculates that, "A strong gift economy can crowd out the market if exchange depends entirely on reciprocal inclusion. This is a strong argument for liberalism, for the impersonality of the market, the law, the public service, and the vote." In the case of the former Soviet Union, corruption may have bolstered the economy. The Eastern European economies under the Soviet regime relied upon a network of "fixers," acting as brokers in a gift economy (*blat*) incumbent upon their access to resources, relationships, and reputations (Offer 1997, 454, 467–469).[8]

Conclusion

Primitive people took the first big step toward trade and commerce, when they learned to exchange goods peacefully. Inherent in an ongoing trading relationship was observing some elementary rules. Reciprocity and the desire for repeated transactions helped keep opportunistic behavior within bounds. Behavior, therefore, was motivated by a strong utilitarianism. Primitive people learned that the rewards from repeated transactions often outweighed any temporary gains from cheating or stealing.

This realization should not be underestimated. For primitive people to understand the future consequences of their decisions required a jump in intellectual development. Had humans' groups remained insular, it is unlikely that living standards would have improved much. We owe much to the first exchangers, even if their ethical behavior emanated from pragmatic considerations.

Notes

1. We are ignoring the possibility that one or both of the parties made a mistake in judgment; the highlander, for instance, may find fish less tasty than anticipated.
2. The distribution of the overall gains or surplus, assuming the quantity transacted remains the same, is also a zero-sum game.
3. Another example is found in Radcliffe-Brown (1933, 84).
4. Tomas Sedlacek reflected on the Genesis story of Adam and Eve. Presumably, the Garden of Eden was so bountiful that scarcity should not have been an issue. But even in the Garden, Adam and Eve sought more: "it will still not be enough for us, and we will have a constant tendency completely unnecessarily, to consume what we do not need to consume or even are forbidden to consume, and to open Pandora's boxes." The serpent, using an early form of advertising, inspired a desire that Eve did not have previously and did not need, but Sedlacek suggests that the serpent "did not create desire but awakened it…that the original sin had the character of over *consumption*" [italics his] (Sedlacek 2011, 216).
5. The itinerant trader would have to convince the unfamiliar group that he or she would be willing to return, otherwise the situation is a one-time game instead of a potentially repeated game.
6. The gain in prestige or by placing people in one's debt is a form of profit (Posner 1980, 17; Grierson 1971, 74–79; see also Winter 1962, 457–461; Colson 1962, 601–607).
7. Henaff described Socrates' choice when faced with the possibility of evading his death sentence; he contrasted Socrates' attitudes with those of the Sophists, who were knowledge professionals selling their knowledge (Henaff 2010, 2–5, 9–10).
8. Overseas Chinese, too, use family and gift reciprocity (Offer 1997, 468–469).

Bibliography

Barach, Jeffrey and John Elstrott. "The Transactional Ethic: The Ethical Foundations of Free Enterprise Reconsidered." *Journal of Business Ethics* 7(7), July 1988, 545–551.

Benet, Francisco. "Explosive Markets: The Berber Highlands." *Trade and Market in the Early Empires: Economies in History and Theory*, edited by Karl Polanyi, Conrad Arensberg, and Harry Pearson (Glencoe, IL: Free Press 1957), 188–217.

Bernstein, William. *A Splendid Exchange: How Trade Shaped the World* (New York: Grove Press, 2008).

Colson, Elisabeth. "Trade and Wealth among the Tonga." *Markets in Africa*, edited by Paul Bohannan and George Dalton (Evanston, IL: Northwestern University Press, 1962), 601–616.

Dalton, George. "Economic Theory and Primitive Society." *American Anthropologist* 63(1), February 1961, 1–25.

Dalton, George. "Aboriginal Economies in Stateless Societies." *Exchange Systems in Prehistory,* edited by Timothy Earle and Jonathon Ericson (New York, NY: Academic Press, 1977), 191–212.

Ember, Carol. "Myths about Hunter-Gatherers." *Ethnology* 17(4), October 1978, 439–448.

Finley, Moses. "Anthropology and the Classics." *The Use and Abuse of History* (New York, Viking Press, 1975), 102–119.

Fort, Timothy. *Prophets, Profits, and Peace: The Positive Role of Business in Promoting Religious Tolerance* (New Haven, CT: Yale University Press, 2008).

Goldschmidt, Walter. *Nomlaki Ethnography.* University of California Publications in American Archaeology and Ethnology (Berkeley, CA: University of California Press, 1951).

Grierson, Philip. "Commerce in the Dark Ages: A Critique of the Evidence." *Studies in Economic Anthropology*, edited by George Dalton (Washington, D.C.: American Anthropological Association, 1971), 74–83.

Harding, Thomas. *Voyagers of the Vitiaz Strait: A Study of a New Guinea Trade System* (Seattle, WA: University of Washington Press, 1967).

Henaff, Marcel. *Price of Truth: Gift, Money, and Philosophy*, translated by Jean-Louis Morhange and Anne-Marie Feenberg-Dibon (Stanford, CA: Stanford University Press, 2010).

Hogbin, Herbert. *Transformation Scene: The Changing Culture of a New Guinea Village* (London, UK: Routledge & Paul, 1951).

Meeks, M. Douglas. *God the Economist: The Doctrine of God and Political Economy* (Minneapolis, MN: Fortress Press, 1989).

Nieboer, Herman. *Slavery as an Industrial System* (New York, NY: Burt Franklin, [1910] 1971).

Nietzsche, Friedrich. *On the Genealogy of Morals and Ecce Homo*, edited by Walter Kaufmann, translated by Walter Kaufmann and R.J. Hollingdale (New York, NY: Vintage Books, [1967] 1989).

North, Douglass. "Government and the Cost of Exchange in History." *Journal of Economic History* 44(2), June 1984, 255–264.

O'Connell. *Soul of the Sword* (New York, NY: Free Press, 2002).

Offer, Avner. "Between the Gift and the Market: The Economy of Regard." *Economic History Review*, New Series 50(3), August 1997, 450–476.

Oliver, Douglas. *A Solomon Island Society: Kinship and Leadership among the Siuai of Bougainville* (Cambridge, MA: Harvard University Press, 1955).

Pinker, Steven. *The Better Angels of Our Nature: Why Violence Has Declined* (New York, NY: Viking, 2011).

Posner, Richard. "A Theory of Primitive Society, with Special Reference to Law." *Journal of Law and Economics* 23(1), April 1980. 1–53.

Pospisil, Leonard. "Kapauku Papuans and Their Law." Yale University Publications in Anthropology 54, 1958.

Radcliffe-Brown, Alfred. *The Andaman Islanders* (Cambridge, UK: Cambridge University Press, 1933).

Sahlins, Marshall. *Stone Age Economics* (Chicago: Aldine-Atherton, 1972).

Saller, Richard. "Framing the Debate over Growth in the Ancient Economy." *The Ancient Economy*, edited by Walter Scheidel and Sitta von Reden (New York, NY: Routledge, 2002), 251–269.

Seabright, Paul. *The Company of Strangers: A Natural History of Economic Life* (Princeton, NJ: Princeton University Press, 2004).

Sedlacek, Tomas. *Economics of Good and Evil: The Quest for Economic Meaning from Gilgamesh to Wall Street* (Oxford, UK: Oxford University Press, 2011).

Smith, Adam. *An Inquiry into the Nature and Causes of the Wealth of Nations*, edited by R.H. Campbell and A.S. Skinner (Indianapolis, IN: Liberty*Classics*, 1981).

Smith, Adam. *The Theory of Moral Sentiments*, edited by D.D. Raphael and A.L. Macfie (Indianapolis, IN: Liberty Fund, 1982).

Viner, Jacob. *The Role of Providence in the Social Order: an Essay in Intellectual History* (Philadelphia, PA: American Philosophical Society, 1972).

Winter, Edward. "Livestock Markets Among the Iraqw of Northern Tanganyika." *Markets in Africa*, edited by Paul Bohannan and George Dalton (Evanston, IL: Northwestern University Press, 1962), 457–468.

CHAPTER 4

Ancient Trade in the Near East

Civilizations in the Near East and along the Nile developed sophisticated trading networks well before the Greeks and Romans. What can we learn about business ethics from the Babylonians? Many westerners' perceptions of Babylon may be tainted by Old and New Testaments excoriations, such as "Whore of Babylon!" The ancient Babylonian governments, however, provide us early written records of trade and commerce, as well as examples of unacceptable and presumably unethical behavior. Along with other ancient societies, the Babylonians enacted regulations that helped facilitate trading and promoted ethical behavior.

Other ancient civilizations, especially the ancient Israelites, recognized basic ethical and unethical aspects of trade and commerce. False weights and measures, limitations upon lending at interest, and the inculcation of simple honesty loomed large. Old Testament prophets waxed indignant at perceived and actual malfeasance by traders and government officials. Many of their tirades resonate in our modern world.

Pragmatism and fear of punishment underlay these rules and precepts. The concept of acting ethically for its own sake was rare and may have struck these people as bizarre, although the Israelites of the Old Testament began to create moral values and duties.

D. G. Surdam, *Business Ethics from Antiquity to the 19th Century*,
https://doi.org/10.1007/978-3-030-37165-4_4

Conflicting Viewpoints

Did the ancients have markets? Polymath Karl Polanyi claimed: "a market is a meeting place for the purpose of barter or buying and selling. Unless such a pattern is present at least in patches, the propensity to barter will find but insufficient scope: it cannot produce prices" (Polanyi [1944] 1957, 56).[1]

Polanyi argues that the Babylonians lacked market places and, therefore, did not form a functioning market system. He bases his argument on a *single* sentence in Herodotus; the historian had described Cyrus the Persian king's taunt about the Greeks setting up "marketplaces in which to buy and sell:" "the Persians do not frequent market places and in effect, do not possess in their country a single market place" (Herodotus 1987, 103; Polanyi 1957a, 16; 1957b, 64–65).

Economist Morris Silver disputes Polanyi's assertion that there was no indication of a development of markets until the seventh century BCE in Greece. Although Near Eastern and Egyptian societies maintained large-scale trade, Polanyi believed they did so without the "regulator of supply and demand" and instead relied upon prices negotiated by treaties. Silver notes, "It should be made clear at the outset that the specification of prices in advance—as opposed to determining them by spot transactions at the point of exchange—does not mean that forces of supply and demand are absent or irrelevant." Silver cites examples of price changes for commodities and slaves. There were seasonal changes in prices in Mesopotamia and even in Egypt. Silver, therefore, thinks the markets were responsive to standard supply and demand factors (Silver 1983a, 796–799, 808).

Silver argues that "the specification of prices in private long-term contracts serves to limit uncertainty and opportunism and to fill gaps in markets. Government treaties, a form of contract, might also be employed, yet would still acknowledge forces of supply and demand." Silver presented price data that suggested that there were fluctuations in the prices of grain, wine, and oil—basic commodities for Greek consumers. Government officials and merchants noted price fluctuations, and such fluctuations affected the timing of their sales of grain (Silver 1985, 73, 77–78). Polanyi asserted that ancient producers did not produce with the intent of reaping profits, and, therefore, capital accumulation was rare. Scattered writings, though, suggest that ancient people acted as profit-seeking, if not maximizing, actors. Silver points to Babylonian textile manufacturers (in Eshnunna), who employed hundreds of workers and exported throughout the Near

East. Landowners, too, displayed decision making that implied a search for profit; the Hammurabi Code and other documents describe landowners who converted grain fields into date orchards and pollinated these new orchards. An Egyptian farmer named Hekanakht wrote his family and outlined how they were to manage their lands in his absence. His advice covered not only how to manage the land and servants but how to market the crop (Silver 1983a, 810–811; 1985, 138–139).

There were other indications that ancient people were economically sophisticated. Mesopotamians and Egyptians recognized the role of time in making loans; they saw that grain prices exhibited a seasonal pattern, rising up until just before the harvest season. Grain loans often occurred just before harvest and repaid after the harvest. To reflect for the seasonality in grain prices, lenders charged a much higher rate of interest on such grain loans than on silver loans. Second-millennium Babylonia "knew negotiable loans of a two-party promissory-note type…specifying repayment not to the creditor but to the 'bearer of this table.'"

The participants in the Near Eastern slave trade understood the risks inherent in such trade. The contracts often had stipulations, whereby the seller provided a warranty as to both the slave's fitness and the seller's legal ownership; other contracts included clauses pertaining to a slave running away or having illnesses. The Hammurabi Code discussed suitable compensation to buyers of slaves, whose slave developed epilepsy within a period of the date of purchase. Economists would recognize these clauses as similar to the purchase of a durable good, whose quality cannot be ascertained without experience. The Romans, too, attempted to resolve the adverse selection problem inherent in the slave trade; the current owner (similar to a modern-day owner of a used car) knew more about the slave than did the prospective owner. Romans sold skilled and therefore, expensive, slaves in permanent shops rather than in the temporary stalls for auctions of unskilled slaves. Slaves wore placards listing their health status, nationality (slaves of some nationalities had a higher incidence of running away), and other information. The Hammurabi Code, paragraph 18, hints at similar legislation.

Although some scholars believe that the labor markets of the ancient Near East were not true markets, Silver lists evidence demonstrating that employers of labor understood the need to create incentives to work hard (such as piecework rates). Rulers from Hammurabi to Greek enacted rules covering apprentices (Silver 1985, 79, 88, 102–106, 112; *Hammurabi Code*, paragraphs 278 and 279).

Even the Old Testament refers to speculation in the marketplace, an action that implies that forces of supply and demand affected markets. In 2 Kings 7:1–2, Elisha announced the end of a siege, and, in a ninth-century BCE example of insider knowledge (from which he did not profit), proclaimed: "Tomorrow about this time a measure of fine meal shall be sold for a shekel, and two measures of barley for a shekel, at the gate of Samaria." He added, somewhat ominously, "You shall see it with your own eyes, but you shall not eat of it." Proverbs 11:26 contains the admonition against speculators: "The people curse him who holds back grain, but a blessing is on the head of him who sells it."

By 3000 BCE, there was a trading bloc comprising Africa, Crete, and across the Middle East to India. Improvements in transport and road building facilitated trade, with people moving such bulky items as alabaster and stones from the Mediterranean coasts to Babylonia and Assyria. Officials of city states were involved with planning trade and transport and the role of individual merchants. These individual merchants quickly learned to make careful accounting of transactions. Money had displaced barter for many transactions but not all. Merchants and traders became specialized occupations, and participants formed merchant associations. The older forms of trading, such as "silent trade, conventional mutual robbing operations, and group-barter almost disappeared under the rule of the Ancient Oriental cities" (Heichelheim 1958, I:116–117, 126).

Role of Deities

Societies used deities to reduce transaction costs: "The syncretistic process so often noted and condemned both in the Bible and by modern commentators may…be understood in terms of the creation of a new public capital good, 'trust.'"[2]

Ancient vendors found it advantageous to congregate in temples or marketplaces. The proximity of many vendors and buyers meant that people could accumulate information about each other, in a sense investing in market knowledge. The accumulation of information reduced transaction costs and reduced price dispersion, as economist George Stigler theorized: "Price dispersion is a manifestation—and, indeed, it is the measure—of ignorance in the market" (Stigler [1968] 1983, 172; Silver 1985, 128).

Near Eastern merchants often congregated at temples to promote honest and secure dealing. The presence of the gods provided scrutiny that promoted scrupulous behavior, although one wonders whether the irreverent were deterred by the gods' presence. Vendors often brought offerings for the temple, including foodstuff. "[T]hese offerings constituted a kind of payment to the temple for the privilege of carrying out their loan and other business transactions under the auspices of the gods." Money changers and spice dealers in medieval Europe followed a similar tradition, as they conducted business in a cathedral square and swore "to commit no theft, nor trick, nor falsification."[3]

The use of temples and religions to inculcate ethical practices came with a potential drawback: Using temples as trading places made it easier for producers of similar goods and services to collude by keeping trade practices secret. The use of taboos against revealing such trade secrets might have retarded diffusion of knowledge; on the other hand, the monopoly profits attendant upon developing new trade secrets might have spurred technical innovations. Morris Silver conjectured that the secrecy within the trade may have been a forerunner of patent laws. Two economists argued that the divine sanction may have helped maintain cartel pricing by discouraging individual producers from cheating on the fixed price. The religious strictures may have exerted a declining effect upon producers, as by the sixth century in Babylonia, skilled craftsmen "frequently embezzled or misallocated materials despite legally binding exclusive work contracts and the possibility of heavy fines" (Silver 1985, 8–9; see also Ekelund and Tollison 1981, 115–119).

Babylonian merchants of the second millennium used the temple of Shamash to settle accounts. Hammurabi's code stipulated that partners distributing their profits or losses should do so in god's presence. Some of the extant loan contracts listed gods as witnesses. Failure to live up to a contract could invite the wrath of gods. Sumerian hymns to gods excoriated such individuals. Some daring individuals, perhaps tempted by the gains from breaching a contract or who did not fear the gods, took and then violated oaths, but the use of oaths appeared to be widespread and presumably exerted suasion among parties to contracts. Modern-day people have not dispensed with the scrutiny of gods, as our "taking the oath" in courtrooms attests. Such diverse religious states as ancient Egypt, Babylonia, Israel, and others used similar tactics. Hammurabi's Code and the Laws of Eshnunna required merchants to swear by the gods that they had been robbed, before they would be released from loans covering merchandise. Exodus 22:10–12 is representative of the practice: "If a man delivers to his neighbor…[livestock]…to keep, and it dies or is hurt or is driven away, without any one seeing it, an oath by the Lord shall be between them both to see whether he has not put his hand to his neighbor's property; and the owner shall accept the oath, and he shall not make restitution. But if it is stolen from him, he shall make restitution to its owner."

Because of the temple's reputation, merchants, traders, and producers often chose to deposit surplus money there. Temples began to perform banking services, such as extending loans. As debtors might be wary of defaulting on a loan owed to a temple (and, therefore, to the gods), the temple might be able to charge lower rates of interest. Temples stored goods for private owners; these valuables were marked with private seals that served to protect property rights (Silver 1985, 14–19; *Hammurabi's Code*, paragraphs 98, 103; Goetze 1956, 39).

Rise of Governments and Ancient Codes

States offer protection and justice in exchange for revenue (taxes, user fees, and so on). A state may have economies of scale in providing these services (it may not cost twice as much to defend twice as many people); if there are economies of scale, then state-provision may be more beneficial than if smaller groups sought to produce these services. The state can also mimic a price-discriminating monopolist by charging different groups of constituents varying amounts and by devising property rights for each group in order to maximize state revenue. The state's ability to squeeze more revenues out of its constituents is restricted by the possibility of rival states or individuals entering the market, so to speak, and offering similar services at (initially) lower prices (North 1981, 23–24).

Rulers and elites in many ancient (and not-so-ancient) societies contrived to extort goods and land from the mass of peasants. Courts and elite landlords desired certain types of agricultural produce, especially produce that was easily taxable. Peasants often would have been better off raising subsistence crops, but the royal court and the elite demanded taxes and levies that required cash crops. Cash crops often posed greater pecuniary risks for the peasants, especially as they had to sell their crops during or right after harvest season, when prices tended to be low. Merchants and creditors, however, benefited from the increased volume of transactions and greater need for consumption loans. The royal court needed revenues to supply its military and police power. Such taxes and impositions could take half of the agricultural produce. Peasants seeking consumption loans frequently lost their ancestral land or became debt slaves (Barrera 2013,

38–40). One wonders what the peasants got in return. True, the royal court may have protected the peasants from foreign invaders and plunderers, but given the high rate of taxation, it is a fair question whether foreign plunderers would have been more deleterious.

Pharaoh appears to have been a parasite upon the foragers turned farmers along the Nile. The farmers reaped larger harvests than they had collected as foragers, but Pharaoh's tax and rent collectors skimmed a portion of the harvest. The burgeoning output also boosted population, creating a pool of labor. Pharaoh justified this confiscation by claiming to control the Nile's flood, but modern-day minds find this highly dubious. As the labor pool increased, Pharaoh began conscripting labor for large-scale projects. When Egypt was underpopulated, Pharaoh had difficulty collecting taxes and labor, as farmers could move away (Allen 1997, 141–146).

The Lagid rulers of Egypt (300 BCE to 30 BCE) controlled the economy. The state maintained monopolies upon grain seeds, charging farmers to borrow seed at 24% in terms of money or 50% in terms of seed. The government also controlled the Royal Bank. The government's other monopolies included purchasing, sale, and warehousing of oil-grain seeds (Levy 1967, 40–41).

The shift from hunter-gathering to agricultural lifestyles led to the development of complex and sophisticated societies. Some societies found it useful to codify existing canons of acceptable behavior or to expand regulations to ensure orderly market transactions. Rulers, of course, often had their own self-interested agendas in issuing codes of behavior.

The Laws of Eshnunna date roughly to the IIIrd Dynasty of Ur (twenty-second to twenty-first centuries BCE). It begins with a tariff of prices, although some scholars believe these prices were maximum prices, given the fluctuations found in prices. The Laws dealt with the principle of responsibility and negligence in such business transactions as hiring a boat. There was a fixed fee of 20% for transporting silver. Other details revolved around paying harvesters of grain in contrast to paying regular laborers or hired hands. The latter categories received wages and provender and were members of the household, while the harvesters received only wages (typically higher than that of laborers, due, in part, to the greater demand for harvesters during the season and the lack of in-kind goods). With regards to loans, interest was not mentioned but "is from the outset added to the amount owed." The rate appears to be 33.3% per year, a rate similar to that in the Code of Hammurabi (Goetze 1956, 24–25, 32–39, 55, 66).

Sumerians were familiar with age-old tricks of the trade. A Nanshe hymn describes the cheating merchant, who "Substitutes the small weight for the large weight; Substitutes the small measure for the large measure." Ur-Nammu's law code attempted to prevent the merchants' sleazy tactics by standardizing weights and measures, but he was not uniformly successful: "The merchant—how he has reduced prices! How he has reduced the oil and barley." The merchant apparently practiced a "bait and shrink" tactic, making an *apparent* price reduction (Kramer 1959, 265–266).

Morris Silver contends that private property and trade "appear to have reached a stage of high development" as early as Ur III (2112–2004 BCE) and continued under Hammurabi (1792–1750 BCE). Hammurabi's code implemented some reforms, including government involvement in real estate transactions, price controls on foodstuffs, and interest rates (Silver 1983a, 828; Heichelheim 1958, I:185). Hammurabi's code demonstrates that "not only was there private property in land, and the leasing and hiring, the buying and selling that such a system would require, but also that there were individuals and procedures in trade as distinct from agriculture that prove the existence of business as a specialized individual enterprise working for profits. The Babylon of Hammurabi may well be likened to leading towns in feudal Europe in the Middle Ages."

The code contains a fair amount of information regarding merchants and suggests that merchants were widely traveled people carrying valuable cargoes. Some merchants, though, remained in Babylon but engaged agents. One clause in the code reads, "If the merchant give to an agent corn, wool, oil, or any sort of goods with which to trade, the agent shall write down the value and return (the money) to the merchant; the agent shall take a sealed receipt for the money which he shall give to the merchant." The code (and presumably the authorities enforcing it) took a stern view of cheating, although there were quirks. If an agent tried to cheat a merchant and was found guilty, the agent had to pay triple the money involved; if a merchant cheated an agent, the merchant had to reimburse the wronged agent six-fold. Behind all of these edicts, the king was the regulator of the market. "The Code stipulates wages of labor in various occupations and charges for services. Storage rates are set as are the prices of various products," in addition to the previous remark regarding market values (*Bulletin of the Business Historical Society*, April 1938a, 25–27).

To forestall disputes and possibly to allow the government to know what was going on, Hammurabi's Code mandated that sales and deposits had to be recorded in writing. The Code prohibited oral agreement under pain of death. Merchants' guilds sometimes created courts to adjudicate disputes between members (Heichelheim 1958, I:132).

Enforcing compliance consumes resources, as Douglass North commented: "Compliance costs in addition consist of the cost of enacting penalties for nonperformance. Because measurement is costly (and the costs of perfect accuracy prohibitive) and because there are also costs of enforcement it pays parties to an exchange to maximize with respect to deviations from the agreement." Compliance and coercion required organization: "a state is an organization with a comparative advantage in violence….The essence of property rights is the right to exclude, and an organization which has a comparative advantage in violence is in the position to specify and enforce property rights." Unfortunately, creating property rights that foster "sustained economic growth" is rare (North 1981, 18–23).

Laws and governments were not the only way to maintain trust. Residues of ancient customs that encouraged trust persist in today's society. The handshake remains a signal of trust. In the past, though, handshakes were just part of a more elaborate process. Concluding a business deal was a significant event marked by sharing a meal, anointing each other with oil, and shaking hands. Often these rituals took place before witnesses, testifying to the importance placed upon the deal. Another way to create trust was to appeal to status; traders might consider themselves gentlemen or some other such appellation. Being a gentleman meant living up to the standards inherent in being a gentleman. Throughout the Near East, merchants' and traders' reputations mattered, as trade was often an ongoing intimate relationship. The code of gentlemanly behavior might include such prohibitions as charging trading partners' interest or censuring someone for failing to reciprocate a favor with a favor or a gift with a gift. One function of the favor- and gift-reciprocity served as an insurance policy against illiquidity; another was to reduce the need to continually incur the costs of formal contracting (Mettinger 1976, 216; Silver 1985, 37–38).

The hope for repeated transactions also helped constrain opportunistic behavior. As we've seen, so-called primitive societies often used gift giving as the mechanism for exchange; not reciprocating led to trouble, so tying gift exchange to regular trade might have been a useful way to keep people adhering to agreements (Oppenheim 1973, 264–265). The exchange, then, promoted trust and continuation of relationships; increased the demand for luxury goods; and spread technology.

Ancient Mesopotamia and Sumer

Two thousand years prior to the apogee of the Athenians, the Assyrians and then the Babylonians developed sophisticated economies. They had written languages and central states. These states maintained voluminous records pertaining to business transactions, land holdings, slaves, and, of course, taxes. Gold and silver coins provided the lubricant to grease economic transactions; there was less need for barter in these economies (Pearson 1957, 7).

Karl Polanyi described Assyrian merchants, known as *karum*—"businessmen who made profit" on various transactions. The merchants were middlemen with regard to trade between their home city of Assur and central Anatolia. They were hereditary traders. The businessmen made profits from selling and buying commodities and making short- and long-term loans. A wealthy "big man" in Assur financed the businessmen's efforts. He consigned goods to the Kanish trader. Given the changing prices and interest rates, the members of the *karum* needed alertness and astute assessment of the business environment. Disputes between merchants were resolved by arbitration, but authorities imposed severe penalties upon defaulters. Polanyi noted that the *karum* trading with Cappadocia did not make profits directly from buying and selling but rather from commissions. If this was correct, then the *karum* would have been shielded from the direct effects of varying prices and interest rates, but presumably their backer would have expected them to be careful in disposing of the consignment of goods or in purchasing goods. Polanyi concluded, "It was exciting as an occupation, but risk-free as a business." One is entitled to suspect, however, that a disappointing venture left a *karum* vulnerable to the "big man's" ire. Morris Silver, though, quotes sources demonstrating that these traders were expected to obtain the best prices for buying and selling, not only for their merchant masters but for themselves. The merchants were known for being risk-takers and "go-getters" (Polanyi 1957a, 18–23; Silver 1983a, 821; 1985, 134–135).[4]

The Babylonian trade featured standardized weights and measures (such as minas and shekels) and notaries recording commercial contracts. The Babylonians used their wealth and capital to create a lending market. Borrowers could obtain money or (barley) seed, with the former incurring 20% interest and the latter 33%. Men with few tangible assets could offer their labor as collateral by agreeing to potential contractual slavery. If the borrower failed to repay, he could "enter the house" of the creditor. Hammurabi's Code, paragraph 117, described such contracts, as did the Eshnunna Code. To spread risk, Babylonians invented limited partnership, often involving a partner providing capital and a partner doing the traveling and work. The Babylonians, however, did not participate much in seaborne trade (Silver 1985, 89–91; Levy 1967, 9–10).

Although the presence of weighing and measuring devices may suggest mistrust, such tools reduced transaction costs and misunderstandings. Ancient people quickly created means to verify metals and grains. "A series of verification processes had to precede payment: ringing, testing by touchstone, to tell the kind and grade of metal; and objects were weighed….To avoid weighing or proving the metal, various advances were gradually made. It may be that certain peoples, such as the Greeks of Asia, used preweighed metals to avoid having to weigh it, and paid with current utensils (tripods, cauldrons, brooches, axes, rings)" (Levy 1967, 17).

Even in this early trade, complications arose when traders acted opportunistically, as a clay tablet dating back almost 4000 years ago recounted. The Code of Hammurabi tried to compel investing merchants to share the risks with the traveling merchant, but apparently to no avail. Losses were frequent, given the hazards of trade and the high costs of transportation. Because of the risks, only specialized traders could run the risks inherent in the trade. Traders naturally tried to spread the risk and created variations of insurance. In some cases, merchants complained about bad faith on the part of their trading counterparts. Telmun shipped copper to Ur during the Old Babylonia period. One Ea-nasir promised to give the anonymous writer's messenger good copper ingots. Ea-nasir contemptuously provided the messenger with bad copper and added, "the Old-Babylonian equivalent to our 'take it or leave it.'" The writer was outraged and retorted, "Who am I that you are treating me in this manner and offend me?" He added that this was no way for gentlemen to interact with each other before exclaiming, "Who is there amongst the Telmun traders who has (ever) acted against me in this way?" The writer reminded Ea-nasir that the transaction had taken place in the temple of Shamash. The aggrieved trader's reminder of their mutual gentlemanly status recurs in other letters, "which one merchant reminds the other of the obligation of being a *mar awelim*…to adhere to certain ethical and social standards in business transactions" (Oppenheim 1954, 6–12).

Babylonians and Persians used a system of courts to adjudicate disputes. Although oral testimony by witnesses was permitted, the main sources of evidence rested upon written documents. Babylonian businesses accumulated a trove of written records to assist them in defending themselves or to press for damages from an errant trading partner. A Near East scholar views the "close relationship between the state, the temples, and these families [who operated family firms that] was mutually advantageous economically. While the state kept a watchful eye on the economic and social power of Babylonian temples, including, in the Persian period, taxing the temples, they were careful to manage the relationship so that temples remained economic engines in their respective areas of southern Mesopotamia….It is significant that the Persians continued in broad terms the Neo-Babylonian policy towards Babylonian temples" (Bedford 2007, 321–322).

Ancient Israel

The Pentateuch and prophets provided much commentary regarding the ethics of trade and commerce. Some Israelites must have prospered, as many prophets inveighed against the perils of wealth.

Ancient Near East kings were, in theory, supposed to be defenders and advocates of the poor. Hammurabi boasted of fulfilling these roles. Father Albino Barrera noted, though, that, "there is not a single piece of legislation in the entire Code of Hammurabi that provides relief or extra protection for the poor." These prologues and epilogues were "self-promoting royal propaganda…intended to create a public image of the king, not only as just, but also as a champion of the poor and the marginalized. Such royal propaganda was intended for the consumption of the gods, the public, and posterity" (Barrera 2013, 256–257).

Morris Silver describes the ancient Israelites' experiences and the repercussions: "the destruction of the Jewish state and the dispersal of its citizens. An ironic postscript is provided by the sharp upsurge in genuine moral values and concern for the poor among the brutal but plunder-wealthy Assyrians." Sargon II and Sennacherib, however, gained the reputation for aiding the needy (Silver 1983b, 242–243).

Unlike the ancient Near Eastern kingdoms, though, all Israelites were responsible for ensuring justice; justice was not just the king's responsibility. Part of this difference was due to early Israelites being a group of herders and small farmers lacking a central government. One scholar, Pheme

Perkins, argues that the purpose of the Old Testament economic statutes was to restrain accumulation of goods in a society with severe constraints on goods; there was a zero-sum aspect to the amount of goods available. Therefore, if a rich person accumulated goods, it was directly at the expense of poor people. "There will therefore be an easy transition from asceticism to a 'class morality' in which almsgiving is a merit for the rich man, who shows himself obedient to God's commandment, but not a right for the poor. God has called on the rich to give, he has not willed that the poor be poor no longer. Furthermore, it remains understood that the rich man gives if he wants to and what he wants to." Leviticus 25:36–43, conversely, demonstrated solicitude for the poor, and not only the poor among the Chosen People. Even those people who sold themselves into bondage were to be treated with respect. The prosperous were not to exploit the hungry and impoverished by lending at interest or selling food at a profit. Barrera speculates that the code described in Deuteronomy (Chaps. 15 and 24) helped Israelite peasants retain their land. The example of a seventh-year remission of debts and the respect expected from lenders toward borrowers (such as allowing borrowers to decide which assets to use as collateral) pointed to a desire to keep the gulf between the wealthiest and the poorest within tolerable limits (Veyne 1990, 33; Perkins 1994, 47–49; Barrera 2013, 71; Deuteronomy, chapters 15, 24; Exodus 20:19–23).[5]

Landowners were to help the poor by not stripping the harvest fields bare. Deuteronomy 24:19–21 admonished landowners to recall when God's people were slaves in Egypt. Therefore, landowners should leave any unharvested sheaves of grain, olive boughs, or grapes for the "sojourner, the fatherless, and the widow." These verses are ambiguous in the sense that the poor are inadvertently aided; a scholar adds that rabbinical commentary suggests, "the true intent of these laws was seen to be the molding of character: people should learn not to want every last piece of produce and profit" (Plaut 1981, 1500).[6]

Proverbs 13:7 contained various nuggets of wisdom regarding wealth. "One man pretends to be rich, yet has nothing; another pretends to be poor, yet has great wealth. The ransom of a man's life is his wealth, but a poor man has no means of redemption." Proverb 13:11 notes, "Wealth hastily gotten will dwindle, but he who gathers little by little will increase it."

A number of verses in Proverbs are attributed to Hezekiah, the thirteenth king of Judah. He espoused the need for charity to the poor and the pitfalls of wealth, although some verses such as 28:6 and 28:8 are ambiguous. "Better is a poor man who walks in his integrity than a rich man who is perverse in his way" and "He who augments his wealth by interest and increase gathers it for him who is kind to the poor." The latter verse is intriguing, as it implied that wealth will somehow end up in the hands of the benevolent, although the verse did not indicate how such a transfer would transpire. In verse 28:18, Hezekiah revealed that "someone who is perverse in his ways will fall into a pit." Verses 28:25 and 28:27 described the extreme fates of those who were good to the poor and those who were not but "will get many a curse." Hezekiah may have been a venerated king, but he was no soothsayer.

The Biblical wisdom literature sometimes hews to the belief that the virtue precedes wealth and prosperity. Destitute people deserve their lot. Barrera cites Proverbs 26:27 and Psalm 7:15, with their virtually identical statements about a man digging a pit, falling into it, and being buried by a stone (Barrera 2013, 240).[7] Certainly God promises long life and prosperity to Abraham and his descendants, but, of course, there were conditions. The covenant between God and Abraham, though, was pretty clear-cut.

These provisions reflected Israel's time as a stranger and in bondage in Egypt. In a sense, the Israelites were to practice a form of the Golden Rule based upon their ill-treatment in the past; by remembering how poorly they were treated, the covenant exhorts them to treat members of Israel and strangers fairly and humanely (Barrera 2013, 69–70).

With regard to unethical behavior, Torah authors were familiar with the simple trick of adroitly using different weights to cheat in transactions. Ancient governments expended much effort toward standardizing weights and measurements. Such government actions, if fairly and uniformly applied, could facilitate trade by reducing transaction costs. Deuteronomy 25:13–16 prohibited the use of weights for fraudulent gain. Hammurabi's Code also dealt with the issue of different weights in the context of making loans of grain or money. Sometimes lenders and borrowers might mutually conspire to use differing weights. The lender would use the small weight or measure and then use the large weight or measure for repayment; in this way, the lender might evade the legal maximum rate of interest (Silver 1983b, 237).

Old Testament writers discussed ethical treatment of workers. In Deuteronomy 24:14–15, employers are advised, "You shall not oppress a hired servant who is poor and needy, whether he is one of your brethren or one of the sojourners who are in your land within your towns; you shall give him his hire [wage] on the day he earns it, before the sun goes down (for he is poor, and sets his heart upon it)."

Ancient Israelites and Usury

Although ancient Near Eastern kings occasionally and arbitrarily granted debt forgiveness, they usually did so to celebrate some notable event or to win public support. Israel regularized debt release and return of land to the original holders, at least in theory. The Jubilee Law and seven-year debt forgiveness were "structural measures" that kept disparities in wealth from getting too large. The jubilee year occurred every 50 years, which roughly matched the average life span for people who survived infancy. The Code of Hammurabi had a similar edict (but it allowed the charging of interest). The prohibition on interest can be seen as a recognition that many of the poor had to borrow to pay for subsistence. Perhaps because almost everyone might need a loan for subsistence at some point, borrowers were not to be saddled with interest payments. If the loan was for purpose of investment, as became prevalent in later years, then the ethical significance of banning interest on loans changed (Barrera 2013, 258–259; Sedlacek 2011, 77, 83–84; Leviticus 25:35–37).

Ancient Israelites, as with people throughout the Near East, frequently needed consumption loans or loans for small investments. Deuteronomy 15:7–8 implies that there was a duty for those with a surplus to lend to the poor: "If there is among you a poor man…you shall not harden your heart or shut your hand against your poor brother, but you shall open your hand to him, and lend him sufficient for his need, whatever it may be."

The ancient Near East was familiar with the concept of charging interest on loans. The Israelites, too, were familiar with the concept. In Ezekiel 18:10–13, a wayward son who is a robber, murderer, philanderer, oppressor of the poor, and lender at interest and taker of increase is condemned; the classification of lender at interest with these other sins is telling.

Exodus 22:25 (Leviticus 25:35–37 bears a similar message) appears to imply that a lender to the poor should not necessarily expect repayment along with the admonition not to charge interest: "If you lend money to any of my people with you who is poor, you shall not be to him as a creditor, and you shall not exact interest from him." This passage seems to imply that it was permissible to lend at interest to the non-poor.

Although economists might dispute the efficiency of a ban on charging interest on loans—even consumption loans—in the context of the early Israelite society, a ban made sense. People dependent upon volatile agricultural harvests for their daily bread with limited ability to store or transport food could easily find themselves facing starvation without loans. Limiting interest also served to retard any tendency toward concentration of land. Mandatory loans to the poor represented a form of insurance against famine, although if a crop failure was widespread, it is difficult to fathom who would be in a position to loan grain. Morris Silver counters that the strictures in Deuteronomy fail to explain the continued prohibition on charging interest during more prosperous, market-oriented periods. According to Silver, Deuteronomy 23:19–21 does not make a distinction upon the economic status of the borrower in ruling out interest on loans. Deuteronomy states: "You shall not lend upon interest to your brother, interest on money, interest on victuals, interest on anything that is lent for interest. To a foreigner you may lend upon interest, but to your brother you shall not lend upon interest; that the LORD your God may bless you in all that you undertake in the land which you are entering to take possession of it." In the Deuteronomy passage, what is the definition of "brother": actual kin by blood or by marriage or figurative? To some extent, Deuteronomy forestalls this criticism by disputing the need for capital loans for such projects as water irrigation by promising that the Lord will supply sufficient rain. Interestingly, the verse, Deuteronomy 28:12, concludes with the promise, "and you shall lend to many nations, but you shall not borrow."

Prohibitions on interest payments likely wreaked havoc on various economies, so people attempted to evade prohibitions by promising labor services as partial payments of loans. In the eighth century BCE, Bakenranef, who ruled in the Egyptian Delta, tried to reform lending practices by canceling many debts, freeing workers tied by debt-servitude, and limited interest rates to 33.3%. Bakenranef's reforms proved ephemeral (Silver 1983b, 230–237; see also Posner 1980, 11–13; Glaeser and Sheinkman 1998, 19).

Some Old Testament passages laud the refusal to take interest on loans as a positive virtue; Psalm 15:1–5 describes those who, "shall sojourn in thy [the Lord's] tent? Who shall dwell on thy holy hill?....[He] who does not put out his money at interest, and does not take a bribe against the innocent." As a simple rule, then, a virtuous Israelite did not charge interest on consumption loans extended to the poor, but it was permissible (if not necessarily virtuous) to charge interest in the course of trade with foreigners (Plaut 1981, 579).

The ancient Israelites also considered debt relief. Deuteronomy 15:1–5 commands: "At the end of every seven years you shall grant a release." Such debt forgiveness was not extended to foreigners, although this was not as discriminatory as it appears. The edict may have been distinguishing between consumption loans and commercial loans, with foreigners being prominent in the latter class of loans (Silver 1983b, 233).

As the seventh year approached, one can imagine that creditors became worried that their loans would not be repaid. Deuteronomy 15:9–11 warns creditors against dunning their debtors for repayment before the seventh year: "Take heed lest there be a base thought in your heart, and you say, 'The seventh year, the year of release is near,' and your eye be hostile to your poor brother, and you give him nothing, and he cry to the Lord against you, and it be sin in you. You shall give to him freely, and your heart shall not be grudging when you give to him; because for this the Lord your God will bless you in all your work and in all that you undertake." A related question was whether it was ethical for a debtor to purposely delay repaying a loan until the seventh year and debt forgiveness?

Jewish rabbi Hillel introduced "Prosbol, by which the sabbatical year does not release the debt, and the creditor has the right to demand his loan." Hillel introduced the Prosbol to "encourage loans to the needy" by "protecting the creditor from losing his loan; first when the creditor received a note which he did not deposit with the court, secondly when the loan was transacted without witnesses" (Zeitlin 1947, 342, 347–348).[8] Hillel apparently realized that if creditors could not get their money back, they would be unwilling to extend loans in the first place.

The Torah's edicts on forgiving debts were not unique. Calls for debt forgiveness recurred throughout the Near East. The question of enforcement arises: How prevalent was actual debt forgiveness? Did lenders evade the law? Babylonian kings enforced debt remittances, so Israelite kings might have been able to do so, too. An eighteenth-century BCE loan that included a clause explicitly mandated repayment even if the ruler decreed debt forgiveness, as did a Neo-Assyrian contract a millennium later.

One way to mitigate the prohibition on charging interest or a maximum interest rate was to include labor services as partial payment. Near Eastern lenders accepted a combination of money (or grain) and labor services in fulfillment of loans. The Laws of Eshnunna were just one source citing such arrangements. As the Israelites began to feel the inconvenience and economic losses associated with prohibiting interest charges, they sought for other means to charge interest indirectly. One attempt was to argue that only the deduction in advance of interest was prohibited (Silver 1983b, 233–241).

Scolding Prophets

Critics of business activities are rarely as scathing as those found in the Old Testament. Then again, many of the diatribes against merchants and traders were contrived by prophets; a prophet did not gain many adherents with reasoned discourse (a lesson not lost on modern-day demagogues). Zephaniah 1:9–13 proclaimed that the Lord warned, “On that day I will punish all…who fill the temple of their gods with violence and deceit… Wail, you who live in the market district; all your merchants will be wiped out, all who trade with silver will be destroyed….I will search Jerusalem… and punish those who are complacent….Their wealth will be plundered, their houses demolished.” Jeremiah 6:13 chides the people of Jerusalem: “every one is greedy for unjust gain; and from prophet to priest, every one deals falsely.” Amos 8:4–7, too, quotes God as condemning those “who trample upon the needy, and bring the poor of the land to an end, saying, ‘When will the new moon be over, that we may sell grain? And the Sabbath, that we may offer wheat for sale, that we may make the ephah [dry weight measure] small and the shekel great, and deal deceitfully with false balances, that we may buy the poor for silver and the needy for a pair of sandals, and sell the refuse of the wheat.’” The Lord, as related in Micah 6:10–12, excoriates the use of “the treasures…and the scant measure that is accursed…wicked scales and with a bag of deceitful weights…your men are full of violence.” Isaiah 23:15 lauds, “He who walks righteously and speaks uprightly, who despises the gain of oppressions, who shakes his hands, lest they hold a bribe.” According to Ezekiel 16:49, even that icon of depravity—Sodom—may have been condemned not only for sexual licentiousness, but for their “pride, surfeit of food, and prosperous ease, but [they] did not aid the poor and needy.”

Rabbi W. Gunther Plaut relates that the Midrash attributed leisure time indulgence in depravity, including “new thrills” and “sexual aberrations,” to “unbounded affluence:” “Hand in hand with material prosperity went an overbearing attitude toward God, whom people judged to be incapable of hearing prayer and of enforcing moral standards.” Morris Silver suggests that many of the allegations of the wealthy exploiting the poor arose from polemical verses, and that the prophets may not have depicted economic conditions in an objective light: "From the perspective of the prophets, any economic transaction between a rich and a poor person had to be robbery, whether it was legal and uncoerced or not" (Plaut 1981, 61; Silver 1983b, 113–114).

Trouble arose for the Israelites, when they strayed from the Covenant. The prophet Amos bemoaned the self-indulgence he witnessed. Israelite society had developed a central government with an accompanying bureaucracy. Urban-based aristocrats, royal officials, tax collectors, and merchants were likely to be among the self-indulgent cited by Amos. It is worth noting that these worthies may have acquired their wealth, not from pleasing consumers but through exploitation, oppression, and appropriation. In any event, Amos' accusations appear to be supported by archeological evidence. The houses of the rich were much larger and more lavish than the shabby houses of the poor. The wealthy confiscated the lands and property of the poor, often through interest-bearing loans. Debtors ended up as slaves. The corruption spread to the temple, where people provided banking and lending services. Pre-exilic Israelites used neo-Assyrian temple practices in providing a convenient place for lenders and borrowers to meet. The temple gained revenue, too. Amos believed the Israelites were destined to be punished for their neglect of the Covenant.

Jeremiah also scolded Israelites. He had the temerity to criticize King Jehoiakim of Judah, who lived opulently by cheating workers, oppressing the poor, and so on. For this king and many others, workers, and the poor were objects to be used, abused, and exploited. Jeremiah warned that unless the King and Judah reformed, big trouble lay ahead. Jeremiah (22:19) predicted: "With the burial of an ass [Jehoiakim] shall be buried, dragged and cast forth beyond the gates of Jerusalem."[9] As comeuppances go, this is strong stuff.

Job and Proverbs, though, portray the causes of poverty differently. Proverbs tends to blame the poor for their poverty, due to their sloth and frivolity; Job attributes the plight of the poor to oppression. Indeed, Job 21:7 and 9 turns the argument around and associates wealthy people's riches to God "choosing not to punish wickedness:" "Why do the wicked live, reach old age, and grow mighty in power? … and no rod of God is upon them." In fact, these wealthy people taunt God according to verses 21:14–16: "They say to God, 'Depart from us! We do not desire the knowledge of thy ways. What is the Almighty, that we should serve him? And what profit do we get if we pray to him? Behold, is not their prosperity in their hand? The counsel of the wicked is far from me." Job becomes bitter regarding his experiences with evil and injustice and figuratively shakes his fist at God; Job is an early social activist (Barrera 2013, 87–88, 97, 113).

Phoenicians and Carthaginians

Among the Near Eastern people, the Homeric Greeks especially held the Phoenicians, the dominant traders in the Mediterranean, in odious repute, although the reverse was quite likely equally accurate. Homer mentions commodities traded in the Mediterranean, presumably by professional traders. Such traders were reviled, although itinerant traders held an even worse reputation. In the *Odyssey*, Odysseus relates falling in with a Phoenician man, "well skilled in beguilements, a gnawer at others' goods, and many were the hurts he inflicted on men, and by his wits talked me over." Odysseus decides to sail with the Phoenician to Libya; the Phoenician lied about the purpose of the trip, claiming they could "win a cargo," but in fact he was hoping to sell Odysseus there and "take the immense price for me" (Homer [1965] 1967, 217–218). The Phoenicians at least had desirable trade goods, as they made purple dyes and had cedar forests that were desired by other people. The Phoenicians were also favorably situated. One commentator cautioned that Homer's Odysseus "saw the merchant through a farmer's eyes." Xenophon praised the way Phoenicians loaded their vessels "as an example of good order, which to the Greeks was the essence of good management" (*Bulletin of the Business Historical Society*, September 1938b, 58, 60).

For their part, the Homeric Greeks had little to offer in return for Phoenician goods, except for slaves taken in the perpetual Greek raids and wars. Naturally such trade in people, "makes for low standards of morality. This will explain why the Homeric Greeks regarded the professional merchant with distrust and contempt, and how the Phoenicians got their evil reputation as kidnappers." Were the Phoenicians as unscrupulous as described by the Greeks? The itinerant nature of many traders created insufficient incentive to be honest, as the trader was unlikely to encounter the same trading partners in the future: "there was nothing in such commerce to make for the establishment of fixed principles or business standards." Economists would view this as a case where repeated transactions might have inculcated an incentive for honesty and fair dealing, but such one-time traders might not have sufficient incentive to behave thusly.

Greeks began loading their surplus boats into boats and traveled along the coastline for other landowners' surplus (Calhoun 1926, 13–15, 39–41).[10] Mutual distrust and vigilance were prevalent.

Along the North Africa coast, Carthaginians became well-known traders. One historian describes Carthage's commercial methods "to have been diverted more toward small profits dishonestly acquired than to progress in commercial techniques." He thinks the Romans' attribution of "Punic bad faith" to have been reasonably accurate. The Carthaginians bought luxury items from barbarians at low cost; the barbarians were "dazzled their [by the Carthaginians] trumpery wares," but this may have been unfair to the barbarians. Levy also maintains that the Carthaginians were late-comers to issuing money; when they did mint coins, "their coins were quite ugly and did not spread far afield" (Levy 1967, 45).

Conclusion

Ancient civilizations advanced the informal trading of primitive peoples. The advent of writing and centralized government exercising coercion benefited trading by lowering transaction costs. On the other hand, governments could establish monopolies and levy burdensome taxes. In some cases, the government-provided benefits outweighed the costs, but all too frequently, the costs outweighed the benefits.

The ancient Israelites introduced the idea that wealthy people had duties toward the poor, an early example of deontological thinking. If the prophets were at all accurate in describing their milieu, ancient Israelites faced and often succumbed to temptations to behave unethically.

Notes

1. Barter does create prices by the terms of exchange. If I exchange two bananas for three coconuts, the price of a banana in terms of coconuts is one banana for 1.5 coconuts. Prices are a relative measure and do not have to be stated in monetary terms.
2. Morris Silver used the example of the pastoralist Israelites and the grain-growing Canaanites (Silver 1985, 12; Genesis 34:21–22).
3. Modern American religious radio stations require financial pledges from the faithful rely on the ever-present scrutiny of God to prevent free riding (Silver 1983b, 67).

4. Polanyi seemed to contradict his point regarding no professional traders made in *The Great Transformation*.
5. F. Charles Fensham remarked that believes that all people in ancient Near Eastern societies had responsibility to care for the poor; the rich and power were explicitly admonished not to oppress the poor (Fensham 1962, 138).
6. Deuteronomy (14:28–29, 23:25–26) extended this concept of generosity to individual travelers and Levites, allowing them to satisfy themselves with crops in the field; they could eat their fill but not take any with them.
7. Barrera characterized this as "a near mechanical correspondence in which wrongdoing brings about punitive consequences."
8. See 346 for the requirement that the creditor had to deposit a note stating the creditor's intent to collect his debt. Steven Levitt emphasized that the loan forgiveness policy induced potential lenders to refuse loans in the years just before and to make most loans in the years just after the year of loan forgiveness, creating a "cyclical credit crunch that punished the very people the law was intended to help" (Levitt and Dubner 2009, 140).
9. The brief biography of Jehoiakim described a nasty tyrant, whose lust and greed compared with many tyrants. There was no mention of his being buried with an ass.
10. Jean-Philippe Levy compared the Phoenicians with the Dutch of the early-modern era; both were "carriers of the seas." Levy, too, noted the Phoenicians flexibility: they could practice piracy and abduction or they could behave themselves most correctly (Levy 1967, 11).

Bibliography

Allen, Robert. "Agriculture and the Origins of the State in Ancient Egypt." *Explorations in Economic History* 34(2), 1997, 135–154.

Barrera, Albino. *Biblical Economic Ethics: Sacred Scripture's Teachings on Economic Life* (Plymouth, UK: Lexington Books, 2013).

Bedford, Peter. "The Persian Near East." *The Cambridge Economic History of the Greco-Roman World*, edited by Walter Scheidel, Ian Morris, and Richard Saller (Cambridge, UK: Cambridge University Press, 2007), 302–329.

Bulletin of the Business Historical Society. "Business in Babylon." XII(2), April 1938a, 25–27. No author.

Bulletin of the Business Historical Society. "The Phoenician Merchantman." XII(4), September 1938b, 58–60. No author.

Calhoun, George. *The Business Life of Ancient Athens* (Chicago, IL: University of Chicago Press, 1926).

Ekelund, Robert Jr. and Robert Tollison. *Mercantilism as a Rent-Seeking Society: Economic Regulation in Historical Perspective* (College Station, TX: Texas A&M University Press, 1981).

Fensham, F. Charles. "Widow, Orphan, and the Poor in Ancient Near Eastern Legal and Wisdom Literature." *Journal of Near Eastern Studies* 21(2), April 1962, 129–139.

Glaeser, Edward and Jose Sheinkman. "Neither a Borrower Nor a Lender Be: An Economic Analysis of Interest Restrictions and Usury Laws." *Journal of Law and Economics* 41(1), April 1998, 1–36.

Goetze, Albrecht. "The Laws of Eshnunna." *The Annual of the American Schools of Oriental Research* XXXI, 1951–52 (New Haven: Department of Antiquities of the Government of Iraq and the American Schools of Oriental Research, 1956).

Hammurabi Code. Avalon.law.yale.edu/ancient/hamframe.asp.

Heichelheim, Fritz. *An Ancient Economic History: From the Palaeolithic Age to the Migrations of the Germanic, Slavic, and Arabic Nations*, translated by Joyce Stevens (Leiden, Netherlands: A.W. Sijthoff's, 1958). 2 vols.

Herodotus. *The History* (Chicago, IL: University of Chicago Press, 1987).

Homer. *The Odyssey of Homer*, translated by Richmond Lattimore (New York, NY: Harper & Row, [1965] 1967).

Kramer, Samuel. *History Begins at Sumer: Twenty-seven "Firsts" in Man's Recorded History* (New York, NY: Doubleday, 1959).

Levitt, Steven and Stephen Dubner. *Super Freakonomics: Global Cooling, Patriotic Prostitutes, and Why Suicide Bombers Should Buy Life Insurance* (New York, NY: William Morrow, 2009).

Levy, Jean-Philippe. *The Economic Life of the Ancient World* (Chicago, IL: University of Chicago Press, 1967).

Mettinger. Trygve. *King and Messiah: The Civil and Sacral Legitimation of the Israelite Kings* (Copenhagen, Denmark: CWK Gleerup, 1976).

North, Douglass. *Structure and Change in Economic History* (New York, NY: W.W. Norton, 1981).

Oppenheim, A. Leo. "Seafaring Merchants of Ur." *Journal of the American Oriental Society* 74(1), January–March 1954, 6–17.

Oppenheim, A. Leo. "Towards a History of Glass in the Ancient Near East." *Journal of the American Oriental Society* 93(3), July–September 1973, 259–266.

Pearson, Harry. "The Secular Debate on Economic Primitivism." *Trade and Market in the Early Empires: Economies in History and Theory*, edited by Karl Polanyi, Conrad Arensberg, and Harry Pearson (Glencoe, IL: Free Press 1957), 3–11.

Perkins, Pheme. "Does the New Testament Have an Economic Message?" *Wealth in Western Thought: The Case For and Against Riches* (Westport, CT: Praeger, 1994).

Plaut, W. Gunther. *The Torah: A Modern Commentary* (New York, NY: Union of American Hebrew Congregations, 1981).

Polanyi, Karl. *The Great Transformation* (Beacon Hill, MA: Beacon Press, [1944] 1957).

Polanyi, Karl. "Marketless Trading in Hammurabi's Time." *Trade and Market in the Early Empires: Economies in History and Theory*, edited by Karl Polanyi, Conrad Arensberg, and Harry Pearson (Glencoe, IL: Free Press 1957a), 2–26.

Polanyi, Karl. "Aristotle Discovers the Economy." *Trade and Market in the Early Empires: Economies in History and Theory*, edited by Karl Polanyi, Conrad Arensberg, and Harry Pearson (Glencoe, IL: Free Press 1957b), 64–94.

Posner, Richard. "A Theory of Primitive Society, with Special Reference to Law." *Journal of Law and Economics* 23(1), April 1980. 1–53.

Sedlacek, Tomas. *Economics of Good and Evil: The Quest for Economic Meaning from Gilgamesh to Wall Street* (Oxford, UK: Oxford University Press, 2011).

Silver, Morris. "Karl Polanyi and Markets in the Ancient Near East: The Challenge of the Evidence." *Journal of Economic History* 43(4), December 1983a, 795–829.

Silver, Morris. *Prophets and Markets: The Political Economy of Ancient Israel* (Boston, MA: Kluwer-Nijhoff, 1983b).

Silver, Morris. *Economic Structures of the Ancient Near East* (Totowa, NJ: Barnes & Noble Books, 1985).

Stigler, George. "Economics of Information." *The Organization of Industry* (Chicago, IL: University of Chicago Press), [1968] 1983), 171–190.

Veyne, Paul. *Bread and Circuses: Historical Sociology and Political Pluralism* (London, UK: Allen Lane/Penguin Press, 1990).

Zeitlin, Solomon. "Prosbol: A Study in Tannaitic Jurisprudence." *Jewish Quarterly Review* 37(4), April 1947, 341–362.

CHAPTER 5

Greek Society

Greek thinkers developed the concept of virtue and raised some basic ethical questions regarding business. What constituted the good life? Was it even virtuous or ethical to be engaged in business? Were profits ethical? What was a just price? Was usury permissible? From a business ethics perspective, Greeks helped shape the western world's attitudes toward commerce, wealth, labor, and other economic aspects.

We know much about how Greek thinkers and leaders thought about business, but the mass of people, even citizens of Greece, left little documentation about their beliefs and experiences. Greek society had flows of goods that were distributed by various means—gift, taxation, plunder, and market exchange. Greeks often relied upon plunder and not voluntary exchange.

Overview of Greek Economy

Economists recognize the influence of Grecian sources upon their discipline. Economics is derived from *oikos* and *nem*, regulation of a household. Xenophon's *Oikonomikos* detailed how gentlemen landowners should run their estates, including aspects of "virtues and leadership qualities necessary for the householder….Fundamentally, this is a work of ethics." Xenophon wrote, "economy was the name of some science; and this science…was one that enabled a man to add to his resources; and his resources were all his possessions; and possessions, we said, were everything

D. G. Surdam, *Business Ethics from Antiquity to the 19th Century*,
https://doi.org/10.1007/978-3-030-37165-4_5

that benefited a man for the maintenance of life" (Xenophon [1876] 1971, 37; Finley 1973, 17–18; Smith 1981, 25).

Economics revolves around scarcity. Karl Polanyi argues that the modern concept of scarcity does not apply to the Greeks. He argues because Aristotle's notion of the good life was based upon non-physical goods and enjoyments, it meant there was no relevant scarcity. The activities, such as theater going, participation in the political system, festivals, and adventure, are never "hoarded nor physically possessed." Discretionary time (which was scarce)—what we might denote as leisure—required the elite to have their needs produced by slaves and free labor. For Aristotle and most Greeks, slavery was natural, and even the kidnapping of people for enslavement was permissible. Of course, political participants needed their bread and wine; the specter of scarcity likely never disappeared among the Greeks. The growing need for imports of food with the attendant commercial traders and a growing acceptance of the idea of physical pleasures through consumption—a "false notion of the good life"—began to transform the Greek conception of the good life (Polanyi 1957, 81–82).

Pirates and Traders

The classical Greeks vaguely knew what their predecessors did centuries previously. They knew that their ancestors faced wild, untamed land and sea, where commerce and trade were risky (Starr 1977, 21). The Greeks began to establish trading posts and developed the land. Their economy developed. Cyrus of Persia reputedly told a Spartan herald, in response to Sparta's claim of retaliation for Persian attacks on Greek cities, "I never yet feared men who have a place set apart in the midst of their cities where they gather to cheat one another and exchange oaths, which they break." Herodotus comments on this quote, "This taunt of Cyrus was directed against all of the Greeks, because they set up marketplaces in which to buy and sell. The Persians themselves do not have such places, nor is there any such marketing among them" (Herodotus 1987, 103).

Greeks, as with previous civilizations, had not completely shunned using force in acquiring desirable assets and goods. A historian commented, "commercial and military activity were not sharply opposed.... Pillage and commerce were two complementary and interconnected methods of exchange and...it was a long time before the ancient world established a clear distinction between them." "Homeric *basileis* led the community's young men in war bands, rewarding them with plunder and honor in drinking parties and feasts….A *basileus* constantly had to justify his position. So long as he did so, the people honored him" (Nicolet 1980, 122; Morris 2007, 232–233).

The Greeks transformed from raiders to a cosmopolitan collection of states with widespread international trade. The legends of Homer celebrated prowess in battle, theft, and pillage. As with all literary authors, Homer aimed at a particular audience. His depictions have to be filtered through these lens. Wealth obtained through piracy was worth boasting about, more so than wealth accumulated through peaceful trade. For many Homeric Greeks, "when commerce was almost non-existent, or at best on a very small scale, the only ready means of obtaining wealth or novelties from other peoples was to go and get them. The code was a simple one and…effective. If the other side was too strong to overcome peaceful trading ensued; if it was open to strong methods, plundering was resorted to" (Michell 1957, 307; see also Cartledge 2002, 27; Calhoun 1926b, 12).

War was so endemic, that leases in Attic gave a partial acquittance of the rent, if an enemy disrupted planting or harvesting or destroyed part of the crops. Aristotle considered piracy as a means of subsistence, along with fishing and hunting. He observed how sailors associated in order to gain money by trade, but soldiers went out to obtain "money, a victory or a town." So dependent were some of the Greek states upon plunder, that Athenians wondered, in the wake of alliances with neighboring states, "how [they] would be able to support themselves through economic means in the future." The old notion that the State was to provide for the citizens needed to be revised, so that instead of State conquests, the citizens needed to earn money in order to buy slaves and live off the slaves' work (Bolkestein 1958, 144–146).

Greeks initially held being a merchant or a trader in contempt. In order to get Odysseus to indulge in some games, Laodamas and Euryalos insulted Odysseus: "No, stranger, for I do not see that you are like one versed in contests, such as now are practiced much among people, but rather to one who plies his ways in his many-locked vessels, master over mariners who also are men of business, a man who, careful of his cargo and grasping for profits, goes carefully on his way. You do not resemble an athlete." The insult bites, and Odysseus retorts that he is not unfamiliar with games: "I think, I have been among the best when I still had trust in youth and hands' strength." Over time, though, as the Greeks gained control of the seas, they morphed into relatively peaceful, law-abiding seafarers. They developed relationships with people around the Aegean (Homer [1965] 1967, 125–126, 159–164, 180–181; Starr 1977, 50–51).

Seafaring was a long-established venture in Europe, Asia, and Africa, dating back at least to the third millennium BCE. The ancient Greeks roamed the Aegean; they met, traded, or warred with innumerable peoples. Their motives were a mixture of gain, adventure, and perhaps curiosity. Historian Chester Starr contended that seeking gain was probably a prime consideration, even if the Greeks did not "calculate his profit from a voyage by modern bookkeeping." In the *Hymn to Apollo*, the Cretans were asked, "Are you for traffic or pirates wandering at random, who put their own lives in jeopardy by mischief to foreigners?" Historian Fritz Heichelheim wrote, "plunder, booty, political presents, trophies for athletes, and keepsakes acquired by sailors, merchants, mercenaries, and travelers were more common imports [until the seventh century] than proper trade goods" (Starr 1977, 56–60; Evelyn-White n.d., 453–455; Heichelheim 1958, 1:225).

A historian disagrees with the interpretation that Menelaus in the *Odyssey* was sailing the seas for commerce; the *Odyssey* makes it plain that Menelaus was engaged in piracy.[1] Historian Paul Cartledge notes that Hermes "was patron god of thieves as well as of merchants." Aristotle considered war as a way of production; in the "science of acquiring slaves," he compared the "just acquiring of slaves, being like a sort of warfare or hunting." Cartledge states, "it is difficult to overstate the Greeks' engrained booty-raiding mentality." Not until 600 BCE did the Greeks begin to develop trading networks and techniques that rivaled those used by the Phoenicians and Etruscans for centuries before (Aristotle 1944, 31, 37; Cartledge 2002, 27–28).

Some Greek regions "openly practiced piracy" and would then negotiate protection money from other states; Athens and Rhodes fought piracy as unlawful and deleterious, especially during the fourth century, when pirates began threatening Athens' already worsening grain situation. In his *Politics*, Aristotle off-handedly states, "Other men live from hunting, and different people from different kinds of hunting, for instance some from brigandage." Even if the Greeks and Romans ostensibly repudiated piracy, they were willing to serve as middlemen for pirate treasure; victims sometimes purchased their goods stolen by pirates (Aristotle 1944, 35; see also Migeotte 2009, 25; Engen 2010, 86).[2]

Aside from piracy, the Greeks practiced other forms of seizure, some sanctioned by law and requiring witnesses. As the Greek economy developed, though, the right of seizure diminished and occurred mostly when there was a public grievance. The Greeks realized that the threat of seizure might deter outside merchants from doing business in areas with seizure laws. A scholar notes that Aristotle also lauded warfare for its stimulating productivity in military goods; this may be one of the earliest instances of someone lauding military spending, because it is "good" for the economy. The fallacy of the observation is in its failure to recall the opportunity costs—what could have been produced instead of military goods (Aristotle 1944, 37; Migeotte 2009, 26–27).

But new seafaring characters were in the wings. In fact the term *emporos* first appears in the *Odyssey*; an *emporos* was a passenger who paid a fare and was usually a merchant. The word eventually became applied to merchants (Hasebroek 1965, 17; Homer [1965] 1967, 67; Michell 1957, 210–211).

Attitudes Toward Work

The large landowners and participants in Greek democracies constituted a minority of the population. Those afforded leisure time for contemplation pondered basic questions underlying civilizations. With regard to business ethics, was it even ethical to be a merchant or trader? Could a seller charge more than or a buyer pay less than the just price? Was charging interest on loans ethical? Greek and Roman attitudes toward all of these questions influenced later Christian, Jewish, and Muslim thinkers for two millennia (Finley 1973, 48; Davies 2005, 151).

Greek philosophers thought the highest aspiration for a citizen was to be involved in politics and civic duties. What is good? Aristotle wrote, "[M]ost men, and men of the most vulgar type, seem (not without some reason) to identify the good, or happiness, with pleasure; which is the reason why they love the life of enjoyment." He continues, "But people of superior refinement and of active disposition identify happiness with honour... Further, men seem to pursue honour in order that they may be assured of their merit." Tomas Sedlacek claims that Aristotle would have disagreed with current economists' fixation on maximization of utility, as Aristotle considered moderation to be a cardinal virtue and unlimited wants or desire to be evil (Aristotle [1893] 2004, 5, 25; Sedlacek 2011, 122–123).[3]

Many Greeks denigrated working for a living; those engaged in arduous labor (*ponos*) were diminished. To live without *ponos* was to live "like the blessed immortal god." Aristotle distinguished between forms of labor.

Labor was vulgar, when it rendered free men unable to pursue "the employments and actions of virtue." A task and also an art or a science must be deemed vulgar if it renders the body or soul or mind of free men useless for, "the employments and actions of virtue." It was moral to follow a pursuit, "for the sake of oneself or one's friends, or on moral grounds, it is not illiberal, but the man who follows the same pursuit because of other people would often appear to be acting in a menial and servile manner" (Cartledge 2002, 23; Aristotle 1944, 639).

Hesiod, in contrast, associated work with riches: "Work is no disgrace; the disgrace is in not working; and if you do work, the lazy man will soon begin to be envious as you grow rich, for with riches go nobility and honor. It is best to work, at whatever you have a talent for doing, without turning your greedy thought toward what some other man possesses, but take care of your own livelihood, as I advise you" (Hesiod 1959, 55).

A truly virtuous person needed to be free of the humdrum daily struggle for sustenance. But even contemplating philosophers and deeper thinkers required their daily bread. Their attitude, of course, did not mean that philosophers eschewed good food and wine. In fact, they liked to eat good food, but this required the efforts of metics, foreigners, and slaves to provide food. A concern for citizen status in Athens made many citizens eschew lending, trade, and financial services as being somehow dubious; this, of course, left such activities to foreigners, women, freedmen, and slaves, or equestrians (Morris et al. 2007, 3).

Slavery undergirded Greek societies. Aristotle believed there was a separation between natural ruler and natural subject, based upon the former's ability to use his mind and the latter's use of his body. Given the complementarity between natural ruler and natural subject, "master and slave have the same interest." Slavery and its output afforded the man who "can foresee with his mind" plenty of time for leisurely contemplation and involvement in politics.

The philosophers scorned merchants, traders, artisans, and other workers. Aristotle, Plato, and Xenophon shared the upper-class disdain of merchants, especially merchants plying the seas. They characterized merchants and traders as low-class and common, sometimes lumping them with fullers and shoe-makers. The Greek elites viewed themselves as political creatures, who lived off income from their lands using the labor of others (Aristotle 1944, 5, 283–285, 295–297; Plato 1960, 310–313; Plutarch [1909] 1956, 12; Hasebroek 1965, 8, 30).

Although the wealthy did not condescend to sullying their hands with commerce, they were not averse to making money from commerce; they invested in commercial ventures, often hiring a professional merchant. These ventures remained small. Most of the commercial class had to borrow funds in order to participate in commerce. Merchants and traders hoped to get sufficient returns in order to retire as quickly as possible. One could envision Greek commerce, then, as a roll of the dice. If the small trader was fortunate and enjoyed a safe passage and return of the vessel carrying their goods and favorable market conditions, then he might be able to retire. A modestly successful trader would then, in turn, become a small lender (Hasebroek 1965, 9–10).[4]

Aristotle reserves scorn for *obolostates*, the Greek equivalent of loan sharks. Greeks may have found the petty lender useful, even at the seemingly high interest rates charged. For Aristotle, lending money and earning interest upon the principal was unnatural and hated: "because its gain comes from money itself and not from that for the sake of which money was invented." Aristotle viewed the purpose of money as for exchange only, so payment of interest was, of the routes to wealth accumulation, "the most contrary to nature" (Aristotle 1944, 51; Finley 1970, 16).

One historian states that, "Aristotle, who merely expressed the general view" on the subject of interest loans, distinguished between loans for consumption and loans for production. He argues that Aristotle condemned the former and tolerated the latter (Levy 1967, 25–26).

Deep Thinkers' Animus Toward Commerce

Modern commentators' belief that the Greeks and Romans were hostile toward commerce was based, according to Jacob Viner, "on the texts of a few poets" exercising personal animus. Horace, for instance, excoriated "impious barks [ships] bound across the waters that should not be touched." Viner describes Horace's personality and penchant for seasickness, in concluding that Horace was a poor reporter of Roman views toward commerce. Viner cites another Roman poet, Propertius, as documenting Roman animus toward the sea and their disdain toward commerce. Viner remarks, "Propertius...was an uplander, with an agrarian bias, and, like Horace, susceptible to seasickness." As amusing as Viner's examples are, they represent a sample size of two. His general point, though, needs to be kept in mind, when we discuss Greek thinkers' attitudes toward trade and commerce. Greek philosophers and poets rarely discussed the possible economic benefits from international trade, although they surely enjoyed consuming products from other countries (Viner 1978, 35–36).

The Greek writers and philosophers left a bounty of information, but how far their attitudes and ideas reflected those of or percolated down to the general public is difficult to deduce. Because many of the literate class characterized small-scale business owners in derogatory terms, the possibility exists that a form of social snobbery colored opinions. Greek writers often characterized the small shopkeepers in the agora (the *kapeloi*) as dishonest and greedy. The *emporoi* bought and sold goods, often for export. They provided financing for shipowners (*naukleroi*). A few *emporoi* are immortalized, because their cities honored them for donations or for selling grains at a discount during shortages. Our understanding of the *emporoi* and *kapeloi*'s attitudes is obscure. The Greek thinkers were more approving of wealthy and large-scale merchants and producers. These business owners were expected not only to be competent managers of wealth but to be educated, benevolent, and active in civic affairs. The owners wanted to enlarge their wealth and maintain their social status. Doing the latter, of course, proved expensive: "[T]he generosity that was expected of them, their outlay of unproductive expenditure, demand huge financial assets." Merchant elites, however, gained fame primarily through their political actions and beneficence, not their business prowess (Migeotte 2009, 137, 141).[5]

For Aristotle and many of the Greek elite, the good life entailed landownership and a desire to be self-sufficient. Exchange for household use was natural, nor was it "any branch of the art of wealth-getting, for it existed for the replenishment of natural self-sufficiency." Eventually, the landowners found themselves importing "things in which they were deficient and exporting those of which they had a surplus, the employment of money necessarily came to be devised" (Aristotle 1944, 43).

Xenophon concludes that agricultural pursuit was the "finest occupation and science" for the true gentleman, as it "allowed the mind full leisure to have some care for both friend and country." In addition, agricultural pursuits provided an "incentive to bravery." For Xenophon, good management of the land is not only profitable but virtuous: "the land willingly teaches justice, for it ever awards its highest prizes to those who serve it best" (Xenophon [1876] 1971, 33, 38). A clearer explication of stewardship would be hard to find.

Wealth, then, is a means to an end: "men do not acquire and preserve the virtues by means of these external goods, but external goods by means of the virtues." Men acquired happiness in measure of their, "virtuous and wise action." What is the wealth for? Wealth allowed free men time for leisure and the pursuit of virtuous actions, which was "the best life." Wealth, therefore, could distract the individual from pursuing the true path to happiness and lead individuals to obtain wealth, "by some other means, employing each of the faculties in an unnatural way." The attempt to gain wealth, such as embodied in coin, may lead an individual to "die of hunger, like the famous Midas in the story" (Aristotle 1944, 45–47, 535–539).

Xenophon, using the device of an imagined conversation between Socrates and Critobulus, describes the advantage accruing to Socrates of having sufficient to subsist; Socrates explains that, "I am rich enough. You, on the contrary, Critobulus, I consider very poor….I heartily pity you sometimes." Socrates admits that Critobulus' estate is easily worth a hundred times that of his estate. But Socrates has a sufficiency, and he has friends who would help him if he were in want. Critobulus, on the other hand, needs his wealth to preserve his status and his friendships (Xenophon [1876] 1971, 9–12).

Although Plato and Socrates displayed some reservations about the desirability of wealth, most ancient Near Eastern sources approved of wealth. Of course, it is difficult to know whether the masses approved of their leaders and oppressors' wealth. Socrates did not believe that wealth was important in living the good life, and Plato, in *The Republic*, thought the philosopher-rulers should not hold property. As classicist Moses Finley remarks, "'Blessed are the poor' was not within the Graeco-Roman world of ideas." He points out that the Greek words *ploutos* and *penia* were more nuanced than simple "wealth" and "poverty." "A *plousios* was a man who was rich enough to live properly on his income, a *penes* was not. The latter need not be propertyless or even, in the full sense, poor." The true distinction was the latter's need to toil for a living (Finley 1973, 38–40).

While it is tempting to view the Greek thinkers' disdain of mundane merchants as a form of snobbery, Xenophon demonstrates why large landowners were potentially virtuous from the perspective of the Greek state: "the state…imposes on you duties of no little importance,—to breed horses for its service, to pay the expenses of a chorus, to superintend the gymnasia, or to be a foreign consul." In time of actual warfare, large landowners were a convenient source of funds to finance the navy. Such contributions were compulsory, although ostensibly voluntary. Xenophon lauded landowners who produced grain instead of wine and oil, as they supplied the basic necessity for cities, and therefore, "It is the most honored profession because it supplies the city with its finest citizens." Arboriculturalists produced wine and olives oil, because of greater profit potential, but since Greece depended upon grain, the agriculturalists were entitled to greater honor (Xenophon [1876] 1971, 10–11; Levy 1967, 28–29).

Growing Importance of Traders and Merchants

Historian Johannes Hasebroek contrasts ancient Greece with the European Middle Ages; in Greece, full-time professional traders transferred goods between producers and merchants. Such middlemen activities were anathema to Europeans of the Middle Ages, who insisted that the producer sell their products themselves. Such an insistence led to much inefficiency, but traces of anti-middlemen sentiment persist to this day. The Greek traders, it is true, were rarely exalted, but their role was sufficiently tolerated to allow Greek society the benefit of their services. Greek and Roman writers inveighed against "the derivation of income by a merchant from purely middleman activities." The early Church Fathers shared a similar attitude. St. Jerome claimed that "the riches of the earth" were "unjust riches" and attempts to own such came at the expense of other people (Hasebroek 1965, 4–5; Jerome quoted in Viner 1978, 35–36).

If the ancient Greek thinkers and citizens disdained trading as a profession, they held skilled craftsmen in somewhat greater respect. Among the ephemera still extant, Greek vases predominate. During the Age of Tyrants, the skilled craftsmen who made and sold such items apparently practiced a rudimentary branding of their products. They inscribed the vases with their names. Over time both the manufacturers and merchants gained greater esteem from their fellow Greeks, especially as trade and manufacture began assuming a larger role in the Greek economy. Businessmen participated in politics, and their contributions to Greek public finance grew in importance. By the fourth century BCE, the need for wealthy men with capital to invest in large-scale projects also amplified their importance. Men of skill, determination, and a dash of luck could rise from slavery to prominence. To further encourage capitalist endeavors, the Athenians created special courts to handle cases involving wronged businessmen and to speedily protect their property rights. The intent of these courts was to encourage "free and ready employment of capital in filling the various needs of metropolitan life" (Calhoun 1926b, 39).

The Grecian elites' denigration of merchants and traders rested, in part, upon the peripatetic lifestyle of merchants. Merchants often traveled extensively and did not own land (aside from a domicile perhaps). "To be a merchant one had to be homeless....But the citizen of a City-State had a home and a country, which demanded his whole energies and attentions, and to leave it was to abandon all things that made life worth living. No commercial or industrial gains could compensate for the loss of home and citizenship." The citizens and philosophers were not oblivious to the need for metics, and Xenophon urged his fellow citizens to provide incentives for metics to settle in their cities (Hasebroek 1965, 42; see also Michell 1957, 145; Xenophon n.d. iii, 3–6).

Over time, though, the Greeks began to respect and admire wealthy traders, and Greek nobility began to become more involved in producing for profit, although they still stopped short of engaging directly in merchant's activities. Hasebroek disputes the idea of the Greek aristocracy becoming a commercial aristocracy. Plutarch, however, suggests that in Solon's time, merchants were respected and honored, but by Plato and Aristotle's era, money-seeking was held disreputable (Hasebroek 1965, 17; Starr 1977, 192; Plutarch 1889, 68–70).

Just Price

What was justice in exchange? Aristotle's sense of justice was related not only to the act but to the person: "[T]here must be the same 'equality' between the persons and the things: as the things are to one another, so must the persons be. For if the persons be not equal, their shares will not be equal; and this is the source of disputes and accusations, when persons who are equal do not receive equal shares, or when persons who are not equal receive equal shares. This is also plainly indicated by the common phrase 'according to merit.'" Aristotle calls this a geometric proportion (he uses two ratios): "That which is just, then, in this sense is that which is proportionate; but that which is unjust is that which is disproportionate. In the latter case one quantity becomes more or too much, the other less or too little. And this we see in practice; for he who wrongs another gets too much, and he who is wronged gets too little of the good in question. This then is one form of that which is just." To rectify injustice, one should transfer the unjust gain to the wronged party (Aristotle [1893] 2004, 95–97).

Aristotle recognizes that "to be fair" may be likened to a balance, and he ties unjust to unfair and just to fair. Moses Finley suggests that Aristotle considers what is unfair in a voluntary transaction (such as a sale) would be a fraud or breach of contract. At this juncture, he does not consider an "unjust price" in the same way: "An agreement over the price was part of the agreement or 'transaction' itself, and there could be no subsequent claim by the buyer of unjust gain merely because of the price…'The law gives the better bargainer *adeia* (security)'" (Aristotle [1893] 2004, 94; Finley 1970, 6).

Aristotle does not argue that a shrewd bargainer acts unjustly. He cites the exchange between Glaukos and Diomedes in *The Iliad*: "Zeus the son of Kronos stole away the wits of Glaukos who exchanged with Diomedes the son of Tydeus armour of gold for bronze, for nine oxen's worth the worth of a hundred." Aristotle commented, "he that gives, as Glaucus gives to Diomede…does not suffer injustice; for the giving rests with him, but suffering injustice does not rest with one's self; there must be some one to do injustice" (Homer [1951] 1974, 159; Aristotle [1893] 2004, 110). The situation, though, may strike modern readers as an injustice of some sort, since Zeus "stole away the wits" of Glaukos. It would be, perhaps, too much to compare Glaucus' temporary loss of wits with the beguilements of modern advertising, but if the gods influence someone into making a disadvantageous trade, injustice would seem to be an appropriate description.

Aristotle understood the rudiments of how forces of supply and demand affected prices, and how petty traders or middlemen adapted to the changes in prices, according to Finley. Even Plato conceded the importance of middlemen petty traders (*kapeloi*), "who will give money for goods and goods for money because neither farmers nor artisans can count on finding someone with whom to exchange whenever they bring goods to the market. Aristotle focused on justice in the exchange being a situation when neither party gains at the expense of the other party" (Finley 1970, 13–14; Plato 2004, 55–56).

For Aristotle, then, trade is natural when it fosters self-sufficiency within the community, according to Karl Polanyi; the mutual sharing of surpluses helps maintain community survival. Whatever exchange transpired within the community needs to be done out of *philia*—goodwill, lest the community splinter. Reciprocity and "just price" are elements of maintaining the community, and "prices are justly set if they conform to the standing of the participants in the community." If there must be gainful retailing, it was better to let the non-citizens do the dirty work, so to speak (Polanyi 1957, 79–82). If Polanyi's description is correct, the difference between how modern economists view the role of prices with that of the Greeks is stark. For the Greeks, prices were to be a means of fostering community good-will and cohesion; whereas economists think of prices in terms of allocating resources.

Traders and Merchants

One consequence of wealthy Greeks avoiding mercantile and trading activities was that the vacuum was assumed by less educated people. Most merchants were illiterate and operated without written contracts; they also lacked basic bookkeeping tools. They did, however, make sure there were witnesses to verbal contracts and fulfillment of contracts. Despite the presence of witnesses and oral contracts, Greek courts were filled with lawsuits. One exception to the lack of written contracts was in bottomry loans; these loans were complicated and required written contracts (Hasebroek 1965, 89).

One historian disputes the traders' alleged illiteracy. Astrid Moller highlights new evidence that showed that traders wrote business contracts: "archaic and early classical trade was more sophisticated and better organized than Hasebroek and Finley thought." These traders needed to inform each about prices and used information to make better profit-maximizing decisions, although evidence of their bookkeeping remains elusive.[6]

Aristophanes satirized merchants and traders, relying on now time-honored clichés, such as placing ripe figs on the top of a basket of figs, while hiding the bad ones underneath. In another play, a dealer "takes payment in the heavy coins of one state and gives change in the light coins of another" (Moller 2007, 368–372). While the audience may have recognized such antics, one wonders how prevalent such rather blatant tricks were. The supply of naifs presumably was not inexhaustible.

The wealthy, upper-class Greeks may have scorned traders and merchants, but they did not scorn the products such lowly people provided. "[T]he friendliness of a state or city towards strangers is in inverse proportion to the ability of its own citizens to run their manufactures and their commerce for themselves." The Greeks actively sought to get foreign skilled artisans and grain traders to settle among them, as the foreigners provided valued products. Greeks offered such incentives as the potential for citizenship and high wages. Once the Greeks attained the ability to produce what the foreigners did, their attitude changed toward repression and hostility: "The foreigner, in fact, is regarded as the intruder, the rival whose intolerable competition must be at all costs and as far as possible eliminated" (Hasebroek 1965, 23–25).

Moller argues that recent evidence disproves Johannes Hasebroek's claim that the Athenian metics and foreigners dominated the Athens' trade. Evidence suggests that Athenian citizens participated in the trade. Athenian citizens engaged in money lending to shippers, but such "risky business required inside knowledge, so there were many former traders among the lenders, whereas *emporoi* and *naukleroi*, the shipowners, were probably not all as poor as is sometimes suggested….Greek trade was a private initiative and private money went into it, although sometimes (as in the case of grain) magistrates supervised it closely" (Moller 2007, 369).

Greek Business Ethics

Greeks sometimes held a reputation for cheating in trades. Cyrus (not King Cyrus of Persia) commented on the cheating nature of Greek merchants. "Neither the gods of Hellas nor its nobles ever cultivated truthfulness as a primary virtue." Historian Chester Starr expressed the opinion that "the power of the merchant is the greater the more primitive commerce is. For the merchant alone is cognizant of the distant market." A merchant making many transactions gains experience and expertise at making deals; a consumer makes fewer transactions and has less knowledge of market conditions. But over time, consumers may identify trustworthy merchants. The local producers, too, often lacked the information held by merchants; by being tied to one market, the local producers may have held less bargaining power. In both cases, local producers of fish and grain may have considered the merchants exploitive (Starr 1977, 84, 107, 138).[7]

Historian George Calhoun suggested that there were opposing views of Greek business ethics. Calhoun disagrees with H.G. Wells' depiction of the Hellenes as, "as unworthy rabble snarling at the heels of a tiny Periclean circle of pure and lofty souls." Calhoun considered the contrast as ignoring the Greeks' economic efficiency, "and to picture them as brilliant visionaries, constantly preoccupied with eternal beauty and metaphysics, but deplorably impractical when confronted with the stern necessities of daily life. The other is to make them a race of clever, unscrupulous sharpers and swindlers, lacking even in the first principles of honesty and common decency." He noted that textbooks of the 1920s painted a picture of majority of Greeks thinking deep thoughts and having their material needs met by, "The little minority who preferred wealth to metaphysics or spiritual ecstasy [who] were a frightful exemplification of the old maxim, *corruptio optimi pessima*, for they turned out to be the cleverest cheats and rascals of the ancient world."

Calhoun, in contrast, lauds the Greeks, not only for their philosophical achievements, but also for their contributions to economics and commerce. He argues that we should not ignore the many Athenians engaged in manufacture and finance, who bequeathed advances in ethical business practices. He does acknowledge that Athens, as with all societies, had its rapacious, opportunistic businesspeople. Calhoun relates that Greek sources not only include anecdotes about traders and merchants' good and bad behavior, but considerable passages describing what conducts were approved or disapproved; he believes these writings show what the public considered, "'good business' and what it reprobated. The ideal business man here put before us is not the clever, unscrupulous sharper." Greeks valued the man who honorably conducted business without running afoul of litigation and earned the trust and respect of his clients. "The great thing in the world of trade and finance, Demosthenes tells us, is to combine diligence with honesty" (Calhoun 1926a, 11–16. 94–95; Wells 1920, 343–350).

Despite the early Greeks' penchant for raiding, warfare, and enslaving, Calhoun believed that within five or six centuries, Hellas had created a culture and economy that surpassed previous civilizations. He lauded the generally high ethical behavior of Athenian business practices. The real question for Calhoun was how the Homeric Greeks transformed from sly, unscrupulous traders and became exemplars of ethical business behavior. In a sense, Calhoun contradicts his claim that the classical Greeks bequeathed a legacy of business behavior and sophistication by attributing the Greeks' advancement to their study of their eastern neighbors' business methods and standards in developing their own corpus of mercantile law. The Greeks succeeded in creating a system of mercantile laws that the Romans adopted (Calhoun 1926a, 41–42, 47–48).

Although city-states began regulating the *agorai* and *emporia* trading centers from the archaic period, the agora received more scrutiny, possibly reflecting the ill-repute ascribed to it by Aristotle and other Greek writers. Fourth-century Athens prohibited fraudulent behavior in the agora. Aristotle believed such enforcement of contracts and maintenance of good order was paramount. In fairness to the merchants in the agora, Aristotle also advocated superintendence of building and roads and of property rights to land. The magistrates—*agoranomos* and *epimeletai*—maintained discipline (*eutaxia*) and order (*kosmos*) and ensured that all participants acted in good faith. They also adjudicated disputes between vendors and buyers. The tax farmers—*telonai*—verified merchants' statements of their merchandise and helped identify fraud. After Aristotle's time, Messene in 92 BCE passed regulations designating the place for sales. The regulations charged the *agoranomos* to ensure "that the salesmen sell products that are not adulterated or doctored and use weights and measures that conform to the public weights and measures; let him fix neither the price nor the time of the sales and let no-one insist on any dues from the salesmen for their pitch; if people do not abide by these sales rules, let him whip the slaves and charge the free men a fine of twenty drachmas, and let this judgment be made by the *heiroi*" (Migeotte 2009, 144–145, 172; see also Aristotle 1944, 519–521; Oliver 2007, 29).

Greek bankers, in contrast, depended upon a reputation (if not the reality) for honesty and probity. Bankers and their customers often transacted business without witnesses, as customers relied upon their banker's honesty and accuracy in record keeping. Bankers' records were considered strong admissible evidence.

The Greeks conducted ordinary day-to-day transactions without too much controversy. Calhoun states that the presence of "market commissioners and official inspectors of weights and measures" are not evidence "of a low moral standard in retail trade, for we ourselves are as yet unable to dispense with such functionaries as these." There were "occasional complaints of attempted extortion, but as a general rule fair prices on a basis of supply and demand seem to have prevailed, with very little governmental price-fixing." Levy, too, remarked upon the relatively free rein accorded traders: "The Athenian legislator showed himself to be very liberal, except in respect of trade in grain, whose cornering and export he forbade. Otherwise he limited himself to ensuring the honesty of business activity by enacting a simple form of commercial law and by controlling weights and measures" (Calhoun 1926a, 99–100; Levy 1967, 23).

Themistocles became a useful figure. For some Greeks, he was the Bernard Madoff of his time; however, Themistocles was a war hero, driving away the Persian navy. Was he a corrupt individual engaged in nefarious activities, including graft, bribery, and extortion? Herodotus accused Themistocles of engaging in bribery (he was the recipient and also a payer) with other naval commanders. Classicist Leslie Kurke maintains that Herodotus and Plutarch misrepresented Themistocles: "figures like Themistocles enter the literary tradition always already mythologized—always already bearers of a cultural signification that exceeds their historical reality" (Herodotus 1987, 557–558; Kurke 2002, 88).

In Kurke's re-fashioning, Themistocles' use of money disrupted the existing social and cosmic orders that proscribed individuals seeking profits. During the sixth and fifth centuries, Greece transformed. The rise of cities created the "summit of the long-term transactional order, to which citizens owe their loyalty and their lives. Thus, for example, gift-giving, so positively valued in elitist terms, becomes negatively inflected as 'bribery' (*dorodokia*) when it is felt to interfere with a citizen's obligations to his civic community." In opposition with this view, the elitist tradition excoriates coinage and the agora for their fixture on economic matters and not its political aspect. The elitist tradition couples "coinage with kapeleia [petty huckstering], deceit, and profit unconstrained by social value… [coinage is also associated with] counterfeiting, prostitution and general lowlife criminality." Themistocles' activities, even if accurately recounted, are imbued with this clash between established elitist traditions and the transformation in Greek culture. In the sixth and fifth centuries, men with wealth were indispensable, as their concentrated wealth were convenient sources of funds from which to build Athenian state fleets.

Playwright Timocreon had reasons for disliking Themistocles, including the latter accepting a payment (bribe) from Timocreon but not delivering the services. Timocreon portrayed Themistocles as a money-grubbing innkeeper instead of a war hero. Timocreon uses the tropes of money as corrupting and being used against the aristocratic *xenia*. He transforms Themistocles' generosity in providing feasts to that of "innkeeping" and "furnishing cold meats [presumably a social faux pas]" (Kurke 2002, 93–95, 100–102). Timocreon undoubtedly used these characterizations knowing that his audience would accept the rather heavy-handed analogy. According to Plato, innkeepers were disreputable, as they "set up his quarters in some solitary spot remote from everywhere; there he entertains the famished traveler and the refugee from tempests with welcome lodging, and provide them with calm in storm and cool shelter in heat. But what comes next?" Instead of treating his guests as friends, "he behaves as though he were dealing with captive enemies who had fallen into his hands, and holds them to the hardest, most iniquitous, most abominable terms of ransom."[8] No noble generosity infuses Themistocles' actions; he treats his guests not as guests with accompanying gifts but rather as hostages held ransom until they pay. Philosopher Theophrastus denigrates innkeepers, too, tarring such persons with such aspersions as pimping and tax farming: "He will turn his mother out of doors, be apprehended for larceny, spend longer time in the lock-up than in his own house" (Plato 1960, 311–312; Theophrastus 1929, 55; Kurke 2002, 103). Nothing is too debased for a profit-seeker.

Although Themistocles organized the navy and fed its sailors, he allegedly did so while capturing a large profit for himself. If the allegation is true, Themistocles is a forerunner of many later corrupt military leaders; history is replete with officers siphoning off money intended for supplying or feeding their troops. Commentators disagree on Themistocles' inordinate thirst for making money. Was he such a lover of being generous (possibly with other people's money), that he constantly needed to replenish his funds for further acts of generosity? Or was he a miser willing to even sell gifts sent to him (Kurke 2002, 105, 110; Plutarch [1909] 1956, 9)?

Profits

What did the Greeks consider profits? Aristotle defined profits as the difference between the costs and the sales price. He countenanced natural exchange in order to acquire what was "necessary for life and useful for one's community of city or household." Once people began using a commonly accepted commodity to sever the double coincidence of wants inherent in barter, exchange took on a different character, whereby traders sought to accumulate as much money as they could. Aristotle's distinction between natural exchange (mutually beneficial trade) and "unnatural" exchange whereby someone ends up with more money than he originally has (profit) is erroneous. Under barter or purchase with money, both parties are usually better off from making a voluntary transaction. Money is simply a way of keeping score.

Aristotle uses Thales of Miletus as an example of a man capable of wealth-getting, who preferred to devote his time and energy studying astronomy. When people taunted him for his poverty, he used his knowledge of astronomy to deduce that there was going to be a bumper crop of olives. He went and paid deposits upon olive presses (at low rents) and, when the crop came in, he charged premium prices to use his leased presses. He therefore demonstrated that philosophers could use their knowledge to enrich themselves but that such worthies generally disdained such use of their knowledge (Aristotle 1944, 39, 43, 55–57). Aristotle's point is instructive, although he did not express an opinion whether it was honorable for Thales to use his knowledge to create a monopoly of sorts. Would present-day regulators have accused Thales of being an "insider trader?"

Xenophon recommended bestowing honors upon traders instead of relying upon profits. Honors took the intangible form of a good reputation among peers and also tangible forms: "it would also be an excellent plan to reserve front seats in the theatre for merchants and shipowners, and to offer them hospitality occasionally, when the high quality of their ships and merchandise entitles them to be considered benefactors of the state. With the prospect of these honours before them they would look on us as friends and hasten to visit us to win the honour as well as the profit, such as preferred seating at the theater and banquets" (Xenophon n.d. 3.4).

Ways to Wealth in Athens

There were various paths to wealth in classical Greece. Ancient Greek business owners held a variety of motives. There was the desire for wealth-getting and seeking profit from trade. Business owners, though, also sought status. Max Weber believed that the quest for status predominated the narrower quest for wealth-based class (Weber 1968, 307; Engen 2010, 21, 36).

Wealthy Athenians had an unquenchable thirst for land, whether owned or leased. With more land, a landowner might be able to deploy his labor force more efficiently, possibly through specialization. More land raised the possibility of diversifying crops and other products. Warfare, too, could bring in booty and more land to occupy, but, of course, the fortunes of war were not certain. Athenians might also gain wealth through manufacturing and mining. The need for liquidity meant there was "a high degree of monetization" in the Athenian economy (Osborne 2002, 127–130).

Another route to wealth in Athens was to invest in the Laurium mines during the fifth century. Investors could invest directly in the mines or by leasing slaves. Even small-scale mining concerns could receive grants of concessions from the Athenian government upon payment of an upfront lump sum or a rental rate, so the industry was open to a broad swatch of Athenians. In the scramble for wealth, some unethical activities probably transpired, although the record is vague. The industry, though, was tightly regulated. Miners were prohibited from mining without a grant and paying for concession rights; if an informer revealed information leading to conviction of violators of the concession rules, he would receive a reward. The regulations served to curb cutthroat competition and negligence that could lead to accidents and poaching of ore from another miner's concession. One rule prohibited directing smoke into neighboring shafts. Failure to pay the lump sum or annual rents might entail loss of civic rights (Calhoun 1926b, 164–165).

Aristotle criticized the desire for acquiring money. The normal course of trade, exchange for the purpose of getting an article desired, is not a part of wealth-getting. Exchange was meant, "for the replenishment of natural self-sufficiency." The goal of amassing *chremata*—useful things, including precious metals, land, livestock—was to afford a life where one did not have to do *physical* labor. The *plousios* were not so fortunate and had to work for sustenance. What sources exist condemn the wealth-seeking aristocratic classes, citing unscrupulous efforts to gain wealth that included looting and extortion (Aristotle 1944, 41–43; Starr 1977, 49 and 54).

Hesiod condemned envy that leads to theft, but he also believed such greed led to only temporary gains: "[A] man's shameless spirit tramples his sense of honor; lightly the gods wipe out that man, and diminish the household of such a one, and his wealth stays with him for only a short time." Hesiod is remarkably practical and clear-headed, when he advises, "When you deal with your brother, be pleasant, but get a witness; for too much trustfulness, and too much suspicion, have proved men's undoing" (Hesiod 1959, 57, 61–63, 380–381).

Greek philosophers' concern with virtue was not unique. On the other side of the world, Confucius (Kong Qui, 551–479 BCE) formulated ethical standards for human conduct. Key to his system of ethics was respect for the social institutions. He made a statement demonstrating some ambivalence regarding wealth and the pursuit of wealth. "I would rather look upon wealth and high position as nothing more than a floating cloud, if they are gotten unrighteously." For Confucius, attempts to gain wealth or to escape poverty had to be done "within the limits of the stipulated ethical criterion," lest one become unrighteous. He exhibited a certain fatalism, arguing that poverty or wealth were determined by "Heaven" and "fate," and people had little leeway to "push his own claim," so a person "ought to be 'contented with poverty,' and 'know one's own fate." The ruling class, of course, subscribed to this contentment with regard to one's own fate. He also stated, "Only the superior man understands righteousness. The inferior man understands only material benefits."

Confucius believed that "men of letters" should not participate in production. He saw no need for a man of letters to know about farming, which was, after all, a humble man's activity. "The superior man looks for knowledge, not livelihood." There was, however, a pragmatic aspect to his thinking, "For him to be engaged in tilling may mean suffering from hunger, but learning will bring him an official post and emolument. What a superior man really worries about is the keeping of his principle, not poverty."[9] Confucius appears to have tolerated the literati participating in commercial activities. One of his pupils, Duanmu Ci was a rich merchant. In fact, Confucius stated, "I'll sell! I'll sell! I am waiting for a good price to sell myself." Unlike Greek and subsequent philosophers, Confucius' *Analects* does not carry any disapproval of commerce (Hu 1988, 43–48).

Grain Supplies and Speculation

One way to accumulate wealth was successful speculation in the grain market. The biggest challenge for Grecian cities was to ensure a sufficient and reliable flow of grain. Because the demand for grain was not overly sensitive to the price, a shortfall could dramatically raise prices; a surplus, conversely, could send prices plummeting. State officials recognized the potential danger of volatile prices, especially high prices, that could trigger civil unrest. Athens issued edicts prohibiting the export of home-grown food, among other tactics. Due to the volatile prices of grain and oil, self-sufficiency in staples may have been a prudent strategy for a landowner (Finley 1973, 128; Halstead 2002, 68).

Wars disrupted the Athenian grain supply. The surrounding areas in Attica sustained Athens, but eventually the *polis* required imports of grain. With the descent of Athens in the interminable wars of the fourth and third centuries BCE, ensuring the grain supply became a pressing issue. Athenian traders faced enhanced risks during the upheavals. The Athenians may have needed to import as much as one-third of their grain supplies, especially as Attica was not the most fertile grain-growing region. (Oliver 2007, 4–6).[10]

The growing need for imported foodstuffs and products gave rise to the importance of prices. Haggling was a feature of the agora, and the Greeks began to ponder the emphasis placed upon bargaining. Karl Polanyi notes, "the sharp eye of the theoretician had discerned the links between the petty tricks of the huckster in the agora and novel kinds of trading profits that were the talk of the day." Still, he insists that the supply–demand price determination, even for international trade, did not really come into play until the third century BCE (Polanyi 1957, 87).

Plato understood that prices fluctuated on a day-to-day basis, but he thought it wrong for people to haggle and "praise up" commodities. Astrid Moller notes that, "prices reveal their role by a complex of factors, including personal relationships and ideology. While grain was in the hands of the *emporos*, grain traders could ask a price that seemed appropriate to him. Thus Xenophon could claim that the *emporoi* are *philositoi* (fond of gain), buying grain where they heard that it grew in abundance, and selling it not wherever they were without thinking, but wherever grain had the highest value. Some poleis seem to have bought grain from the *emporoi* at a 'just price.'" On rare occasion, authorities might have attempted to fix prices during extreme scarcity, but Moller observes, "there is no hint that anyone ever tried to regulate the wholesale price. The aim of the 'official price' was stabilization, escaping unpredictable oscillations and, most frequently, preventing speculation and unjustified profits." Five *agoranomoi* (market magistrates) scrutinized the agora and ferreted out goods that were not in marketable condition and genuine; they had the authority to fine anyone lying. Athens had ten *metronomoi* (measure magistrates) to monitor weights and measures (Moller 2007, 373).

On occasion, a shortfall in supply was matched by a surplus in nearby regions. Speculators in the outlying regions may have hesitated to send in foodstuffs during a famine, fearing potential seizure by authorities or a missed opportunity to reap even higher prices by waiting. Economists demonstrate that astute speculators can alleviate the worst effects of famines, but state officials often deterred speculators from fully realizing this potential. Difficulties in transportation or civil unrest and other turmoil could create obstacles in shipping grain to hard-pressed cities. Moses Finley recognized that speculative "greed" was not the sole culprit for famines (Finley 1973, 127).[11]

Xenophon describes the risk-taking speculators—merchants who were "fond" of corn. "For it is their exceeding love of corn that makes merchants sail to wherever they hear there is most of it….And whenever they want money, they are not likely to throw away their corn at the first opportunity; but wherever they hear that corn is dearest and most thought of by the inhabitants, thither they carry it, and sell it there" (Xenophon [1876] 1971, 124–125).

Because a secure food supply was paramount, Athenians created corn-guardians to inspect the quality and quantity of bread loaves and to maintain a just price. On other occasions, corn buyers, *sitonai*, were appointed to buy grain wherever (and possibly however) they could. Historian Robin Osborne writes, "The more securely a city could meet its own food needs from its own land the easier it was to maintain political independence" (Osborne 2002, 116; Finley 1973, 169–170; Migeotte 2009, 145–147; Austin and Vidal-Naquet 1977, 293).

The Greeks took a dim view of traders and merchants, who speculated in the grain market and prosecuted attempts to corner the grain market, perhaps inspired by Kleomenes (Cleomenes, according to Google), a governor of Egypt appointed by Alexander. This character prohibited exports of wheat and bought up the entire harvest. He then gradually shipped the grain to Greece, where there was a dearth, and made a profit (Levy 1967, 36; Michell 1957, 276). In this case, you have a tyrant, who knew in advance that he was going to issue an edict on exports and using his insider knowledge to make a huge fortune; apparently, the public outcry led to his death and execution, when his patron, Alexander, died. Kleomenes' use of inside information was to be repeated by legislators through the ages.

Regulators attempted to prevent hoarding and stockpiling grain for speculative purposes. Lysias accused grain dealers of withholding grain and forcing prices to rise; the authorities passed a grain tax law in 375/374 BCE to combat the rising prices allegedly manipulated by hucksters.[12] Informants, dubbed "sycophants," brought charges against dealers; many of the charges were false, but the informers may have been motivated by "personal enmity, oftener still by the hope that they would be privately bribed to withdraw the complaint; in case the prosecution succeeded, they had in prospect of collecting a share of the fees." Demosthenes complained about speculators and high prices; if he was not the first demagogue in history to do so, he certainly continued a tradition that has never ceased. Speculators are reviled throughout history. The Athenians attempted to fix grain prices, but one can imagine that such efforts were futile in the face of significant shortages (Lysias [1876] 1886, 78–79; Oliver 2007, 27–29).

Demosthenes' "Oration against Dionysodorus" refers to Dionysodorus and Parmeniscus, who borrowed 3000 drachms from Darius and Pamphilus for purpose of obtaining a cargo of corn abroad and bringing it back to Athens. Parmeniscus sailed to Egypt and purchased corn. En route to Athens, Parmeniscus stopped in Rhodes, where he received word that the price of grain had fallen in Athens due to large imports from Sicily. Parmeniscus sold the cargo and did not return to Athens. In doing so, he violated a stipulation in the contract with Darius and Pamphilus and also under Athenian law not to discharge the cargo at any port besides Athens; the penalty included paying double the amount owed (Michell 1957, 276–277).

To ensure their supplies of grain or to promote public works, Greek authorities encouraged *leitourgia* (liturgies). The Athenians developed the practice of bestowing honors and privileges. These honors were inscribed on *stelai* that were placed in public places (surviving *stelai* are an important source for our knowledge of the awarding of honors and privileges). Initially, traders did not receive such honors. Some of the privileges were lucrative, such as protection from seizure (*asylia*) and exemption from obligations (*ateleia*). The value of friendship served an insurance aspect; a shipper who provided grain during a significant shortfall might be promised *boetheia*, an obligation of the Athenians to come to the aid of the benefactor should such need ever rise.

Ptolemy helped the Athenians in 282 BCE; he sent a large shipment of grain to Athens and may have moderated any upsurge in grain prices. By honoring Ptolemy for his actions, the Athenians undoubtedly served both political and economic purposes (Oliver 2007, 42–43, 246, 261; Engen 2010, 11–12, 182–183; Migeotte 2009, 155, 169). The Athenians eventually proved open-minded in awarding such honors and privileges. Certainly wealthy, well-connected men who arranged for shipments of grain and timber as gifts gained honors, but wealthy professional traders and small professional traders also gained honor when they sold their grain at discounted prices or for reasonable prices during shortages. The awarding of honors and privileges reflected Athenians' changing attitudes toward profit-seeking traders, who were once "disesteemed" but became literal life-savers during grain shortages. With respect to foreign rulers, the Greeks were willing to lavish honors upon foreigners who agreed to export grain to the city-states (Engen 2010, 32–35, 79, 186–187; Oliver 2007, 241–242; Finley 1973, 161).

Seaborne Trade

Seaborne trade was prominent in the Greek economy. Lenders may have charged sea-going merchants a high rate of interest, because until the borrower returned with a cargo that would serve as security, the lender held no security. George Calhoun suggests that the persistence of such loans implies that the borrowers collectively established a reasonable record of repaying loans and were therefore honest and honorable men (Calhoun 1926b, 45–49).

Besides the risk inherent in any particular borrower, there were risks endemic to seaborne trade, such as fluctuating demand for goods, shipwrecks, capsizing, piracy, war, and covetous governments. Each successful seaborne journey was cause for celebration and relief. The typical seafaring merchant set out with some goods; often he did not have a set itinerary or plan. At each stop, the merchant would display his wares and trade for what was available. If he accepted local money, he ran a risk with the currency exchange. No wonder many Greek traders were content with one successful journey (Hasebroek 1965, 83).[13]

Despite this lack of collateral, traders with a proven record of honesty were able to borrow funds, at rates even as low as 12%. Although 12% is higher than most modern business borrowers face, the Greeks' interest rate does not imply "excessive moral risk." Calhoun suggests that even men lacking credit or inability to pay interest might acquire sufficient capital from friends, who were relied upon his honor. To renege on a debt was to besmirch one's reputation. In a sense, a man's reputation and honor were his collateral.

Although Calhoun asserted that the majority of merchant adventurers must have been honest, otherwise the *respondentia* would not have survived for so long, Greek orators described some scoundrels and swindlers. In one case, Zenothemis conspired with a ship captain to obtain a large loan by pretending another merchant's (Protus) cargo was theirs. They decided to scuttle the ship and cargo. The conspirators planned to bore a hole in the ship bottom and escape in a small boat. Unfortunately, another passenger caught them, although the ship's captain drowned. Zenothemis was brazen and claimed that Protus' cargo was his; he asserted that the now-deceased ship captain had borrowed money from him to buy the cargo. The existing records do not state whether Zenothemis got away with his amateurish and yet daring plot. Calhoun observed that such behavior could not have been common, otherwise capitalists would have demanded more security before extending loans. He concluded, "The speeches give us…an interesting picture of various sorts of swindlers who were undoubtedly to be met with all too often in the cosmopolitan crowds of traders and sailors who thronged the Piraeus." He argued that such characters recur throughout history, and to assume that their flamboyant criminal activities were indicative of the whole is dubious (Calhoun 1926b, 54–56; 60–61; 96–98; Levy 1967, 25–26). Calhoun did not mention that such former merchant adventurers might be admirably suited to ascertain the merits and morals of prospective borrowers.

Greek Bankers and Lending at Interest

The Greeks, of course, had plenty of reasons to seek loans, many of them unpleasant. Taxes, food, burials, and other expenses kept occurring (Meikle 2002, 243).

Greeks practiced a form of cronyism with regard to lending. A merchant might extend an *eranos* loan to a well-known and trusted borrower. The merchant would not charge interest. The expectation was that eventually, aside from paying back the loan, the borrower would be expected to extend a similar, interest-free loan to the merchant. The *eranos* loans were a tit-for-tat system. Daniel Friedman and Daniel McNeill speculate that the animus to interest-bearing loans emanated from emotional sources. The *eranos* loans allowed the lender to feel virtuous; because of the implied reciprocity, the borrower, too, could avoid feeling exploited or vulnerable. Borrowers dealt with moneylenders at times of vulnerability, and people feel discomfort at being vulnerable. Friedman and McNeill conclude that the rules governing collateral and default reflected incentives; once the borrower had the funds, the incentive was to delay or avoid paying back the loan (Friedman and McNeill 2013, 68–70). The situation is a classic "moral hazard" case. If enough borrowers fail to repay, the lenders' willingness to loan may disappear; the absence of lenders hurts borrowers in general.

Money changing was a key occupation in Athens. The Greek isles issued a variety of currencies. Money changers presumably had some means of secreting and protecting their money. Traders and merchants might have need for depositing their money for safekeeping. Some money changers began to offer such depository services. Obviously, these money changers had to have a stainless reputation for people to be willing to leave money with them. At times, Athenians required witnesses for all business transactions, but witnesses were rarely enlisted for transactions between banker and depositor. The money changers, recognizing that not all deposits were likely to be withdrawn on any given day, began to transform into bankers by loaning out some deposits, in the expectation and hopes that loans would be repaid before the depositors requested their currency. A money changer/banker might advertise his probity and credibility by investing in a costly and sturdy vault; the mere act of investing in a non-movable asset would signal his intent to remain in the community.

The bankers naturally had to keep accurate records. The reputation for accuracy of the bankers' records allowed them to be used by courts as prima facie evidence of transactions, and litigants could request records be examined. Then as now, banking could be quite profitable; as long as the banker was prudent, his wealth was likely to increase reliably. The courts were designed to quickly settle cases involving business transactions and served to encourage investment, as potential investors would be reassured that their funds would not be frozen in extended litigation: "It must have been very important to afford the banker every possible element of security, and thus to encourage him to keep his money invested" (Calhoun 1926b, 90–91, 98, 114).[14]

Even former slaves, such as Pasion, could aspire to become prosperous bankers, especially if they had prudence, acumen, and integrity. Pasion was accused of defrauding Isocrates, who sought to conceal his father's wealth by having Pasion to keep it from the hands of unscrupulous Athenian officials. Pasion agreed to conceal the wealth but later denied having it currently in his possession. There is no record of the outcome of the trial. Pasion, however, had long enjoyed an excellent reputation, even by people who feuded with him; after the allegations by Isocrates, Pasion continued to be respected and admired by Athenians for his rise from the dregs of society to a position of esteem. Sadly for Pasion, his son, Apollodorus, was a demoralized spendthrift. Pasion's selection of his ex-slave Phormion to inherit the banking business triggered a long-running lawsuit. Phormion's esteem and integrity was such that the members of court hearing the case "refused to hear a single word from the plaintiff and hooted him from the speaker's stand" (Calhoun 1926b, 108, 119–124).[15]

State Policies

Trade in Greek cities was tightly supervised. Sometimes the state policies benefited traders and merchants, but sometimes the state acted predatorily.

One interesting aspect of the Greek regulations was a decree prohibiting "bringing a man's trade in the market into disrepute, no doubt with business rivalry in view. (We hear of 'defamation in the emporium' as a feature of commercial life even in those days.) Secondly, there was a law, protecting a citizen who plies his trade in the market against contemptuous comment upon his means of livelihood—for such a livelihood was universally despised" (Hasebroek 1965, 174).

Ancient states, including Greece and Rome, were willing to create monopolies with regard to mineral resources. Although monopolies are sometimes more efficient than competitive firms—if there were economies of scale—the ancients were more interest in the fiscal aspects than in efficiency. A monopoly over precious metals helped finance governments; governments, too, monopolized minting coins. If the purpose of minting coins was to facilitate trade, many, if not most, ancient governments failed to issue enough coinage to meet the needs of trade. Merchants and consumers alike resorted to loans in the absence of coinage. A lack of uniformity with regard to weight and purity of coins contributed to confusion and created arbitrage opportunities; the notorious money changers presumably were experts in recognizing various coins and knowing their respective values. Even an honest money changer could easily be perceived as cheating relatively ignorant customers. With regard to the ethics of coinage, impecunious rulers have frequently debased their coins by a variety of methods (Finley 1973, 165–167). Lest the reader feel smug about today's currencies, Americans of the early nineteenth century were not too much better off than the Greeks and Romans of antiquity with regard to coinage and currency.

In comparison with private traders and merchants, Greek city-state governments and leaders were capable of dubious business practices. Greek city-states also minted their own coins and propped up the value of the coins, even after debasing the currency. Dionysius, tyrant of Syracuse, reportedly resorted to a particularly nasty trick: "Having borrowed money from the citizens under promise of repayment, when they demanded it back he ordered them to bring what money any of them possessed, threatening them with death if they failed to do so. When the money had been brought he issued it again, after stamping it afresh so that each drachm had the value of 2 drachms, and so paid back the original debt and the money which they brought him." Some researchers think the story inaccurate and surmise that Dionysius may have borrowed debased coins and repaid under a new, not necessarily fraudulent, standard. No such re-stamped coins have been found, but Dionysius had a sufficiently nefarious character to warrant such suspicions reasonable (Michell 1957, 332).

On occasion Greek city officials would buy up all of the corn under an edict that fixed the price below the market price; the officials then turned around and repealed the prohibition upon the export of corn and sold the corn for a profit. In other words, the officials acted opportunistically in creating and exploiting monopoly power. Some Greeks urged governments to create a state monopoly of the mines or to manipulate the markets for gain. In other cases, Greek city officials seized corn-ships or encouraged pirates to steal corn (Hasebroek 1965, 148–150, 155–157). A double standard for business practices existed in Greece.

Greeks' Legacy

The Greek philosophers' discussion of the ethics of business resounds even today. Thinkers from medievalists to modern-day thinkers have examined some basic issues and often based their ideas upon these Greek philosophers of 2500 years ago. The Greeks evolved from raiders and pirates to practicing relatively ethical business behavior. To be sure, much of their economy rested upon slavery and lower status for many of the residents.

Although the Greek philosophers remain the glamor boys with their unsullied hands, thinking deep thoughts, one wonders how the rest of Greek society viewed trade and commerce. Most of the residents of Greek cities had to devote their time procuring food and shelter. They may have grudgingly accepted their need for toil and went without contemplation.

Aristotle and other Greek philosophers, however, considered the nature of virtue and endowed us with a new approach to ethical considerations. These ideas differed from the pragmatic, if not opportunistic, ethical approaches used elsewhere in the ancient world.

Notes

1. Humfrey Michell described how Menelaus and Odysseus boasted of their piracy; they doubted that there had been more successful pirates than themselves (Homer [1965] 1967, 67, 216; Michell 1957, 210).
2. Although the normal progression of events was for pirates to become traders, sometimes the process was reversed. China dealt with piracy for centuries, but there was an eruption of piracy between 1550 and 1567, when

Chinese merchants responded to heavy-handed edicts by resorting to piracy (Kung and Ma 2014, 510–534).

3. Solon's explanation of virtue *arête*, contrasted with wealth *chremata*, disappointed the wealthy Croesus, who wanted Solon to praise him because of his extreme wealth (Herodotus 1987, 45–48).
4. Johannes Hasebroek claimed that our knowledge of these small traders was limited, as most were illiterate.
5. Karl Polanyi described how satirists ridiculed hucksters. One might imagine Greek audiences laughing at the antics of hucksters getting their comeuppance (Polanyi 1957, 92).
6. Leopold Migeotte argued that business participants must have been among the earliest users of writing. "By bestowing a fixed and durable form upon all kinds of documents, writing made it possible not only to create archives but also to produce evidence in the event of disputes" (Migeotte 2009, 9).
7. Humfrey Michell described fishmongers as "a rough lot, cheats and cutthroats, and a sharp look-out had to be kept on them by the police and market officials to prevent swindling. One ordinance forbade them watering the salt fish" (Michell 1957, 289).
8. Presumably, the value added of providing a comfortable, safe resting place in an isolated region would be quite significant.
9. Similar to the Greek thinkers, the Chinese philosophers expressed a variation of the old Greyhound bus lines slogan, "Go labor and leave the thinking to us."
10. See Migeotte for a slightly different interpretation (Migeotte 2009, 148).
11. Here's a brief lesson in economics (no graphs, I promise). Perceived future prices affect both current supply and demand; the differing expectations of future prices create an incentive for speculation. Modern people, who are not familiar with the mechanics of speculation, think speculators are making paper profits and not earning profits through production of useful goods and services or by the sweat of their brows. There is a hilarious depiction of speculators in *Trading Places*, where Don Ameche and Ralph Bellamy's characters are explaining to Eddie Murphy's streetwise character how speculation works; alas, they are planning to cheat—by bribing officials—in order to gain an advantage in the futures market. Let me shock or offend you—we are all speculators. If you have ever driven by the local gas station, taken a look at the current price, and muttered, "I think I'll fill the tank today, since a news report said that a large oil refinery burned down last night," then you are speculating. You are guessing that gasoline prices would be greater in the near future.
12. If such speculations are successful, the obvious question becomes, why didn't the ordinary Athenians do the same? In one case, the Athenians gave

a group of grain retailers a temporary right to form a cartel to negotiate with the importers—a bi-lateral monopoly (Michell 1957, 272).

13. One ramification of this nascent trade was the possibility of one-shot interactions; the merchant might figure he would never again transact with a party, so opportunistic behavior might have been tempting.
14. Humfrey Michell, too, argued that some of the money changers and bankers must have been honest, since they were used as expert witnesses in currency exchange disputes (Michell 1957, 388).
15. Apollodorus' demoralization was a bane that all-too-frequently afflicted heirs of wealth, but at least such situations provided inspiration for numerous plays, novels, and motion pictures.

Bibliography

Aristotle. *Nicomachean Ethics* (New York, NY: Barnes & Noble, [1893] 2004). Translated by F.H. Peters.

Aristotle. *Politics* (Cambridge, MA: Harvard University Press, 1944). Translated by H. Rackham.

Austin, Michael and Pierre Vidal-Naquet. *Economic and Social History of Ancient Greece: An Introduction* (Berkeley, CA: University of California Press, 1977).

Bolkestein, Hendrik. *Economic Life in Greece's Golden Age* (Leiden, Netherlands: E.J. Brill, 1958).

Calhoun, George. *The Ancient Greeks and the Evolution of Standards in Business* (Boston: Houghton Mifflin, 1926a).

Calhoun, George. *The Business Life of Ancient Athens* (Chicago, IL: University of Chicago Press, 1926b).

Cartledge, Paul. "The Economy (Economies) of Ancient Greece." *The Ancient Economy*, edited by Walter Scheidel and Sitta von Reden, (New York, NY: Routledge, 2002), 11–32.

Davies, John. "Linear and Nonlinear Flow Models for Ancient Economies." The Ancient Economy: Evidence and Models." *The Ancient Economy: Evidence and Models*, edited by J.G. Manning and Ian Morris. (Stanford, CA: Stanford University Press, 2005), 127–156.

Engen, Darel Tai. *Honor and Profit: Athenian Trade Policy and the Economy and Society of Greece, 415–307 B.C.E.* (Ann Arbor, MI: University of Michigan Press, 2010).

Evelyn-White, Hugh. n.d. Editor. *Hymn 3 to Apollo*. http://www.Perseus.tufts.edu/hopper/text?doc=Perseus:abo:tlg,0013,003:450, viewed April 2, 2018.

Finley, Moses. "Aristotle and Economic Analysis." *Past & Present* 47(no number), May 1970, 3–25.

Finley, Moses. *The Ancient Economy* (Berkeley, CA: University of California Press, 1973).

Friedman, Daniel and Daniel McNeill. *Morals and Markets: The Dangerous Balance* (New York, NY: Palgrave Macmillan, 2013). 2nd edition.

Halstead, Paul. "Traditional and Ancient Rural Economy in Mediterranean Europe: plus ca change?" Reprinted in *The Ancient Economy*, edited by Walter Scheidel and Sitta von Reden. (New York, NY: Routledge, 2002), 53–70.

Hasebroek, Johannes. *Trade and Politics in Ancient Greece* (New York, NY: Biblo and Tannen, 1965), translated by L.M. Fraser and D.C. MacGregor.

Heichelheim, Fritz. *An Ancient Economic History: From the Palaeolithic Age to the Migrations of the Germanic, Slavic, and Arabic Nations* (Leiden, Netherlands: A.W. Sijthoff's, 1958), 2 vols. Translated by Joyce Stevens.

Herodotus. *The History* (Chicago, IL: University of Chicago Press, 1987).

Hesiod. *The Works and Days* (Ann Arbor, MI: 1959). Translated by Richmond Lattimore.

Homer. *The Iliad of Homer* (Chicago, IL: University of Chicago Press, [1951] 1974). Translated by Richmond Lattimore.

Homer. *The Odyssey of Homer* (New York, NY: Harper & Row, [1965] 1967). Translated by Richmond Lattimore.

Hu, Jichuang. *A Concise History of Chinese Economic Thought* (Beijing, China: Foreign Languages Press, 1988).

Kung, James and Chicheng Ma. "Autarky and the Rise and Fall of Piracy in Ming China." *Journal of Economic History* 74(2), June 2014, 509–534.

Kurke, Leslie. "Money and Mythic History: The Contestation of Transactional Orders in the Fifth Century." *The Ancient Economy*, edited by Walter Scheidel and Sitta von Reden. (New York, NY: Routledge, 2002), 87–113.

Levy, Jean-Philippe. *The Economic Life of the Ancient World* (Chicago, IL: University of Chicago Press, 1967).

Lysias. *Select Orations of Lysias*, edited by William Stevens (Chicago, IL: S.C. Griggs, [1876] 1886).

Meikle, Scott. "Modernism, Economics and the Ancient Economy." Reprinted in *The Ancient Economy*, edited by Walter Scheidel and Sitta von Reden (New York, NY: Routledge, 2002), 233–250.

Michell, Humfrey. *The Economics of Ancient Greece* (New York, NY: Barnes and Noble, 1957).

Migeotte, Leopold. *The Economy of the Greek Cities* (Berkeley, CA: University of California Press, 2009).

Moller, Astrid. "Classical Greece: Distribution." *The Cambridge Economic History of the Greco-Roman World*, edited by Walter Scheidel, Ian Morris, and Richard Saller (Cambridge, UK: Cambridge University Press, 2007), 743–768.

Morris, Ian. "Early Iron Age Greece." *The Cambridge Economic History of the Greco-Roman World*, edited by Walter Scheidel, Ian Morris, and Richard Saller (Cambridge, UK: Cambridge University Press, 2007), editors, 211–241.

Morris, Ian, Richard Saller, and Walter Scheidel. "Introduction." *The Cambridge Economic History of the Greco-Roman World* (Cambridge, UK: Cambridge University Press, 2007). Walter Scheidel, Ian Morris, and Richard Saller, editors, 1–12.

Nicolet, Claude. *The World of the Citizen in Republican Rome* (Berkeley, CA: University of California Press, 1980). Translated by P.S. Falla.

Oliver, G.J. *War, Food, and Politics in Early Hellenistic Athens* (Oxford, UK: Oxford University Press, 2007).

Osborne, Robin. "Pride and Prejudice, Sense and Subsistence: Exchange and Society in the Greek City." Reprinted in The Ancient Economy, edited by Walter Scheidel and Sitta von Reden (New York, NY: Routledge, 2002), 114–132.

Plato. *The Laws*, edited by A.E. Taylor (London, UK: J.M. Dent & Sons, 1960).

Plato. *Republic*, translated by Benjamin Jowett (New York, NY: Barnes and Noble Classic, 2004).

Plutarch. *Plutarch's Lives of Themistocles, Pericles, Aristides, Alcibiades and Coriolanus, Demosthenes and Cicero, Caesar and Antony* (New York, NY: P.F. Collier & Son, [1909] 1956).

Plutarch. *Plutarch's Live of Romulus, Lycurgus, Solon, Pericles, Cato, Pompey, Alexander the Great, Julius Caesar, Demosthenes, Cicero, Mark Antony, Brutus, and Others, and His Comparisons with Notes, Critical and Historical*, edited by Rev. John and William Langhorne (New York, NY: Wm. L. Allison Company, 1889).

Polanyi, Karl. "Aristotle Discovers the Economy." *Trade and Market in the Early Empires: Economies in History and Theory*, edited by Karl Polanyi, Conrad Arensberg, and Harry Pearson (Glencoe, IL: Free Press 1957), 64–94.

Sedlacek, Tomas. *Economics of Good and Evil: The Quest for Economic Meaning from Gilgamesh to Wall Street* (Oxford, UK: Oxford University Press, 2011).

Smith, Adam. *An Inquiry into the Nature and Causes of the Wealth of Nations*, edited by R.H. Campbell and A.S. Skinner (Indianapolis, IN: Liberty*Classics*, 1981).

Starr, Chester. *The Economic and Social Growth of Early Greece, 800–500 B.C.* (New York: Oxford University Press, 1977).

Theophrastus. *The Characters of Theophrastus*, edited by J.M. Edmonds (London, UK: William Heineman, 1929).

Viner, Jacob. *Religious Thought and Economic Society* (Durham, NC: Duke University Press, 1978).

Weber, Max. *Economy and Society: An Outline of Interpretative Sociology* (New York, NY: Bedminster Press, 1968).

Wells, Herbert G. *The Outline of History: Being a Plain History of Life and Mankind* (New York, NY: Macmillan, 1920).
Xenophon. *The Economist of Xenophon*, translated by Alexander Wedderburn and W. Gershom Collingwood (New York, NY: Burt Franklin, [1876] 1971).
Xenophon. n.d. *On Revenues*, translated by H.G. Dakyns (*Poroi*). www.gutenberg.org/files/1179/1179-h/1179-h.htm, viewed October 31, 2019.

CHAPTER 6

Roman Society

Rome dominated the Mediterranean world for centuries. The Romans transformed from small landowners to conquering militarists, whose conquests provided a base for the Roman economy. The Romans, however, developed ways to facilitate trade and commerce. The Romans also bequeathed a sophisticated system of laws affecting trade and commerce. The often misunderstood concept of caveat emptor arose in Rome.

Although often cruel, Romans created a large trading bloc that incorporated a variety of different peoples. Roman elites professed disdain for sordid business, but they did not disdain profits. Roman senators were not supposed to involve themselves in large-scale trade, so they often resorted to subterfuges, such as having slaves act on their behalf. The senators and other wealthy Romans avidly sought to expand their landholdings and wealth. The interaction between Roman legislators and businesspeople sometimes created temptations to plunder residents and enrich legislators.

Overview

Before empire, before the Coliseum, Romans were hard-working, small landholders. Families eked out a modest living from their land. "Hard work and calloused hands were not shameful things, as they were in the sophisticated eastern cultures, but badges of honor for Romans" (Madden 2008, 42).

D. G. Surdam, *Business Ethics from Antiquity to the 19th Century*,
https://doi.org/10.1007/978-3-030-37165-4_6

Rome became a military state. The quests for slaves, land, and booty were omnipresent. Roman legions stole or confiscated "a steady stream of movable wealth…Looted treasure, art works, and slaves by the thousands, many of them captured in Roman campaigns." Once conquered, forever taxed proved the fate of many territories. A scholar observed, "Imperial tribute was demanded based on the principle of obtaining as much as possible with the least effort." Roman governors often simply usurped the conquered territory's current taxation system. The flow of taxes was not met with a flow of services: "The profits from empire were not going to be squandered on providing demanding, and potentially expensive, services to imperial subjects" (Bang 2012, 199–201).[1]

Rome's early military conquests appear to have gained more than the costs of the conquests. Rome acquired such valuable assets as mines in Spain. Even better, from Rome's perspective, was the capture of developed agricultural land; Roman citizens displaced the conquered people and became landowners. In addition, the indigenous farmers provided cheap slave labor. The military buildup also helped Italy, at least, through the improved infrastructure (primarily through military roads) that lowered transportation costs. With increased international trade, Rome's market increased in extent that, in turn, generated economies of scale, division of labor, and urbanization (Kay 2014, 279–280 and 324). The drawback, though, of an economy resting in large part upon military conquest was the Romans' recurring need for new conquests. The Mediterranean basin was a fruitful region to assimilate within the Roman empire, but much of northern Europe was, relative to Rome, not as well developed. There were natural resources, but additional military conquests might not have yielded as beneficial outcomes as the earliest conquests.

Even as the Romans continued to practice "steal" in acquiring desirable land, commodities, and slaves, they sometimes tolerated piracy. As with China in the 1700s and 1800s, Roman officials were ambivalent regarding pirates. The pirates supplied Rome with slaves, but by the time of Pompey, piracy threatened the supply of corn. Given the importance of the latter trade, Pompey quickly, and one imagines ruthlessly, squelched piracy (Finley 1973, 156).[2]

For Roman men, war was a path to accumulating wealth. Rome, as with Greece, was still taking a multi-faceted approach to "exchange." Serving in the Roman army was a "bridging occupation" that could gain a soldier sufficient land and capital to retire comfortably. Many Romans did not view involuntary exchange as unethical or immoral. The lures of war booty plus gaining ownership of conquered lands remained attractive. A swarm of people followed Roman legions. Some of these were the usual camp followers—wives, girlfriends, professional women, sutlers—but many were traders willing to purchase plunder from the soldiers, who were more than happy to divest their booty for ready cash. Some soldiers eventually became traders and sometimes usurers themselves (*negotiatores*). French historian Claude Nicolet observed, "the two professions [servicemen and *negotiatores*] are by no means incompatible and basically involve the same behavior and attitudes." For Rome, "Pillage and commerce were two complementary and interconnected methods of exchange and the transfer of wealth, and it was a long time before the ancient world established a clear distinction between them" (Von Reden 2012, 269; Nicolet 1980, 121–122).

There were indirect benefits from military conquest. "[T]he creation of more peaceful and safer conditions translated to a marked decrease in transaction costs. The suppression of piracy in the final decades of the Republic, the diffusion of a 'technology of measurement' and of common metrological systems, and above all the creation of a unitary monetary zone and of common legal rules, especially in the field of commercial law, were all quite remarkable contributing factors" (Lo Cascio 2007, 626).

Other scholars argue that the Romans were too interested in flaunting their wealth, rather than investing in productive endeavors. Too many resources were devoted to a "display of luxury, and unproductive waste: feast days, games, and building of monuments." Rome's economy was capable of producing surpluses, but the system was still susceptible to shortages of grain. Rome, itself, became an economic black hole, sucking in grain and produce in order to placate the often indolent masses. "The proud ideal of the Conquering City, mistress of the world, and the uneasiness of the government in face of this idle, greedy mob incited by continual intrigue, combined to turn her citizens into recipients of relief...fed at low prices and stupefied with public entertainments....About 200,000 heads of families were supplied with a kind of ration card and received free wheat" (Levy 1967, 77).

Attitudes Toward Trade

Many historians believe that elite Romans held "heavy prejudices against trade and traders." Oxford Fellow Philip Kay rebuts this position by demonstrating that Cato "said nothing whatever in his *De Agricultura* about the disreputability of *mercatura*, talking only of its profitability and its risks. 'The merchant, however, I consider to be an energetic man and one bent on making money; but, as I said before, it is a dangerous career and one liable to disaster (Kay 2014, 92; Cato 1967, 9).'" Cicero wrote, "Trade, if it is on a small scale, is to be considered vulgar; but if wholesale and on a large scale, importing large quantities from all parts of the world and distributing to many without misrepresentation, it is not to be greatly disparaged. Nay, it even seems to deserve the highest respect." Did Cicero's opinion reflect Roman society as a whole? Being a large landowner himself, Cicero was unlikely to denigrate his peers (Cicero 1928, 1:151; Morley 2012, 312; Finley 1973, 43–44).[3]

Historian Jean-Philippe Levy paints an unflattering portrait of Romans involved in commerce: "they were greedy and brutal rather than clever, and thus aroused hatred against themselves….It was above all the kings who were the businessmen." The *lex Claudia* of 218 BCE precluded nobles from taking part in maritime commerce or being publicans (tax collectors), but, similar to modern-day contractors using minorities as "front men or women" in order to snare minority-designated construction contracts, Roman nobles enlisted their slaves or other intermediaries in commerce endeavors. Whatever the ethics of circumventing the *lex Claudia*, these plutocrats amassed large fortunes by "subordinating everything to money in whatever were its most corrupt aspects. Market-cornering and speculation were continual" (Levy 1967, 60–61).[4]

Roman senators also largely refrained from participating in public contracts, "from what had possibly become the most profitable form of imperial exploitation"; some senators eventually succumbed to the profits from such activities, largely through societas. The prohibition on senate participation undoubtedly stemmed from the obvious potential for what modern-day people dub conflict-of-interest. The prohibition may have also emanated from the perception that it was "unaristocratic" to make money in such fashion; it was much better to have senators engaged in the more prestigious realm of wartime riches. The *Lex Claudia* prohibition may have also been created to placate wealthy non-senators, who wanted to reduce the competition. Roman governors and legates were also prohibited from engaging in the slave trade, aside from buying replacement slaves for those who had died while serving their master in the provinces (Harris 1979, 90–91).

As mentioned, although elite Romans disdained direct involvement in trade, they were more than happy to skim the profits. The Roman legal system created advantages for employing slaves and agents to conduct business instead of dirtying one's own hands. Early in Roman history, owners entrusted their slaves with a small amount of money, the *peculium*; over time, owners provided their slaves with larger amounts of money. The master was "liable on the slave's contracts, but, apart from express authorization only to the extent of the *peculium*, by the action de *peculio*. Thus the risk was limited to the amount of the *peculium*. Any profit belonged in law to the master, and he could always recall the *peculium* at any moment [and avoid exposure to further liabilities], subject to the rights of existing creditors, so that he could always get back what was left of his money, an advantage not always open to the shareholder or common stockholder" (Buckland and McNair 1936, 25–26, 229; see also Johnston 1999, 108).

Wealthy People's Disdain of Labor

Cicero made distinctions between types of occupations. Free men should disdain work that "arouse people's dislike," such as collectors of harbor duties or usurers. He also excoriated "those who buy whole lots from wholesalers to retail immediately. They would not make a profit unless they indulged in misrepresentation, and nothing is more criminal than fraud." This would seem an early criticism either of speculators, middlemen, or retailers. "All mechanics work in contemptible professions because no one born of free parents would have anything to do with a workshop." But the least worthy of approval are those who pander to pleasure: "'Fishmongers, butchers, cooks, sausage-makers, fisherman,' as Terence says. Add to this list, if you like, perfume makers, stage dancers, and the whole musical stage" (Cicero 1974, 68–69; Giardina 2007, 764–765).

Cicero expressed disapproval of artisan labor, beginning with its manual effort, work in unsalubrious conditions, and free citizens working alongside slaves. Worst of all, artisans sold their products themselves, which exposed them to the same criticisms as Cicero directed to small retailers. In addition, the effort devoted to production kept the artisan-owner from engaging in truly honorable pursuits, such as being with friends and engaging in public life.

According to historian Andrea Giardina, Christianity transformed the perception of artisans' work by overturning the traditional Roman (upper-class) view of accumulation of profits and large-scale traders and merchants. Other early Christian figures, though, such as Gregorius of Nissa, still held retailers and usurers in low regard, especially since many people did not understand "the mechanism of price formation between producer and consumer." Although some church leaders did not approve of large-scale traders and merchants, others who accepted Roman and pagan morality regarded such vendors more favorably: "the customary reasons for commendation (or moderate disapproval)—their courage, their civic function—found support from the Christian point of view in its appreciation of the substantial charitable donations that large-scale merchants were able to make." A cynic might view this as the church leaders' willingness to accept, in a sense, "blood money" (Giardina 2007, 765–766).

There was a paradox in Greek and Roman elites' thinking regarding respectable occupations. The elites often relied upon foreigners for grain; for Roman *equites* in the collection of taxes; and artisans and merchants for the luxuries and necessities of life. The elites "lacked the will; that is to say, they were inhibited, as a group by over-riding values. It is then decisive to notice that, in the familiar denunciation of freedmen and metics, from Plato to Juvenal, the invariable theme is moral, not economic" (Finley 1973, 60).

One classicist cautions, "we should be wary of judging Roman distribution in terms of the absence of merchant princes and trading companies; for the high empire, the existing structures were clearly adequate for the purpose of keeping the army and cities regularly supplied. It is notable that the state was generally content to ensure Rome's supply through incentives to merchants and ship owners, rather than through the punitive regulation of traders, retailers, and millers that characterized many medieval and early modern cities with similar concerns about placating the hungry masses." Only after the state's incentives to shipowners and traders failed to adequately supply Rome and the army, did the Roman state begin to rely upon compulsion. The Annona became a hereditary obligation by the fourth century CE. The state revealed its "lack of faith in the reliability of market-driven supplies to the city as much as the emperors' need for popular support." Goods such as olive oil, wine, and pork began to be forcibly distributed. "Diocletian's Price Edict of the late third century and the increasing reliance on requisitions in kind from the fourth century onwards, reveal a similar lack of faith that merchants [could] be trusted to further the state's interests" (Morley 2007, 586–590).

Trading as a Path to Wealth

One path to wealth was international trade. By bringing grain to Rome, traders benefited their fellow Romans. Roman grain traders and merchants could not sail with every one of their cargoes. As with most international traders, these owners faced the challenge of finding competent and honest agents to act on the owners' behalf without close scrutiny. Buying and selling grain required a practiced eye; merchants faced temptations to offer low-quality grain, perhaps camouflaged with a veneer of good-quality grain. Given the economic concept of adverse selection, such as George Akerlof's "Markets for 'Lemons (whereby poor-quality grain might drive out good-quality grain),'" it is not surprising that overcoming the disadvantages inherent in not being physically present at points of sale was a major challenge. Hiring an agent to deal with the adverse selection did not resolve all of a merchant's potential difficulties. The owner (denoted as the principal) hiring an agent to work on the owner's behalf needed to monitor the agent or at least create an incentive structure to ensure the agent's compliance with the owner's wishes. Such biological factors as having a pool of trusted and competent sons and nephews might help a merchant. Trusted friends or co-religionists also helped (Akerlof 1970, 488–500; Temin 2013, 98–99).

Roman traders and government officials compiled information regarding grain cargoes by issuing receipts. In addition to specifying who owned the grain and who was to receive the grain, the officials also specified the year and quality of the grain. Economic historian Peter Temin observes that the receipt not only helped convey information but made the grain harder to steal. Merchants and traders also exchanged information, especially between friends and family. They also relied on the Roman legal system, government office of the Annona, or merchants' organizations. The Prefect of the Annona issued contracts for grain and gathered information. Because the Prefect dealt with merchants, he gleaned information from them. By extending public contracts, the Prefect could help merchants ascertain trends in prices and market shortages or surpluses. Temin likens the Prefect's announcements or dissemination of information as similar to the American Federal Reserve Board chairperson's remarks.

Agents had plenty of opportunities to act in ways that injured their principals' interests. On the long overseas journeys, there were stochastic events such as pirates, storms, shipwreck, and fluctuating prices. An agent could, for instance, find prices were significantly higher than anticipated upon arrival; after selling the grain at the high local price, the agent could report a good but lower price to the principal and skim the difference. The principal might or might not hear of the true level of prices only well after the relationship with the agent had concluded.

Because monitoring agents was difficult, especially with respect to international trade, merchants devised ways to forestall trouble. Receipts were a standard feature of most international transactions. Grain merchants started sending samples in sealed pots or pouches to deter agents from adulterating grain with barley or dirt. The recipient could then compare the samples against the grain in a ship's hold to see whether the grain had been switched. Merchants often used seals signed by the granary official, the merchant, and a witness. The sealed samples protected the merchant sending the grain and the merchant purchasing the grain. Merchants also drew a line on the inside of a ship's hold to indicate how much grain had been loaded. Merchants also labeled amphorae containing wine and sacks of grain with their marks, just as modern producers use labels on their containers.

Having an aristocrat involved in a project was often useful. A prominent person could lend prestige and credibility to a company. A millennia-and-a-half later, European and American corporations would employ similar tactics; by inviting prominent (and wealthy) people to sit on their boards, these corporations reaped benefits…as long as the prominent person did nothing to besmirch the company's reputation. In any event, the merchant groups could effectively mitigate some of the effects of an errant agent. They could replace a misbehaving agent or threaten criminal action. In addition, they could blacklist agents. The government helped by refusing to work with known unscrupulous agents and by punishing them (Temin 2013, 105–110).

The use of friends and social dependents alleviated the difficulties in enforcing formal and informal contracts. If the principal–agent problem was too hard to surmount, property owners might have been reluctant to engage in potentially beneficial ventures because of the difficulty in monitoring their agents. An imperfect solution would have been to let the agents undertake the venture and for the property owner to rake off some of the profits (Frier and Kehoe 2007, 134).

Less Savory Routes to Wealth

Late third-century BCE Romans were avid pursuers of wealth, according to classicist John D'Arms. The Elder Cato proclaimed to his fellow Romans that it was laudable that a Roman "upon his death bed, could show that he had added more to his patrimony than he had inherited." Polybius described Romans' pursuit of money: "at Rome the most disgraceful things of all are to accept bribes and to show greed for gain from disapproved activities; for no less strong than their admiration for money-making from the proper sources is their disapproval of greed for gain from forbidden sources." He also stated, "So unusual and extreme is [the Romans'] exactitude about money" (D'Arms 1981, 20–21; Harris 1979, 90).[5]

Roman civil administrators found that governorships paved the way to wealth. Cicero, author of *De Officiis*, proved an honest governor, who contented himself with the honest profits of the office. Many other Romans used cash and loans to create a network of alliances and guarantees in order to wrangle political offices. In a sense, the process resembled "can you top this," as politicians sought to outdo each other. The Roman political sphere was a high-risk endeavor, and an aspirant who overextended could find himself bankrupt at an unpropitious moment. Such worthies as Crassus, Caesar, and Cicero played the game (Finley 1973, 53).[6] Although true friendships probably existed, one cannot help but think that this networking was based upon opportunism and self-seeking.

Juvenal and Horace employed "vulgar maxims" lauding money-seeking. Juvenal satirized Vespasian's greed; Vespasian was such a greedy legislator that he put a tax on urine, and then taunted his disapproving son, waving the money under his son's nose and saying: "Does this stink somehow?" Juvenal wrote:

> If your bowels move at the sound of horn or of trumpet,
> Try to find something to sell for a profit, say fifty per centum;
> Don't turn up your nose at a business that has to be banished
> To the far side of the Tiber, and don't make any distinction
> Between the odor of hides and attar of roses; a profit
> Always smells good, no matter what possible source it may come from.
> Here is a slogan for you, a maxim worthy of poets,
> Even if Jove himself turned bard: No one asks where you get it,
> *But money is what you must have* (Erasmus 2005, viii, 13; Juvenalis 1958, 173–178, 201–207).

Horace wrote, "O citizens, citizens, money, you first must seek; virtue after pelf." Such crass expressions were rarely uttered publicly by sensible Roman senators. Instead, Tacitus and others urged diligence and thrift as routes to honorable and respectable wealth accumulation. Tacitus displayed scorn towards seaborne trading. Philostratus quoted Apollonius of

Tyana in echoing Tacitus' scorn regarding "the ill-starred breed of traders and shippers, who secrete themselves in the hold of a ship and think of nothing but cargoes and petty bills of lading" (Horatius [1926] 1978, 255; D'Arms 1981, 152–153).

Verres was known for his corruption as governor of Sicily; he stole many works of arts and precious stones; in his defense, Verres claimed to have "purchased" these items. Cicero rebutted Verres' claim: "A sterling defense, by heaven! We have sent a trader to a province with the insignia of a governor." Verres' hiring of a vessel drew a withering retort that he intended to "go into shipping" (D'Arms 1981, 3–4).[7] Given Verres' scale of plundering, one wonders whether Cicero, by his own remark, should have admired Verres. After all, Verres stole big.

Crony business relationships were common. When the town of Salamis (Cyprus) borrowed money from Scaptius, they lived to rue the day. When the town fell into arrears, Scaptius got his friend, who was the governor of Cilicia and Cyprus, to allow him to lead cavalry and despoil the town, leading to starvation. Cicero, who was notably honest, replaced the governor and tried to relieve Salamis' debt load, but he discovered that Scaptius and Brutus (of Julius Caesar infamy) were business associates; Cicero backed down.

Another route to wealth was tax collection; the government enlisted tax farmers (publicans). For a set fee, the chosen tax collector enjoyed almost free reign to plunder the taxpayers under his aegis; this legalized theft was supported by the courts: "[W]hen a tax-payer complained, the judge assigned by the governor to resolve the dispute was always another publican." One must admit that this was a nifty arrangement for the publicans (Levy 1967, 63–64).

Tax farming was a lucrative but risky route to wealth. There was a conundrum within the Roman tax situation: low taxes coupled with widespread complaint. Although conquests acquired slaves and booty, maintaining the military required a more stable source of financing. The Roman state proved voracious, and Plutarch cited figures showing that between the second century BCE and 62 BCE, state income increased six-fold. The tax rate, though, remained well below 10%. The taxes were supposed to be levied upon the wealthy, but since many wealthy, politically powerful Romans were involved in tax farming, they could easily shift the tax burden upon the politically powerless. Modern-day Americans complaining about the IRS are fortunate not to endure the tender mercies of Roman tax collectors, who were accused of torturing wives and children of reluctant taxpayers.[8] Conquests helped keep tax rates low and provided benefits for not only the common soldiers but Roman citizens. Roman citizens received subsidized wheat from 122 BCE and free wheat after 58 BC (Hopkins 2002, 204–205). As long as the Romans continued to conquer new territories, such a system was viable. Of course, the costs of defending an ever-larger empire grew, too.

Price Controls

Roman law considered that "price was entirely a matter to be determined by free contract….subject only to the limitation that the seller was bound to reveal faults interfering with the proper enjoyment of the thing sold." Other Roman laws were "aimed only at protecting the *seller*. It was enacted that when a thing was sold for less than half its value, the seller could recover the property unless the buyer chose to make up the price to the full amount." This protection for the seller probably applied only to land and was intended to protect landowners from the injustice associated with forced sales (Ashley 1913, 131, 133).

Roman authorities occasionally intervened in the wheat market, according to Peter Temin, if the price of grain was too high; their ultimate goal—which was not too different from modern-day economic stabilization policies—was to moderate price increases. Another classicist, Elio Lo Cascio suggests that the "decurions were supposed to play [a role] in ensuring the local food supply, [and] contain the notion that a fair price is 'fair' precisely because it was set by the market, and that only speculative behavior can alter it." The purpose was to regulate the market in such a way "to avoid speculative behavior, and even an artificial lowering of the prices" (Temin 2013, 101; Lo Cascio 2007, 627).

Roman authorities were not alone in trying to stabilize grain prices. In China, around the sixth century BCE, rather than have the government dictate prices when prices were too high or too low, Fan Li, an advisor to King Goujian of Wu, suggested that the government should "participate in grain trade not for profit-making but for stabilizing undue fluctuations in prices" by releasing stored grains during a supply shortfall and buying grain when the price was too low. He dubbed this a policy of "stabilizing grain prices" (Hu 1988, 38–39).

By the end of the third century CE, Rome's finances and economy were teetering. Diocletian attempted to stymie rising prices by issuing widespread edicts *setting maximum prices*. As a reflection of the complexity of the Roman markets, the edict of 301 CE covered over 1000 items. In his edict, Diocletian bemoaned the rising prices. He cited the "wantonness in prices [which] had progressed to such a point that the unbridled greed for plundering might be moderated neither by abundant supplies nor by fruitful season." Naturally, he did not attribute rising prices to the debasement of the currency. He identified the speculators and hoarders as the culprits—a time-honored tactic. These avaricious men allegedly conspired to raise prices "to such a degree that human language cannot find words to set a proper evaluation upon their action." By doing so, they robbed the soldier of "his bounty and of his pay…so that our soldiers seem to yield the entire fruit of their military career…to these profiteers in everything, in order that the pillagers of the commonwealth may from day to day carry off all that they resolve to have?"

Diocletian did not fix prices, because, as he noted, "sometimes very many provinces exult in the good fortune of the low prices which they desire." Instead, his edict set maximum prices, so that "avarice, which could not be checked…might be confined by the bounds of our statute and the limits set in the law promulgated to control them." He believed that the maximum price would force international traders to moderate their prices, knowing that they could not sell for more than the Roman maximum. He also mandated that it was a crime to withhold goods or to ship goods from where prices were low to where prices were high (Kent 1920, 41–45).

The edict proved effective in *discouraging* trade and production, as people feared they would be forced to accept unremunerative prices. Of course, people surreptitiously broke the law or hoarded their goods when confronted by binding price controls. Such behavior is hardly specific to Romans. Between the spiraling increase in prices and onerous taxes, small landowners lost their land; land lay fallow, as people refused to maintain irrigation and drainage. The ill effects of the tax included, "a great increase in slavery, and the liberties even of the free towns were restricted or lost. And the results of such taxation made increasingly difficult the raising of the taxes. The product was a vicious circle, not only of difficulty in securing the taxes, but of increase in the cost of articles of trade" (Kent 1920, 37–38; see also Rostovtzeff [1926] 1957, 424–425).

The irony of Diocletian's edict can be seen in his setting maximum prices denominated in denarius (copper coins) instead of silver. Previous Roman emperors had continually debased the currency and triggered price increases. One can easily imagine that speculators and hoarders were convenient scapegoats. Diocletian inherited a fiscal mess; some of his edicts were attempts to maintain security and to create stability. He was forthright enough to announce that the new denarius was made of copper; the new currency stabilized prices but at a level he deemed too high. As subsequent emperors could not resist the gains from debasing the currency, the denarius eventually became a purely copper coin worth perhaps 1/40 of the original silver coin (Kirchberger 1942, 631–632).

Business Organizations

Greeks and Romans formed "private-order enforcement networks" to create a system of establishing and maintaining reputations based on good behavior. The associations set high membership fees, sometimes as much as a fifth of the annual gross earnings of Roman artisans. The high fees helped ensure that members were of good repute and who intended to remain so. In a sense, the high fees were an investment in signaling one's reputation. The private-order enforcement networks transmitted details regarding individual's reputations on a timely basis. Individuals who "refuse to accept the decisions of arbitrators quickly acquire negative reputations."

Individual entrepreneurs contracted with each other for intermediate goods and services in manufacturing. These entrepreneurs interacted with members of a well-defined network. These networks provided the benefit of lower transaction costs through the use of peer pressure. Members relied upon the reputation of other members in choosing reliable partners. Bad behavior could easily cost a member their reputation and get them ostracized. Membership, therefore, sent a signal of quality. The membership imposed two costs; members had to pay a fee and they also suffered an opportunity cost by refusing to engage non-members as economic partners (Hawkins 2012, 177, 190–191).

Roman merchants developed enforcement-based and reputation-based mechanisms in dealing with agents. The merchants used both methods; Peter Temin believes that these merchants developed sophisticated ways of monitoring and constraining agents that rivaled what their medieval peers would use a millennium later.

Guilds could enforce good behavior even on the part of members who might have normally cheated. In addition, cheaters rarely ascended to guild officer positions. Guild members exchanged information regarding agents. Cicero informed his fellow merchant, Titus, about an agent,

Avianius. "Avianius worked for Pompey, one of Cicero's friends and also a merchant principal: 'What I beg of you is this—that you would accommodate Avianius as to the place and time for landing his corn: for which he obtained by my influence a three years' license whilst Pompey was at the head of that business.'" What is notable is that, "This letter contains two instances of the reputation mechanism. First, Cicero clearly used his social ties to Pompey, another merchant principal and member of the senatorial circle, to secure Avianius a contract in the first place. Second, Cicero, with his personal reputation, persuades Titus to give Avianius a favorable reception. Cicero's letter brands Avianius as a trustworthy agent, just as a personal endorsement from a standing president might brand a candidate 'honest' or 'trustworthy'" (Temin 2013, 109–113; see also Hawkins 2012, 189). One can imagine later-day business owners exchanging similar favors.

Contract Law

The Romans used many of Grecian laws pertaining to trade, commerce, and credit. Similar to the Greeks, ancient Romans disliked loans at interest. Cato the Elder "rounded up the usurers" (Levy 1967, 58). In later life, though, he invested in maritime loans, presumably at interest. An economist points out that "lending was not practiced at a professional level; however, it was readily accepted as an activity to supplement agricultural income, and at times openly encouraged and considered almost preferable to mercantile activity" (Vivenza 2012, 30).

Unlike the Greeks, who required a written record of transactions, Romans did not mandate written records. Legal scholars William Buckland and Arnold McNair noted, "It is the contrast between *Romana fides* and *Graeca fides*: no Greek trusted another unless he had the matter set down in writing." Over time, Romans began putting transactions into writing, so the *Romana fides* [a complex value that carried connotations of trust, obligation, loyalty, and reliability] disappeared (Buckland and McNair 1936, 211).

The ordinary contract of sale (*emptio venditio*) implied some legal protections for the buyer. The basic contract of sale implied a warranty that the seller had title to the goods. Earlier a buyer had to insist on a specific *stipulatio* (promise or series of promises) for such protection. Despite what people assume they know about caveat emptor, there was a warranty as to the quality of the goods. A buyer previously had to have an expressed *stipulatio* regarding the absence of particular defects. "Only if the seller had fraudulently concealed the presence of defects in the goods would the buyer have a remedy, as this was of course a breach of good faith." Over time, the aediles-magistrates who oversaw the markets developed "a liability for defects which was independent of the seller's knowledge or lack of good faith." This edict, however, only applied to the sale of slaves and cattle. A legal historian, David Johnston, ties the gradual evolution of warranties from the buyer having to list defects that the seller promised were not present to an implied warranty (Johnston 1999, 80–81). The Curule Aedile (magistrates) monitored the slave and livestock markets at Rome and dealt with asymmetrical information between buyers and sellers. They allowed a buyer rescission of the sale, but only within six months (tantamount to a six months' warranty) or the restitution of the difference in price had the buyer been aware of the defect. The purpose of these edicts was to restore confidence in the markets. Such edicts were not perfect, as the aggrieved buyer faced the obstacles in finding the seller and demonstrating that the defect existed when the sale was consummated (Frier and Kehoe 2007, 120).

The fear of being caught doing something deceitful or injurious kept many merchants and agents from engaging in malfeasance. The Roman legal system enforced judgments against agents, who proved untrustworthy; having such backing, merchants could take more confidence in enlisting agents, even agents they did not know intimately (Temin 2013, 104).

Banking and Moneylending

Romans frequently loaned and borrowed money. There were professional bankers (*argentariae*), who owned and ran institutions similar to deposit-taking banks. Banking was their full-time endeavor. There were also individuals, often aristocrats, who loaned their surplus funds to fellow members of the social elite. These loans were ways to help friends or to ingratiate themselves with politicians. The risk of extending loans, of course, was that of default; lenders had to discern how likely a potential borrower was to repay a loan. Aristocratic financiers might have had an advantage making loans to friends and families, given their familiarity with such people. On the other hand, *argentariae* might have been better situated to perform the role of financial intermediary, who connected people with surplus funds with potential borrowers and was an expert at assessing risks of less familiar borrowers. An intermediary connected people with surplus funds with potential borrowers (Kay 2014, 235–236). Without financial intermediation, many potentially socially useful loans would not have been made, thereby, in effect, throwing grit into the economic machinery.

Roman legislators of the fifth century CE enacted laws against usury. Under Justinian, interest rates were reduced to 6, 8, or 12%, depending on whether the loan was for civil affairs, trade, or maritime purposes respectively. These rates of interest were historically very low. The Romans also outlawed compound interest (*anatocism*) (Levy 1967, 95).

With regard to security for loans, Romans typically used personal security or real security. Modern-day borrowers usually have to provide real security, some sort of collateral as a guarantee of repayment. Romans, however, tended to use personal security, in which a friend or family member pledged to back the loan. If the borrower had a wealthy Roman willing to serve as personal security, such was the bond of a wealthy Roman's word that the security was deemed as good as real security. "Roman friends made mutual claims on each other which would in many cases cause a modern 'friend' to break off the friendship without delay." Often the payment of interest was an informal agreement, perhaps to avoid explicitly violating the edicts on usury (Johnston 1999, 86–87).

Playwrights lampooned bankers. Plautus' play, *Curculio*, portrays the banker character Lyco as "cunning and crooked." The title character, Curculio, proclaims, "by heaven, I put you people [pimps and bankers] in the same category; you match them perfectly. They, at least, do business in private, you in the open forum. You mangle men with interest; they do it with solicitation and dens of vice. The people have passed bills without number against you, and once they pass them, you smash them; you always find some loophole." Although Lyco is a Greek banker, Plautus is aiming at the Roman *agentarius* (bankers). That Roman audiences understood the gibes suggested that bankers were well-known to them and so were the caricatures. That the bankers openly conducted business at the forum and had the ability to evade or ignore regulations were also commonplaces. The play also refers to the bankers making profits with paper transactions. Roman and Greek bankers were also reputed to be dilatory in paying deposit requests while enthusiastic in demanding money from borrowers; such proclivities were depicted in another play: *Casina*. Bankers were also well-known for lending out deposits at interest (Kay 2014, 118, 120–123; see also Von Reden 2012, 281).

Besides wealthy people needing occasional (or perhaps regular) infusions of borrowed funds, where did poorer Romans go to cover cash shortfalls? What was the equivalent of modern pay-day loan places? Cicero's *faeneratores* may have been small professional bankers, who granted credit to small-scale merchants and farmers. Such borrowers may have offered collateral for their loans. Then again, *faeneratores* was used as a generic term for anyone providing credit.

Roman legislatures occasionally dealt with the credit market. The Twelve Tables attempted to cap the legal rate of interest and to forbid compound interest, whereas previously the rate "had been determined by the whim of the rich." Both lenders and borrowers conspired to circumvent the law by "ingenious schemes." Historian Philip Kay suggests that the negative attitude toward credit emanated from the Roman veneration of the Cincinnatus ideal: small, self-sufficient farmers, who did not need money. Of course, as the Americans would discover in the 1800s, the (Jeffersonian) ideal ran contrary to an evolving and growing economy. But the Roman ideal faded slowly. Cato the Elder compared lending to murder. Kay criticizes the legislators for not understanding the role banks or credit played in economic growth. These legislators also proved myopic on the supply of bullion and coins in circulation; they had little or no comprehension that bank lending led to a greater amount of money in circulation. Similar to a present-day modern central bank constricting the money supply, Roman legislation squelching bankers' ability to lend placed a brake on economic growth (Kay 2014, 258–260).

The Roman Republic was as keen to control interest rates as the Catholic Church was a millennium later. The republic passed 27 bills to either prohibit loans or limit interest rates. The republic also sought to ameliorate treatment of debtors, and the Twelve Tables (451–449 BCE) indicated that usury and loans threatened the social fabric. Livy indicated that citizens seeking to evade the prohibitions transferred loans to *socii*, who were exempt from the legislation. Another attempt to halt lending at interest included an edict that *socii* should divulge publicly to whom they had lent money; the debtors could then choose which Roman state's jurisdiction they wanted to be under. Marcus Sempronius, tribune of the people, stated on behalf of the Senate that such allies (*socii*) should be under the same laws as Roman citizens. As regulators would discover again and again in the millennia to come, financiers proved adept at using stratagems to circumvent laws (Kay 2014, 114).

Labor, Slavery, and Slave Agents

Slavery was prevalent in the Roman economy. Slaves were endowed with contractual power, when acting on behalf of their owners. Historian Gloria Vivenza characterizes the slaves' position as "less than completely subordinate," but the slaves were not *sui iuris* (legally competent). She adds, "the Romans considered the running of the economy a service, a task to be delegated to designated categories of actors rather than to be performed directly. Thus slaves were afforded the legal power to perform duties from which their owners were to be relieved in order to devote themselves to other matters" (Vivenza 2012, 31).

Legal historian David Johnston highlights Roman law's "great contradiction:" "on the one hand slaves were property, just like a book or a dog; on the other, they were also human, and to make full use of them required that their human characteristics—their intellect and the opportunities it offered—be recognized." As with slave owners throughout history, there was disdain and suspicion of slave dealers. Such dealers had to "warrant that the slave was free of defects; eventually this warranty was implied in the contract of sale. Much the same regime applied to cattle. Nothing could make it clearer that the slave was property than the elaborate discussions of the jurists about whether an ailment, disease or impairment amounted to a defect in the goods and so a breach of contract." Slave owners could treat the slave in any manner he or she desired, but given that slaves were costly assets, so to speak, "one should not get carried away with the idea that they were constantly maltreated or inhumanely overworked. There were, however, gradual humanitarian developments: the prohibition of excessive harshness; the requirement introduced by Hadrian that an owner should obtain the approval of a state magistrate before killing his slave who had committed crimes" (Johnston 1999, 42–43).

Roman slavery differed from American slavery with respect to education. American slave owners feared educated slaves, although a few owners surreptitiously educated chosen or favored slaves. Wealthy Romans often sent promising young slaves to various schools. They expected these slaves to gain facility with letters and numbers; for slaves destined for domestic service, education might instill "the finer arts of elegant domestic service." Owners anticipated that their more intelligent and diligent slaves would serve as their agents, managing the farms and other tasks requiring intelligence and education. For employers, slave labor in many respects was more attractive than free labor employed in similar roles, because owners held a greater power of discipline over slaves (such as physical punishment). Of slave, freedmen, and freeborn laborers, slaves were most overrepresented in administrative positions. There was an irony involved in that although freeborn were not formally precluded from training and education, they rarely received such; in fact, female slaves appear to have had better opportunities in this respect. John D'Arms notes the usefulness of a manumitted slave; the freedman could perform tasks for his former master that the latter would hesitate to be seen in public performing (Saller 2012, 78–79; see also Harris 2007, 527; D'Arms 1981, 44–45).

Slave prices, even with conquests and the enslavement of thousands, typically ran between four and eight times mean annual, per-capita GDP. The high prices may have discouraged owners from manumitting their slaves. Manumission did, however, occur. Some Roman slaves did very well for themselves after manumission. They had built-in ties with their former owner and could prosper enough to own their own slaves. On occasion, their descendants joined the political ruling class (Scheidel 2012, 99–100).

A key challenge facing the principal in dealing with any principal–agent relationship is creating the correct incentives, whether positive or negative, to motivate the slaves. By giving a slave money to use, the owner wanted to reduce the likelihood of the slave squandering the money. The *peculium* allowed a slave to manage a business independently and to share in the rewards (or the loss). The slave manager, therefore, had an incentive to use the money wisely, so the owner did not have to exert as much time and energy monitoring the slaves or other employees. The slave manager became what economists denote a residual claimant (the party keeping the profits or absorbing the losses) (Frier and Kehoe 2007, 132).

Charity

Connected to the Greco-Roman disdain of the poor, when the wealthy gave generously, their beneficence was directed to the community and not to the poor. Moses Finley notes, "The very poor aroused little sympathy and no pity throughout antiquity" (Finley 1973, 39). Romans were keen to climb up the social ladder; on the other hand, they were perhaps more anxious not to slip down the ladder. As late as the fourth century CE, patronage was paramount. The Roman notion and practice of charity was more explicitly calculated with respect to social status. Whereas Christians considered giving to the poor in terms of laying up treasure in Heaven, a Roman, similar to the Greek, sought honor and esteem in the here and now. For Romans, public giving was a form of competition. Biblical scholar Peter Brown describes how Romans were not particularly interested in the material poor, such as slaves, non-citizens, tenants, and servants. “If the rich had victims, these victims were not thought to be the poor: they were their fellow rich. The rich feared that they might at any time be made to feel ‘poor’—in the sense of helpless—in the face of overmighty members of their own class.” Philanthropy to social equals took on the character of making personal loans to a friend or family member and was a form of insurance. Even in situations where Romans made charitable donations, the sense of social status was present. “Alms implied outreach to perceived inferiors. Indeed, the very act of giving alms stressed the helplessness of those who received them” (Brown 2012, 58–60; Woolf 1990, 210).

Brown argues that Roman Christians of the early centuries did not separate commerce and religion into separate spheres, “Purely earthly gifts moved…on a quick circuit. Money exchanged hands. Clients and patrons exchanged favors and support.…All of these exchanges happened in this world only.…They hoped that their glory might last on earth, but there was no thought that their gifts might ever follow them to heaven.” Brown describes the uniqueness of the Christian portrayal of gifts to the other world. Such gifts were so “divorced from human time as to leave the imagination haunted by thoughts of incommensurability. What was the relation between the earthly gift and what it might bring in a world beyond the stars?…Earth and heaven were brought together by the Christian gift. And this was done though the daring extension of the earthly language of exchange, commerce, and treasure to the unimaginable world of heaven.” He concludes, “seldom in any literature have money and images borrowed from commerce bulked so large as in the literature of late Roman Christianity.” There were ramifications of this gifts to the other world concept. Such largesse was no longer confined to the wealthy, so the concept “empowered the average donor.” Any treasure placed in heaven would be rewarded, “Utterly out of proportion to the gift itself” (Brown 2012, 85–86).

Conclusion

The Romans codified much of what could be considered acceptable and unacceptable business behavior. The rulers and populace, of course, had not completely discontinued practicing “steal” in seizing land, people, and goods through military conquest. The Romans succeeded, however, in creating a vast trading network that would not be rivaled in Europe for a millennia.

Romans formalized contract and other forms of business law. Although the Roman elite disdained labor and trade, they discreetly participated in potentially profitable endeavors. Their disdain, however, led to an amelioration in the conditions of slavery and created opportunities for talent and ambitious slaves to accumulate wealth through *peculium*. Roman elites often demonstrated rapacity in government-sanctioned endeavors such as tax farming.

Romans relied upon punishment and a sense of honor (or at least concern regarding one's reputation) in eliciting ethical behavior. The quest for status imbued their charitable donations, although Christian influences began transforming charitable motives in Rome.

Notes

1. Jean-Paul Morel characterized Roman rulers, businessmen, and "wheeler-dealers" as engaging in "robber capitalism" (Morel 2007, 504). Roman confiscation of valuables was a tradition preceding them and following them. Even twenty-first-century warfare has its share of looting, as Germany, the Soviet Union, and even the United States stole art work, transferred skilled workers, including top scientists, and removed economic assets (Zuckerman 2004, provides a thorough discussion; see 142–182 for deportation and 218 and 261–262 for stolen equipment).
2. At about the same time, Japanese authorities were fighting piracy, although sometimes inapt government policies pushed small traders into piracy (Beasley 1999, 135–136, 138).
3. John D'Arms argued that Cicero's passage in *Verrines* was not intended as being derogatory toward traders and manufacturers. "In fact, Cicero was here implying that *mercatura* is *honesta*—an implication which is confirmed by passages in the philosophical works, where he either juxtaposed commerce and agriculture as equally desirable means of acquiring wealth" (Cicero 1966, 653; D'Arms 1981, 22).
4. See Kay and D'Arms for interpretations of the *plebiscitum Claudianum* of 218 (D'Arms 1981, 5–6; Kay 2014, 134).
5. Roman Polybius had the temerity to criticize Carthaginian scruples. He claimed that Roman customs and rules regarding money-making endeavors were better than those of Carthage. The Carthaginians allegedly had no lower limit with respect to profit-seeking (Harris 1979, 88).

6. Aristotle defended similar behavior among the Greeks (Aristotle [1893] 2004, 99–100).
7. Proclus proved a contrast to Verres (D'Arms 1981, 4–5).
8. See Plutarch 1958, 180–181 for state income.

Bibliography

Akerlof, George. "The Market for 'Lemons:' Quality Uncertainty and the Market Mechanism." *Quarterly Journal of Economics* 84(3), August 1970, 488–500.

Aristotle. *Nicomachean Ethics*, translated by F.H. Peters (New York, NY: Barnes & Noble, [1893] 2004).

Ashley, William J. *An Introduction to English Economic History and Theory. Part 1: The Middle Ages* (New York, NY: Longmans, Green, 1913). 9th Edition.

Bang, Peter. "Predation." The Cambridge Companion to the Roman Economy, edited by Walter Scheidel (Cambridge, UK: Cambridge University Press, 2012), 197–217.

Beasley, W.G. *The Japanese Experience: A Short History of Japan* (Berkeley: University of California Press, 1999).

Brown, Peter. *Through the Eye of a Needle: Wealth, the Fall of Rome, and the Making of Christianity in the West, 350–550 AD* (Princeton, NJ: Princeton University Press, 2012).

Buckland, William W. and Arnold D. McNair. *Roman Law & Common Law: A Comparison in Outline* (Cambridge, England: Cambridge University Press, 1936).

Cato, Marcus. *Porcius Cato on Agriculture; Marcus Terrentius Varro on Agriculture* (Cambridge, MA: Harvard University Press, 1967).

Cicero, Marcus. *De Officiis*, translated by Walter Miller (London, UK: William Heinemann, 1928).

Cicero, Marcus Tullius. *De Officiis*, translated by Harry Edinger (Indianapolis, IN: Bobbs-Merrill, 1974).

Cicero, Marcus Tullius. *The Verrine Orations: In Two Volumes* (Cambridge, MA: Harvard University Press, 1966).

D'Arms, John. *Commerce and Social Standing in Ancient Rome* (Cambridge, MA: Harvard University Press, 1981).

Erasmus, Desiderius. *Collected Works of Erasmus: Adages*, edited by John Grant, translated and annotated by Denis Drysdall (Toronto, Canada: University of Toronto Press, 2005). 86 vols.

Finley, Moses. *The Ancient Economy* (Berkeley, CA: University of California Press, 1973).

Frier, Bruce and Dennis Kehoe. "Law and Economic Institutions." *The Cambridge Economic History of the Greco-Roman World* (Cambridge, UK: Cambridge

University Press, 2007). Walter, Ian Morris, and Richard Saller, editors, 113–143.

Giardina, Andrea. "The Transition to Late Antiquity." The *Economic History of the Greco-Roman World*, edited by Walter Scheidel, Ian Morris, and Richard Saller (Cambridge, UK: Cambridge University Press, 2007), 743–768.

Harris, William. *War and Imperialism in Republican Rome, 327–70 B.C.* (Oxford, UK: Clarendon Press, 1979).

Harris, William. "The Late Republic." *The Cambridge Economic History of the Greco-Roman World*, edited by Walter Scheidel, Ian Morris, and Richard Saller (Cambridge, UK: Cambridge University Press, 2007), 511–539.

Hawkins, Cameron. "Manufacturing." *The Cambridge Companion to the Roman Economy*, edited by Walter Scheidel. (Cambridge, UK: Cambridge University Press, 2012), 89–113.

Hopkins, Keith. "Rome, Taxes, Rents and Trade." Reprinted in *The Ancient Economy*, edited by Walter Scheidel and Sitta von Reden (New York, NY: Routledge, 2002), 190–230.

Horatius Flaccus, Ouintus. *Horace: Satires, Epistles and Ars Poetica*, translated by H. Rushton Fairclough (Cambridge, MA: Harvard University Press, [1926] 1978).

Hu, Jichuang. *A Concise History of Chinese Economic Thought* (Beijing, China: Foreign Languages Press, 1988).

Johnston, David. *Roman Law in Context* (Cambridge, UK: Cambridge University Press, 1999).

Juvenalis, Decimus. *The Satires of Juvenal*, translated by Rolfe Humphries (Bloomington, IN: Indiana University, 1958).

Kay, Philip. *Rome's Economic Revolution* (Oxford, UK: Oxford University Press, 2014).

Kent, Roland. "The Edict of Diocletian Fixing Maximum Prices." *University of Pennsylvania Law Review* 69(1), 1920, 35–47.

Kirchberger, Hans. "An Ancient Experience with Price Control." *Journal of Farm Economics* 24(3), August 1942, 621–636.

Levy, Jean-Philippe. *The Economic Life of the Ancient World* (Chicago, IL: University of Chicago Press, 1967).

Lo Cascio, Elio. "The Early Roman Empire: The State and the Economy." *The Cambridge Economic History of the Greco-Roman World*, edited by Walter Scheidel, Ian Morris, and Richard Saller (Cambridge, UK: Cambridge University Press, 2007), 619–647.

Madden, Thomas. *Empires of Trust: How Rome Built—and America Is Building—a New World* (New York, NY: Dutton, 2008).

Morel, Jean-Paul. "Early Rome and Italy." *The Cambridge Economic History of the Greco-Roman World*, edited by Walter Scheidel, Ian Morris, and Richard Saller (Cambridge, UK: Cambridge University Press, 2007). 487–510.

Morley, Neville. "The Early Roman Empire: Distribution." *The Cambridge Economic History of the Greco-Roman World*, edited by Walter Scheidel, Ian Morris, and Richard Saller (Cambridge, UK: Cambridge University Press, 2007), 570–591.

Morley, Neville. "A Forum on Trade." *The Cambridge Companion to the Roman Economy*, edited by Walter Scheidel. (Cambridge, UK: Cambridge University Press, 2012), 309–317.

Nicolet, Claude. *The World of the Citizen in Republican Rome*, translated by P.S. Falla (Berkeley, CA: University of California Press, 1980).

Plutarch. *Fall of the Roman Republic: Six Lives by Plutarch* (Harmondsworth, UK: Penguin Books, 1958).

Rostovtzeff, Michael. *The Social and Economic History of the Roman Empire* (Oxford, UK: Clarendon Press, [1926] 1957). Second edition.

Saller, Richard. "Human Capital and Economic Growth." *The Cambridge Companion to the Roman Economy*, edited by Walter Scheidel (Cambridge, UK: Cambridge University Press, 2012), 71–86.

Scheidel, Walter. "Slavery." The Cambridge Companion to the Roman Economy, edited by Walter Scheidel (Cambridge, UK: Cambridge University Press, 2012), 89–113.

Temin, Peter. *The Roman Market Economy* (Princeton, NJ: Princeton University Press, 2013).

Vivenza, Gloria. "Roman Economic Thought." *The Cambridge Companion to the Roman Economy* (Cambridge, UK: Cambridge University Press, 2012). Walter Scheidel, editor. 25–44.

Von Reden, Sitta. "Money and Finance." *The Cambridge Companion to the Roman Economy*, edited by Walter Scheidel (Cambridge, UK: Cambridge University Press, 2012). 266–286.

Woolf, Greg. "Food, Poverty and Patronage: The Significance of the Epigraphy of the Roman Alimentary Schemes in Early Imperial Italy." *Papers of the British School at Rome* 58(1), 1990, 197–228.

Zuckerman, Larry. *The Rape of Belgium: The Untold Story of World War I* (New York, NY: New York University Press, 2004).

CHAPTER 7

Jewish and Christian Attitudes

Since Jews and Christians shared most of the books comprising the Christian Old Testament, many of their attitudes toward business were similar. The ethical beliefs of both groups rested, in part, to their belief in an all-seeing deity, although both religions imposed duties upon adherents.

Jewish attitudes were shaped by their shared cultural experiences of being a relatively weak group of outsiders. Christians, too, initially faced persecution, but within a few centuries found themselves embraced by Rome's leaders. The ascension to power affected Christian attitudes toward trade and commerce, as did the unfulfilled *Parousia* (Second Coming). The earliest Christians' anticipation of an imminent *Parousia* initially influenced their attitudes toward business endeavors.

Jewish religious thinkers held a more favorable attitude toward business endeavors. They associated doing good with doing well. Christians struggled with attaining wealth in the here and now versus storing treasures in the afterlife.

General Religious Beliefs Pertaining to Business Behavior

It is instructive to compare Judeo-Christian beliefs with other religions' beliefs regarding business ethics. Edward Zinbarg disagrees with some clergy, who hold that religion is against the ethic of caveat emptor, as he sees evidence in most religions that traders are not supposed to be naifs.

D. G. Surdam, *Business Ethics from Antiquity to the 19th Century*,
https://doi.org/10.1007/978-3-030-37165-4_7

Buyers and sellers are assumed to take the time and effort to learn about each other's knowledge and intentions. The *Qur'an*, too, provides practical advice: "Do not follow that of which you have no knowledge." Maimonides argues that sellers did not have to reveal "every possible negative characteristic of their goods" but could "accentuate the positive" aspects. Maimonides states that "oral deception is more heinous than monetary fraud," because one can restore monetary fraud but injuries to a person's reputation are difficult to restore. The exceptions are professions, where the buyer is entitled to presume the professional is advising them in their best interest. Of course, the seller (or the buyer) is not permitted to deliberately mislead the other party. Honesty is prized by all religions, and in Muhammad's view, "In the day of Judgment the honest, truthful Muslim merchant will take rank with the martyrs of the faith" (Zinbarg 2001, 80–81, 98).

Jewish and Christian ethicists interpret Leviticus 19:14, "you shall not place a stumbling block before the blind," as prohibiting sale of harmful products, even if the product is legal. Whether a product is harmful, though, depends upon the user and the amount consumed. For most people, alcohol provides satisfaction, but for some, alcohol can create havoc. A lawnmower is a relatively safe product for most users, but there are some who insist on using their hands to unclog a clot of grass. If Christians and Jews rely on Leviticus, Hindu have the Laws of Manu: "One thing mixed with another should not be sold, nor anything that is spoiled, deficient, far away, or concealed" (Zinbarg 2001, 88–89; Buhler [1886] 1967, 290).[1]

Jewish tradition emphasizes buyer's responsibilities in a transaction. Many retailers complain that customers come in, ask a lot of questions, and then go to another merchant from whom they had planned to buy in the first place. Questioning the first merchant is unfair, as it wastes that merchant's time: "his very humanity would be violated." Along the same lines, Confucian tradition developed the concept of *hsin*. *Hsin* requires that people speak truthfully, sincerely, and honorably; just as important, *Hsin* urges people to speak or act in ways that promote social harmony. A person who falsely claims to be a serious buyer is deceitful and violates social harmony, as such buyers unethically, "take up the time and psychic energy of the salesperson," when "they have no intention of buying." Zinbarg makes the interesting point regarding modern technology; buyers surfing the internet do not violate *hsin*, because they do not waste the seller's time. The seller, indeed, invites buyers to browse his or her website (Zinbarg 2001, 98–99).

Zinbarg remarks that all of the religions he studied forbid making or implying promises that cannot or will not be kept. The *Qur'an* is explicit that people who keep their promises will enter Paradise. *Hsin* goes beyond doing what one has promised, but insists that the promisor do so skillfully. "This aspect of *hsin* puts a substantial ethical burden on sellers, who too often promise what they are unable to do skillfully."

Judeo-Christian and Islamic writers inveighed against community leaders and officials taking bribes. Zinbarg thinks that the Old Testament passages imply that accepting bribes must have been a frequent occurrence in ancient Israel. Islam puts it memorably in the Hadith of the Prophet: "Any official who takes anything from the public funds without justification will meet his Lord carrying it on himself on the Day of Judgment." Zinbarg suggests that Islamic jurists used this passage to cover unethical behavior of not just public officials but also to other people in positions of trust. Westerners often characterized the eastern world as rampant with bribery, but Confucian and Buddhist ethics specifically prohibited such behavior, and public officials in the east are often forced to resign in disgrace when caught accepting bribes.

Westerners also criticized Confucian values for its alleged cronyism and the prevalence of gift giving to public officials. The purpose of the gifts, at least from an Asian perspective, is to honor "dedicated service to the commonweal" and as a means of demonstrating "communal individualism." Westerners perceived the gift giving as bribery (Zinbarg 2001, 101, 108–109, 127).

The major world religions appear to have been in basic agreement regarding charging interest on loans. Lenders are exhorted to treat borrowers with sensitivity. As we shall see, Islam maintains its strictures upon usury to this day. Jews and Christians eventually emphasized excessive rates of interest as usurious, and the *Laws of Manu* appears to have held similar views.

The monotheistic religions emphasized using honest weights and measures. Jewish teachings go a little bit further, adding that not only should the weights and measures be accurate; they had to be easy to see and understand. Modern-day food labels probably fail the Jewish edicts, since the labels are difficult to read and the list of chemicals and grams are unfathomable for many people (Zinbarg 2001, 84–85, 111–112).

A Key Jewish Question

The Talmud relates that the dead awaiting the final judgment faced three questions asking whether they dealt faithfully, studied the religious works regularly, and had children. Jewish scholars believe the question, "Did you deal faithfully?" refers to business dealings, such as a verse in Yeshaya (33, 6): "Did you display integrity when dealing with other people?" The question relates to conducting business matters honestly and with integrity, although Rabbi Chaim Palagi broadens the question to cover all activity (Parsha Pages n.d., no pages). This question may demonstrate how important Judaism considers ethics in the marketplace. The sages conclude from Leviticus 25:14 that urges people to deal honestly in property transactions, that "if one is honest in his business dealings and people esteem him, it is accounted to him as though he had fulfilled the whole Torah."

The application of this general question could be difficult. Maimonides carefully parsed the fine line between permissible puffery ("gilding the lily") and outright deception. He stated that that a merchant, "should not deck out…old vessels so that they appear new, but he may deck out the new ones by polishing, ironing, or beautifying them all they require." Business executive and author Edward Zinbarg admits the dictum is somewhat vague, but he considers it a good starting point (Zinbarg 2001, 37, 40).

Jewish Attitudes

The Hebrews were charged with doing good, regardless of any benefit. Doing good was its own benefit. Immanuel Kant's "moral dimension of ethics" puts a different perspective on the matter of calculated "goodness." Calculated acts of goodness lose their ethical content. Despite the belief that leading a moral life and prosperity were inter-related, they really weren't correlated. "Good (incoming) has already happened to us. We must do good (outgoing) *out of gratitude* [italics his] for the good (incoming) shown to us in the past." Socrates exemplifies the concept; he chose to drink the hemlock instead of running away. "He would rather have evil done to himself than do something he himself considers wrong." Again, Kant suggested that doing good to reciprocate for good is nothing virtuous, "because the increase in our utility (whether precalculated or unexpected) negates the morality of our acts."

The Hebrews believed that leading a moral life would benefit them materially. In most business situations, there was a potential benefit from cheating, to exploit other participants' trust and adherence to the rules. In the case of the Hebrews, since there was little discussion of heaven or hell, the rule-enforcing promise of an afterlife for the virtuous did not come into play. "If God desires to punish or to reward, He must do so during man's lifetime. The righteous therefore is prosperous here, and the wicked here suffer punishment." Such a belief, of course, differs from Christianity and many eastern religions (Sedlacek 2011, 67–68, 70–71). But, as in so many cases, there were verses contradicting the Hebrews' fixation on their earthly lives. In Exodus (20:5–6), there was explicit mention of future punishment, albeit indirect: "for I, the Lord your God, am a jealous God, visiting the iniquity of the fathers upon the children to the third and the fourth generation of those who hate me, but showing steadfast love to thousands of those who love me and keep my commandments."

There is a strong sense of community in the Jewish tradition. Economist Meir Tamari believes that the Jewish ethos of community creates, "an obligation to provide food, shelter and basic economic goods for the needy, it has a moral right and duty to tax its members for this purpose. In line with this duty, it may have to regulate markets, prices and competition, to protect the interest of its weakest members. Judaism does not distinguish between deserving and non-deserving poor. Its protection extends even to those suffering through their own faults" (Tamari 1997, 52).

Rabbi Daniel Lapin asserts that, "Jews were never ever handicapped by the theological notion that somehow wealth was a vice or evidence of wrongdoing. Rather to the contrary, it was the notion that wealth was a reward, not necessarily on an individual basis, but rather on a group basis, for a group of people who commit to one another and create a moral legal framework in which property and rights are preserved and in which trust and integrity are rewarded." In addition, he recognizes the importance of, "The respect of ownership of property emerges as a very basic principle, a very realistic assessment of human nature which says people care most for the things that they own." He continues by observing that Jewish people care about spiritual things, but that such care "is the single most important contribution to Jewish business success…this is the Old Testament concept that in business you are succeeding in direct proportion to the extent that you believe you are acting selflessly."

Lapin acknowledges that sheer self-interest often bothers people, but businesspeople who combine self-interest and service are people he trusts, "Because this is the kind of people that human beings are; we do better when we are focused on the good, than when we are focused on ourselves. And the Jewish approach to business is driven by this basic idea that business is a way of becoming obsessed with the needs of other people." Lapin answers the question of whether God wants people to be rich. "The answer in Jewish tradition is that the good Lord is very preoccupied and that is not at the forefront of his mind; however, what he does want is for human beings to become obsessively preoccupied with the needs and welfare of other human beings." The outcome of meeting people's wants and needs is often a reward of wealth (Lapin 2005, 187–190). In contrast to the Epicureans, who sought to maximize their utility without regard to rules, "Judaism comes therefore to train or educate the unbounded desire…for wealth, so that market activities and patterns of consumption operate within a God given morality" (Sedlacek 2011, 71; Tamari 1997, 45).

Jewish people inculcated moral habits. The emphasis on learning Jewish intellectual heritage helped in "educating the emotions, for the more time and energy spent considering aspects of the Law, the more likely it becomes that its moral content will influence working memory during everyday appraisal and coping events, and therefore the less likely it becomes that individuals will default to the self-centered inclinations of intuitive morality. Virtue becomes second nature in those who know the Law." The shared heritage also provided protection against "the ongoing competition of social life [that] wears away at overlaps of self-interest…the collective affirmation of a shared story may restore them at the level of ultimate truth and value. By the power of myth, I become whole and we become one" (Rue 2005, 164, 180).

Jewish Traders and Merchants

Jewish people settled in Muslim Spain, Italy, France, and Germany by 1000. These Jewish people engaged in trade, especially long-distance commerce, and handicrafts. They were involved in extending credit in their roles as shopkeepers and merchants. A century later, Jews were specializing in lending money. The usual explanations for Jewish specialization in money lending revolved around the papal prohibition on charging interest or the removal of Jews off the land. Economists Maristella Botticini and Zvi Eckstein, though, disputed these explanations. They argued that

Jewish emphasis upon reading (and understanding) the religious texts and the Jewish uniform code of law (the Talmud) created comparative advantages for them with respect to European Christians. Jewish communities and traders understood contracts (and enforcement of such), networking, and arbitrage. Before migrating to Western Europe, Jews had accumulated wealth from their livelihoods in the Muslim Middle East.

Between 750 and 900, better economic opportunities pulled Jewish farmers off the land and into the towns and cities, where their literacy and contract-enforcing institutions made them adept at crafts and trade. During this time, there were no restrictions on Jewish property-holdings. Jews in Mesopotamia and Persia could own and dispose of land, and some remained farmers. They engaged in a wide range of occupations, some 450 urban occupations noted in the Cairo Geniza documents. The ability to read and write in Hebrew was carried over in learning other languages. As Jews dispersed in order to conduct long-range trade, they created a network externality. "Literacy was a prerequisite for implementing community sanctions and accessing the Jewish court system." Botticini and Eckstein stress that economic opportunities motivated the diaspora, not persecutions or expulsions. Because Jewish fathers had to bear the expense of educating their sons, the literacy requirement spurred fathers to find more remunerative occupations. As the Jews' abilities and ethical conduct became known, local rulers in Europe began inviting Jewish families to relocate. These families then engaged in crafts, trade, tax collecting, banking, and money lending. They sometimes became royal treasurers.

The thesis that Muslims and Christians were proscribed from charging interest on loans and thereby opened up opportunities for Jewish lenders does not fit the timeline. During the eighth and ninth centuries, Jews were leaving farming and entering urban occupations, including money lending, in Mesopotamia and Persia. The theory may explain why urbanized Jews became money lenders, but it does not address why Jews left the land. In any event, Jews became employed in many occupations and not just money lending. The Catholic Church's ban on usury took its fullest form well after Jews were already well established as moneylenders: "The usury ban on Christians was enforced too late to explain the selection of European Jews into the most skilled and profitable occupation" (Botticini and Eckstein 2011, 58–60, 65–71).

Just Price and Fair Trade

The Talmudic concept of the just or fair price revolves around Leviticus 25:14: "And if you sell to your neighbor or buy from your neighbor, you shall not wrong one another." In some translations, "wrong" is replaced by "oppress." Some of the scholars of the Mishna thought the verb referred to "exploitation through price deceit." Economist Ephraim Kleiman asserted that the "relevant standard was none other than the going market price." If either party to a transaction was defrauded, the deceived party could legally revoke the deal within a set time limit. Both buyers and sellers were protected from deceitful bargaining. The rabbis attributed deceit to ignorance of what the price should be, and they understood that either a buyer or a seller might not possess such information, although some rabbis argued that a merchant was unlikely to be ignorant of such information.

The purpose of the Jewish rules was "to prevent inequality of information from having distributional effects," but the rules did not question the price system itself. The rabbis also recognized a good's value with respect to its opportunity costs: "the market price represented the value of the benefit forgone by selling an object or obtained by acquiring it." In this context, deviating from the just price cheated the buyer or the seller "of the benefit it could obtain in an alternative deal in the same market." This differed from the Greek and Roman notion of a "fair" exchange as simply one that satisfied the participants.

The rabbis did not apply the rules governing pricing to transactions involving slaves, bills, and real estate. These items faced a thin market, in the sense that they were transacted sporadically, so there was a lack of uniform market prices. The items also varied in quality and attributes (Kleiman 1987, 25–27, 30, 39–40).

The rabbis classified speculators who tried to corner the market with usurers and light-weighters. These characters were sure to suffer heavenly wrath. The ban on hoarding pertained only to subsistence goods and also did not apply to primary producers (even of subsistence goods). The rabbis were most concerned about professional speculators trying to monopolize basic staples, such as wine, oils, and flour. For other goods, although the rabbis might personally disapprove, it was permissible to engage in speculation. Perhaps because it would have been difficult to ascertain whether a producer was indulging in speculation or simply storing his own produce for his family's needs, the rabbis also permitted storing up one's own produce.[2]

In a stagnant economy, the just or administered price may reflect a sort of inertia, a reliance upon market prices established in the past. Such prices provided everyone a "stock of general information." The stagnant price might be thought of as similar to Daniel Kahneman, Jack Knetsch, and Richard Thaler's reference price. The Mishna, though, provides evidence that price changes were frequent. Because prices changed, the prohibition of usury (a nominal interest rate of zero) could mean an (implicit) real rate of interest different from zero. Such a possibility created difficulty in time-bridging transactions.

The Mishna identified typical fraudulent trading practices. These practices recurred throughout history and across cultures. The prevalence of such practices may have been indicative of a certain low cunning on the part of merchants; presumably reasonably alert customers caught on rather quickly, although some of the practices undoubtedly persist today. "Produce may not be mixed with other produce, even new with new, needless to say new with old. He whose wine became diluted with water should not sell it in his shop unless he informs [the customer]. Nor to a merchant, even if he informs him, because [the latter buys it] only to cheat with it. [A shopkeeper] should not pick the refuse from the top of the bin, because the only purpose [of doing so] is to deceive the eye. One should not dress-up men, cattle, or utensils" (Kleiman 1987, 29, 33–37).

Jewish and Christian Attitudes Toward Charity

Providing charity could be considered an act of self-interest. King Monobaz dispersed his family's wealth among the poor. His relatives were understandably perturbed at the dissolution of the family estate. He explained: "My fathers stored something which produces no fruits, but I have stored something which does produce fruits....My fathers accumulated treasures of money, but I have accumulated treasures of souls... My fathers piled up for life in this world, but I have piled up for life in the hereafter" (Finkel 1999, 555).

The book of Sirach, which is in the Catholic Bible but not the Protestant or Jewish canons, offers a somewhat different perspective. Sirach acknowledges the advantages of being wealthy, including the observation that people are more tolerant of wealthy people's mistakes (Sirach 10:30–31, 13:3, 21–23).[3] Sirach makes a point that is not always mentioned: rich people have a network of people able (and willing) to help them; poor people may lack such resources. In modern-day America, with its social distance between wealthy and impoverished, the latter suffer not only from lack of income and wealth but also often lack of prosperous friends with the financial ability to succor them: "A rich man beginning to fall is held up of his friends….When a rich man is fallen, he hath many helpers." Poor people work and work but receive meager earnings. Sirach strikes a discordant note to our modern sensibilities, with the claim that being a beggar is worse than being dead (Sirach 31:4; 40:28–30). Despite these seemingly hard-hearted statements, Sirach warns people that wealth can be a snare, creating arrogance and a neglect of one's relationship with God (Sirach 5:1–3 and 8). With regard to business, the lure of profits can tempt participants into acting unethically and sinfully. Trade and commerce are closely related with sin. Sirach doesn't comment that consumers would face similar temptations as vendors.

Sirach encourages generosity and tithing. "One is not to think of this as bribing God or putting God in one's debt on account of such offerings" (Barrera 2013, 117). Sirach (35:10–12) states: "Give unto the most High according as he hath enriched thee; and as thou hast gotten, give with a cheerful eye. For the Lord recompenseth, and will give thee seven times as much. Do not think to corrupt with gifts; for such he will not receive; and trust not to unrighteous sacrifices; for the Lord is judge, and with him is no respecter of persons." Sirach appears to tie generosity to future rewards.

Gospel Interpretations

Early Christian attitudes reflected Jewish attitudes to a degree, given that many of Jesus' early followers were Jews. The New Testament presents a somewhat different moral code. The Gospel of Matthew presents the paradox. The disciples are expected to have "a self-forgetful response" to Jesus' invitation. In Matthew 25:31–46 (King James version), at the separation of the goats from the sheep, the King will laud those who gave succor to the hungry, thirsty, and stranger, and these people will reply quizzically, "'Lord, when did we see thee hungry and feed thee, or thirsty and give thee drink? And when did we see thee a stranger and welcome thee, or naked and clothe thee? And when did we see thee sick, or in prison and visit thee?' And the King will answer them, 'Truly, I say to you, as you did it to one of the least of these my brethren, you did it to me.'" The converse holds true, too, when those who neglected their duties ask the same question and get the scathing reply in verse 45: "'Truly, I say to you, as you did it not to one of the least of these, you did it not to me.'" The denouement for the latter group is grim, indeed, as verse 46 states: "And they will go away into eternal punishment, but the righteous into eternal life." Thus, those who desire eternal life must help the unfortunate ones, but not with the expectation of a quid pro quo: "Matthew ethics is not about a contrived, rewards-seeking, works-righteousness, but a virtuous, self-forgetful righteousness." How one does this is the crux of the matter. The key, revealed later in Matthew, is God's grace. "The entire Gospel is founded on the gratuitous gift that is the kingdom of God. Ethical righteousness is merely a response to this earlier divine gift." The self-forgetful aspect clashed with the contemporary Greco-Roman idea of ostentatious giving. The prosperous gave in order to achieve honor and acclaim. Economist and theologian Albino Barrera refers to this as "negative almsgiving" that was "driven by expediency and expected returns." Jesus commands that people emulate him in being the servant of all (Barrera 2013, 167, 268; Matthew 6:1–4, 20:28; Luke 22:25).[4]

Luke's Gospel, though, diverges from Matthew's self-forgetfulness. The disciplines are told to "Sell your possessions, and give alms; provide yourselves with purses that do not grow old, with a treasure in the heavens that does not fail, where no thief approaches and no moth destroys. For where your treasure is, there will your heart be also" (Luke 12:33–34). Since some of the disciples are men of means, this admonition is costly in terms of earthly goods. Throughout Luke 16, Jesus teaches that almsgiving is a way to be a good steward of God's gift; even donations of "unrighteous mammon" should be used to help the needy. Luke takes a swipe at the Pharisees, characterizing them as "lovers of money," and makes them foils for Jesus' teachings.[5] Luke's gospel exhorts people to go beyond parity in exchange and a move from "ethics of strict reciprocity" to "generous self-giving." Calculations based on utility violate this spirit of disinterested generosity. Barrera identifies this as a distinctively Christian virtue (Barrera 2013, 264–265).[6]

St. Augustine and others argued that instead of such largesse limited to fellow citizens, wealthy people should donate to the "faceless mass of the poor…a gesture that owed nothing to the claims of one's hometown or of one's fellow citizens—would earn the rich 'treasure in heaven.'" Redirecting donations, of course, provoked resistance. Wealthy people enjoyed the fame and prestige of lavish benefaction upon their fellow citizens. Certainly today's wealthy people often subsidize such prestigious institutions as ballet, symphony orchestras, opera, or Ivy League universities and bask in the acclaim.

St. Augustine understood the attraction of financing popular spectacles, but he was arguing that one should store up treasure in heaven by giving to the poor and to the church. He was savvy enough to pitch his argument in language that risk-taking wealthy Romans could understand: "God wishes you to invest what you have [by sending it to heaven], not to throw it away." Wealthy African Christians near Hippo and Carthage were used to investing in overseas trade and dealing with complicated loans. St. Augustine employed a metaphor of a merchant: "Our Lord God wishes us to be merchants of a kind. He proposes a long-distance deal," exchange treasure on Earth for treasures in heaven—metaphorically a very long distance (Brown 2015, 87, 90–92).

St. Augustine fought the Pelagians, who, according to St. Augustine, believed only a complete disbursement of wealth would save a wealthy person's soul. The Pelagians lauded Pinianus and Melania, a wealthy and prominent Roman couple for selling most of their possessions after a joint dream that they were passing through a crack in the wall; they decided to rid themselves of most of their possessions in Rome, although they retained sufficient to endow churches and monasteries in Africa. Their ostentatious generosity rankled St. Augustine, who was trying to get the great masses of Christians to donate on a steady, if modest, basis, rather than for showy excess (Brown 2015, 94–95).

Christians, Work, and Charity

Wealthy Greeks and Romans eschewed manual labor. Homer stated that Zeus imposed work as an oppressive misfortune upon men. Christians, on the other hand, believed that work was dignified and obligatory. The Apostle Paul took a pragmatic stance. He made this explicit in 2 Thessalonians, when he stated that the abled-bodied who do not work should not be fed. Paul faced a conundrum; many of his fellow believers expected the Parousia was imminent, but he argued that people should still work for one's subsistence and not free-ride on other people (1 Thessalonians 4:9–12, 5:14; 2 Thessalonians 3:6–12). Work also reduced the temptation to steal (Ephesians 4:28). People also needed to continue to work in order to render unto Caesar that which is his (Romans 13:6). Paul recognized that if people quit working, the ability to succor the truly needy would be overwhelmed; indeed, believers were to see first to their dependents or relatives in need (1 Timothy 5:8 and 11–13).

Albino Barrera explains that Paul, similar to John Wesley's views of the 1700s, differs from many of the other authors in the New Testament. He does not harshly criticize the wealthy, and he does not advocate voluntary divestment. Although goods are provided to everyone, he advises providing for oneself and then sharing the excess. The goal is to avoid being a burden on others. The author of the letter of James offers advice very similar to modern-day authors, Thomas Stanley and William Danko. James 2:2–4 read: "For if a man with gold rings and in fine clothing comes into your assembly, and a poor man in shabby clothing also comes in, and you pay attention to the one who wears the fine clothing and say, 'Have a seat here, please,' while you say to the poor man, 'Stand there,' or, 'Sit at my feet,' have you not made distinctions among yourselves and become judges with evil thoughts?" Judging people's wealth by their outward appearance can be mistaken. James, of course, is aiming at a different point that Stanley and Danko (who argue that ostentatious spenders often have low net wealth while many millionaires are indistinguishable from middle-class people), but the similarity is useful to note. James (2:2–4) dislikes the fawning over the rich and shunning of the poor, and he claims that everyone "shares a fundamental equality" based on their "being made in the likeness of God" (Barrera 2013, 219, 227; James 3:9; Stanley and Danko 1996, 28–29). James chides the rich for defrauding their workers and using the justice system for their own ends (James 5:4). He believes the wealthy become arrogant and deluded in believing they control their destinies, but he warns, in the prophetic tradition, "Come now, you rich, weep and howl for the miseries that are coming upon you. Your riches have rotted and your garments are moth-eaten. Your gold and silver have rusted, and their rust will be evidence against you and will eat your flesh like fire" (James 5:1–3). James also warns that coveting wealth creates competition and conflict, dividing the society into haves and have-nots (James 4:1–4, 13–17). To say that James is scathing of the rich hardly does justice to his rebukes.

Since wealth has snares, should one go the opposite way and assume voluntary poverty? Divestment needs to be tied to putting one's trust in God. To romanticize poverty is to misunderstand God's intentions. "The invitation to radical divestment is associated with the call to follow Christ." The New Testament's discussion of radical dispossession and voluntary poverty diverge from the Old Testament teachings. In both the ancient

Near Eastern literature and Old Testament, private property rights are permissible, and even the prophets held property. Wealth was not inherently good or bad, but how one obtained and used wealth determined whether a wealth holder was virtuous or not. This focus on how the wealth was obtained presaged Robert Nozick's process theory of distributive justice. Scholars hold different interpretations of the New Testament passages regarding divestment. Some view it as tied to the expectation of an imminent return of Jesus or only for the initial period of the Church. Others see the divestment as continuing a tradition of wandering charismatics. Barrera notes that "radical dispossession is merely part of a much larger proleptic living of the end-time in the here and now" (Barrera 2013, 284, 290–294, 296–297).

Attitudes Toward Traders and Merchants

Although New Testament readers are familiar with Jesus' rage toward the money changers in the temple, other religions countenanced similar activities. In the Roman empire, holy days often coincided with market days, where pilgrims first paid their respects to the gods and then went shopping. Medieval Lucca witnessed moneychangers in the square of the San Martino cathedral. The moneychangers had to swear not to resort to chicanery and fraud (Silver 1985, 8).

Jesus' anger at the moneychangers in the temple sparked two interpretations; one was that the money changing itself was sinful, and the other was that Jesus was angry that moneychangers were profaning the temple. Overall, Jacob Viner suggests that the Old and New Testaments held little advice as to the desirability of trade "either for salvation or for temporal welfare." Some Church Fathers relied upon Psalm 71:15, whereby the writer states, "For I have not known tradings." St. Augustine analyzed this passage and concluded that the passage implied a condemnation of trading for Christians, although he adds that some versions of the verse use "learning" or "literature" ("letters") instead of "trading" (Viner 1978, 35; Augustine n.d., 10; Michell 1957, 338).[7]

Aside from the usual deceit and fraud involved in trade, St. Augustine seemed to be condemning the concentration upon gain instead of praising God. "Therefore if this man for this reason speaketh the praise of God all the day long, because he hath not known tradings; let Christians amend themselves, let them not trade." St. Augustine discounted the argument that traders brought desirable merchandise from abroad and asked to be compensated for their labors. But even craftsmen were guilty, as St. Augustine mocked: "I will be a shoemaker, I will make shoes for men. Are not they too liars? Are not they too false-swearers? Secondly, in the very sewing do they not commit as many frauds?" Even farmers hoped for a famine in order that their crops would fetch a high price. "For they that are active traders, rely as it were upon their own action, they praise their works, they attain not to the grace of God. Therefore traders are opposed to that grace which this Psalm doth commend. For it doth commend that grace, in order that no one may boast of his own works" (Augustine n.d., 10–12).

St. Ambrose inveighed against false weights, short measures, fraudulent agreements and contracts, and dishonesty (Dudden 1935, 548). The sharp practices prohibited by imperial laws incurred his ire. His main attack on commerce was that it distracted people's thoughts from virtue and focused them on making money, thereby tempting business participants to engage in sinful activities. He urged clergy to avoid participation in commerce, which was somewhat difficult, since the Church owned so much land.[8] Later thinkers elaborated upon St. Ambrose's condemnation of merchants by relying upon a passage in Ecclesiasticus (26:29, 27:2): "A merchant shall hardly keep himself from doing wrong; And a huckster shall not be freed from sin….As a nail sticketh fast between the joining of the stones, So doth sin stick close between the buying and the selling."

St. Augustine denotes a difference in attitudes toward prosperity. He describes a man who has a healthy family, "barns full of corn," and so on. He asks whether this should be sufficient for a man's happiness. In contrast, another prosperous man may feel restless, worrying or considering how to acquire even more than the amount needed to be happy. The concept of "enough" apparently does not resonate with this restless rich man (nor does it seem to resonate with plutocrats throughout history). What is the purpose of the wealth, what ultimate ends will a property owner put their property? As one can imagine, for St. Augustine, a person's use of their wealth is an indication of their love—as a person's love is, so is the person. "It is the ends chosen which determine and define the morality of human acts," so a person must not "lose sight of eternity and its prior claims." A person should be thankful for the "unmerited gifts that God bestows," and so the property owner who takes joy in having enough is the one to emulate. The other rich man is doomed by his "*cupiditate flagrans*;" this person is "aflame with covetousness," and whose flames are difficult to extinguish. For the restless rich man, there can never be enough riches for there may always be another person with greater riches or greater fame (MacQueen 1972, 201–203).

Of the texts that were not included in the canon, apocryphal, or pseudepigraphical sources associated wealth with injustice with such pithy remarks as, “Wild asses in the wilderness are the prey of lions; likewise the poor are pastures for the rich” and “Deceitfulness is another common trait of the wealthy: ‘A rich man will exploit you if you can be of use to him, but if you are in need he will forsake you.’” Other writers employed snide remarks, such as the amusing, “My son, the rich man eats a snake, and they say ‘He ate it for medicine.’ And the poor man eats it, and they say, ‘For his hunger he ate it (Schmidt 1987, 71).’”

Conclusion

Jewish and Christian thinkers introduced an all-knowing (even your inner thoughts) and all-seeing God, who urged altruistic compassion for the poor. As with the Greeks, these religions warned against undue concentration upon amassing wealth, whether by means fair or foul. The opportunity cost of amassing wealth had to be weighed against the loss of time spent contemplating and worshiping God.

Jewish commentators often held more positive views of traders and merchants than did Christian writers, although Paul was an exception among the Christians (and, of course, he was a converted Jew). Jewish and Christian writers, though, noted the pitfalls of over-earnest pursuit of wealth that incited unethical behavior while neglecting God. They also highlighted duties owed to the poor.

Notes

1. Zinbarg noted that Buddhism has a stricter do-no-harm tradition, “extending do not kill” to animals as well as humans (Zinbarg 2001, 89).
2. Kleiman (1987) also described other ways to undercut a rival’s price on pages 34–35, including handing out parched corn and nuts to children.
3. Sirach 8:12–13 gave some good advice: “Lend not unto him that is mightier than thyself; for if thou lendest him, count it but lost. Be not surety above thy power: for if thou be surety, take care to it.” Although lauding those helping the impoverished, Sirach cautioned lending to a sinner, who “will overthrow the good estate of his surety” (29:16). Sirach suggested that one not give children their inheritance, lest the parent end up needing the

children's help; only when death was imminent, should a person distribute inheritance (Sirach 33:20–23).

4. See also Barrera (2013, 130) regarding Greco-Roman ways.
5. As with other scholars, Albino Barrera described Jesus' interactions with people of means. Some scholars argued that Jesus himself may have been bourgeoisie (Barrera 2013, 205; Schmidt 1987, 105–106, 110–13; Judge 1960, 61). Even Jesus' birth in a lowly manger might be misinterpreted (Buchanan 1964, 208, see also 195–196; Drower 1937, 41). The Apostle Paul provided another clue that Jesus may have been a man of means in 2 Corinthians 9: "For you know the grace of our Lord Jesus Christ, that though he was rich, yet for your sake he became poor, so that by his poverty you might become rich."
6. But Jewish people would seem to practice a similar virtue.
7. The Revised Standard Version and King James translations of this verse do not contain the phrase, "For I have not known tradings, or learning."
8. Ambrose's vehemence against commerce went to the extreme that he made a bizarre claim that the seas were not intended for commerce (Dudden 1935, 548–549).

Bibliography

Augustine. n.d. *Exposition on the Book of Psalms—St. Augustine*. http://biblehub.com/library/augustine/exposition_on_the_book_of_psalms/psalm_lxxi.htm.

Barrera, Albino. *Biblical Economic Ethics: Sacred Scripture's Teachings on Economic Life* (Plymouth, UK: Lexington Books, 2013).

Botticini, Maristella and Zvi Eckstein. "Religious Norms, Human Capital, and Money Lending in Jewish European History." *The Oxford Handbook of the Economics of Religion* (Oxford, UK: Oxford University Press 2011), 57–70.

Brown, Peter. *The Ransom of the Soul: Afterlife and Wealth in Early Western Christianity* (Cambridge, MA: Harvard University Press, 2015).

Buchanan, George. "Jesus and the Upper Class." *Novum Testamentum* 7(3), June 1964, 195–209.

Buhler, Georg, translator. *The Laws of Manu* (Delhi, India: Motilal Banarsidass, [1886] 1967). Vol. 25 of 50 vols. of Sacred Books of the East Series.

Drower, Ethel. *The Mandaeans of Iran and Iraq: Their Cults, Customs, Magic, Legends, and Folklore* (Oxford, UK: Clarendon Press, 1937).

Dudden, F. Holmes. *The Life and Times of St. Ambrose* (Oxford: Clarendon Press, 1935). Vol. II.

Finkel, Avraham, translator. *Ein Yaakov: The Ethical and Inspirational Teachings of the Talmud compiled in the sixteenth century by Rabbi Yaakov Ibn* Chaviv (Lanham, MD: Rowman & Littlefield, 1999).

Judge, E.A. *The Social Pattern of the Christian Groups in the First Century* (London, UK: Tyndale Press, 1960).
Kleiman, Ephraim. "'Just price' in Talmudic literature." *History of Political Economy* 19(1), 1987, 23–45.
Lapin, Rabbi Daniel. "An Explanation for Jewish Business Success." *Business and Religion: A Clash of Civilization?*, edited by Nicholas Capaldi (Salem, MA: M & M Scrivener Press, 2005), 184–191.
MacQueen, D.J. "St. Augustine's concept of property ownership." *Recherches Augustiniennes* VIII, 1972. 187–229.
Michell, Humfrey. *The Economics of Ancient Greece* (New York, NY: Barnes and Noble, 1957). Cited by Finley 1973.
Parsha Pages. n.d. "The Six Ultimate Questions." www.parshapages.com/./The%20Six%20Ultimate%20Questions.doc.
Rue, Loyal. *Religion Is Not About God: How Spiritual Traditions Nurture Our Biological Nature and What to Expect When They Fail* (New Brunswick, NJ: Rutgers University Press, 2005).
Schmidt, Thomas. *Hostility to Wealth in the Synoptic Gospels* (Sheffield, UK: JSOT Press, 1987).
Sedlacek, Tomas. *Economics of Good and Evil: The Quest for Economic Meaning from Gilgamesh to Wall Street* (Oxford, UK: Oxford University Press, 2011).
Silver, Morris. *Economic Structures of the Ancient Near East* (Totowa, NJ: Barnes & Noble Books, 1985).
Sirach, Book of http://www.sacred-texts.com/bib/apo/sir010.htm.
Stanley, Thomas and William Danko. *The Millionaire Next Door: The Surprising Secrets of America's Wealthy* (Atlanta, GA: Longstreet Press, 1996).
Tamari, Meir. "The Challenge of Wealth: 'Jewish Business Ethics.'" *Business Ethics Quarterly* 7(2), March 1997, 45–56.
Viner, Jacob. *Religious Thought and Economic Society* (Durham, NC: Duke University Press, 1978).
Zinbarg, Edward. *Faith, Morals, and Money: What the World's Religions Tell Us about Money in the Marketplace* (New York, NY: Continuum, 2001).

CHAPTER 8

Islam and Business Ethics

The people of the Arabian Peninsula had long practiced raid or trade. Muhammad and Islam held different attitudes toward merchants and traders than did Christians. Muhammad's background as a trader probably imbued his more favorable views toward merchants and traders than did Christian thinkers. The *Qur'an* contains business-like precepts. Later Islamist rulers were more than tolerant of Jewish businessmen. As with Jewish and Christian ethics, Islam disapproved of lending at interest. Islam remains theologically opposed to lending at interest, a stance that eventually proved onerous.

Islamic Traders

The *Tales of the Arabian Nights* chronicled a traveling trader's adventures. The Sinbad legends in *The Thousand and One Nights* depicted the hero as stocking trade goods before venturing on his expeditions seeking adventure and profits, even in the face of pirates, dangerous waters, and other calamities (Bernstein 2008, 89). Historian Robert Lopez admits the tales are fascinating, but he considers them misleading. "They see Baghdad in the age of Harun al-Rashid through a magnifying glass. Actually most roads were poor or nonexistent, ships were small, coinage was barely adequate, and the conspicuous consumption of a few rich people did not make up for the destitution of the masses." What was correct was that the Arabs despised farming and had long practiced traveling commerce (such

D. G. Surdam, *Business Ethics from Antiquity to the 19th Century*,
https://doi.org/10.1007/978-3-030-37165-4_8

as Muhammad had done). By the early Middle Ages in Europe, "the economic pace of the Islamic world was distinctly faster than that of Catholic Europe, if only because it drew its resources and techniques from an incomparably larger range of lands and cultures" (Lopez 1971, 24–25).

Merchants in Ottoman Syria sometimes attained the status of folk heroes, and people recounted clever merchants' feats. Sinbad's adventures demonstrated how a clever person, even one of modest background, could travel to far-off lands and, through luck and pluck, gain a fortune. "Good business sense, then, and not valor, was the trait most often glorified and extolled. The rich merchant was the society's paragon of success, but more than that, he represented a universal everyman on whom fortune had smiled" (Masters 1988, 45).

Before Islamic trade, tribes living on the Arabian Peninsula, similar to other places around the world, faced a tough existence for survival. One strategy for survival was to prey upon weaker groups. "Recall the trilemma of trade: whether to trade, protect, or raid. In the absence of any authority beyond the tribe, entrepreneurs will invariably choose to raid." The group or tribe was paramount for an individual's survival, and the attitude mimicked the Three Musketeers' slogan, "All for one, and one for all." An offense to one member was an offense against all members. A murderer's "entire clan was held accountable for retribution" (Bernstein 2008, 67; see also Armstrong 1992, 60–61). Raiding became prevalent.

The Quraysh tribe, headed by Qusayy, opted to trade and to protect. He recognized that it was better to offer protection for caravans than was raiding them. The Quraysh traded protection in return for taxes; although one can wonder about the dubious ethics of offering such "protection," which was, in a sense, a promise not to raid (albeit also not to allow others to raid). The procedure, however, worked. The Quraysh settled in Mecca and became traders instead of pastoral nomads. Mecca was the site of the annual hajj, which brought large numbers of pilgrims to the city, even before the rise of Islam (Bernstein 2008, 69; Bulliet 1990, 28–36; Armstrong 1992, 62–63, 66–67).

Muhammad and Islamic Attitudes

Christian tradition claims Jesus was a carpenter, so he may have been familiar with business practices; Muhammad, however, was clearly familiar with trade. His uncle was a trader and Muhammad worked for a widow (who later became his wife) operating an ongoing caravan trading venture.

Muhammad served as the widow's agent in Syria. Muhammad became acquainted with Jewish and Christian traders and peoples and their holy writings. The Arabs of the Arabian Peninsula both lacked a holy book of their own and found the commercial elite of Mecca becoming alienated from the traditional tribal behavior (Armstrong 1992, 66–67).

Whereas Jesus preached a possible wiping clean of a person's slate recording good and bad deeds, Muhammad used an accounting approach, if one may. There was a strict and accurate running debit–credit account for each person. At the end, the account must have a final settlement; this idea was paramount for Muhammad. The balance sheet approach was familiar to Arabs in Muhammad's time; they were accustomed to the idea that everything had a price and could be paid for. With regard to God, though, "God cannot be cheated, and must himself, in common fairness, deal honestly." The idea of "payment from God, including punishment and reward, is naturally very prominent in Muhammad's theology." There will be an "exact requital," and no good deed or bad deed is left out of the final settlement. The believer earns recompense for each good deed, and historian Charles Torrey suggests that "earning" is Muhammad's "favorite" word. "How far the trade idea was present here to Muhammad is a question not easily answered." Muhammad's conception of God as revealed in the *Qur'an* resembles "a somewhat magnified and idealized picture of a Mekkan merchant" (Torrey 1892, 14, 17, 29).

Muhammad's familiarity with business affected the sacred texts. Mecca's importance in trade, "secured for the merchant a great deal of influence on the affairs of the state. Many learned men had, at some stage of their careers, earned a living as merchants." One of Muhammad's closest friends, Abu Bakr, was "an honest and upright merchant of substance" (Saunders 1965, 24). "Islam is perhaps the one great religion which affords the merchant a highly honoured place in society, and even the theological terminology of the *Qur'an* contains a number of words borrowed from the commercial usage of the time" (Lieber 1968, 230). Unlike some of the eastern religions, where there is disapproval of people engaging in commerce, Islam stresses commerce. The *Qur'an* (4:29) states, "O you who believe! Do not devour your property among yourselves falsely, except that it be trading by your mutual consent." A similar tradition holds that, "I shall meet God before I give anyone the property of another without the latter's consent, for trade requires mutual consent" (*Qur'an* 1997, 4:29; El-gamal 2006, 9). Mutual consent is a necessary but not sufficient condition for a valid economic transaction.

The *Qur'an* contains many passages with commerce and trade motifs. For instance, 2:194 states, "Every man will at last be confronted with his 'reckoning;' unbelievers are 'the losers.' Allah 'buys' the service of his people, every soul is 'held as security' for its debts," are a few examples. Muhammad speaks glowingly of the "ship (tikis) as a vehicle of trade." He permitted trade during the pilgrimage. Verses 83:1–9 emphasize fairness in bargaining as a key attribute for a virtuous man, and "the invective against those who give short weight" match those of the Old Testament prophets. Having been involved in trade, Muhammad had a keen appreciation of participants' behavior. He proclaims that "Allah will surely pay each soul its full due" (Torrey 1892, 1–2; *Qur'an* 1997, 52:40, 68:46).

The theme of "loss" recurs in the *Qur'an*. Sometimes the loser incurs the loss through making a foolish bargain, but at other times the loss results from unfair dealing. Torrey notes that "loss" occurs three times in the *Qur'an* with regard to actual trading, but on other occasions it is used as a metaphor. "The unbeliever is the 'loser' par excellence," but Allah "will not defraud in any smallest degree in settling man's account."

Allah deals in a businesslike manner with mankind, including "actual bargaining, buying, and selling, as well as payment, keeping an account." Muhammad encourages believers to "not make the bad bargain of misusing our revelations, or withholding them for your own purposes!" Other verses maintain that, "The mutual relations between God and man are of a strictly commercial nature. Allah is the ideal merchant….All is counted, everything measured….he has made himself the pattern of honest dealing." Allah is not a hard creditor and sometimes forgives debts. "The Muslim makes a loan to Allah; pays in advance for paradise; sells his own soul to him, a bargain that prospers. The unbeliever has sold the divine truth for a paltry price, and is bankrupt." At the end, Allah will calculate the final reckoning for each person. Our actions "are read from the account-book, weighed in the balances; each is paid his exact due, no one is defrauded" (Torrey 1892, 29–32, 35–36, 48).

Islamic Trade

Islamic success in spreading trade to southeast Asia emanated from its system of laws that covered day-to-day conduct, including conduct of commerce, according to historian William Bernstein. "Thus, the new monotheism from Arabia was especially attractive to those engaged in any organized economic activity that flourished wherever rules were plainly visible and vigorously enforced by disinterested parties—again, as in the more secular English common law. Even if one was not moved by religious fervor, embracing Islam at least did wonders for one's credit rating."

In the aftermath of conquest, the Umayyad and Abbasid empires created free-trade regions stretching from Asia to the Mediterranean. Muslim traders arrived in China. Bernstein identifies the Muslim's commercial advances, including "bills of exchange, sophisticated lending institutions, and futures market." On the other hand, he believes that the failure of Islamic states to create national or central banks proved a key drawback (Bernstein 2008, 75–76, 108).

Because Muslims were required to make a pilgrimage to Mecca, there was a well-developed system to serve travelers, as well as traders. Mecca became, to use today's parlance, a tourist center. People came for serious religious reasons and stayed to sample the cultural sites, including the wondrous centers of learning. Because Mecca became a crossroads for travelers, Arab merchants and scholars learned about a variety of subjects. Ethnographer Shelomo Goitein notes that "The standing wish for a Muslim pilgrim was: 'May your *hajj* be accepted, your sin be forgiven, and your merchandise not remain unsold'" (Watson 1974, 20; Goitein 1967, I:55).

Economic and Moral Developments

The *Qur'an* considers economic development to be part of moral development, as there is no cleavage between religion and the pursuit of prosperity, which is good in itself. Islam urges believers to strike a balance between individual and social duties, material and spiritual needs, "so that all activities are oriented toward the achievement of well-being in this world as well as in the afterlife." Such a balance is compatible with "moderation in consumption habits, altruistic behavior, and seeking personal peace." Muslim business owners are called to be fair and generous, as such behavior is more respected than sheer profit maximization. Justice is important in the economic and business realms, as business actors seek "a harmony between the various interests and proportionality between needs and rewards. Each Muslim contributes to his well-being by contributing to the collective well-being. Social justice, too, is important in Islam."

Muslims are to be stewards or managers of Allah's property; as the universe is Allah's and has been "given" to people, who have been given rights of (temporary) ownership. Any prosperity is to be handled as Allah would, to benefit the community. Each Muslim is individually held responsible for the management of Creation, so each is a trustee of the natural resources that he or she needs. With wealth, comes greater responsibility to Allah (Dion 2002, 161–162; *Qur'an* 1997, 2:30, 2:256, 7:54, 7:166, 12:40).

Because of his strong adherence to property rights, Muhammad refused to intervene during a famine in Media. He did not believe it right to override the market-driven prices. "Allah is the only one who sets the prices and gives prosperity and poverty. I would not want to be complained about before Allah by someone whose property or livelihood has been violated" (McMillan 2002, 90).

Islamic tradition views producers of basic goods more positively than producers of luxuries. Merchants and traders are esteemed, and the *Hadith* calls them "couriers of the world" and "trusted servants of God upon earth." The merchants are lauded for bringing distant goods to the local market. On the other hand, Islamic traditions take a dimmer view of finance than did Catholicism. Islam views finance as suspect, and participants in financial actions are "at the lower end of the ladder of occupations considered to be socially useful." Aspects of finance resemble gambling. "Selling short" is considered illegal by many Islamic jurists. In general, though, when Muslims meet in the bazaar, people have moral obligations: "Not only prices but men's reputations are set, reset, and continually adjusted in the bazaar." Bazaar and mosque are twin aspects of Islamic communities (Zinbarg 2001, 55–56; see also Mottahedeh 1985, 34–35).

Credit arrangements existed from the earliest Islamic era, and, in all likelihood, well before the Prophet. Sarakhsi, an Islamic scholar, quoted the Prophet as saying that credit was permissible and perhaps necessary for all but local trade. Sarakhsi considered credit sales as the "surest, if not always the swiftest, method of achieving profit…[because] 'a thing is sold on credit for a larger sum [than] it would be sold for in cash (Udovitch 1970, 77–80).'"[1]

As with Christianity and Judaism, monopolistic behavior is proscribed under Islam, although the reasoning differs slightly. Muslims believe that monopolies "show a lack of harmony between private and social interests and impede on the moral and spiritual development of human beings. Monopolistic practices are allowed only to the extent that it is clear that they will create a greater collective good." In addition to generally prohibiting monopoly, Muslims discourage sheer profit maximization and needless consumption of goods and services: "economic life is only a means for a spiritual end and prosperity is a means to live a virtual [virtuous] life."

The *Qur'an* says that prosperity should not be the province of the few; those who are prosperous must use their wealth according to Allah's will, as well as fulfill social responsibilities toward the poor. Islam discourages the accumulation of capital and encourages a just distribution of wealth. Islam recognizes that greed and love of material prosperity are "the source of all evil." Muslims are exhorted to be temperate in consumption and not to indulge too much in consuming luxury goods and services (Dion 2002, 163–164; *Qur'an* 1997, 51:19, 57:20, 59:7).

A pillar of Islam is almsgiving. Muhammad was appalled at the callous attitude displayed to the poor by "selfish fortune-seek[ers]s" in Mecca. A main motivation for his ministry was to redress the "glaring injustices of Meccan society. It is therefore not surprising that the means for redressing social injustice—almsgiving—would find a central place in the new religion." Islam associated charity with worship. The principle of zakat is to "purify or increase." In other words, "by giving alms, individuals may purify their own wealth—the more you give, the more god approves of what you keep. Almsgiving also increases the rewards one may expected in the afterlife—the more you give, the higher your station in heaven." The believer would fare well by doing good. Zakat started as "a graduated annual tax," but even in modern times, "zakat continues to provide self-esteem motivation—God still loves a cheerful giver—for supporting various philanthropic enterprises" (Rue 2005, 236; *Qur'an* 1997, 2:43, 5:55; 9:71).

Contractual Agreements

A simple *commenda* consisted of an investor or investors and an agent. The agent might not provide any capital and would instead provide labor. The investors and the agent agreed upon how to share the profits. The investor(s) bore the risk of loss, and the agent only risked his time and effort (or possibly his life, if traveling to a dangerous place). A bilateral *commenda* meant that the agent contributed some capital, possibly because the main investor wanted more capital involved in the project or because the main investor figured the agent would be both more cautious and more enterprising with some of his [the agent's] own capital at risk.

Incidental expenses created disputes with regard to *commenda* contracts. As in modern times, agents might find government officials demanding "favors." Some Islamic jurists disallowed such payments from the *commenda*, even if necessary to protect an investment from confiscation, but the agent could make such payments from his own funds. This Hanifa and Shaybani opinion was reversed between the eighth and eleventh centuries, and Sarakhsi attributed the change in opinion to the "deteriorated moral quality of political rule." Bribes had not been acceptable under past rulers, "when the power of political authority was exercised justly," but by Sarakhsi's time (eleventh century), bribes were necessary to protect investments. The Malikis went a step further; because they considered such extortion by government officials akin to robbery, they absolved the agent from any responsibility.

There were restrictions upon *commenda* contracts. The Islamic jurists were less concerned about economic efficiency than about maintaining the peace. Some Islamic jurists, Shafi'i for instance, opposed partnerships where one partner did not supply any capital. The Shafi'i view considered limited investment partnership as permissible, if the partners each provide capital and the profits were divided in direct proportion to the amount of capital supplied by each. Such a restricted partnership was adequate only for partners who were able to communicate frequently, thereby relegating them to residing close by. This edict meant that commercial partnerships lacked flexibility in the distribution of profits, nor could a partner supply labor, skill, connections, or knowledge in lieu of capital. This interpretation was an obstacle to the flow of investment capital. Not all of the Islamic jurists agreed with prohibiting partnerships where a partner provided labor or other non-cash assets. Kasanni defended such partnerships by pointing out that businesspeople had been using credit and work partnerships for centuries, and the Prophet had advised that his community would not unanimously agree upon an error.[2]

Their opposition toward using goods and commodities as investments in such contracts rested upon concerns for the inherent risk and potential unjustified enrichment and an adherence upon Islamic law that mandated that the object of any contract be determined, that is, clearly known and defined. Partnerships based on goods, therefore, were not permitted, since the value of the goods often was unknown until it became time to split the profits. Such a state might trigger disputes. Coins, gold, and silver were permissible, as they were usual means of exchange. This edict posed a disadvantage to merchants involved in long-distance trade, since merchants often had most of their capital tied up in goods. One commentator, Kasanni, wrote that contracts involving goods faced uncertainty as to the future value of such goods: "And uncertainty in turns leads to dispute, and dispute leads to discord." Because the goods and commodities might not be divested for an extended period of time, their market values might change considerably, creating an inequitable advantage and enrichment for one partner and corresponding disadvantage for the other. In fact, if prices were volatile enough, one partner might lose all of his profits. The potential for discord, then, was palpable.

Hanafi law identified commercial partnerships as *mufawada* (unlimited investment partnership) and *'inan* (limited investment partnership). Both of these partnerships had the drawback of unlimited liability, although the partners were "liable in proportion to their share of the total investment," even if such liability exceeded their share of the assets. One key aspect of the *mufawada* is the freedom of action and the seeking of profits by each partner; if one or more of the partners do not have full freedom of action, the partnership is not allowed.

Although men with capital might employ an agent or employee, the cultural distaste for working for another created a problem. "I eat bread in the service of others; every minute of the day I gulp the cup of death because of my degradation and that of my children." A *commenda* contract whereby the capitalist put up money and the agent pledged his services could help maintain the agent's dignity.

As with their Catholic peers, Islamic jurists were vigilant in guarding against use of a *commenda* as a vehicle for unlawful usury. The Malikis strenuously disapproved converting a debt into a *commenda* investment held by the debtor. False *commenda* contracts gave creditors both the certainly of his debt and an illicit gain from, "the guise of his share of the *commenda's* profits."

Similar to the Christian passage whereby Christians were not to be unequally yoked in marriage, Islamic law discouraged *commenda* contracts between a believer and non-believers. The *mufawada* partnership does not allow a Muslim to partner with a non-Muslim. Such a proscription ruled out the advantage of having a *dhimmi* (a non-Muslim) around, who could handle some goods, such as pork and wine, that a Muslim could not own or profit from. Some legal scholars, however, permitted a *mufawada* partnership between a Muslim and a *dhimmi* but recommended against it. Sarakhsi argued that there was nothing inherently wrong with Muslims receiving investments from Christian under a *commenda* contract, but the reverse was reprehensible. However, Sarakhsi cautions that Christians were unlikely to be scrupulous in obeying Islamic usury proscriptions and to be tempted to deal in prohibited substances, such as wine and pork (Udovitch 1970, 40–47, 62, 170–172, 180–188, 228–235).

There was an explicit announcement of profit-seeking, as parties created written documents for many commercial transactions. Written documents might contain two phrases: "This contract is a contract of fidelity, the aim of which is the attainment of profit; and this is attained by the fear of God and mutual fidelity." The fidelity aspect was reflected in the case of a loss. If the loss was incurred in the nature and scope of the business, the partner was not liable for restitution. If, instead, the money was lost because of an action outside the "realm of acceptable business conduct," then the erring partner was liable. The phrase "aim of which is the attainment of profit" was critical. If an action was done with the purpose of attaining a profit (or if it was in line with the practice and customs of the merchants), then it was permissible, even if it compromised some religious-ethical aspect. Such pragmatism gave the *commenda* agent and members of commercial associations a wide freedom of commercial action (Udovitch 1970, 86–87, 93, 252–253).

Usury

Historian Abraham Udovitch cautions that, "Any assumed harmony between medieval Islamic law and the actual practice of that period has been brought into serious question, and even completely denied by several eminent Islamists." Usury was an example, as the practice was prohibited throughout the Islamic world, but people devised subterfuges to avoid the charge. In other cases, "systematic legal reasoning [was] suspended because of the 'custom of the merchants' or 'because of the needs of merchants'" (Udovitch 1970, 4, 11–13).

Although the *Qur'an* prohibited the taking of interest, economist Subhi Labib described the widespread practice of usury: "Usury and excessive profit played an important role in Islamic capitalism. Neither Muslims nor Christians nor Jews shunned usurious business dealings. Even Caliphs, Sultans, and Emirs received loans carrying too high an interest rate." Among the Ottomans, Muslim men of religion often lent at interest, and some jurists argued that interest could legitimately be charged on precious metals. Lending to rulers was risky. Rulers often failed to repay loans or explicitly repudiated their debts; on some occasions, they went a step further and confiscated their creditors' assets! Labib notes, "Confiscation in times of unrest and invasion was the order of the day."

The creditors, though, were often willing to assume the risk (assuming the loan was not a "forced loan"), because the "privileges and advantages received from the heads of state brought such high profits that some creditors were able to amortize the debts and cover even the losses" (Labib 1969, 90, 93; see also Inalcik 1969, 101).

Islamic law forbids charging interest (*riba*) and stipulates that all transactions entail sharing risk; therefore, a fixed return on capital is forbidden. An economist might respond that even a "fixed return" is subject to the risk of inflation and also loss or default. Islamic banks cannot simply lend capital to businesses and charge interest; instead banks have to enter into joint ventures (Fort 2008, 16).

Early fourteenth-century Islamic Jurist Ibn Taymiyya identified the two key attributes that determine whether a contract is valid or not: *riba* and *gharar*. The prohibition on *riba* has inspired much comments by non-Islamic scholars, some of whom confess befuddlement. Their befuddlement emanates from the loss of efficiency in observing the prohibition on *riba* and *gharar* (El-gamal 2006, 8–9).[3]

The *riba* prohibition restricts Muslims in their financial management. Such modern financial conveniences as credit cards, savings accounts, and fixed-income investments are precluded. Because stock ownership entails risk, Muslims can invest in mutual funds, once such funds are investigated for being halal (acceptable). Conservative Christians might find themselves wishing they had mutual funds that avoid firms selling or having an interest in alcoholic products, gambling, pornography, or profiting from interest. A Sharia board comprised of Islamic scholars determines whether the investments are halal (Fort 2008, 16).

Transfer of credit and risk are crucial for a well-functioning economy. Mahmoud El-Gamal seeks to explain the prohibition on *riba* and *gharar* by arguing that "in finance—the forbidden *riba* is essentially 'trading in credit,' and the forbidden *gharar* is 'trading in risk,' as unbundled commodities. In other words, Islamic jurisprudence uses those two prohibitions to allow only for the appropriate measure of permissibility of transferring credit and risk to achieve economic ends." These activities can be beneficial but also financially dangerous, especially as assuming credit and risk can shade into becoming "ruinous gambling behavior." The aim of the prohibitions is "to protect individuals from their own greed and myopia."

Riba al-nasi'a and *riba al-fadl* are common types of riba. *Riba al-nasi'a* was similar to the Jewish prohibition on charging interest on loans to co-religionists (Maimonides later extended the prohibition to interest-based lending to non-Jews). Pre-Islamic lenders could charge interest, but eventually jurists considered the prohibition on charging interest to cover all interest-bearing loans. In any case, strictures against charging excessive rates of interest are found in Hammurabi's code, as well as in India, where a lender could only charge interest up to the doubling the principal. The jurists worried that interest could exploit the poor debtors; trading money faced fluctuating currency values and uncertainty; and trading food today for food tomorrow might lead to shortages in spot markets. *Riba al-fadl* dealt with trading goods of the same genus, such as gold, silver, wheat, and basic commodities. Under these trades, one might borrow an amount of gold today in return for repaying an amount of gold in the future. Some forms of interest, though, were permissible, such as mark-up credit sales and lease financing. On the other hand, *riba al-fadl* demonstrates that some "forms of forbidden riba…do not include interest." Trading an ounce of gold today for a future price of an ounce of gold in the future would be considered *riba*, even though the interest rate is zero. The jurists understood that such a transaction would normally never be made, since the ounce of gold today is typically more valuable than the ounce of gold in the future (a recognition of opportunity cost of foregoing an ounce of gold today). The transaction would never be made, unless there is some other consideration involved (El-gamal 2006, 46–52).

Islamic jurists disagree on the legitimacy of various "ruses" to evade the edict on usury. The same-item, sale-repurchase contracts remain controversial. Some jurists find them valid while others find them valid but reprehensible. Because of the controversy, some financiers developed the *tawarruq* contract.

More understandable is the purpose of paternalism with regard to *riba*. The edict on *riba* helps to keep people from getting hopelessly in debt, a situation that many modern-day Americans find themselves. Some jurists think that interest-free lending might be seen as charitable and be permissible: the person extending the loan sacrificed the time value of their money or property, which underlies a *qard hasan* (beautiful loan). This belief led the Prophet's companions and jurists to prefer the process of lending and having their loans repaid to outright charity, although they were prepared to absolve debtors unable to repay. Such transactions also have the advantage of allowing a borrower to retain their dignity, while the lender earned "religious credit" by donating the foregone "time value" of the loan and risking not being repaid (El-gamal 2006, 44–45, 55; *Qur'an* 1997, 2:245, 5:12, 57:11, 57:18, 64:17, 73:20).

The *Qur'an* urges a lender to consider the debtor's plight. "If a debtor is in want, give him time until his circumstances improve; but if you forgo the debt as charity, that will be to your good, if you really understand." Edward Zinbarg explains that if the *Qur'an* told lenders they *could* not legally retrieve their money from distressed debtors, they would probably not extend any loans, interest-bearing or not. Extinguishing consumption loans would not help poor people. He comments, "religious ethics asserts that just because a creditor has the legal right to demand payment, he is not bound to exercise that right" (*Qur'an* 1997, 2:280; Zinbarg 2001, 114).[4]

Gharar and Risk

The Prophet prohibited *gharar* sales and rendered them defective. The problem with *gharar* is that it can lead to "dispute, hatred, and devouring others' wealth wrongfully. However, it is known that this corrupting factor would be overruled if it is opposed by a greater benefit." *Gharar* is also allowed if it "cannot be avoided without incurring an excessive cost, or if *gharar* is trivial." *Gharar* involves "trading in risk" or, more colorfully, "That which has a pleasant appearance and a hated essence." *Gharar* covers a variety of dubious trade practices, including fraud, cheating, and selling possibly undeliverable goods. In essence, *gharar* addressed the uncertainty inherent in most transactions that gave rise to opportunistic behavior arising from asymmetric information. Risk and uncertainty pose the possibility of unanticipated loss to one or more parties and may transform into a form of gambling or a source of future dispute. *Bay' al-gharar*—the sale of *gharar*—attempts to reduce the hazards and temptations of risk.

The concept of *bay' al-gharar* with its characteristic trading in risk means that Muslims may be precluded from insurance and derivatives. In the former case, such a prohibition was ironic, since insurance served to reduce risk; some jurists recognized that "safety" or insurance was based upon a "contingent claim, akin to an option," and was therefore forbidden. Even maritime insurance, a longstanding type of contract, was suspect, and so were options such as calls and puts. The jurists considered the insurance premium or option price as certain, but the compensation was contingent upon an uncertain outcome. The jurists permitted warranties, viewing such as a "bundled sale of insurance."

The two major prohibitions against *riba* and *gharar* "are in fact prohibition of trading in unbundled credit and unbundled risk, respectively. We have further argued that the paternalistic nature of those prohibitions is understandable, in light of human idiosyncrasies that would lead to dynamically inconsistent behavior." Despite the jurists' countenance of bundled activities, they warned against using "apparently legitimate means toward illegitimate ends." That is why so many jurists opposed *tawarruq*, "where the stated purpose is to extend credit and provide liquidity to some customer. Economic activities camouflaging the underlying sale of credit (two spot sales and one credit sale of some commodity) do little to protect individuals from borrowing or lending excessively, for the wrong reasons, or at the wrong interest rate" (El-gamal 2006, 59–62).

International Trade Among People of Different Faiths

A resurgent Europe posed problems for the Islamic states. Religious animosity inspired political and military campaigns. Despite the intermittent warfare, trade between Jewish, Christian, and Muslim vendors continued apace; the peaceful example set by the traders, unfortunately, was not emulated by the rulers. Spanish traveler Ibn Jubayr observed in 1184 that even during heavy fighting between the Christians and Muslims, traders enjoyed unmolested transit between the lines. Merchants conducted business without interference, and each paid the taxes or customs as usual. "Reciprocity prevails and equal treatment in all respects. The warriors are engaged in their wars, while the people are at ease" (Goitein 1967, I:70).

Jewish people played a prominent role disproportionate to their numbers in medieval Islam. The Vizier 'Ubaidallah b. Sulayman wrote to his Caliph explaining that he employed Jews to official positions, "not because of any sympathy…for Judaism or Christianity did I take the Unbelievers into civil service, but because I found them to be more faithfully attached to thy dynasty than Muslims." These Jews and Christians found themselves serving as physicians and bankers.

In the tenth-century Abbasid empire, two Jews, Joseph b. Phineas and Aaron b. Amram, were frequently mentioned as serving the Caliph al-Muqtadir. These two were merchant-bankers, who had conducted financial transactions pertaining to the revenues of the Ahwaz province.

High officials, including Viziers of the Caliphs, often entrusted their wealth to such moneylenders/bankers. Aaron b. Amram and Joseph b. Phineas gained the trust of al-Muqtadir and Ibn al-Furat. These operations required inordinate levels of trust, as the deposits were not (could not) be entered into the books. Ibn al-Furat, for instance, sought secrecy for his deposits (Fischel [1937] 1968, 7–9, 13–15).

Amram and Phineas may have originally been merchants. Successful merchants gradually accumulated sufficient funds that they could feel comfortable storing or lending. Amram and Phineas proved dependable and discreet in their roles of court bankers. As honest as they were, however, they were willing to handle illegal monies on behalf of Ibn al-Furat. "The Vizier, of course, avoided creating any evidence of the existence of such an account in the form of book-keeping entries." The bankers used Hebrew characters which were used in the bulk of Jewish-Arabic writings of the Middle Ages, adding an element of secrecy. The existing documents show that the Vizier's ill-gotten funds led to a legal inquiry against Aaron b. Amram and Joseph b. Phineas, but they apparently escaped unscathed.

In their unquenchable thirst for revenues, Islamic rulers often appealed to bankers for loans. Vizier 'Ali b. Isa asked Amram and Phineas for such, although the request appeared to be ill-cloaked by a threat: "Do you want to avoid my inflicting penalties on you that may affect you and your heirs for ever?" The Vizier suffered from a mismatched cash flow. He requested a loan of 150,000 [silver] dirhams, which he assured the bankers, "an amount that you, as you know, will get back in the course of the month from the Ahwaz revenue." The two bankers apparently did not like the proposition and intended to refuse, as they worried about the state's solvency, but they knew refusal could trigger reprisals, including violent acts; the Vizier also proved persistent.

Amram and Phineas successfully navigated the uncertain shoals of Islamic politics and served for 25 years of the Caliph's reign. During those years, the Caliph changed Viziers 15 times. A large part of Amram and Phineas' success was their ability to draw upon the credit of other rich merchants. The Caliph could have relied upon Christian or Muslim bankers, as Jews did not have a monopoly on such services, during those prosperous years, so Amram and Phineas' longevity marked them as especially talented and reputable bankers (Fischel [1937] 1968, 23–24, 27–29).

An earlier Jewish merchant/banker, Ya'qub b. Killis served the Egyptian court for a number of years in the tenth century. Kafur, the ruler of Egypt, had business transactions with Killis. Killis was knowledgeable regarding the agricultural situation in Egypt and shared his knowledge, making him a valued advisor. Killis used his knowledge to accumulate wealth, and "his reputation for ability, cleverness, and trustworthiness reached Kafur himself, who 'was astonished by it.' It would seem that Kafur was looking for just such a man in order to take him into the service of the state." Killis demonstrated his honesty early in his relationship with Kafur. News reached Killis of a buried treasure belonging to a deceased merchant who lacked relatives. Islamic law stated that in such cases, the estate belonged to the state. Killis informed Kafur and asked permission to retrieve the treasure. Kafur agreed and supplied pack animals. Killis found the treasure, but it was worth 30,000 dinars not 20,000. He wrote Kafur: "O Ustadh, I knew only of 20,000 dinars; now I have found 30,000." Such honesty endeared Killis to Kafur. While on this mission, Killis also investigated a similar treasure owned by a deceased Jewish merchant. He found the treasure, and Kafur rewarded him with a large sum. Ya'qub "returned all but 1000 dinars, saying, 'That is enough for me.'" Such honesty and fidelity were rare traits among any people, Jewish, Muslim, or Christian. Kafur was not the only person to hold Ya'qub in deference.

Kafur was so enamored of Ya'qub that he considered appointing him as Vizier, after all, "What vizier could compare with him?" Ya'qub's religion was a stumbling block, and Kafur would not have hesitated if Ya'qub had been a believer. Killis finally declared himself a Muslim and ascended to the post. Kafur noticed that Ya'qub was not consumed by a desire to make more money, but perhaps he realized that ambition burned within his Jewish friend. Years later, after Kafur died and his successor, Ibn al-Furat, was less sympathetic to Killis, the former vizier fled to Maghrib and associated himself with the Jewish community there, who were aligned with al-Mu'izz. Ya'qub went to al-Mu'izz and offered to serve him (Fischel [1937] 1968, 46–49).

Two Jewish brothers, Abu Sa'd Ibrahim and Abu Nasr Harun, became renowned for their roles in "sale transactions and the reporting to heirs of the secret deposits received by them from merchants from near and far, upon the latters' death. This honesty on their part secured them a good name in every land." Abu Sa'd Ibrahim purchased a black female slave, who he gave to az-Zahir. The slave girl became az-Zahir's favorite, and she bore a son, al-Mustansir. The brothers continued their business and earned a reputation for scrupulous business ethics and integrity. The brothers catered to the Caliph's demands for rarities; az-Zahir died and was succeeded by his son, al-Mustansir. Since al-Mustansir was only seven years old, the former slave girl, now queen, sent for Abu Sa'd Ibrahim and appointed him to a high political office; eventually Abu Sa'd Ibrahim became the vizier for the regent and his mother (Fischel [1937] 1968, 72, 76–79).

Geniza Merchants

Shelomo Goitein described how Jewish merchants and traders flourished in Islamic lands during the Middle Ages. He used documents to describe business practices and experiences of a Jewish community in Geniza.

International traders required a network of friends and family. Because most business transactions were better carried out face-to-face, a businessman needed to have trusted agents, often family members, scattered throughout the Mediterranean. Where he could not have family members looking after his interests, he relied upon trusted friends. Such friendships entailed reciprocal duties. Such activities on behalf of friends might seem onerous, but, of course, the merchant relied upon his friends to do likewise: "he serves there and I serve here" and "you are in my place there, for you know well that I am your support here." Goitein summarizes the Mediterranean trade as depicted in the Cairo Geniza papers as based upon, "the human qualities of mutual trust and friendship." Within the business community, at least, reputations for reliability and honesty were paramount. Whether such qualities as reliability and honesty carried over to dealings with customers is a separate issue. The Geniza collection, however, shows that merchants knew their customers fairly well and apparently depended upon continued relationships with customers to remain in business.

Scrupulous behavior was also enforced by family ties. One disgraced family member reflected upon the family. On occasion, family members made restitution or faced shame because of the actions of an errant family member. On one occasion, however, businessmen did not hold a sister accountable for her brother's misbehavior (Goitein 1967, I:157, 167–169, 182–183).

Islamic Slavery

The *Qur'an* allows slavery but also declares emancipation a "meritorious act," and, in any event, slavery pre-dated the holy book. Slavery in Islamic lands often differed from the variant practiced by Europeans in the New World. Because Islamic rulers were sometimes distrustful of their subjects, they imported slaves and other people from far-off lands. Isolated from their kin and communities, these imported people relied upon their masters, but Shelomo Goitein relates the slaves "very often became the masters of their masters." In one case, a black eunuch ruled Egypt, while the Fatimids and Ayyubids "made copious use of European, Turkish, and other slaves for the highest posts of confidence." The Mamluks were a longstanding body of slaves, who were given military training and proved loyal to their masters. The reality for female slaves was quite different, as Islamic slave masters had a different attitude than Jewish and Christian owners toward sexual exploitation of their female slaves; of course, some Jewish and Christian owners proved as sexually predatory as Muslims (Goitein 1967, I:131–132; see also Saunders 1965, 120).

The Islamic market for slaves featured a broker, who collected commissions for his services and a sales tax. The broker acted as an expert with regard to an individual slave's quality but also served the government by making evasion of the sales tax impossible. Apparently, the buyer "undertakes to acquiesce in all defects the slave might have, who under no circumstances might be returned," although sometimes contracts would specify a slave's defects. The seller, on the other hand, guaranteed to "protect the buyer against any claims that may be raised against him with regard to the proprietorship of the slave in any court, Jewish or Gentile."

Maimonides, the esteemed Jewish thinker, wrote in his code of law that pious masters should be "merciful and just towards his slave" and to exercise leniency and respect. The master should also avoid humiliate and corporal punishment. Goitein added that Muslim and Christian sources voiced similar ideas, but Maimonides' humane treatment of slaves evaded the issue of free will and begged the question of how many owners acted humanely. At least from the Geniza records, many masters employed their slaves as business representatives; these slaves were referred to in the records identically as respected merchants. Such employment suggested that masters viewed their slaves as reasonably intelligent, diligent, and trustworthy agents; there may have even been "a strong family attachment between the master and his slave." Even with respect to punishment,

Goitein pointed out that flogging was not unique to slaves, as even viziers were flogged (Goitein 1967, I:140–143).

Business Practices in the Islamic Middle Ages

Although two key aspects of Islamic trade were "friendship and mutual trust," these were insufficient to sustain a developed economy. Long-distance trade required more than personal relationships, and merchants and trades needed to rely upon "the professional representative of the merchants." The representative of the merchant acted on the merchant's behalf as legal representative with power of attorney. The representative could also represent the merchant in court.

Because most transactions were not recorded, participants ensured having trustworthy people around as witnesses. Muslim and Jewish laws required just two witnesses, but often a much larger number of witnesses would be enlisted. The witnesses were usually from similar religious community as the participants, which was important as disputes would be handled in a court of that community (Goitein 1967, I:186–187, 196).

The Maghribi traders of northern Africa used business associates to reduce the uncertainty and complexity of trade. These business associates were not typically bound by contract but by mutual trust. Economist Oliver Williamson predicted that if cooperation can increase efficiency gains that the market and the legal system were unable to capture, then "private order" economic institutions would arise. In the case of Maghribi traders, they created a "private order" institution based on trust. A key aspect was the repeat nature of relationships. Unlike the neoclassical one-off relationship, investors and agents often engaged in multiple transactions. There were two types of reputation. One depended upon God or an innate ideology of honesty; an agent signaled that he was trustworthy because he feared God or was inherently honest. The second mechanism "enables an agent to establish *ex ante* that his most profitable course ex post is to be honest. This mechanism allows an agent credibly to commit himself ex ante to be honest ex post. The merchant can thus trust the agent—the agent possesses a reputation as honest agent. The *geniza* reflects the importance of the second mechanism, where an agent remains honest out of desire to retain his position as an agent." Merchant-investors needed to make the agent's position attractive; the merchant-investor could do so by creating "a gap between the expected lifetime utility of an agent employed by him and the agent's best alternative elsewhere." Often this entailed giving an agent a premium, thereby raising the opportunity cost of cheating on the agreement. "The merchant would offer the agent an *optimal* premium—the lowest cost premium for which the long-run gain was not less than the short-run gain."

As an added inducement not to cheat, the coalition members could agree to ostracize an agent who cheated one of the coalition. In the case of a dishonest agent who was also an investor in some transactions, "coalition agents who cheated in their dealing with him will not be considered by other coalition members to have cheated. This implicit contract improves upon the simple reputation mechanism. It reduces the optimal premium that a merchant has to pay an agent to keep him honest, all other things being equal (since it reduces the probability that a cheater will be able to receive the premium somewhere else)."

These coalition members each created numerous links with other coalition members. With the widespread net of members, one of the duties of each member was to provide trade-related information, including prices, ship arrivals and departures, and other economic and political news. The information helped members make business decisions but also served as a check upon cheating by agents. With the flow of information, investors had a general idea of market conditions facing an agent; fellow members, knowing that an agent represented a member of the association, would send such information to the merchant-principal. With this flow of information, agents knew they were under scrutiny: "Without such monitoring…the reputation mechanism could not have functioned…if monitoring agents is costly, the merchant's claim that he will monitor [the agent] is not credible." If an agent knew the principal couldn't easily monitor him, the agent's temptation to cheat rose (Greif 1989, 864–868, 880).

Merchants need both technical ability and ethical behavior, as, "'Your actions are not those of a merchant,' was a reproach made to a business friend, when the writer was 'very angry' with him." From the Geniza records, however, there were few complaints about unethical activities. Goitein found that complaints of "tampering with the weight of shipments" were extremely rare, and most shippers paid their customs without deception. The shibboleth, "May God reward me for what I do with my fellow merchants. I do not aspire to a compensation from men," appeared to have been honored. Merchants often helped out fellows who were teetering upon bankruptcy. Authorities and prominent locals arranged loans, arbitration, and settlement of debts for merchants were struggling; sometimes merchants would donate cash to succor a bankrupt.

One of the prevalent lapses of ethics reflected in the Geniza letter was "the pernicious habits of procrastination and delay of payments." Often the more important the person, the more difficult it was to dun them for repayment. Although a domino analogy may be too simplistic, delaying payment to a creditor could jeopardize the creditor's ability to conduct business (causing him to delay payment to and injuring another person). Writers continually begged their correspondents to collect past-due payments. Creditors sometimes required collateral for loans, and the list of collateral was varied. Some poorer people pledged their children, an extremity exercised by people of all faiths in the Mediterranean (Goitein 1967, I:202–204, 258–259).

Conclusion

Islamic attitudes toward business ventures were both more and less benign than those of Christians. Moslems maintained a strict interpretation of usury laws that persisted well after the Catholic church loosened its strictures. For centuries, Moslem rulers demonstrated considerable tolerance for Jewish and Christian businesspeople, who exhibited talent and scruples. Islam often proved open-minded about non-believers advancing to positions of influence, often based upon their reputations for probity and honesty in business. Islam also took a more favorable view of business activities in general than did Christians.

Islamic ethics stressed the good of the community, and Muhammad emphasized the need for reform of wealthy people's disregard of the poor. To preserve harmony within the community, Islam prohibited a variety of business practices that could rupture the harmony and spark ill-will.

Notes

1. *Qur'an* (1997, 2:282) contained a passage that advised people to keep a written record of their debts.
2. The Jewish scholar Maimonides held somewhat similar views as Shafi'I (Udovitch 1970, 39).
3. *Riba* and *gharar* can be loosely translated respectively as interest and uncertainty.
4. Zinbarg presented a similar edict from the Laws of Manu: "if a man is unable to pay a debt and wishes to make a new contract, he may pay the interest that is due and turn around the legal instrument" (Buhler, *Laws of Manu* 8:154).

Bibliography

Armstrong, Karen. *Muhammad: A Biography of the Prophet* (San Francisco, CA: HarperSanFrancisco, 1992).

Bernstein, William. *A Splendid Exchange: How Trade Shaped the World* (New York: Grove Press, 2008).

Buhler, Georg, translator. *The Laws of Manu* (Delhi, India: Motilal Banarsidass, [1886] 1967). 50 vols. of Sacred Books of the East Series.

Bulliet, Richard. *The Camel and the Wheel* (New York, NY: Columbia University Press, 1990).

Dion, Michel. "Business Ethics and Spirituality among Jews, Christians, and Muslims." In *Ethics and Spirituality at Work: Hopes and Pitfalls of the Search for Meaning in Organizations*, edited by Thierry Pauchant (Westport, CT: Quorum Books, 2002), 159–167.

El-Gamal, Mahmoud. *Islamic Finance: Law, Economics, and Practice* (Cambridge, UK: Cambridge University Press, 2006).

Fischel, Walter. *Jews in the Economic and Political Life of Mediaeval Islam* (London, GB: Royal Asiatic Society for Great Britain and Ireland, [1937] 1968).

Fort, Timothy. *Prophets, Profits, and Peace: The Positive Role of Business in Promoting Religious Tolerance* (New Haven, CT: Yale University Press, 2008).

Goitein, Shelomo. *A Mediterranean Society: The Jewish Communities of the Arab World as Portrayed in the Documents of the Cairo Geniza* (Berkeley, CA: University of California Press, 1967). 6 vols.

Greif, Avner. "Reputation and Coalitions in Medieval Trade: Evidence on the Maghribi Traders." *Journal of Economic History* 49(4), December 1989, 857–882).

Inalcik, Halil. "Capital Formation in the Ottoman Empire." *Journal of Economic History* 29(1), March 1969, 97–140.

Labib, Subhi. "Capitalism in Medieval Islam." *The Journal of Economic History* 29(1), March 1969, 79–96,

Lieber, Alfred. "Eastern Business Practices and Medieval European Commerce." *Economic History Review New Series* 21(2), August 1968, 230–243.

Lopez, Robert. *The Commercial Revolution of the Middle Ages, 950–1350* (Englewood Cliffs, NJ: Prentice-Hall, 1971).

Masters, Bruce. *The Origins of Western Economic Dominance in the Middle East: Mercantilism and the Islamic Economy in Aleppo, 1600–1750* (New York, NY: New York University Press, 1988).

McMillan, John. *Reinventing the Bazaar: A Natural History of Markets* (New York, NY: W.W. Norton & Company, 2002).

Mottahedeh, Roy. *The Mantle of the Prophet: Religion and Politics in Iran* (New York, NY: Simon and Schuster, 1985).

Qur'an. *Interpretation of the Meanings of the Noble Qur'an in the English Language*, edited by Muhammad Taqi-ud-Din Al-Hilali (Riyadh, Saudi Arabia: Darussalam, 1997). Sixteenth Edition.

Rue, Loyal. *Religion Is Not About God: How Spiritual Traditions Nurture Our Biological Nature and What to Expect When They Fail* (New Brunswick, NJ: Rutgers University Press, 2005).

Saunders, John. *A History of Medieval Islam* (London, UK: Routledge and Kegan Paul, 1965).

Torrey, Charles. "The Commercial-Theological Terms in the Koran." Ph.D. Dissertation, University of Strasberg, 1892.

Udovitch, Abraham. *Partnership and Profit in Medieval Islam* (Princeton, NJ: Princeton University Press 1970).

Watson, Andrew. "The Arab Agricultural Revolution and Its Diffusion, 700–1100. *Journal of Economic History* 34(1), March 1974. 8–35.

Zinbarg, Edward. *Faith, Morals, and Money: What the World's Religions Tell Us about Money in the Marketplace* (New York, NY: Continuum, 2001).

CHAPTER 9

Medieval Business Ethics

Medieval Europe struggled in the wake of Rome's decline. Trade and commerce dwindled and became unimportant in most people's lives. The idea of engaging in such endeavors receded, and such participants that remained were usually held in disrepute.

The rediscovery of prominent Greek thinkers influenced medieval scholars. Thomas Aquinas and others distinguished between commutative and distributive justice in forming their opinions regarding the ethics of various business practices.

Medieval theologians and authorities focused on the "just price" and prohibition on taking interest from loans (usury). These topics reflected a tension between efficiency and perceived equity. Too strict a regime on curbing "unjust prices" or charging interest could hamper trade and even leave poor people, the putative beneficiaries, worse off. Societies decided how much efficiency to trade in return for a perceived improvement in equity. On occasion, however, intervention both decreased efficiency and diminished equity.

Modern-day economists often view the Catholic Church's shifting positions regarding lending at interest with skepticism and cynicism. They are perplexed at why the Church would enact such economically inefficient edicts that stymied economic growth.

This chapter focuses upon the usury issue. The following chapter examines the just price and its application, among other topics.

D. G. Surdam, *Business Ethics from Antiquity to the 19th Century*,
https://doi.org/10.1007/978-3-030-37165-4_9

Overview

Historian Henri Pirenne suggests that there was little trade and few merchants, in Europe with the decline of the Roman Empire. Ports in southern Europe continued to interact with "oriental" merchants, dealing in luxury goods but also, in the case of Marseilles, goods for general consumption. Gaul and Marseilles were major ports during the Merovingian years; Paris had some professional merchants operating in markets or bazaars in 585. Because of the decline in trade from the apogee of Rome's power, trade became more localized. The great demesnes disposed of their excess produce in the towns and cities (Pirenne [1925] 1974, 20–22, 45).

Traders and merchants in Europe regained importance after the decline of the Roman Empire. Many medieval lords remained contemptuous of trade in the eighth and ninth centuries. The lords were more interested in acquiring land and harvesting produce; they scorned traders and merchants but not the products put on sale. The medieval lords were not keen on economic growth that might have proved disruptive; instead they sought security and stability. The European commercial revolution that transpired after the tenth century resulted from an unanticipated chain of events in some Italian towns.

The Church owned much land throughout Europe. The clergy involved in overseeing these landholdings often became proficient "in collecting real and movable estates as in attracting devoted souls." They were less willing to engage in commerce. The clergy, too, hesitated to get involved with buying and selling. Society was bifurcated between the clergy and nobility versus the laborers. Merchants fell in between, as most clergy believed it was easier for paupers to enter Heaven than merchants; in fact, wealthy merchants needed paupers as objects of almsgiving to gain Heavenly favor, a weird symbiotic relationship, indeed. People emphasized consumption not production and indulged in largesse. How the small middle group of traders, artisans, and merchants succeeded, if inadvertently, required, "exceptional men in exceptional circumstances to break the spell and make commerce the most rapidly expanding, if not the largest frontier of the medieval West."

The animus toward commerce and trade held by Christian nobility sometimes took bizarre turns. Emperor Theophilus, ruler of Constantinople in 829, found out that "a beautiful merchant ship entering the port" belonged to his wife. He became angry and criticized her: "God made me an emperor, you would make me a ship captain!" He then commanded that ship and cargo be destroyed. Robert Lopez thought the emperor recalled the Roman law forbidding nobles to own ships for the purpose of commerce; the Byzantine code inherited such an attitude. The Byzantine code provided a rationale: "so that the plebians and merchants may more easily transact their affairs." Rather than view Theophilus' action as ridiculous, subsequent Byzantine historians lauded him (Lopez 1971, 56–60, 65–66).

Changing Medieval Thoughts Regarding Commerce

Libanius in the fourth century viewed seaborne commerce as beneficial. He lauded overseas trade's role in creating peaceful and mutually beneficial interaction between people of different regions. God distributed products across different regions, so that, "men might cultivate a social relationship because one would have the need of the help of another."

Libanius' ideas influenced two of his students, who became prominent Christian leaders: St. Basil and St. John Chrysostom. This outcome contained a measure of irony, given that Libanius was a pagan. Libanius, though, was more favorable toward commerce than many of the early Church leaders, who associated commerce and trade with fraud and exploitation because of the dangers of avarice and lust for luxury. By the fourteenth century with the growth of international fairs in Europe, some clergy returned to the idea that international trade was beneficial, with one stating, "God has wished that no country should be able to be completely self-sufficing....in order that they should all become united by friendly ties" (Viner 1972, 36–38).

Catholic thinkers rediscovered Aristotle in the thirteenth century and started developing ideas somewhat more favorable toward private enterprise. The idea that private property was not needed in Heaven but was useful on Earth in order to make life more tolerable proved persuasive. Some church thinkers began to view private property as better than a necessary evil, even something natural and good. Albert the Great favored private property as being for "the convenience and utility of man." His pupil, Thomas Aquinas, also embraced the Aristotelian idea that private property was, on utilitarian grounds, necessary.

Eventually the scholastics determined that, "an honest, modest, charitable merchant was indeed able to lead a good, Christian Life." The scholastics were not extending a blanket approval of merchants, as witnessed by the three adjectives. Another line of reasoning with regard to whether being a merchant was legitimate posed the question whether they were engaged in creative work. The early Christians placed a premium upon creative work. Some scholastics recognized and lauded merchants' ability and willingness to shift goods where plentiful to regions facing scarcity. Others referred to St. Augustine, who drew a distinction between trade and traders. Some traders were dishonest but such actions did not mean trade itself was disreputable. Scholastics eventually decided that honest merchants deserved the profits they made, assuming they had earned the profits honestly and in absence of fraud or deceit. The idea of "an honest, modest, charitable merchant" was paramount. A merchant should seek only a modest profit honestly acquired, only enough to sustain his needs and those of his family; merchants who sought, even honestly, large amounts of profits and wealth were not justified. Presumably any excess should be donated to charity (Little 1978, 176–179).

San Bernardino of Siena in the early fifteenth century held a more complicated view of merchants. True, he denounced greed and evil practices, but he recognized that merchants could and should possess some positive qualities that served both their Christian duty and their business endeavors. San Bernardino understood that merchants needed a combination of abilities, including diligence, "by which he means that they should be well informed about qualities, prices, and costs, and be 'subtle' in calculating risks, 'which few are able to do.'" Merchants also need to pay attention to details. He lamented the reality that traveling abroad meant that merchants neglected their wives and families, and he invoked the specter of "living in carnal sin or even in 'filth' with infidels as well as with believers." Despite his ambivalence with regard to merchants, San Bernardino believed they were entitled to compensation for their risk and labor, but such compensation was to be limited to these and no more, "because the only justification of profits lay in the service and utility of the commonweal." He recognized that merchants had to maintain meticulous records of their accounts; he urged them to balance their books annually if not more frequently. Among his other admonitions, he stated it was morally wrong to denigrate a rival's goods in order to sell one's own. He disliked bargaining, because bargainers often resorted to misrepresentation and blasphemies. "A seller should state his price and tell the buyer 'to take it or leave it'" (De Roover 1974b, 343–344).

Aquinas' Theories

By the thirteenth century, Thomas Aquinas and the scholastics based their theory of social justice upon a distinction between distributive and commutative justice. Distributive justice examined the individual in the context of the social order, so equality was not a paramount concern. Distributive justice, therefore, meant that individuals were, "entitled to a share of the goods of this world according to his station in life. …the basis of this distribution depended upon the social structure and could vary from one society to another." This was in contrast to commutative justice, which elevated the "principle of absolute equality [between individuals], since justice required that the thing delivered be the equivalent of the thing received. Consequently, the exchange of goods, as in buying and selling, was within the province of commutative justice. Hence the latter applied to the theory of value and price" (De Roover 1951, 495–496).

Moralists made points regarding the sinfulness of trade. Chrysostom thought it was wrong to sell something that had not been altered, presumably improved, for gain. The process of trying to buy as cheaply or sell as dearly as possible was inherently sinful. Saint Jerome warned of priests acting as merchants and transforming their poverty into prosperity. Aquinas tempered these warnings by identifying such actions as the vices of the particular traders and not of the occupation. He then made the distinction that it was okay to provide necessities but simply trading for the sake of gain was wrong, unless the gain is to be used for something honorable.

Dealing with specific situations, Aquinas considered the question whether a seller was required to reveal information not of his product's quality but also of availability of similar goods. Aquinas conjured the scenario whereby a trader brought wheat to a market, where the supply was skimpy. The trader knew that other people were bringing wheat to the market, an event that would lower the price considerably. Was the trader duty-bound to inform the buyers that there were wagonloads behind him? Aquinas concluded the trader did not have to divulge the information, although doing so would be the virtuous thing.[1] With regard to revealing defects, Aquinas differed from Saint Ambrose, who argued that faults were destined to become known at some point. What duties did the seller owe the buyer? Aquinas identified three cases: a defect in substance, a defect in measurement, or a defect in quality. If the seller sold a defective product, he had to make restitution. If he sold an item with a defect that he was genuinely unaware of at the time, he was still required to make restitution, but at least he had not sinned. Aquinas thought it just, if a seller kept quiet about secret faults of an article that would unduly lower the price, even though the concealment and defect did not cause peril or loss to anyone. He also thought that obvious defects, such as a one-eyed horse, absolved the seller of having to reveal the defect. Historian William Ashley thought Aquinas' explanations were a concession to the growing commercial spirit of the medieval period (Ashley 1913, 140–147).

Aquinas draws some very fine distinctions. In dealing with Question 77—"fraud committed in the course of buying and selling"—he generally casts buying and then reselling a commodity as wrong. However, people who initially purchased with the intent of consuming the good themselves but, who subsequently changed their mind, "is not strictly engaging in a commercial transaction, even though he is now asking a higher price. And he is entitled to do this either because he has improved the thing in some fashion, or because prices have gone up in response to local changes or the lapse of time, or because he has incurred risks in transporting it about or in having it delivered. In such cases neither the purchase nor the sale is unjust." This passage is fascinating in its parsing "just" and "unjust" resale. The clause about prices having gone up in the interim is especially striking, as many people would consider it wrong to make such a windfall profit. Modern economists would say that the opportunity cost of continuing to use the now-more expensive good has increased, even though the purchase price remained the same. The lapse of time argument also smacks of contradicting the argument surrounding charging interest, although admittedly Aquinas is referring to reselling goods and not money (Aquinas 1964, 38:229–231; Viner 1978, 82).

Aquinas viewed private ownership of property as necessary because people "more intently tend to things if they possess them, rather than the goods or duties being held in common; second, because possession promotes order rather than confusion, as responsibility can be established; and third, private possession promotes peace, since 'quarrels arise more frequently where there is no division of the things possessed.'" Aquinas, though, also believed that "the use of goods must be in common, or must be at the service of the common good, so that man 'is ready to communicate them to others in their need.'" He cited the Apostle Paul's admonition, "Charge the rich of this world…to give easily."[2]

Aristotle and Aquinas also claimed that property be transferrable, either through a "purely gratuitous transfer" or by selling and buying, renting, loaning, and so on. Scholastics' defense of private property did encounter an exception. A person driven by extremity could steal necessities in order to sustain life. Such drastic situations, of course, should not arise if the wealthy fulfilled their responsibility to succor the poor (Dougherty 2003, 487–488; 1 Timothy, 6:17, 18; Little 1978, 179).

Theologians Struggle with Usury

The scholastics' great weakness was their usury doctrine. Historian Raymond de Roover argued that the Scholastics and later Schoolmen overemphasized the usury question. Early in the Middle Ages, loans were primarily made for consumption purposes, but as business became more sophisticated and widespread, "[the usury doctrine] became a source of increasing embarrassment. Tied to their definition, the Doctors was [sic] sucked deeper and deeper into a quagmire of contractions. It is not that the Church ever seriously hampered business investments, but practical necessity placed before the moralists the well-nigh impossible task of legitimizing means for taking interest while safeguarding the principle that loans were gratuitous contracts" (De Roover 1974a, 318).

When harvests failed, peasants faced unenviable choices. They faced starvation or they could take out a consumption loan. A peasant could be forced to repay a loan by selling grain before it was harvested at set prices. Often the peasant lost control over their land. Robert Lopez observed, though, that transfer of land from inefficient to efficient owners benefited society, although individual (former) landowners were worse off. Even larger landowners, however, could find themselves dispossessed of land (Lopez 1971, 156).

Before confronting a choice between famine and consuming seed corn, peasants could try to borrow from manorial lords (in a sense, the lord acted as a "lender of last resort" or as an insurer), selling off assets such as land. They could resort to theft, riots, or rebellion or rely upon Church insurance schemes, charity, or taking loans at high rates of interests. Many of these choices had obvious drawbacks and could leave poor families worse off than before. The Church, of course, provided a variety of social programs, but in an economy where the surpluses were small, the ability to alleviate widespread suffering was sometimes overwhelmed. Poor families might have relied upon extended family, but such help was likely insufficient. Another expectation for wealthy landowners was to donate to the church: "feudal lords granted land to the Church with the expectation that the Church would maintain social order by guaranteeing sustenance to the poor." When landowners perceived that the Church failed to maintain its end of the bargain, a king such as Henry VIII could strip it of its land (Reed and Bekar 2003, 353; see also Le Goff [1986] 2004, 25).

Europe's fixation on usury was not shared everywhere. The Western Zhou Dynasty (1046–771 BCE) differed from western civilizations in that it openly practiced usury for certain types of loans. Loans made so that people could fulfill the needs of sacrifices to the gods or for funeral rites were not charged interest, although there was an expectation of quick repayments. Loans for productive activities, however, required the payment of interest that was "calculated on the basis of the tax payments the debtor generally owed." The rates of interest charged under the monopolized usurious lending was often omitted from the official documents. Although no definitive historical sources exist, private usury probably existed; there appears to have been no explicit law prohibiting even private usury. Thus the Western Zhou Dynasty differed from European and Islamic practices (Hu 1988, 10–12).

Church and lay officials, though, were trying to balance the needs of the traders (and economic growth) with the necessity of protecting the mass of poor people seeking consumption loans on a recurring basis. Historian Richard Tawney painted a poignant picture: "For loans are made largely for consumption, not for production. The farmer whose harvest fails or whose beasts die, or the artisan who loses money, must have credit, seed-corn, cattle, raw materials, and his distress is the money lender's opportunity. Naturally, there is a passionate popular sentiment against the engrosser who holds a town to ransom, the monopolist who brings the livings of many into the hands of one, the money-lender who takes advantage of his neighbor's necessities to get a lien on their land and foreclose." Medieval historian James Davis indicated that the evidence strongly suggests Church officials were cognizant of the dilemma facing poor people (Tawney 1926, 37–39; Davis 2012, 68).

Some scholars view the Roman Catholic edicts on usury as a means to promote consumption smoothing. Economists Clyde Reed and Cliff Bekar characterize the Church's strategy as relying on: charity and informal pooling in providing economy-wide consumption smoothing and averting social/economic crises, and the Church's use of usury prohibitions to create a negative tie-in between salvation and consumption lending at interest (Reed and Bekar 2003, 348).[3]

In dire cases, peasants offered to pay interest, but Aquinas denied that if a borrower voluntarily contracted to give interest on a loan, it was not usury. Aquinas appeared to think that borrowers were at the mercy of lenders with respect to bargaining power. He pronounced a borrower, who agreed to borrow at interest, sinful. He admitted that lenders may contract for compensation in the case of a loss on the capital lent, but he condemned compensation for "surrendering the possibility of gain which otherwise might have been procured through the use of the money lent." He stated, "He must not sell that which he has not yet and may be prevented in many ways from having." Jacob Viner described some inconsistencies in Aquinas' analysis of usury. Medieval traders sometimes charged more for credit sales than for cash sales. The additional sum was to compensate for the deferred payment, but Aquinas considered this usury. On the other hand, if the seller offered a rebate to induce earlier payment, this was not usury (Viner 1978, 93–94; Aquinas 1964, 38:233–253).

Loans for investment purposes were handled differently. Merchants willingly lent money to tenants; they understood the needs of the tenants and often extended reasonable, mutually beneficial terms (Lopez 1971, 156).

The strictures against usury ebbed and flowed across the centuries. During the mid-thirteenth century, canon lawyer Sinibaldo Fieschi (the future Pope Innocent IV) asserted that usury should be prohibited, because it produced the evils of poverty while corrupting the soul. He associated usury with avarice. Aquinas, echoing Aristotle, used a sophisticated argument that "selling" the substance of and use of money was inherently fraudulent, as the lender was selling something, "that does not exist or sells the same thing twice" (Little 1978, 180). But even as these scholars wrote, other scholars noticed that Roman law allowed interest in the form of a penalty paid by the borrower who was delinquent. Scholastics studying Roman law made a rather fine distinction between interest that was not intrinsic to the loan, but simply incidental to the loan. The justice of the penalty was that the lender may have been placed in a worse financial position because of the dilatory repayment than if he had not made the loan at all. Such a loophole was denoted as *poena conventionalis* (standard punishment) (Mele 1999, 180–181).

The Salamanca School of the fifteenth and sixteenth centuries recognized opportunity costs inherent with lending. During the thirteenth century, the definition of usury evolved so that the term meant only lending at exorbitant rates of interest. A legal historian, though, highlighted the fact that usury cases in the royal courts demonstrated that even moderate profits on money loans or sales on credit was sufficient for conviction. On the other hand, the Church and secular courts often dealt informally (but effectively) with manifest usurers while infrequently pursuing moderate usury. Davis thought the Church's policy might have been a recognition that "communities wanted to protect certain sources of credit provided at moderate rates" (Gilchrist 1969, 67–70; Seabourne 2003, 32–34; Davis 2012, 214–215).[4]

The *poena conventionalis* spurred legal scholars to insinuate it within the laws pertaining to loans. At first, some scholars deemed *poena conventionalis* as legal but that the penalty be paid to the poor rather than to the original lender. Another avenue justifying *poena conventionalis* or other forms of interest was *lucrum cessans* (profit ceasing), a situation where the lender lost out on profits during the time his money was out on loan. Scholars grappled with this concept. Eventually Aquinas and other scholars gradually came to accept *lucrum cessans* and *damnum emergens* (loss occurring, because of a loan) as justifiable compensation to a lender, "on the basis of the utility of money and the just price of its value" (Little 1978, 181).[5]

Acceptance of the *lucrum cessans* idea, which is somewhat similar to the modern-day economic idea of opportunity cost, caused consternation among canonists and theologians. A historian wrote, "that to admit *lucrum cessans* as a valid title would throw the doors wide open to usury. Most of them, therefore, including Thomas Aquinas, initially rejected this title." Sant'Antonio (early thirteenth century) and some others, though, gave it some approval, but the lender must have incurred a loss or damage from being deprived of his capital. If a lender merely intended to keep his capital inactive, he was not entitled to compensation. One theologian added the caveat that *lucrum cessans* did not entitle the merchant a maximum profit but only a probable profit.[6]

While theologians grappled with the issue of usury, laypeople held their own beliefs. Robert Lopez notes that medieval people distrusted and despised "alien moneymakers." They perceived such lenders as making money "with nothing but a pen and an inkpot." Peasants and kings believed that the lenders bled them of their material wealth (Lopez 1971, 166). Such sentiments persist, as modern-day people view financiers as making money from paper transactions and not from real labor.

The *Ayenbite of Inwyt* contains a lengthy discussion of the evils of usury, the practice falling under the heading, "The Fifth Head of the Beast."

Usury is a form of avarice and covetousness. The first root is usury and has seven "outcastings" described graphically (Michael 1889, 28–30).

Medieval thinkers displayed considerable imagination in concocting torments for usurers and corrupt people. Historian Lester Little described a particularly nasty variation of "The Myth of Sisyphus"; in this case, the protagonist was a corrupt lawyer. This character was forced to swallow burning coins while being tortured with an iron cart-wheel, "studded with spikes and nails, against his back and whirled it around." This discomfiture caused him to vomit the burning coins, whereupon he was forced to swallow them again, starting the cycle anew. The motif of swallowing burning coins appeared to have been a popular depiction of the fate awaiting the avaricious (Little 1978, 39–40).

Enforcement of Usury Laws

Depending on when a lender lived, the church's strictures against usury might or might not have led to excommunication and other unpleasantness. Clyde Reed and Cliff Bekar identify six phases of the church's evolving attitude toward usury. Between 500 and 1050, usury was a vague concept and what prohibitions existed applied to clerics.[7] Thereafter until 1175, the church cited Old and New Testament passages to define usury in a broad way, including a "desire for a return beyond the good itself," as sinful. The church recognized potential evasions of the law by also defining charging higher prices for credit instead of cash sales as usury. Restitution was mandatory to avoid damnation. Between 1175 and 1350, the church employed more drastic measures to eradicate usury, including refusal of sacraments and excommunications. Reed and Bekar believe social policy motivated the church's more explicit stance against usury: "First, the only individuals or groups singled out by the Church for public denunciation and punishment were lenders dealing primarily in consumption loans. Second usury prohibitions restricted the flow of loanable funds into consumption lending, but not into other uses." The Church's efforts against usury dwindled between 1350 and 1500, as withholding sacraments from professional usurers became less prevalent, and some loan contracts became permissible. Usury became associated with charging excessive interest rates. The church also began helping the poor secure access to credit by creating the *monti di pieta*, private pawnshops backed by charitable donations. The Church allowed interest charges on these loans to defray expenses. In the wake of the Reformation, the pendulum swung back toward strict interpretation of usury as a sin meriting severe punishment; after 1600, though, theologians began revising the interpretation of usury laws. By 1830, the Sacred Penitentiary "issued instructions to confessors not to disturb penitents who lend money at the legal rate of interest" (Reed and Bekar 2003, 350–351; De Roover 1942, 104–105, 151); 1974a, 306–335.

Reed and Bekar hint that Church officials were cogent of the potential drawbacks of discouraging loans for investment purposes. Strict prohibition of lending at interest for investments would retard economic development that suppressed incomes and possibly charitable giving while possibly boosting the demand for charity.[8] Another scholar wrote that giving to the Church or to the poor was a way to redeem sins: "It was the solemn duty of those who exercised power and of those involved in lucrative activities, especially activities of a morally dubious nature, such as money-lending" (Reed and Bekar 2003, 364–365; Geremek 1994, 23).[9]

Ways to Evade and to Foil Evasions of Usury Edicts

Because lending at interest was so mutually advantageous for borrowers (as opposed to not getting a loan at all) and lenders, people tried evading the usury laws. A common tactic was to charge a penalty for late payment; such "late" payment might be agreed upon in advance as a connivance. Sometimes, though, courts mandated a penalty for late repayment. Courts and clerics alike realized that lenders were unable to use the money they lent for potentially profitable ventures. Lenders, moreover, charged interest at some risk to themselves. Edward I, for instance, evicted the Jews from his kingdom in 1290 and pontificated that the Jews had "wickedly conspired and conceived a new species of usury more pernicious than the old" (Seabourne 2003, 60). On occasion, those accused of usury took their accusers to court for slander. At times, convicted usurers were punished by humiliation, such as being led through the city, "with their heads uncovered, unshod and without girdle, upon horses without saddles" (Davis 2012, 213; see also Lopez and Raymond [1955] 1970, 157–158).

Professional moneylenders were in an advantageous position to surreptitiously charge interest. Contracts of exchange (*cambium*) arose to spare merchants the inconvenience and risk of carrying large sums of money during their travels. The complicated nature of currency exchange afforded unscrupulous (with respect to the usury laws) parties means by which to hide interest payments within the currency exchange rates. Although unanticipated changes in the exchange rates might upset the intent, interested parties could use the *cambium et recambium* (exchange and reexchange) to protect against such fluctuations. These contracts, somewhat similar to today's use of hedging, eliminated the speculative risk. The contracts were known as *ricorsa* (dry exchange). Most of the sales of bills of exchange were legitimate, but many were fictitious. Scholastics debated whether dry exchange was licit, but such contracts were common in the money market from the Middle Ages to the eighteenth century. In modern times, the practice died out, although some Islamic banking practices are very similar (Lopez and Raymond [1955] 1970, 162–163; Poitras 2000, 234–237).

But merchants were not above deceptive practices, especially with regard to usury. A government desperate for funds could buy goods and pay a higher price than necessary to the merchant and then resell the goods for cash, accepting a lower price. A variation on this was for "distressed sovereigns…[to] find much-needed cash by accepting part of a loan in overrated jewels or diamonds which they then had to peddle around at disastrous prices." Lenders also resorted to charging interest disguised as "service charges," a tactic used in modern pay-day loan businesses. During the thirteenth century, businesses began to reduce concealment of interest rates; they did not use the term "interest," although they used various euphemisms. But with the edict enacted by Pope Clement V in 1312, lenders again donned their cloaks of secrecy. The canon on usury was not often enforced but risk-averse lenders took precautions (De Roover 1974c, 125, 137–140).

Despite church strictures, the gains from new forms of business tactics and specialization proved overwhelming. The economic surge resulted in explicit interest being written into contracts, usury laws or not. Late medieval church officials more commonly possessed business experience and more realistic views. Pope Innocent III and Thomas Aquinas urged moderation in enforcing the Third Lateran council rules, with Aquinas making a rather pragmatic observation, "Human laws leave certain sins unpunished because of the imperfection of men; many useful things would disappear, in fact, if all improper operations were rigorously forbidden. This is why civil legislation has at times tolerated usury, not because usury is thought to be just but so as not to hinder the advantages that so many derive from it." During the thirteenth century, civil and church authorities were choosing not to prosecute usurers, as the authorities were benefiting from usurers, whether through licensing fees, accepting offerings from usurers, or absolving usurers without requiring restitution. Instead of restitution, wealthy businessmen opted to make ostentatious displays of generosity; usury laws increasingly focused on the petty usurer, the pawnbroker on the corner (Aquinas 1964, 38:217, 237; Little 1978, 212–213).

The church found it difficult to deter usurious lenders, admitting such at the Second Council of Lyons. Instead of stopping the usurer during his life, the church focused on getting a confession near the end of his life in preparation of his will.

The church had different penalties for Jew and Christian or layman and cleric. A key distinction between usurers was whether the lender was a manifest usurer, "peculiarly liable to the strictest sanctions in the episcopal courts, the so-called external forum." If, instead, the usurer was an "occult usurer," the church used moral suasion to persuade the usurer to make restitution. The "public manifest usurer" was typically someone whose usury was easily proved, such as operating a pawnshop, or someone who confessed to his crimes. Jurists agreed that "rumor alone is insufficient to convict a public usurer." By the thirteenth and fourteenth centuries, manifest usurers were being compared with prostitutes in a brothel. Such usurers might live in a particular part of town and were willing to lend to all. The bigger players in the usury games were bankers and international merchants, who were discreet in their activities and were available only to a few selected customers. What appalled the church authorities most, then, were the visibility and notoriety of such activities. For such as the Medici, the church was willing to look the other way (while accepting loans at interest from the Medici).

One ironic outcome was that eventually these wealthy merchants bequeathed various religious organizations and other charities out of the periodic interest payments they received from their loans or from government bonds. The leading families of Italy endowed artists, various charities and religious causes, while maintaining a reputation for being humanists; these families often donated money, not out of fear of damnation, but out of regard for "service to society," pride, and conviction "of their worthiness in the sight of God" (Nelson 1947, 104–108, 118–119; see also Ashley 1913, 150).

Besides the occasional, penny-ante, usurers, there were regular, large-scale usurers. One could paraphrase Mario Puzo's epigraph to apply to the Church's attitude toward these big-time usurers: "Behind every cathedral lies a crime of usury." The Church was anxious to cultivate favor with the wealthy lenders, since these worthies had convenient pools of capital from which to borrow. Sociologist Benjamin Nelson observed, "Men of the Middle Ages were not oblivious to the fact that many a usurer succeeded in giving the color of philanthropy to what ought rightly to have appeared as restitution." St. Antonius of Florence, in the early fifteenth century, dubbed this, "distributive restitution," a restoring of what the usurer unjustly received. Writers and other observers did, indeed, bemoan the rampant hypocrisy of clergy "of being more intent on gathering tainted moneys for the sake of financing church construction than upon expediting a genuine return of illicit goods to the actual victims of usury" (Nelson 1947, 111).[10]

Merchants in maritime centers such as Genoa and Venice had more attractive alternatives to lending money at interest than did similar men in Lombardy and Tuscany. Merchants in Genoa and Venice began placing their capital into commercial partnerships, maritime loans, and insurance. All of the merchants, however, became savvy in portraying themselves as earning their profits because of their virtuous "abstinence, enterprise, risk, and divine favor." These men were proud of their professions. Despite their assertions of probity and virtue, a few, from time to time, were forced to provide restitutions on their death beds. Nelson suggests that these few were still haunted by the possibility of eternal damnation for their acts of usury.

The case of Jehan Boine Broke of Douai in 1286–1287, however, showed that even prominent financiers still could face ecclesiastical interrogation. Prior to his death, he left a lengthy list of people he owed restitution. In the main, however, the public and the church authorities distinguished between manifest usurers and merchant-financiers. Florentine merchant-financiers, for instance, were international traders, public officials, confidants of rulers and popes, and benefactors. Cases such as Boine Broke, however, appeared to be less common during the thirteenth century, and Nelson believed the diminution in such restitutions revealed that in Italy, at least, businessmen were gaining in influence versus the clerics and there arose "a clear distinction between the manifest usurer and mercantile elite."[11] Despite the strictures on usury, the papacy was willing to borrow from Italian merchants and bankers at interest rates ranging from 15 to 20%. Such famous banking families as the Medici extended loans and helped the papacy collect taxes and dues from princes, laity, and clergy, as well as providing other services. Church leaders borrowed from Christian, Jewish, foreign, and local lenders. The theologians' cogent arguments notwithstanding, the church often found itself requiring loans at interest. The payment of interest by church authorities was not considered a violation of the tenets regarding usury, as most canonists did not believe it "unlawful to pay interest in case of necessity" (Nelson 1947, 113–117).

Risks of Being Jewish Lenders

Jewish lenders occupied an uneasy perch. Presumably the Deuteronomy verse (23:19–21) allowing the Israelites to charge non-Israelites interest was still in force, but some Christian theologians believed Jewish lenders should be subject to the usury prohibitions. Scholars have pointed out that since charging interest for business purposes seemed inevitable, it probably wasn't feasible to close off Jewish lenders. Some rulers discovered they could exploit the Jewish lenders by offering them legal rights similar to Christians but only upon paying for these privileges via hefty taxes. Pope Nicholas V (1452) granted a dispensation that explicitly permitted Jewish lenders to charge interest (Gilchrist 1969, 111–112).

With the loosening of the strictures on usury, Christian rulers decided they no longer needed their Jewish lenders, and they therefore banished them from England and France in 1290 and 1306. The kings then resorted to Christian bankers. Despite the relaxed attitude toward usury, many successful merchant-bankers hedged their bets, so to speak, and made copious donations to the church and other religious institutions. Businessmen also had their patron saint, in Francis, who had been a merchant of sorts (apparently he worked in his father's silk business). One scholar stated, "Oh, how much good hope there must be for merchants, who have such a merchant intermediary with God" (Little 1978, 216–217).

Jews faced sporadic pogroms, sometimes at the instigation of a government. Lester Little pointed out that during such pogroms, governments valued Jewish financial records, in order to dun borrowers of amounts owed Jews. "No such interest restrained the perpetrators of the relatively unorganized pogroms." In fact, the typical debtor probably desired to see the written evidence of their loans destroyed. Little suggested that the hatred Christians felt toward Jews had a psychological basis, in that Christian guilt regarding attaining profits was projected (and magnified) onto the Jews (who were, of course, interested in profits). Unscrupulous rulers could use such feelings to wring money from the Jews. Peter the Venerable proclaimed that Jews should pay for the crusade of 1149; he claimed that Jews were wealthy but that they did not work. The latter phrase played upon the stereotype common people held toward moneylenders and merchants: Jews (and merchants) did not work the land or engage in honorable labor. Jews allegedly got the money "by stealing from Christians and by receiving goods stolen from Christians by thieves." Little acknowledged that, aside from the baseless accusation regarding stealing, "this was an essentially accurate, if rough, description of those who were successful in the new economy," whether Jewish or Christian. But even church officials, such as St. Bernard, repeated the canard that Jews controlled the entire money trade; accusing the Jews meant that less attention would be paid to errant Christian moneylenders. Sometimes people blurred the two identities, as when St. Bernard wrote, "that where there are no Jews, Christian moneylenders 'Jew,' or 'Judaise,' worse than Jews, if indeed these men may be called Christians and not rather baptized Jews" (Little 1978, 54–55; see also Baer 1966, I:85–90).

Pawnshops

One way to evade the strictures on usury was resort to a pawnshop. Barbarus, the Governor of Perugia, established the first public pawnshop in 1461 (*mons pietatis*); the pawnshops made small loans charging 6% interest that was used to cover the expenses of safekeeping and administrative costs. Within a few decades, there were scores of *montes pietatis* throughout Italy. Later the *montes pietatis* assumed bank-like services such as deposits. The success of the *montes pietatis* aroused the envy of the Italian rulers, who in 1625 forced the *montes pietatis* to act as state "piggy banks," so to speak. Other governments created their own *montes pietatis* (Poitras 2000, 44–45).

Although most Christians obeyed the Church's strictures regarding usury to some degree, the Lombards proved willing to engage in pawnbroking, a particularly odious form of lending even in the Middle Ages. "A pawnshop was entitled to the same grudging toleration as a house of prostitution." Earthly authorities might not intervene, but the general belief was that such practitioners were destined for Hell, unless they repented and paid restitution to the Church, "stewardess of the poor." Although the Lombards charged high rates of interest, these rates were comparable to modern payday loan vendors, and the Lombards likely faced greater risks of default. In any event, the Lombards proved stiff competition for Jewish pawnbrokers (Lopez 1971, 77).

The church also created *montes pietatis*. The Dominicans, however, charged the *monte pietatis* with practicing usury, because the charges were levied upfront and were taken from the truly indigent. Lateran V rebutted the Dominicans and said the "Inter multiplices" permitted the *montes*; historian John Gilchrist noted how far church thinking had strayed from the view that, "Usury means nothing else than gain or profit drawn from the use of a thing that is by its nature sterile, *a profit that is acquired without labour, cost, or risk*."

The church-run pawnshops solved the problem of a lack of consumer credit for the workers and the poor. The poor certainly needed credit; the pawnbrokers and money lenders were proof enough of the need. The Church's prohibition upon charging interest for consumption loans—similar to modern-day usury laws—had the perverse effect of driving out legitimate pawnbrokers and money lenders and forcing the poor to rely on less savory sources of credit, often at much higher rates of interest. "The canonists and theologians overlooked the fact…professional pawnbrokers performed a service that called for a proper recognition. Here alone is where the Church's usury laws had their greatest effect, and it was a moral and social rather than an economic disaster that resulted. The masses blamed the Church for their plight, and the *montes pietatis* came too late to save the Church in regions other than in Italy and Spain, where they were most widespread" (Gilchrist 1969, 115, 121).

Naturally, the scruffier small pawnbrokers and moneylenders were reviled and often prosecuted by the fifteenth and sixteenth centuries. These were the manifest usurers. Benjamin Nelson characterized the church's and public officials' attitude as opportunistic. When it was convenient, Italian authorities evicted the Jewish usurers, in part, to foster the growth of the *monti di pieta*. The contrast between small-time pawnbroker (often Jewish) and merchant prince was pronounced, and the latter was esteemed, or at least respected, for their acts of cultural largesse. Some few started as small-time operators and ended up as merchant princes: "Such miracles of social chemistry are the harbinger of the modern era." There was an unanticipated consequence of the merchant princes' deflection of opprobrium and church punishment: "Modern capitalism could not come of age so long as the agents of church and state were able or especially disposed to require merchants and financiers to disgorge their 'usuries' and 'ill-gotten gains.'" Nelson concluded that attribution of European economic stagnation to church doctrines was overstated, "It was the church's willing assistance to and unwilling compromises with merchants and financiers that helped convert the merchant-usurers of the twelfth and thirteenth centuries into the merchant princes of the Renaissance."

These merchant princes chose to disburse donations during their lifetimes and not just on their deathbeds. They deliberated on what appeals for charity to assist, "with the intention of reaping the greatest returns in service and good will. Such systematic liberality is a far cry from the older practice of showering innumerable petty gifts on widely scattered establishments" (Nelson 1947, 120–122).

Protestant Attitudes Toward Usury

Some Europeans began to question the usury laws. Jean Calvin took a nuanced view of usury. He distinguished between charging interest in the course of a business and being a professional, full-time usurer. Finance professor Geoffrey Poitras argues that Calvin revolutionized thinking about lending at interest. Calvin associated lending at interest with the Golden Rule. Such action was legal if it did not exceed any official maximum, if no interest was charged to the poor, and if neither party to the interest-bearing loan gained an excessive advantage. He stipulated that borrowing and lending be sporadic and not be main activities; under these conditions, lenders could levy "reasonable interest" upon borrowing merchants.

Merchants, lawyers, and the business community wasted no time in quoting Calvin and refuting the scholastics, but reversing usury edicts took time. The scholastics and their allies retreated slowly across the centuries. Even so, by the late sixteenth century, Benjamin Nelson quipped, "we are no longer in the atmosphere of the confessional; we are in the counting house" (Poitras 2000, 10; Nelson [1949] 1969, 77–78, 82–83).

Usury laws gradually receded. By the time Adam Smith wrote *Wealth of Nations*, most people probably agreed with him that the laws were undesirable. Smith argued that prohibiting usury simply increased the evils of usury, since desperate (or not-so-desperate) debtors had to pay an extra penalty for borrowing from lenders who faced potential punishment for usury. Smith carried the argument further to include the drawbacks of putting a binding limit on the rate of interest that could be charged. Usury laws receded faster in England and Holland than in France and Italy. In some cases, usury laws evolved from prohibition to legal limits as to the maximum rates allowable. Since governments were often large debtors, the legal maximum rates may have been more a concern for the governments' finances than for lenders' souls (Smith 1981, 356–357; Poitras 2000, 98, 101).

Conclusion

It is easy for modern-day economists to marvel at the medieval theologians and authorities' edicts regarding usury. Usury was a price control upon loans. The standard prediction was that such a binding price control—and price controls are rarely more binding than a zero price—should have stymied the efficient working of the lending market, injuring borrowers and lenders. For the impoverished person, the absence of a legal interest rate meant taking one's chances with usurers, who, in turn, faced the risks of detection and punishment. The end result was that borrowers paid more and lenders ran risks of church- and civil-imposed sanctions. For borrowers interested in obtaining loans for business endeavors, the usury laws increased the friction within the economy, making the economy less productive.

The Church recognized that loans at interest had to exist, lest the economy grind to a halt. The church also needed to balance the needs of lenders with the interests of the poor, a balancing act facing authorities across time and place. The Church, too, found itself at times lender or borrower.

Notes

1. See Goitein for a similar discussion on the constraint placed on the first shipper to reach a port (1967, I:201).
2. These justifications of property rights presage economist Ronald Coase's stress upon well-defined property rights.
3. If a state or church provided a guaranteed minimum income, poor people might undertake too risky ventures than they otherwise would. Enacting a usury prohibition could ameliorate the assumption of "too much" risk (Reed and Bekar 2003, 349–350; Posner 1995, 301–302).
4. Gilchrist noted that even "gratuitous loans" were not what they appeared (Gilchrist 1969, 67–68).
5. Giles of Lessines followed Aquinas in using natural law in discussing usury. Of more interest was Giles' justification of moneychangers, whose work he considered useful and convenient. He interpreted Christ's scourging of the moneylenders in the temple as directed to the act taking place in the temple—a holy place reserved for spiritual matters—and to not the moneylending itself (Little 1978, 182; Poitras 2000, 87–88 regarding *poena*).

6. Julius Kirshner wrote in the Introduction to De Roover (1974c, 29–30).
7. John Noonan developed two periods: 750–1050 and 1050–1175 (Noonan 1958, 14–17).
8. Economists interpreted the church's varying stances toward usury as exploiting monopolistic power or serving the public interest (Ekelund et al. 1989, 308, 322–323; Glaeser and Sheinkman 1998, 2–5, 9–10, 20–23).
9. Was it ethical for Church leaders to create this ambiguity in order to induce charitable giving? Was deception or obfuscation acceptable?
10. Such willingness not to vet potential donors has haunted many a philanthropic organization, including universities. Selling naming rights to big donors has, on occasion, resulted in embarrassment for the institution, when the donor gets convicted in federal court for business illegalities.
11. Nelson recalled Shakespeare's portrayal of "Shylock, the public usurer, whether or not a Jew, and Antonio, the devout merchant, who proudly boasts that he 'doth neither lend nor borrow upon Advantage'" (Nelson 1947, 117). Robert Lopez characterized Boine Broke as "one of the most wicked exploiters and usurers that has ever lived" (Lopez 1971, 137).

Bibliography

Aquinas, Thomas. *Summa Theologiae* (New York, NY: Blackfriars, 1964). 60 vols.

Ashley, William J. *An Introduction to English Economic History and Theory. Part 1: The Middle Ages* (New York, NY: Longmans, Green, 1913). 9th Edition.

Baer, Yitzhak. *A History of the Jews in Christian Spain. Volume I: From the Age of Reconquest to the Fourteenth Century* (Philadelphia, PA: Jewish Publication Society of America, 1966).

Davis, James. *Medieval Market Morality: Life, Law and Ethics in the English Marketplace, 1200–1500* (Cambridge, UK: Cambridge University Press, 2012).

De Roover, Raymond. "Money, Banking and Credit in Mediaeval Bruges." *Journal of Economic History* 2(1), December 1942, 52–65.

De Roover, Raymond. "Monopoly Theory Prior to Adam Smith: A Revision." *Quarterly Journal of Economics* 65(4), November 1951, 492–524.

De Roover, Raymond. "Scholastic Economics: Survival and Lasting Influence from the Sixteenth Century to Adam Smith." In *Business, Banking, and Economic Thought in Late Medieval and Early Modern Europe* (Chicago, IL: University of Chicago Press, 1974a), 306–335.

De Roover, Raymond. "The Scholastic Attitude toward Trade and Entrepreneurship." In *Business, Banking, and Economic Thought in Late Medieval and Early Modern Europe* (Chicago, IL: University of Chicago Press, 1974b), 336–345.

De Roover, Raymond. *Business, Banking, and Economic Thought in Late Medieval and Early Modern Europe* (Chicago, IL: University of Chicago Press, 1974c).

Dougherty, Richard. "Catholicism and the Economy: Augustine and Aquinas on Property Ownership." *Journal of Markets and Morality* 6(2), Fall 2003, 479–495.

Ekelund, Robert Jr., Robert Hebert, and Robert Tollison. "An Economic Model of the Medieval Church: Usury as a Form of Rent Seeking." *Journal of Law, Economics, & Organization* 5(2), Autumn 1989, 307–331.

Geremek, Bronislaw. *Poverty: A History* (Oxford, UK: Blackwell, 1994).

Gilchrist, John. *The Church and Economic Activity in the Middle Ages* (London, UK: Macmillan, 1969).

Glaeser, Edward and Jose Sheinkman. "Neither a Borrower Nor a Lender Be: An Economic Analysis of Interest Restrictions and Usury Laws." *Journal of Law and Economics* 41(1), April 1998, 1–36.

Goitein, Shelomo. *A Mediterranean Society: The Jewish Communities of the Arab World as Portrayed in the Documents of the Cairo Geniza* (Berkeley, CA: University of California Press, 1967). 6 vols.

Hu, Jichuang. *A Concise History of Chinese Economic Thought* (Beijing, China: Foreign Languages Press, 1988).

Le Goff, Jacques. *Your Money or Your Life* (New York, NY: Zone Books, [1986] 2004).

Little, Lester. *Religious Poverty and the Profit Economy in Medieval Europe* (Ithaca, NY: Cornell University Press, 1978).

Lopez, Robert. *The Commercial Revolution of the Middle Ages, 950–1350* (Englewood Cliffs, NJ: Prentice-Hall, 1971).

Lopez, Robert and Irving Raymond. *Medieval Trade in the Mediterranean World* (New York, NY: Columbia University Press, [1955] 1970).

Mele, Domenec. "Early Business Ethics in Spain: The Salamanca School (1526–1614)." *Journal of Business Ethics* 22(3), November 1999, 175–189.

Michael, Dan. *The Ayenbite of Inwyt* (*Remorse of Conscience*), translated by A.J. Wyatt (London, UK: W.B. Clive, 1889).

Nelson, Benjamin. "The Usurer and the Merchant Prince: Italian Businessmen and the Ecclesiastical Law of Restitution: 1100–1550." *Journal of Economic History* 7 (Supplement), 1947, 104–122.

Nelson, Benjamin. *The Idea of Usury: From Tribal Brotherhood to Universal Otherhood* (Chicago, IL: University of Chicago Press, [1949] 1969).

Noonan, John. *Scholastic Analysis of Usury* (Cambridge, MA: Harvard University Press, 1958).

Pirenne, Henri. *Medieval Cities: Their Origins and the Revival of Trade* (Princeton, NJ: Princeton University Press, [1925] 1974).

Poitras, Geoffrey. *The Early History of Financial Economics, 1478–1776* (Cheltenham, UK: Edward Elgar, 2000).

Posner, Eric. "Contract Law in the Welfare State: A Defense of the Unconscionability Doctrine, Usury Laws, and Related Limitations on the Freedom to Contract." *Journal of Legal Studies* 24(2), June 1995, 283–319.

Reed, Clyde and Cliff Bekar. "Religious Prohibitions against Usury." *Explorations in Economic History* 40(4), October 2003, 347–368.

Seabourne, Gwen. *Royal Regulation of Loans and Sales in Medieval England: 'Monkish Superstition and Civil Tyranny* (Woodbridge, UK: Boydell Press, 2003).'

Smith, Adam. *An Inquiry into the Nature and Causes of the Wealth of Nations*, edited by R.H. Campbell and A.S. Skinner (Indianapolis, IN: Liberty *Classics*, 1981).

Tawney, Richard. *Religion and the Rise of Capitalism* (New York, NY: Harcourt, Brace, 1926).

Viner, Jacob. *The Role of Providence in the Social Order: an Essay in Intellectual History* (Philadelphia, PA: American Philosophical Society, 1972).

Viner, Jacob. *Religious Thought and Economic Society* (Durham, NC: Duke University Press, 1978).

CHAPTER 10

Medieval Ethics and Markets

Along with strictures dealing with usury, medieval authorities concentrated upon the "just price." The "just price" has often been misinterpreted by later commentators; medieval scholars had a somewhat more sophisticated understandings of the forces of supply and demand than is generally realized. The authorities tried to suppress attempts to monopolize the market.

Medieval sellers allegedly resorted to a variety of ageless tricks to gull customers. Then again, the repeat nature of interactions between buyers and sellers may have acted as a brake upon opportunistic behavior. Church and lay officials monitored transactions in the markets for signs of fraud. The poor needed their daily bread, and authorities during the medieval period (as in previous periods) were keen on ensuring an affordable supply of basic foodstuffs. These authorities were intent on inculcating ethical behavior on the part of sellers and buyers.

By the end of the medieval period, developments in renaissance Italy, England, and northern Europe combined with the rise of Protestantism to forge new attitudes toward business and its practitioners.

Rise of Merchants

During the tenth century, throughout continental Europe, professional merchants reappeared. The growing population was one of the possible impetuses for this development, as men became detached from the land.

D. G. Surdam, *Business Ethics from Antiquity to the 19th Century*,
https://doi.org/10.1007/978-3-030-37165-4_10

These men, whether voluntarily or involuntarily, often coalesced into groups of wandering adventurers, and Henri Pirenne claimed, "It is among this crowd of foot-loose adventurers that the first adepts of trade must, without any doubt, be looked for." Pirenne described the career of Godric (of Finchale) from the early twelfth century. Godric was born to peasant parents and left to make a livelihood. He started as a beach-comber (salvager) and graduated to peddler and merchant. He became wealthy as an international trader. Pirenne seems faintly derogatory in describing Godric's and his fellow associates' tactics, which amounted to buying where goods were abundant (and prices were low) and selling goods where scarce (and prices were high). Godric proved adept at this and became rich. What made Godric memorable was his renunciation of his lifestyle and divestment of his wealth. He became a hermit, venerated by many. Although some honored Godric as a merchant saint, Lester Little made the telling point that, similar to St. Francis, the granting of sainthood was predicated upon Godric ceasing to engage in commerce (Pirenne [1925] 1974, 114–117; Little 1978, 214–215).

But were Godric's later actions all that laudatory? If he was helping bring products that his countrymen wanted, then he was serving people. By doing so, he might have arguably benefited his fellow residents more than by being a hermit. Pirenne criticized Godric's accumulation of wealth: "It is preposterous to submit that Godric carried on his business merely to provide for his daily needs. In place of hoarding in the bottom of some chest the money he gained, he used it only to maintain and extend his trading." Pirenne characterized Godric as "completely free of all religious scruple. His zeal in searching out for every commodity the market where it would produce the maximum profit was in flagrant opposition to the disapproval with which the Church looked upon every kind of speculation." By Pirenne's own description, however, Godric and his fellows could be considered heroic. They faced many natural and man-made hazards. The merchants banded together in caravans or convoys for protection against bandits, rapacious rulers, and biased courts, as "Security existed for them only if guaranteed by force, and force was an attribute of collectivity….They [merchant troops] should be pictured as armed bands…bound together by an oath of fidelity." They pooled their capital and used their collective credit to purchase merchandise. Pirenne also neglected to mention that customers benefited from Godric's activities, even if only subjectively (Pirenne [1925] 1974, 118–120).

The further afield Godric and his peers went, the more potentially profitable the venture. The traders' desire for gain was balanced by the "hardships, the risks and the dangers of a wandering existence." Thus arose, at least in the English case, the *piepowdrous* ("dusty-foot"). These travelers upset the traditional roles and introduced shrewd calculation instead of social status. By upsetting the social norms, the trader incurred animus from the social elite, who desired the trader's goods but resented the trader's fortune. For centuries, European social elite disdained careers in commerce and trade. Only the Italian aristocracy enthusiastically embraced mercantile endeavors.

Given their wanderings, merchants and traders needed a new form of law. The traditional court system was ill-equipped to meet the needs of merchants, who needed "a simpler legal system, more expeditious and more equitable." The merchants began developing a commercial code (*jus mercatorum*) to quickly adjudicate disputes between themselves. At the great fairs where there was a gathering of merchants from diverse regions and countries, few had the desire or ability to tarry while waiting for a special tribunal to handle cases. The end result was that the merchant "thus seems to have been not only a free man but a privileged man to boot. Like the cleric and the noble, he enjoyed a law of exception. Like them, he escaped the demesnial and seigniorial authority" that pressed upon peasants.

The Church was displeased with the merchants' growing self-governance. The Church showed little inclination to assist traders and merchants. Pirenne concluded that the Church "may have prevented an understanding of their wants, and given a false impression of their real power." Pirenne approved of the Church's strictures on commercial enthusiasm, as it suppressed the quest for earthly gain. He believed such suppression or constraining protected the poor and debtors and claimed, "The scourge of debts, which in Greek and Roman antiquity so sorely afflicted the people, was spared the social order of the Middle Ages." He lauded the Church's ability to keep "greediness for profits" in check, in part to fears of the Afterlife and in part to their social standing. Godric apparently fell prey to these fears in making his decision to abandon his wealth and assume the life of a hermit (Pirenne [1925] 1974, 122–125, 128–129, 173).

Others acted similarly to Godric. St. Francis of Assisi, of the early thirteenth century, helped his father in the family silk business. The family was well-to-do, but Francis gradually became disillusioned with his life and assumed a life of poverty. St. Bonaventure began using commercial terms in his arguments regarding the usefulness of friars, calling them "trustees for the Christian people, who are like debtors, and whose debt the friars try to pay off, or at least reduce." Another example of a successful merchant elevated to a saint was Omobono of Cremona. Unlike Francis of Assisi, though, Omobono never stopped being a merchant who made profits. He used the profits to support his family and also to support charities. Pope Innocent III declared him a saint in 1199 (Little 1978, 200, 215). This infiltration of religious men with an understanding of business perhaps helped shape the ongoing arguments regarding usury, the just price, and other business practices.

The emergence of traders and merchants was revolutionary in that it created "a man whose normal condition was liberty. From that time on, in place of being subject to seigniorial and demesnial jurisdiction, he was answerable only to public jurisdiction." To a degree, the traders and merchants had the approval of some local rulers, who took these merchants and traders under their protection. The local princes appreciated the benefits merchants and traders wrought, not the least was the tolls they collected. They also recognized that the burghers provided a counterweight to the castellans' [appointed officials] growing strength. The princes' "attitude was almost always one of benevolent neutrality." Charlemagne, among others, granted freedom of circulation to traders (and pilgrims). The local princes sought to encourage trade by eradicating highwaymen in their midst; by the eleventh century, some regions were so safe that a traveler carrying large amounts of goods could feel confident of traveling without being waylaid (Pirenne [1925] 1974, 126–127, 182–183).

Some medieval rulers faced heavy expenses and often acted rapaciously, mulcting merchants and traders. Edward the Confessor enacted laws calling for forfeiture and outlawry as penalties for usury. If a usurer had not repented upon his deathbed, then his chattels were forfeited to the king. Just why the king should get the usurer's property is unclear, although modern-day governments feel free to confiscate estates of the recently deceased, if a proper will is not in force. Over time, though, rulers realized that charging too high tolls or not restraining robbers meant that traveling merchants would detour around the ruler's lands, resulting in no toll revenue and dissatisfied residents bereft of outside goods (Ashley 1913, 195; Lopez 1971, 102).

Grappling with the "Just Price"

Jacob Viner observed that, "The Scholastics also adopted a more tolerant attitude [than did the early Christian Fathers] towards economic inequality and the pursuit of profit and did not question the possibility of engaging in commerce without recourse to sinful practices." Although the Scholastics developed the concept of the just price, Viner thought the application of the concept upon contemporary commerce was mostly in the context of "monopoly, fraud, exploitation of emergency situations for abnormal profit, or overt usury" (Viner 1978, 110–111).

A key question was, "What was the 'just price?'" Historian Raymond de Roover wrote, "the just price was nothing more mysterious than the competitive price, with this important qualification: the Doctors [scholastics] never questioned the right of the public authorities to set and regulate prices." He cited Leonardus Lessius' (1554–1623) definition of the just price, "that which is fixed by public authority in consideration of the common good or that which is determined by the estimation of the community. In the absence of regulation, however, the just price was the one set by common estimation, that is by the free valuation of buyers and sellers, or, in other words, by the interplay of the forces of demand and supply." De Roover admits that the definition depends upon interpreting "'common estimation' as a synonym of market valuation" (De Roover 1951, 495–496; Aquinas 1964, 38:219–221; Viner 1978, 84–85).

Roman law appealed to "nature" in the sense that "every one wishes to buy cheap and sell dear; but what is common to all must be natural, and what is natural cannot be a sin." Aquinas would later disagree with this reasoning and, instead, appealed to *justice*, "the perpetual and constant will of giving to every one that which is his right." Aquinas employs the Golden Rule in answering this question, noting that people dislike paying more for an item than it is worth, so sellers (who were buyers in other transactions) should refrain from doing so. There was a symmetry in Aquinas' thinking, though, as it was similarly unjust to buy something for less than it is worth. He recognized the mutually beneficial aspect of trade inherent in buying and selling, but he believed that transactions should be for *equal* benefit for each party (Ashley 1913, 134).

With regard to the just price, theologian Johannes Nider of the fifteenth century considered the "common estimation" to be too vague, as even within a single community, there could be differences of opinion as to the price of an item. In some cases, too, the item was so unique that the community had not formed a common estimation. Nider lauded grain merchants, who, recognizing a shortfall, sold their grain in such a way to prevent or mitigate a rise in price that would hurt the poor. He excoriated those who were "thinking only of their own gain…sin most gravely." He acknowledged that both buyers and sellers could be guilty of sinful behavior by greedily hoping for a fortuitous change in price that would overly benefit them (Nider 1966, 22–24, 45–46).

Aegidius Lessinus, a student of Aquinas, claimed: "a thing is justly worth what it can be sold for without fraud." De Roover remarked that "without fraud" meant "without cunning devices, in a competitive market." Medieval scholars concluded that price discrimination and monopoly were immoral and that vendors should charge all customers the same price. A monopolist or speculator violated commutative justice by artificially hiking the price. Exploitation was not practicing charity and brotherly love.

Aquinas and later Scholastics used the term "monopoly" with respect to conspiracies to set prices "maximum price above which they refused to buy or a minimum price below which they agreed not to sell." Monopoly was not just a game played by sellers and producers but also by artificers and craftsmen, who could unite and conspire to raise wages above prevailing levels (De Roover 1951, 497–499; Aquinas 1964, 38:219–221).

Nider, as with Aquinas, described the "just price" as being a dual responsibility: "it is clear that it is required (in sound morality) that a man selling his own property not knowingly sell it in excess of its value or dearer than he ought. The buyer, too, should not give too little for a thing, but pay for an article as much as it is worth." The seller was ethically bound to follow the Golden Rule by giving the buyer a product that the buyer expected according to the agreement. Aquinas and others thought fraud could "be committed in the substance of the property or in its appearance, both in quality and quantity." These thinkers argued that a vendor "who commits injustice in selling by fraud is properly held to restitution in proportion to the amount of the fraud. This holds whether in substance or appearance he commits fraud" (Nider 1966, 11–12). They quoted Isaiah 1:22: "Your silver has become dross, your wine mixed with water." The implication was that any adulteration constituted fraud, although they did not seem to address whether *known* adulteration was permissible, if consumers preferred such.

Enforcing the Just Price During Medieval Times

Medieval people produced a bare sufficiency of food; areas with surpluses might move grain to other regions. If the bare sufficiency had been produced with certainty instead of with variance each year, the situation would have been easier to manage.

English medieval marketplaces were thoroughly examined by historian James Davis. The over-riding concern of officials was to ensure reasonable prices for basic foodstuffs, especially grain. English municipal officials understood the precarious nature of food prices; dissatisfied townspeople could violently protest high prices. In Coventry in 1374 and 1387, outraged residents hurled loaves of bread at the mayor, which was certainly a symbolic way to make a point. Davis denied that the authorities were against all price increases or that they set prices arbitrarily. The authorities had a working definition of "common market price" and realized their inability to fully counter supply and demand; at best the authorities knew they could only mitigate such economic forces. Their efforts were frustrated by the medieval economy's vulnerability to "exogenous shocks and disturbance" (Davis 2012, 223, 240, 252).

Davis began by identifying the paradox regarding market traders. Moralists understood that retail traders and middlemen could be rapacious and dishonest, but moralists concurrently understood traders' services to be "essential to the sustenance of society." The medieval English market was developing; sites for regular trade and an apparatus of rules, supervision, and enforcement helped to cut transaction costs and to facilitate trade. The weekly rural or small-town market was a predictable event for both sellers and consumers; such market regularity fostered itinerant traders. One scholar believed that, "most transactions below the level of wholesaling were undertaken on trust and credit, based on communal reputation and contractual morals, which both emphasized and reinforced reciprocal cooperation" (Davis 2012, 2–3, 26).

Davis asserted that medieval thinkers perceived economic activity through a conservative lens; such activity should reflect the traditions of agrarian society and Christian ethical beliefs. Authorities, both religious and secular, assumed that corruption in the marketplace was widespread, so they needed to focus on "combating dishonesty and heightening the level of trust" (Davis 2012, 28–29; Muldrew 2000, 156–177).

Price Setting

Historian Richard Britnell advances a thesis that "prices of grain and fish… were not in fact fixed by free bargaining between buyers and sellers in medieval English markets." In markets for cattle and other commodities, bargaining may have been common, but he concludes, "in most food markets people who tried to bargain risked a fine" (Britnell 1996, 3–4).[1]

The authorities, then, were wary of any perceived or actual attempt to manipulate the market. Authorities promulgated a variety of rules against individuals manipulating markets, as well as collusive agreement to maintain an artificially high price. In the late 1590s, Hugh Alley castigated, "Greedie kinde of people, inhabiting in and about the city, & suburbs of the same, called *Haglers*, *Hawkers*, *Huxters*, and *wanderers* [italics in original], uppe and downe the streets, in buyenge into their owne hands, to rayse the prices, for their owne luker, and private gayne." The activities of such characters redounded to the disadvantage of the poor and held potential for unrest and civil disturbance. There was the obvious point that the poor usually did not have the reserves of cash to protect themselves either by buying in bulk and storing enough to get through periods of dearth, just as in today's world, where super discount stores that require bulk purchases are often beyond the financial means of the poor (Muldrew 1998, 48–51).

Each town or village had a committee of "wise men" who set the just price. These authorities must have been kept busy on some days, when market forces created an impetus for fluctuations in the price. Authorities could change the price during the course of the day, and there may have been opportunities for market officials to act corruptly (but they faced severe punishment for behaving so). Britnell gave some examples of officials using their position to sell their own grain for higher prices than what had been set. On the other hand, the authorities could allow sellers with higher-quality goods to receive a higher price than the set market price. Some towns established three different grades of wheat and set different prices; unscrupulous vendors trying to use the different prices to their advantage faced punishment, including fines. On occasion, authorities might raise prices after the supply ran out, and producers bringing grain in subsequently could receive the revised prices. To forestall speculators, once a vendor offered commodities for sale in the market, the vendor could not withdraw them in hopes of higher prices later in the day. In addition, enforcing the official prices hindered attempts to disguise usurious practices in sales (Britnell 1996, 4–9; Ashley 1913, 188).

Forestalling, engrossing, and regrating described attempts to artificially raise the prices of goods, particularly basic foodstuffs. Medieval authorities spent much effort in preventing these activities, although an economist might view their efforts as misplaced. The forestaller or engrosser met farmers or producers bringing their goods outside of town and purchased their entire stock. Thus having monopolized the supply, the buyer then sold the goods for higher prices. Since there does not appear to be any reason for only one or two parties to play this game, one might anticipate that, once exploited, townspeople or other merchants would lurk outside of town to intercept shipments. One might also wonder why the farmer or producer did not continue into town and reap a higher price for himself. A partial but unsatisfactory answer might be found in the accusation that forestallers deceived merchant strangers with regard to prices to be had in the town. Henry III and Edward I passed ordinances condemning forestalling and engrossing (Ashley 1913, 182).

The market authorities sometimes acted as though they wanted to restrict the flow of market information. "Numerous urban regulations discriminated against outsiders in favour of burgesses, but for the determination of prices the most essential were those intended to enforce ignorance upon them. This was to ensure that the urban authorities could settle with incoming merchants for the lowest possible prices." By making it difficult to get price information, local authorities hoped to prevent forestalling for the purpose of reselling the goods in the market for a better price. A variation on forestalling—regrating—was to buy produce before the opening time, again with the hope of reselling at a higher price (Britnell 1996, 8, 10–11).

From the perspective of some sellers and buyers, though, making transactions outside the towns held attractive advantages. The seller avoided the tolls and faced slightly lower transport and time costs; the buyer (forestaller) gained by reselling the goods at a higher price in the market. Assuming the forestaller lived in the town, he was not subject to the tolls. In one sense, forestalling was a tax evasion mechanism. To some degree, forestallers might help a town make up a deficit in supplies, but the authorities were more concerned with the speculation that might lead to higher prices. The forestallers, therefore, undermined the authorities' efforts to set prices. The efforts to stymie forestalling, engrossing, and regrating created a "violent interference with the liberty…of freedom of contract."

Historian William Ashley terms the efforts "one of the curious follies of the Dark Ages" (Davis 2012, 253–255; Ashley 1913, 184; see also Smith 1981, 534).

Although setting the just price and other medieval regulations ostensibly protected the consumers, such regulation was not even-handed between consumers. Often the price-setting procedures and other edicts favored groups of consumers with higher status, especially the burgesses. In fact, some forestallers defended their actions by testifying that their consignment of goods they had allegedly sold illegally had been acquired for a large household; if true, this purchase could be exempted from the de facto rationing system inherent in the price controls. The accusation of forestalling in order to gain monopoly power was also less than it appeared; juries often ignored whether the forestaller was, in fact, trying to corner the market. Sometimes the mere fact that the seller made a profit by buying to resell was enough for a jury to convict (Britnell 1996, 11–12).

The Assize of Bread

Medieval market laws were based on general ethical and practical principles, including open and public markets. The idea was that secrecy and stealth led to undesirable outcomes. The marketplaces were open spaces, and a market cross was often prominent. At the end of the market day, a bell would sound the conclusion of the market. These measures reduced the cost of search and negotiation. In the larger towns, there might be multiple marketplaces with stalls spread out on adjacent streets. Instead of a single, well-known market day each week, there might be multiple market days in the larger towns. Anglo-Saxon laws stipulated basic guarantees: the seller/warrantor stated that the goods were in marketable condition and were not being fenced. If there was no warrantor, a witness testified that an honest sale occurred and a pledge, who vouched for the seller's reputation. If these persons proved unreliable, they were not allowed to serve in these roles again. These rules provided some protection for consumers.

The assizes were laws governing the price, quality, and quantity of bread, ale, and wine. Over time the assizes concentrated on different aspects. Before the thirteenth century, the assizes focused on weights, measures, and coinage, but the assizes later began to govern prices and other trading practices. The assize of bread was a rather ham-fisted attempt to control the bread market. The compilers assumed a constant turnover in bread sales in terms of loaves sold and allowed bakers to make a profit of 4d. for every 111 farthing loaves sold. The defect was that the price did not vary with the cost of wheat. James Davis suggested that the proponents of the assize of bread mistakenly viewed demand and supply in the market for bread to be stable. Such controls, of course, created distortions in the market for bread. The bakers faced competition from innkeepers that surreptitiously baked bread (horsebread). The bakers cloaked their protest in the public interest, but they were worried about their profits; the bakers eventually persuaded the town authorities to make it illegal for innkeepers to bake bread for sale (Davis 2012, 176–178, 235–236; Ashley 1913, 188–190).

The government sought to protect the poor by eliminating middlemen and having farmers sell corn direct to the consumer in local markets. The corn sales would then be sold under regulations designed to forestall middlemen and speculation. Such regulations prohibited selling corn yet to be harvested, selling corn before the market bell rang, or selling corn before the poor had an opportunity to purchase their small, household needs. Only after the poor had their chance to buy corn could the larger dealers purchase corn in bulk. Along with being prohibited from selling corn that was still in the fields, authorities tried to suppress reselling corn at a profit in the same market or selling by sampling. The millers and bakers were deemed servants of the community, who were not to be intent on making a profit but "a fair allowance." Some of these heavy-handed and often counterproductive edicts continued in operation until the end of the eighteenth century (Webb and Webb 1904, 201; Thompson 1971, 83–84; Westerfield [1915] 1968, 169–175).

The bakers bore the brunt of the Assize of Bread, as farmers and millers were not subject to its regulations. Bakers pleaded that the Assize made it difficult for them to earn sufficient profits to sustain their families and themselves. They argued that they had to resort to the petty cheats, short-weighing, and adulteration, to maintain profitability at an adequate level. If their customers suspected or unmasked their chicaneries, bakers faced swift and harsh judgment, such as damage to their equipment or loss of their stock of output.

The bread riots often followed a general pattern. English consumers had resorted to demonstrations for centuries. "The central action in this pattern is not the sack of granaries and the pilfering of grain or flour but the action of 'setting the price.'" Holders of grain at such time faced an unenviable choice—sell at a below-market price or face the opprobrium of the local populace and authorities. By the time of the English Civil Wars, the practice of having local authorities set prices during times of dearth was diminishing in frequency, although the populace long remembered such measures and would continue to call for them.[2]

There was a mystery surrounding these accounts. Presumably the local baker depended upon customer goodwill and repeated transactions. "Gouging" today might antagonize customers and send them elsewhere, if there was any competition between bakers. Although it was possible that bakers could conspire to raise prices, the temptation to cheat on the collusive arrangement rendered such agreements fragile. Even Edward (E.P.) Thompson recognized this facet, but he did not develop it fully: "The bargaining [between the crowd and a baker] was well understood on both sides; and retailers, who had to hold on to their customers in the fat years as well as the lean, often capitulated at the first sign of crowd turbulence" (Thompson 1971, 106–109, 117).

Thompson recognized the likelihood that the riots boomeranged, when farmers hesitated to bring their produce to the local market. Such reluctance, easily foreseeable, could stymie hopes for moderated grain prices. He cited evidence of prices rising, falling, and not changing much after the riots in the short run, and he identified an unknown factor: Whether the *expectation* of riots affected market prices. Thompson later concluded that, "Such pressures as these, in anticipation of riot, may have been more effective than has been supposed: in getting corn to market; in restraining rising prices; and in intimidating certain kinds of profiteering."

One interesting account, by a sheriff in Gloucestershire in 1766, alluded to the "lowest of the people," whom he identified as "weavers, mecanicks, labourers, prentices, and boys." These people damaged bags of flour at a gristmill and set the price of grain in the main market. Unlike most mobs, however, this group returned a few days later and returned the money to the proprietors who had not resisted. They "behaved with great regularity and decency where they were not opposed, with outrage and violence where they was; but pilfered very little, which to prevent, they will not now suffer Women and boys to go with them."[3]

In some cases, hungry crowds did not keep the bread and grain they stole, seeking only to punish miscreant vendors; they often then disposed of the grain about the countryside instead of eating it. Authorities were perplexed by such behavior, pointing out the obvious that wasting food was not conducive to remedying its dearth. Such disturbances recurred through the years of the Napoleonic wars. The poor had conduits of information. Laborers at the docks, granaries, and mills knew where grain was stored, even clandestine storage sites. When prices were high and local magistrates failed to persuade farmers and grain speculators to supply the market, informers often divulged the location of caches of grain (Thompson 1971, 110–115, 120–122).

Government intervention was no panacea. The seventeenth-century Qing dynasty in China attempted to forestall and mitigate shortfalls in the rice crop. Markets with good access to outside supplies of rice were usually able to maintain lower stocks of rice, than markets with unreliable access to outside supplies. The government's intervention, though, created a perverse incentive structure. Regions with frequent government bailouts began holding smaller stocks of rice than "would have otherwise been chosen in the absence of this implicit insurance relationship with the center [government]….The numerous charges of local corruption with respect to storage, the repeated efforts at monitoring on the part of the central government to raise storage, and the direction of deviation between actual storage and target storage all suggest that the extent to which intergovernmental relief allocation changed local calculations on storage was an unintended consequence of relief" (Shiue 2004, 118).

Attitudes Toward Speculation

Successful speculators benefit society; this is a point worth repeating. As Adam Smith understood, corn merchants helped mitigate short crops. Smith described how successful forestallers benefited society: "By making them feel the inconveniences of a dearth somewhat earlier than they otherwise might do, he prevents their feeling them afterwards so severely as they certainly would do, if the cheapness of price encouraged them to consume faster than suited the real scarcity of the season." In the face of scarcity, consumers generally prefer to smooth their consumption instead of binging and starving. Speculators and the associated price fluctuations help smooth consumption. Such speculation didn't always work, but Smith also demonstrated that society was protected from inept forestallers: "If he judges wrong in this, and if the price does not rise, he not only loses the whole profit of the stock which he employs in this manner, but a part of the stock itself, by the expence and loss which necessarily 'attend' the storing and keeping of corn" (Smith 1981, 533–534).

Authorities worried about the "export" of grain from their locale to another. Speculators moved grain from locales with plentiful grain (and low prices) to those with scant supplies (and high prices). The local authorities facing a market with plentiful grain worried that allowing such exports might leave them vulnerable to scant supplies and high prices (Ashley 1913, 188). Exporting grain out of the country met even greater resistance.

Poor people adhered to a provincial view of the economy. They believed that corn grown locally should remain within the locality. They were loath to see corn exported from their region in times of scarcity. Presumably these same people applauded the *import* of corn, even from other localities facing a dearth. One might argue that their attitude was a violation of the Golden Rule, but economic theory lauding integrated grain markets ran against the reality of fear and resistance to exports. Poor people, more justifiably, especially disliked the export of English corn to foreign ports, often with a bounty paid out of English taxes. The exporters earned an extra measure of opprobrium for his activity for his perceived profiting at the expense of his neighbors (Thompson 1971, 98–99).

With regard to speculators trying to corner the market, Jacob Viner's commentary on Joseph's actions recounted in Genesis is worth quoting at length. Joseph's actions were:

> not for private profit but were carried out in the public name and for the public good. John [Jean] Calvin used this argument, but he carried his defense further so that it should cover Joseph's transactions even if he had acted on his own behalf as a profit-seeking merchant. In the first place, Joseph did not have a complete monopoly, since others were free to store grain if they wished. Secondly, if others out of free choice sold at a low price in time of plenty what they could have held for a time of scarcity, the losses they thus incurred were just punishment for their negligence, presumably in mastering the technique of business forecasting. Calvin did not meet squarely the issue that Joseph, enjoying divine guidance, had kept his inside knowledge to himself, instead of broadcasting it and thus adding to the probability that enough grain would be stored in the fat years to enable the Egyptians to withstand with less suffering the lean years, but he ended his defense of Joseph's conduct with the comment that divine guidance sometimes excuses actions otherwise reprehensible. (Viner 1960, 54; Williams 1948, 227–228)[4]

Nor did Joseph use fraud (Williams 1948, 226).[5]

A different interpretation of the story of Joseph is theologian Douglas Meeks' characterization of Joseph as "the great economist," but who "used famine as a way of centralizing power, gaining control over the land, and creating a labor force." Meeks makes the bold claim that, "those in charge of the economy and those in charge of the religious cult are mutually dependent upon each other. Economic oppression cannot exist without its religious justifications" (Meeks 1989, 78).

Ethics of Sales

Sellers exaggerated the quality and their need to sell at a certain (high) price; buyers denigrated the quality and exaggerated their need to buy at a certain (low) price. Often both parties would baldly change their claims mid-negotiation and reveal their deceptions. Literary contemporaries found it easy to condemn or satirize the proceedings. Some observers thought the hagglers committed perjury, as they often swore that they were telling the truth. A fourteenth-century writer described the process as involving mutually fraudulent statements; he wondered why the haggling was necessary, when many transactions involved relatively known criteria.[6]

Medieval Englishmen often purchased and sold horses. Horse traders were the used car sales representatives of the medieval era; sellers of broken-down nags (similar to "lemons") glossed over the horse's faults ("ridden only by a little old damsel on Sundays"). Potential buyers, of course, responded with criticism. In one amusing anecdote, a trader said the horse "ate everything and would not climb trees," which meant that the "horse bit everything and would not cross wooden bridges." Drapers knew how to present their cloth in, literally, the most flattering light. Tawyers (working with hides) could buff up rotten skins (Davis 2012, 69–72, 76–77).

With so much deceit, what could a hapless buyer (or trader) do? Walter of Henley advocated making transactions with witnesses present. Henley warned of vendors with false scales or weights or with wayward thumbs pressing on the auncel balance. Others went further and agitated for prohibiting the use of auncels. Other writers warned traders that customers were capable of deceit; in some cases, the buyer might know the commodity was worth more than the seller realized, or buyers could be dilatory in repaying debts. Writers advised traders to keep detailed records of their transactions in order to avoid the depredation of "wasters" and the untrustworthy. Such unethical behavior, if as prevalent as depicted, must have adversely affected local and regional economies (Davis 2012, 79, 82).[7]

Merchants earned a just reward by selling "lawful, honorable, and useful" items; the merchant's "diligence, prudence, and [taking] risks" justified the reward. People who sold but did not manufacture defective items still owed restitution to the buyer. A merchant, though, could easily stray from the righteous path and be "suspect of malice" if he sold "to a simpleton or one lacking in expertise; second, when a buyer is forced by circumstance; and third, when by some kind of signs, acts, or words, i.e. intimidation or duping, even if they are true, he induces the buyer to pay more than he otherwise would" (Wren 2000, 114). How a seller could ascertain whether a buyer was uninformed or impulsive was left unsaid, but the seller was presumed to have an advantage in the relevant knowledge. Buyers sometimes faced desperate situations that made buying mandatory (such as a food shortage). Sellers could use a sales pitch that, even if true, unduly influenced the buyer; such actions raised ethical qualms. Finally it was fraud to knowingly offer an item at an inflated price, knowing that the buyer "out of a sense of embarrassment or because he believes that the merchandise is not overrated by more than one denarius gives three denarii for it [instead of the demanded four denarii]." The seller had to pay restitution equal to the difference between the excessive price and the market price (Nider 1966, 13–14, 42–43).[8]

Some merchants of the Middle Ages were experts in practicing trickery and dishonesty, but historian Norman Gras believed the crooked merchants were a minority and that almost all groups of any profession have a few rogues. He went on to answer his own question: "Probably it is because the inefficient ones can succeed in no other way." In any event, local merchants were in need of better public relations. On the other hand, the "sedentary merchants" enjoyed favorable public relations. Their daring and large-scale successes elicited admiration, as did the rich merchants' philanthropic activities. As some merchants grew, they often became associated with the welfare of the state or nation, and public policy often catered to their interests. "There was indeed a failure to distinguish between state policy and business welfare, because, in fact, there was essential harmony." Large merchants enjoyed the esteem of respectable society, including the clergy and intelligentsia (Gras 1945, 109–110).

Medieval author William Langland warned traders to beware of other traders' tricks, such as unwittingly buying stolen goods. If a trader discovered he has purchased stolen goods, he was to return it to the real owner and assume any costs; otherwise, the trader could be considered a thief. If a trader made profits from unknowingly selling stolen goods, he had to make restitution (Davis 2012, 121).

Sellers needed to build a reputation for honesty. In the small English towns and villages, word of mouth was prevalent. A medieval merchant described two virtuous traders. A tailor stayed up all night finishing clothes that he promised would be ready in the morning; a cordwainer worked to maintain the quality of his shoes. Although a trader might be tempted to cheat for a momentary gain, his reputation, once lost, was hard to regain (Caxton 1900, 34–36; Davis 2012, 121–122).

Economist and theologian Tomás de Mercado strove to instruct young men considering mercantile careers to "earn his living in such a way that he does not lose his future life." The Salamanca School was novel in trying to establish practical judgments "that did not depend solely on faith, so as to be useful for everyone," including people of other faiths. The school's ethics "is thus a 'first-person' ethics, as opposed to 'third-person' ethical theories in which it is left to experts to determine what is ethically correct by means of utilitarian calculus or consensus-based procedures….In this respect, the morality proper to a profession is distinct from the morality of the intention of the one who exercises that profession." A medieval writer stated, "Not the profession, but the evil use of the profession, makes commerce evil. The ruin is in the artifice, and the art remains free and blameless" (Mele 1999, 179–180).

The animus Aristotle directed toward merchants as middlemen seeking to buy for resale at a higher price continued into medieval times. Some scholastics, however, understood that for long-distance trade, merchants were necessary in order to obtain desired goods. John Duns Scotus argued traders should be allowed a profit, because they conferred a benefit for the public. Even Aquinas agreed that merchants involved in foreign trade could be without sin, but he obscures the issue by his insistence that such merchants "not seek gain for the sake of gain but as a just reward for their efforts," which was a mighty subtle distinction.

A contemporary of Aquinas, theologian Richard of Middletown, used an example of a horse trader selling a horse to demonstrate trade's benefits. The buyer preferred the horse to the agreed-upon payment; the seller preferred the agreed-upon payment to the horse. Some thinkers even ventured to suppose that God set things up in order to induce nations to engage in peaceful trade. Other thinkers developed a rudimentary explanation of international trade. Some scholastics endorsed the idea that it was permissible for a merchant to ship wine from a country where it was plentiful and fetched a low price to a country where it was scarce and commands a high price. This was not a sinful pursuit of gain, since the merchant bought and sold for the market price in both countries. Middleton proclaimed this profit to be licit, since the merchant did a useful service and was entitled to a profit to cover their troubles and risk (De Roover 1974b, 338–339).

Under certain circumstances, some believed it permissible for a merchant to raise the price above what they paid for the commodity. They recognized the benefit of a merchant or trader, who "transfers things from country to country" in order to take from an area of plenty to an area of dearth. Johannes Nider thought that the risks inherent in transporting goods and the need for judgment and diligence justified a merchant to "justly receive beyond the sustenance necessary for himself and his family not only a price corresponding to his own industry, but in addition something corresponding to his perils." The obverse was that "business dealers who neither transport nor conserve, nor by their industry improve things for sale, are blameworthy and stand properly removable from the commonwealth. Such people do not give an unequivocal assurance concerning the value of goods but merely buy in order to sell without performing the arduous duties mentioned above." Nider's call for banishment arose from his belief that the speculators or middlemen prevented direct exchange from producers and consumers; in doing so, he ignored the services provided by middlemen. In a sense, though, he was ignoring the possibility that merchants and traders who "transport" goods across time provided a socially beneficial service; as shown earlier, astute speculators "transport" goods *when* they were in some abundance to a time when they were in shortfall. Nider viewed speculators as solely gamblers, whose activities raised prices or "to undercut legitimate dealers. Such people cause loss in value to others both in buying and selling" (Nider 1966, 32–33). Nider's inability to see the value of transporting goods across time is not endemic to his milieu or to him. Modern-day people, especially politicians, decry speculators.

Tricks of the Trade and Maintaining a Reputation

In the *Ayenbite of Inwyt*, the monk condemns various fourteenth-century practices. He describes the "eighth bough of Avarice," unfair dealing, with seven ways of sinning in hopes of temporal gains. These include buying low and selling high; exaggerating the quality of goods for sale; cheating with weights and measures, either by false weights and measures; using two sets of weights and measures; and making things look heavier than they are; to "sell to time" (credit sales); "sell[ing] otherwise than one hath showed before, as the scriveners do who begin with words fairly written"; hiding defects; and contriving to make an item "appear better than it is," in which he cites cloth-dealers selling their cloth in "a dim light" (Michael 1889, 36).

If the medieval moralists had been correct regarding the low state of morals within the trading profession, then the costs of monitoring buyers and sellers would have been exorbitant. Buyers and sellers would have faced perhaps insuperable difficulties in conducting transactions. Local traders were dependent upon repeat transactions with villagers. Although villagers could shun a dishonest trader, they might have been inconvenienced. Then again, enough aroused villagers (and their lord) might have exerted moral and physical suasion to discipline an unethical trader.

Literary depictions of petty victuallers were unflattering. They were considered degenerate and desperate characters. Critics chided them for "failing to fufil [sic] their divinely ordained station of providing the community with food and drink at a reasonable price" and for selling bad food. Some speculated that such vendors "would end up in Hell" for their various chicaneries (Davis 2012, 105, 136). Then again, describing honest vendors would have held scant drama or interest for readers.

A historian related the amusing tale of bakers putting bread dough on the counter for their customer to see; underneath was a trap door, where a small lad would retrieve some of the dough, thereby cheating the customer in not-so-plain sight. The authorities sometimes exhibited a puckish sense of humor, as they sought to design punishments befitting the crime. A seller convicted of vending bad wine was ordered to drink it, while a person stealing water was led around the town with a leaky bucket on his head. Historian Louis Salzman considered the "standard commercial morality" to be low. Medievalist Maryanne Kowaleski argued that medieval markets required effective law and enforcement to bolster confidence in both buyers and sellers, although the local burgesses tilted the rules to their advantage; such bias was not necessarily detrimental to consumers, because burgesses were both producers and consumers (Salzman 1927, 75; Kowaleski 1995, 179–221).

Even honest vendors could find their reputations ruined by slander; English courts heard slander cases, whereby plaintiffs alleged the stains upon their reputation cost them credit and deals. Honest sellers took steps to demonstrate and to protect their reputation, including "taking office, oaths, and guild or burgess membership," whereby other people vouched for their probity. Producers also used marks on their goods as means of identification, with the assumption that higher-quality producers willingly marked their goods.

In an era without refrigerators (or expiration dates), vendors with unsold inventory were tempted to hang on to spoiling meat and fish for just a little longer to sell. Some venders violated other rules, possibly out of desperation as many vendors barely eked out a living. Another trick was to reheat or recook meat and other food. Vendors sometimes sold meat from diseased (and deceased) animals. Fourteenth-century Beverly imposed fines for selling such meat. Butchers had to sell meat within four days of slaughtering the animal or else salt the meat. Of course, once a food seller was convicted and publicly identified as selling bad food, his or her tarnished reputation hurt business. Fishmongers, too, could disguise stale fish by using water to make the fish appear fresher. Other merchants resorted to "dubbing" their baskets by using the old trick of placing the best fish or goods on top and putting the dregs below. Alert consumers presumably inspected and detected such simple-minded tricks. Milkwives adulterated their milk and cream with flour. With regard to all of these tricks, presumably there were enough alert and suspicious customers to make these tricks less than panaceas for unscrupulous vendors (Davis 2012, 148, 205, 221–222).

The Crown, as with many rulers in the past, recognized the importance of establishing and enforcing standard weights and measures. As early as Edgar in the tenth century, English monarchs hoped to facilitate trades by reducing the transaction costs involved with a myriad of weights and measures, many of which were accepted as legitimate by various locales. Some jurisdictions required a "heaped" (how much is a "heap") bushel of grain, but others stipulated a level bushel without heaping. Local authorities sometimes created a panel of townsmen to inspect containers and to label them with the owner's name. The royal Exchequer provided standard bushel, gallon, yard, and stone measures to authorities of some towns. These valuable items were kept secure, and it was a crime to tamper with or to abscond with the official measures. Even with these safeguards, people continued to complain about the use of "double measures" and other ways to cheat. On occasion, a trader was caught and convicted. Town authorities had an incentive to maintain the reputation of the town's products and assiduously tried to eliminate false weights and measures (Zupko 1977, 18–19; see also Davis 2012, 190–194).

Controversy Regarding Perceived Avarice

The medieval moralists faced a challenge in pursuing equity and benefits from markets. Could high standards of ethical behavior co-exist with a well-functioning marketplace? Moralists often acknowledged that "commerce was economically necessary and even beneficial for the common good."

To some degree the literate elite distinguished between prosperous wholesale merchants and the petty traders. The literate elite often portrayed the petty traders in unflattering terms and with contempt: "lecherous alewives and faux-friendly innkeepers, to flirtatious peddlers and stinking tanners" (Davis 2012, 34, 38). One historian, Judith Bennett, described how the depictions of alewales and female traders were misogynistic ("the missing piece is misogyny") but another historian disagreed (Bennett 1996, 133; Hanna 1996, 1, 13).

Some medieval writers referred to a halcyon period, where people dealt openly and honestly with each other. These writers lamented the current milieu that was rife with deceit, concluding: "Therefore, one sees nowadays that everything is getting worse-both trades and merchandise." Medieval poet John Gower's lament mirrored the discomfiture of some people during the late medieval years, accusing merchants and traders of being "part of a wider discourse that blamed social disruption on evils that were palpable within every part of society, even if their sins were manifest in differing ways" (Davis 2012, 48).[9]

Moralists used traders to demonstrate the sin of avarice (covetousness), especially in the face of the growing prevalence of money. Modern-day economists often assume that people have insatiable wants, a condition that medieval moralists might have condemned. A person was covetous, when they had an extraordinary and "selfish love of worldly goods." This avarice induced people to engage in a lengthy list of dreadful behaviors, including neglecting their souls, as well as the needs of the poor. Avariciousness was insatiable. The trick was to convert covetousness into something useful; a Lollard delivered a sermon comparing vice to a dunghill. The dunghill stinks from its rotten state, but used as manure, it can bear fruit. "Similarly, accumulation of wealth leads to a rotten soul, but remission can be gained by distributing riches to the poor" (Cigman 1989, 146).

Not only was avariciousness inherent in trading, the merchants did not deserve any profit, since they lacked "transformative skill or extensive labour." These merchants watched the market to ascertain the most propitious time to buy and sell. Some clerics, though, participated in these activities, and John Wyclif denounced them in the fourteenth century. Other critics lumped avarice with "usury, theft, rapine, false claims, sacrilege, simony, treachery, wicked crafts, and gambling." They outlined the sins of buying and selling, including unjust prices, usury, false oaths, false wares, concealment (of faults), misrepresentation, false weights and measures, and "lyther bargaining (exploiting the buyer's need)." Many moralists viewed the average trader as falling into the sin of avarice, as "fraud and an inordinate desire for money were the [traders'] bedfellows" and whose unethical behavior injured the entire community (Davis 2012, 52, 55, 134).

Role of Guilds

Medieval guilds are often thought of as artificial monopolies that charged disproportionate prices and forestalled entry. James Davis surveyed various historians' opinions regarding crafts guilds. He argued that, to some extent, historians viewed craft guilds anachronistically; these historians let contemporary concerns affect their perceptions. Some viewed craft guilds as pioneering trade unions; other historians saw craft guilds as cartels. Among these historians, Heather Swanson thought the craft guilds were "instruments of town councils and had little independent power, but another historian believed she overstated the case" (Davis 2012, 169; Swanson 1988, 29–48; Swanson 1989, 108–120; Rosser 1997, 6). Sylvia Thrupp believed the guild's rules served to primarily benefit guild members by raising prices and erecting barriers to entry although cautioning that such abilities were limited: "Consumers probably over-estimated the economic powers of gilds, giving them an unfair share of blame for upward price trends. Even when they had the support of public authority, their power to raise prices through cartel agreements or suppression of local competitors was limited by conditions that were beyond their control" (Thrupp 1978, 231, 247–249; Davis 2012, 217).[10]

Craft guilds bore a suspicious resemblance to both a cartel and a labor union, even though the guilds tried to foster a benevolent image. These guilds hoped to "bolster the economic potential of individual workshops without destroying their autonomy, each guild endeavored to represent the entire membership as a united front." They tried to achieve these goals by imposing uniformity of output, precluding cutting quality or size in order to undercut competition. There were strictures against advertising: "some medieval regulations even forbade an artisan to attract attention to his products with a nod or a sneeze—the certifying seal of a guild was the best means to bid for distant markets. Only his neighbors might recognize the watermark of a distinguished paper-maker, but Pabriano paper was, and still is, known everywhere." Guilds occasionally acted collectively in purchasing raw materials in bulk or selling output, but the public saw such actions as attempts to manipulate prices. Guilds' alleged social activities often drew opprobrium, but monopoly was not always the policy of craft or market guilds (Lopez 1971, 128; Postan 1972, 216).

Davis relates how guild-induced higher prices injured the producers of lower-quality goods and the consumers with the skimpiest budgets. The guildsmen and more prosperous members of a town benefited. As producers of low-quality goods were eliminated in a village, poor people might go to nearby towns with fewer controls that inhibited producers of lower-quality goods. Non-guild entrepreneurs might also seek towns with weak or non-existent guilds (Davis 2012, 218).

Did the guilds create monopoly power? Economist Gary Richardson found that the thesis was exaggerated. Richardson defended his depiction by describing the competition for customers between guilds in different towns. Richardson adduced other evidence to disprove the guild/monopoly story. Guilds often produced more than what the local market could purchase, so the excess production was sold elsewhere, often to customers hundreds of miles away. A local guild might specialize in what it produced. He attributed the persistence of the historians' thesis to a lack of research "about the legal structure of markets for manufactures." After examining many guild charters, Richardson concluded that the guilds rarely possessed legal monopolies. "At most 5% of all guilds possessed court-enforced, anti-competitive powers." With regard to manipulating prices, the common law prohibited such actions, while courts punished forestallers, engrossers, and regrators who supposedly were trying to manipulate prices. The crown prohibited hindering trade, and wholesalers had the right to sell their products anywhere in the realm.

Guilds were not allowed to create barriers to entry, although guild control over entry into some occupations was a form of barrier to entry. Guilds might set education standards of apprentices and the like, but the guild charters “never allowed some weavers to prevent others from practicing their craft. The charters established inclusive rather than exclusive organizations. They required everyone to join the organization. They did not prohibit anyone from entering the craft.”

Guild members faced competition from outside producers. English rulers granted freedom from tolls in many cases, even to merchants from other countries. Crown and towns usually granted free movements of persons and property. Authorities monitored weights and measures, thereby lowering transaction costs and reducing disputes. The economy was developed enough that there was well-established financial intermediation. Consumers often could walk to more than one marketplace or town (Richardson 2004, 2–5, 8, 13–20).

Another attribute of the guilds, though, may have benefited consumers: the enforcement of minimum product quality and control of who practiced a craft in a town. Such power, of course, could be abused on occasion, but the guilds were intent on protecting the reputation of their collective products, and any substandard or slovenly producer threatened the reputation of all. The guild’s surveyors exercised powers that modern people might find annoying; since many medieval producers worked out of their homes, the surveyor’s right to inspect meant searching homes. Artisans had to maintain the quality of their goods and not bring scandal upon their craft or guild. There were also restrictions on poaching customers from another guild member. These regulations protected both the guilds and, it was argued, the customers. Modern-day regulatory agencies profess to do the same, although many economists suspect a regulated industry’s true motive is to limit competition and to raise prices. Guild members were tempted by a residual consumer demand for cheaper goods, just as modern consumers express desires for a continuum of quality for even the same basic commodity. Guild members were prohibited from denigrating their fellow producers’ products. Richardson cited the guild’s attempts to foster moral integrity among its members by creating links between spiritual ties and behavior (Davis 2012, 170 and 172; Richardson 2005, 139–189).

Monastic Ethics and Rapacious Clergy

The cliché that medieval monasteries were austere places, as exemplified by St. Bernard, was often inaccurate. St. Bernard’s austerity negatively affected his health; after his death, the Cistercian Order declined, because it became wealthy. "Citeaux was on the trading route via Brenner into Italy and commerce damaged the spiritual side of monastic life. While its rentals grew longer, its prayers and austerities grew shorter" (Rowling 1968, 128).

If businesspeople of the medieval years had their ethical challenges, so did monks in various Catholic monasteries. Clergy demonstrated that greed was not only a layperson's vice. Church officials, of course, had their own special category of avarice: simony. Some houses demanded gifts from aspiring monks; the problem so widespread that Charlemagne convened an empire-wide council to deal with the issue of simony. The solution was to use the Rule of Saint Benedict, whereby the entrant could give his goods to the poor or to the monastery, but the choice was his. The council ruled that it was impermissible for the house or monks to charge money for entry. The monasteries' burgeoning wealth diverted monks from spiritual matters to business matters and also began attracting men who were not interested in spiritual values. Although Martin Luther may have represented the culmination of protest against monastic laxity, Italian townspeople had earlier begun criticizing and rebelling against the worldliness of bishops and nobles. This rebellious attitude gradually spread to the Low Countries (Lynch 1976, 61–62; Rowling 1968, 130).

One practice provoked much criticism. Gregory I defined simony as "an improper attainment of ecclesiastical office…whether it was secured by rendering undue services, by giving praise, by promising favors, or by making a monetary gift," whether using actual cash or worth some sort of "calculable monetary value." Simony was considered the buying and selling of sacred things, such as holy orders and church offices. There was debate over whether simony was a heresy. Scholastic theologians agreed that the practice needed to end. Simony was considered a contaminant (Little 1971, 21–22; see also Lynch 1976, 65–67).

The popes, similar to business owners, tapped as many sources of revenues as they could. New revenue resources included transforming "once free communes of the papal states into units of authoritarian papal rule" (Gilchrist 1969, 101). Pope Pius II ruthlessly wrung repayment from debtors, sometimes using the threat of excommunication. The pope monopolized the sale of salt (presumably the demand for salt was relatively insensitive to price, so the price could have increased significantly without too much diminution in purchases) and the production of alum (by trying to stymie imports of Turkish alum). The papacy, of course, was aware of the inconsistency in its alum cartel and justified it, "on the questionable principle that the end justifies the means" (Ekelund et al. 1989, 320; see also De Roover 1948, 49).

Unlike businesspeople who had no similar coercive powers, the Popes sometimes allowed their soldiers the right of pillage, when towns defaulted on loans. Monks in monasteries in England proved keen practitioners of buying low and selling high in the wool market. Professor John Gilchrist noted, "For that day and age these procedures ranked as acceptable business methods, for a later age they have become sources of accusation and sometimes scorn."

This catalogue of dubious ethical practices was counter-balanced by the church's promotion of civil liberties across Europe, and the monasteries' development of neglected lands. The Cistercian Order began large-scale wool production in England, including building a fulling mill. The Cistercian's involvement in business and their methods, however, "were often reprehensible, even to laymen."

The monasteries' monopolistic practices irritated both the merchants and the general populace. The monks cheaply obtained lands given as security to Jewish moneylenders; they used their exemption from customs duties and tolls to act as middlemen in the transport of other merchants' goods. The Cistercians found that their antics left them bereft of defenders in later centuries. Gilchrist concluded that the monks' business activities weakened the laity's obeisance to and loosened interpretation of church doctrine (Gilchrist 1969, 102–104).

Legacies of Scholastics' Arguments

Did the Scholastics' doctrines affect business behavior? Max Weber argues that the doctrines did. Protestants changed the attitudes toward business. The story is much more complicated, since the Renaissance Italian merchants certainly were pioneers and developed sophisticated business practices.

A doctrine can be erroneous and still exert an influence, of course. Raymond de Roover observed that the many wills of merchants and businessmen providing restitution for usury meant that Catholic theologians' precepts exerted some influence upon their secular peers. The usury proscription also affected the development of banking. "Since the taking of interest was forbidden, the discounting of commercial paper was also ruled out, but the bankers cleverly shifted to exchange dealings as the basis of their operations. This shift changed the entire structure of the continental

European banking system up to the time of the French Revolution" (De Roover 1974a, 332; De Roover 1974b, 344–345; Nelson 1947, 104–122).

There was an ironic effect of the public's attitudes toward merchants and traders that, according to business ethicist David Vogel, "not surprisingly, many medieval merchants did in fact act like contemporary drug dealers. After all, if their activity was thought to be immoral to begin with, why should they have tried to perform it ethically?" Another author observed that pre-Reformation capitalism exhibited "rampant individualism which knew few scruples….The capitalist mentality of the medieval business classes rested on the dictum: 'A profit is a profit, however it is acquired.'" Italian merchants were known for using biological warfare, by placing diseased animal carcasses into their rivals' shops in order to injure their rivals, rivals' employees, and rivals' customers. "It was by morally sanctifying the pursuit of profits that Protestantism made business ethics possible" (Vogel 1991, 51). Vogel's thesis is provocative, and, in these politically correct times, quite likely to raise the ire of Catholic readers.

On the other hand, some medieval businessmen were not shy about their motives. Francesco di Marco Datini wrote on the first page of his ledgers: "In the name of God and of profit." For Datini, profit "in this world or in the next, as if the whole of life were one vast counting-house and at its end, the final Day of Accounting" (Origo 1957, vii).

Many merchants and traders during the Middle Ages believed in the teachings of the Church and took seriously the phrase, "In the name of God and profit." De Roover cited the numerous wills providing for restitution for having lent at interest or for unethical gains. The phrase also implied that they hoped and prayed that the Lord would "bless them with profits and to shield them against losses. At the same time they often ask Him to preserve them in good health and to protect them against illness. In other words, our merchants expected that God would give them prosperity in this world and eternal bliss in the next." Not only Catholics but Protestants, too, held similar outlooks (De Roover 1974c, 73). A modern-day skeptic might ask why these businessmen waited until they were almost dead to provide restitution but such criticism may be unduly harsh.

Datini presents an interesting study of a "perplexed medieval businessman." He had a partner, Domenico, and legal counselor, Lapo. Domenico and Lapo served as extreme models of behavior for the perplexed Datini. Domenico was an "enthusiastic 'materialist,'" while Lapo was "so disconcerted by the very existence of business operations that he insisted on Francesco's immediate retirement and the release of his wealth for 'spiritual' purposes." At first Francesco opted to use his wealth to build a new mansion and to enjoy his prestige from being wealthy (Miller 1952, 107).

Datini built new houses for his workers and faced disapproval from friends. One friend made the rather bizarre claim, "If you put them into houses fit for craftsmen they will die of heat." Other landowners despised their tenants and understood that their tenants reciprocated landlords' feelings; Datini was warned to be absent as much as possible and never to visit his lands on feast days: "for then [the workers] are heated with wine and are armed and there is no reasoning with them" (Rowling 1968, 45–46).

Lapo fretted about his friend and client's soul; Domenico was envious of Francesco's wealth. Lapo emphasized the "worry and distraction and vexation of spirit" from wealth, and he counseled his friend to let go of his possessions. As with many wealthy people, Francesco was besieged by friends, family, and associates' requests (demands) for financial help. Lapo, to his credit, only wanted from Francesco a "cask of salted anchovies" and he told his friend, "don't fret about the freight charges."

Domenico appeared to be a bumptious character constantly on the make. One can imagine Domenico envying Datini's wealth without necessarily being willing to expend the energy and effort to attain such on his own. Lapo might have "never been told how money came into the world and had lived too long on institutional overhead to enjoy the embarrassing process for himself." Datini seems to have been shaken from his ambivalence, when another plague struck Florence. He had lost his parents to the plague of 1348, and the plague of 1400 may have seemed a harbinger of the Last Judgment. He donated his mansion and wealth to endow Prato's "Ceppo dei Poveri" (Mainstay of the Poor), a similar institution to where Lapo worked.

Rather than laud Lapo and criticize Domenico, historian Stanley Miller suggests that each was a useful counter for Datini. "[T]he Domenicos—enthusiastic, acquisitive, eager for conflict and glory—see no reason for wasting resources on fol-de-rol. They know how fundamental to society is its economic potential and they want to re-invest to keep the machinery running." In contrast, "the Lapos—mild, judicial, absorbed in meditation—are uninspired by the workings of economics. They feel significance in terms of the long run, and they want to keep distractions away from the solitude of the spirit. Neither breed demonstrates undue curiosity about the other. In fact it is really a little shocking to recognize how thoroughly their own in-breeding prevents them from understanding each other even after performing the same work routine together day after day" (Miller 1952, 115, 118–119, 121).

Conclusion

Historian John Baldwin contrasted "the economic mentality of the Middle Ages with the new 'spirit of Capitalism.'" The medieval period represented, perhaps, the nadir of businessmen's repute, at least with scholars of Catholicism. By the early modern period, businessmen or merchants were "Undisputedly honored and revered as a progressive force in capitalistic society, his role in the Middle Ages was irritating and thankless at best. His worst enemy was the Church, which harassed him with absurd regulations concerning usury and just prices." Traders and merchants faced a dilemma: "To make a profit or even earn a decent living by the commercial profession led the merchant along a morally hazardous road on which he could slip at any moment and plunge into Hell's damnation. Economic gain was inevitably accompanied by propensities toward greed and avarice, which were lethal to the soul. In contrast to the business man of the dawning age of Capitalism, according to some scholars, the medieval merchant was persona non grata, and religion was a millstone around his miserable neck" (Baldwin 1959, 287–288). While Baldwin painted a rather stark portrait, medieval thought and practices resound today, as people argue over the just price for, say, life-sustaining prescription drugs or limits upon interest rates charged by credit card companies, payday loan establishments, or loan sharks.

Much medieval thinking revolved around an all-knowing deity and calculations of punishments and rewards for one's actions. Fears of damnation persisted for centuries after the medieval period, as Protestant theologians and ministers depicted the horrors of Hell in almost loving detail. A growing secularism, however, was slowly altering business participants' motivations for behaving ethically.

Notes

1. The haggling in the market for livestock may have reflected differences in quality.
2. Bread riots that occurred during the American Civil War in Richmond and other southern towns were similar to descriptions of riots in England (McCurry 2010, 181–182, 188).

3. Thompson used the spelling in the original quote.
4. For another discussion of this story, see Sedlacek (2011, 63–65).
5. With regard to Joseph getting the message from God, under today's rigid Securities Exchange Commission regulations, Joseph could have been indicted for "insider trading" and done time at Club Fed with Michael Milken, Charles Keating, and their ilk.
6. Geertz and Muldrew regarding similarities with haggling in Indonesia (Geertz 1968, 32–36; Muldrew 1998, 43).
7. See page 195 for a discussion of auncels versus balances.
8. Daniel Kahneman described how negotiators "often pretend intense attachment to some good, although they actually view that good as a bargaining chip and intend ultimately to give it away in an exchange. Because negotiators are influenced by a norm of reciprocity, a concession that is presented as painful calls for an equally painful (and perhaps equally inauthentic) concession from the other side" (Kahnemann [2011] 2013, 304–305).
9. Their laments for a pristine past might be characterized by borrowing the warning on rear-view mirrors: "Past virtue appears larger than it was."
10. Almost a millennium ago, the Japanese *za* became an institution created to benefit the few by restricting entry into and competition within a particular market. The *za* existed through the sufferance of political authorities, who, in turn, reaped gains from their sponsorship. The *za* was designed to raise the income of the members (Yamamura 1973, 439 and 441, see also 462–463).

Bibliography

Aquinas, Thomas. *Summa Theologiae* (New York, NY: Blackfriars, 1964). 60 vols.

Ashley, William J. *An Introduction to English Economic History and Theory. Part 1: The Middle Ages* (New York, NY: Longmans, Green, 1913). 9th Edition.

Baldwin, John. "The Medieval Merchant before the Bar of Canon Law." *Papers of the Michigan Academy of Science, Arts, and Letters* 44(Part 1), 1959, 287–299.

Bennett, Judith. *Ale, Beer, and Brewsters in England; Women's Work in a Changing World, 1300–1600* (New York, NY: Oxford, 1996).

Britnell, Richard. "Price-setting in English Borough Markets, 1349–1500." *Canadian Journal of History* 31 (April 1996), 1–15.

Caxton, William. *Dialogues in French and English*, edited by Henry Bradley (London, UK, 1900).

Cigman, Glorida, editor. *Lollard Sermons* (Oxford, UK: Early English Text Society, 1989).

Davis, James. *Medieval Market Morality: Life, Law and Ethics in the English Marketplace, 1200–1500* (Cambridge, UK: Cambridge University Press, 2012).

De Roover, Raymond. "Monopoly Theory Prior to Adam Smith: A Revision." *Quarterly Journal of Economics* 65(4), November 1951, 492–524.

De Roover, Raymond. *The Medici Bank: Its Organization, Management, Operations, and* Decline (New York, NY: New York University Press, 1948).

De Roover, Raymond. "Scholastic Economics: Survival and Lasting Influence from the Sixteenth Century to Adam Smith." In *Business, Banking, and Economic Thought in Late Medieval and Early Modern Europe* (Chicago, IL: University of Chicago Press, 1974a), 306–335.

De Roover, Raymond. "The Scholastic Attitude toward Trade and Entrepreneurship." In *Business, Banking, and Economic Thought in Late Medieval and Early Modern Europe* (Chicago, IL: University of Chicago Press, 1974b), 336–345.

De Roover, Raymond. *Business, Banking, and Economic Thought in Late Medieval and Early Modern Europe* (Chicago, IL: University of Chicago Press, 1974c).

Ekelund, Robert Jr., Robert Hebert, and Robert Tollison. "An Economic Model of the Medieval Church: Usury as a Form of Rent Seeking." *Journal of Law, Economics, & Organization* 5(2), Autumn 1989, 307–331.

Geertz, Clifford. *Peddlers and Princes: Social Development and Economic Change in Two Indonesian Towns* (Chicago, IL: University of Chicago Press, 1968).

Gilchrist, John. *The Church and Economic Activity in the Middle Ages* (London, UK: Macmillan, 1969).

Gras, Norman. "Shifts in Public Relations." *Bulletin of the Business Historical Society* 19(4), October 1945, 97–148.

Hanna, Ralph. "Brewing Trouble: On Literature and History—And Alewives." *Bodies and Disciplines: Intersections of Literature and History in Fifteenth-Century England*, edited by Barbara Hanawalt and David Wallace (Minneapolis, MN: University of Minnesota Press, 1996), 1–17.

Kahneman, Daniel. *Thinking, Fast and Slow* (New York, NY: Farrar, Straus and Giroux, [2011] 2013).

Kowaleski, Maryanne. *Local Markets and Regional Trade in Medieval Exeter* (Cambridge, UK: Cambridge University Press, 1995).

Little, Lester. *Religious Poverty and the Profit Economy in Medieval Europe* (Ithaca, NY: Cornell University Press, 1978).

Little, Lester. "Pride Goes before Avarice: Social Change and the Vices in Latin Christendom." *American Historical Review* 76(1), February 1971, 16–49.

Lopez, Robert. *The Commercial Revolution of the Middle Ages, 950–1350* (Englewood Cliffs, NJ: Prentice-Hall, 1971).

Lynch, Joseph. *Simoniacal Entry into Religious Life from 1000 to 1260* (Columbus, OH: Ohio State University Press, 1976).

McCurry, Stephanie. *Confederate Reckoning: Power and Politics and the Civil War South* (Cambridge, MA: Harvard University Press, 2010).

Meeks, M. Douglas. *God the Economist: The Doctrine of God and Political Economy* (Minneapolis, MN: Fortress Press, 1989).

Mele, Domenec. "Early Business Ethics in Spain: The Salamanca School (1526–1614)." *Journal of Business Ethics* 22(3), November 1999, 175–189.

Michael, Dan. *The Ayenbite of Inwyt (Remorse of Conscience)*, translated by A.J. Wyatt (London, UK: W.B. Clive, 1889).

Miller, Stanley. "Business and the Fear of Materialism." *Bulletin of the Business Historical Society* XXVI(3), September 1952, 107–121.

Muldrew, Craig. *The Economy of Obligation: The Culture of Credit and Social Relations in Early Modern England* (New York, NY: St. Martin's Press, 1998).

Muldrew, Craig. "From a 'light cloak' to an 'iron cage': historical changes in the relation between community and individualism." *Communities in early modern England: Networks, place, rhetoric*, edited by Alexandra Shepard and Phil Withington (Manchester, UK: Manchester University Press, 2000), 156–77.

Nelson, Benjamin. "The Usurer and the Merchant Prince: Italian Businessmen and the Ecclesiastical Law of Restitution: 1100–1550." *Journal of Economic History* 7 (Supplement), 1947, 104–122.

Nider, Johannes. *On the Contracts of Merchants* (Norman, OK: University of Oklahoma Press, 1966).

Origo, Iris. *The Merchant of Prato: Francesco di Marco Datini* (New York, NY: Alfred A. Knopf, 1957).

Pirenne, Henri. *Medieval Cities: Their Origins and the Revival of Trade* (Princeton, NJ: Princeton University Press, [1925] 1974).

Postan, Michael. *The Medieval Economy and Society: An Economic History of Britain, 1100–1500* (Berkeley, CA: University of California Press, 1972).

Richardson, Gary. "Craft Guilds and Christianity in Late-Medieval England: A Rational-Choice Analysis." *Rationality and Society* 17(2), 2005, 139–89.

Richardson, Gary. "Guilds, Laws, and Markets for Manufactured Merchandise in Late-Medieval England." *Explorations in Economic History* 41(1), 2004, 1–25. [no month given].

Rosser, Gervase. "Crafts, Guilds, and the Negotiation of Work in the Medieval Town." *Past & Present* 154(1), February 1997, 3–31.

Rowling, Marjorie. *Life in Medieval Times* (New York, NY: Perigee Books, 1968).

Salzman, Louis. *English Life in the Middle Ages* (London, UK: Oxford University Press, 1927).

Sedlacek, Tomas. *Economics of Good and Evil: The Quest for Economic Meaning from Gilgamesh to Wall Street* (Oxford, UK: Oxford University Press, 2011).

Shiue, Carol. "Local Granaries and Central Government Disaster Relief: Moral Hazard and Intergovernmental Finance in Eighteenth- and Nineteenth-Century China." *Journal of Economic History* 64(1), March 2004, 100–124.

Smith, Adam. *An Inquiry into the Nature and Causes of the Wealth of Nations*, edited by R.H. Campbell and A.S. Skinner (Indianapolis, IN: Liberty*Classics*, 1981).

Swanson, Heather. "Illusion of Economic Structure: Craft Guilds in Late Medieval English Towns." *Past & Present* 121, November 1988, 29–48.

Swanson, Heather. *Medieval Artisans: An Urban Class in Late Medieval England* (Oxford, UK: Basil Blackwell, 1989).

Thompson, Edward P. "The Moral Economy of the English Crowd in the Eighteenth Century." *Past and Present* 50, February 1971, 76–136. No issue number.

Thrupp, Sylvia. "The Gilds." *The Cambridge Economic History of Europe. Volume III: Economic Organization and Policies in the Middle Ages* (London, UK: Cambridge University Press, 1978). 230–280.

Viner, Jacob. "The Intellectual History of Laissez Faire." *Journal of Law and Economics* 3(1), October 1960, 45–69.

Viner, Jacob. *Religious Thought and Economic Society* (Durham, NC: Duke University Press, 1978).

Vogel, David. "Business Ethics Past and Present." *The Public Interest* 102, Winter 1991, 49–64.

Webb, Sidney and Beatrice Webb. "The Assize of Bread." *Economic Journal* 14(54), June 1904, 196–218. [54 is correct].

Westerfield, Ray. *Middlemen in English Business, Particularly between 1660 and 1760* (New York, NY: Augustus M. Kelley, [1915] 1968).

Williams, Arnold. *The Common Expositor: An Account of the Commentaries on Genesis, 1527–1633* (Chapel Hill, NC: University of North Carolina Press, 1948).

Wren, Daniel. "Medieval or Modern? A Scholastic's View of Business Ethics, *circa* 1430." *Journal of Business Ethics* 28(2), November 2000, 109–119.

Yamamura, Kozo. "The Development of *Za* in Medieval Japan." *Business History Review* XLVII(4), Winter 1973, 438–465.

Zupko, Ronald. *British Weights & Measures: A History from Antiquity to the Seventeenth Century* (Madison, WI: University of Wisconsin Press, 1977).

CHAPTER 11

Early Modern Europe and Resurging Trade

In the seventeenth and eighteenth centuries, new forms of motivation began to displace the Church's strictures. People began to accept self-interest as a legitimate and even virtuous motivation. Protestants developed modifications to Catholic thinkers' views upon business activities. Religious leaders began to see work and accumulation as virtuous, if ethically earned.

The quest for economic success contained a conundrum. One could ethically amass wealth, but there remained strictures against using such wealth for self-enjoyment. Austerity remained a virtue, which, in turn, contributed to even larger accumulations of wealth.

Business practitioners began to see ethical behavior not solely in terms of potential punishment but also in terms of benefits. Observers advised that acting ethically could pay off. People began using teleological approaches to ethics in terms of whether actions proved, on net, beneficial instead of whether such actions pleased a deity.

European expeditions to the Indian and across the Atlantic oceans created opportunities requiring large-scale capital investments. Opportunities for larger-scale businesses required new forms of financing, and such entities as joint-stock companies arose. Trading stock in such companies was not for the naïve, and a severe learning process ensued. The first two decades of the eighteenth century witnessed succeeding speculative bubbles.

D. G. Surdam, *Business Ethics from Antiquity to the 19th Century*,
https://doi.org/10.1007/978-3-030-37165-4_11

Christian Attitudes Toward Economic Gains

Theologian Pierre Nicole was a predecessor of the idea that "enlightened self-interest, through the medium of commerce resting on mutual exchange of services, meets all the needs of earthly life without any intervention of charity....life is carried on with as complete peace, security, and ease as if one were in a community of saints." Nicole's friend and contemporary, Jean Domat, argued in a slightly different vein. Self-interest might result in corrupt outcomes for those pursuing such, but for society, "it yields genuine benefits." By "the design of Providence, those passions which tend by their nature to destroy the divine order are made to contribute to its conservation." Domat, though, added that self-interested passions did need God-inspired laws to maintain public order (Viner 1978, 135, 138–139). Such ideas presaged Adam Smith's views on how self-interest could inadvertently promote social benefits.

Many Christian moralists possessed a mindset that economic gain was a zero-sum game. A person seeking to enrich him- or herself did so, only by "appropriating an unfair share of what God had intended for the common use of men." The obvious corollary was that, "If a man possessed more than he needed, he was bound to give his superfluity to the poor; for by natural law he had no personal right to it; he was only a steward for God" (Ashley 1913, 128). But these thinkers did not consider the possibility that a person could enrich him- or herself by expanding or improving upon God's providence.

The trick was to reconcile seeking enrichment, which was a sin, with trade. Scholars dating back to Tertullian wrestled with this conundrum: "If covetousness is removed, there is no reason for gain, and, if there is no reason for gain, there is no need of trade." Saint Jerome complained that a trader who did not improve the product but sold at a higher price meant that the buyer lost a commensurate amount as the seller gained. This simplistic, zero-sum game mentality befuddled thinkers for centuries (Tertullian n.d., Chapter 11, no page numbers; Ashley 1913, 128–129). People often clearly benefited from and desired the commodities traders brought to the market.

Many people disagreed with the idea that commerce had benign effects. They denied that interregional and local commerce provided net economic benefits relative to the autarky of regions or of private estates. They cited merchants' temptations to cheat customers, while nations clashed over international trade. The import of luxuries led to demoralization.

International trade exposed people to great hazards and was an impious affront to the gods (defying the winds and the seas). Others objected because trade and commerce triggered avarice and meant association with people of other cultures, leading to the corruption of "the native culture, to give rise to strategic risks, and to breed wars" (Viner 1972, 34).

Protestant Advantages and Prosperity

Martin Luther's excoriation of the Catholic hierarchy echoed criticism of business practices: "the holy sacrament has been turned into mere merchandise, a market, and a profit-making business. On these the priests and monks depend for their entire livelihood." In another passage, he inveighed, "because these two sacraments furnish opportunity for gain and profit, the greed of the shepherds has raged in them with incredible zeal against the flock of Christ." In disputing marriage as a sacrament, Luther cited the greed of the clergy in graphic terms: "What is it that they sell? Vulvas and genitals—merchandise indeed most worthy of rich merchants, grown altogether filthy and obscene through greed and godlessness.…O worthy trade for our pontiffs to ply, instead of the ministry of the gospel" (Luther 1959, 36:35–36, 81, 97). Businesspeople have been accused of many sordid and dishonorable practices, but one is hard-pressed to match Luther's tirade.

New ideas challenged Catholicism's hold upon Europeans. Within a few centuries, Protestant economies surged. Jacob Viner found no writer, Catholic or non-Catholic, who denied (at least by the eighteenth and nineteenth centuries) the claim that Protestant countries were more prosperous than Catholic countries, despite Italian cities' former prosperity (Viner 1978, 182–184).

In his study of Protestants and their effects upon economies, researcher Robert Woodberry defined conversionary Protestants as wanting "people to read the Bible for themselves in their own language, have a 'converted' clergy (clergy chosen for religious reasons, not political reasons), and actively attempted to bring others into their faith." These desires extended to women and the poor, whereas economic and political elites throughout Europe during the nineteenth century "resisted educating women and the poor, fearing it would undermine stability." He observed, "The desire to convert people helped undermine elites' long-term economic and political interests and created a threat to other religious groups that forced them to transfer resources to nonelites."

Woodberry's statistical analysis revealed that Protestant missionary activity "strongly and robustly predicted higher educational enrollments, GDP [gross domestic product], political democracy, government efficiency, secure property rights, and lower infant mortality and corruption." On the other hand, Catholic missionary activity "have little influence on most of these outcomes." He refuted the argument that economic development "explains" mass education (Woodberry 2011, 112–113, 123; Becker and Woessmann 2011, 93–94). Scotland proved an interesting case. Adam Smith and others represented an apogee of Scottish intellectual attainment, but up until the mid-eighteenth century, Scotland was impoverished (Buckle 1904, 784–785; Viner 1978, 187–188).[1]

Other scholars gave the Protestantism argument a twist by suggesting that the Catholic sacrament of penance kept the cost of defaulting on a contract low; the defaulter could simply seek pardon and perform penance. The Protestants jacked up the perceived cost of defaulting by linking default with an elevated possibility of not being saved. Because Protestantism lowered the likelihood of default for even one-time-only contractual exchanges, "To cooperate with others became an unavoidable moral obligation." As greater numbers of business participants adhered to the Protestant beliefs, the Protestant business participants gained important network externalities due to benefits accruing from interacting with a group of similar believers, especially along the northern coastline of Europe and London. Even Jewish merchants and financiers from southern Europe found it "more profitable to do business under Protestant institutions than under Catholic ones by the seventeenth century." The process worked in reverse, too, as French persecution and eviction of Protestants wrecked what small networks of cooperating individuals that had existed within France's borders.

Economists Ulrich Blum and Leonard Dudley concluded that Weber was right "in terms of information networks. Protestant cities, but not Catholic cities, with direct access to the Atlantic were able to take advantage of advances in transportation technology that reduced the cost of ocean shipping." Protestant printing centers were not constrained by the Catholic church, and Protestants tended to have greater literacy. The Protestants had a penchant for honoring contracts, even with people they did not know personally, and these connections were the "random links that converted regional economies with tenuous ties into a 'small world' network" (Blum and Dudley 2001, 217, 221, 229).

There was another possible contributor to England and the Low Countries' growing prosperity; the "emerging middle-class habits of passing moral judgments on neighbors and exerting tribe-like peer pressure" were more common in Protestant Western Europe than in traditional cultures and may have contributed to the economic transformation. These Protestant characteristics sparked imitation, because they facilitated commerce. "[T]hese virtues were not the lucky *cause* of the Industrial Revolution…but rather both *cause and effect*, a part of the runaway dynamic. Moral traits conducive to the new market system were bound to appear somewhere" (Friedman and McNeill 2013, 49–50).

On the other side of the world, seventeenth-century wholesale merchants in Japan prided themselves on their independence and their unabashed profit-seeking motives. "Samurai looked down on townsmen because they thought that it was despicable to earn profits, but [Ishida] Baigan argued that to get business profits was not illegal nor should there be any distinction between samurai and *chonin* [townsmen] as far as their duties were concerned. He exhorted *chonin* to have a high moral sense and consider profits justified if they were earned legally." During the seventeenth and eighteenth centuries, hard-working, industrious *chonin* had a reasonably chance of prospering: "In the middle of the Tokugawa period [1600–1868], in the years when money begat money…men of good credit and capital grew to be begetters of more money" (Takenaka 1969, 152).

Changing Meaning of Credit

The definition of credit in the *New Palgrave Dictionary of Economics* is: "transfer [of] property rights on a given object (e.g. a sum of money) in exchange for a claim on specified objects (e.g. certain sums of money) at specified points of time in the future." Up to the seventeenth, credit meant a person's reputation or trustworthiness, derived from "the Latin *credo*: to believe or trust." This older definition was a more personal one: "it meant that you were willing to trust someone to pay you in the future. Similarly, to have credit in a community meant that you could be trusted to pay back your debts" (Eatwell et al. 1987, I:715; Muldrew 1998, 3).

Benjamin Franklin wrote in *Advice to a Young Tradesman*, "Remember this saying, The good paymaster is lord of another man's purse. He that is known to pay punctually and exactly to the time he promises, may at any time, and on any occasion, raise all the money his friends can spare."

Borrowers sent signals to lenders, as "The most trifling actions that affect a man's credit are to be regarded. The sound of your hammer at five in the morning, or eight at night, heard by a creditor, makes him easy six months longer; but if he sees you at a billiard-table, or hears your voice at a tavern, when you should be at work, he sends for his money the next day....It shows besides, that you are mindful of what you owe; it makes you appear a careful as well as an honest man, and that still increases your credit" (Franklin 1902, 153–155; Muldrew 1998, 1). To modern sensibilities, credit more often means anonymous purchases by swiping a card through a scanner or typing in the card number over the internet. Although interested parties can request your credit score, your credit reputation, although important financially, may not be as much a measure of you personally as in days past.

The emphasis upon faulty human agency loomed large in the sixteenth century and also in the minds of many scholars. To be sure, inept or dishonest managers and investors could cause their own downfall. Scandal gradually transformed from a religious term signifying discredit to the faith to a more secular meaning of "a disgraceful imputation or a grossly discreditable circumstance or event" that damages one's reputation. The Latin *scandalum* was meant to be a "moral offense or stumbling." Scandal served a social purpose in allowing members of the community "to demonstrate their indignation and condemn the offender. Scandal helps a community, therefore, to maintain the limits of acceptable behavior—in essence, to define itself in moral or ideological terms—and to market transgressions as deviant." One scholar argued that "A city that is home to a large and powerful merchant community, such as Augsburg, might be inclined to take a dimmer view of business misconduct and to have a better articulated set of legal or moral sanctions against such behavior" (Safley 2009, 43–44).

Two Different Paths

Spain and Scandinavia took different economic paths. Their respective experiences are revealing.

During the medieval era, the Norsemen transformed from raiders par excellence to traders of note. They ranged from Russia to the New World. In the *Speculum Regale* (*King's Mirror*), a father, who has observed merchants, advised his son that such a pursuit can be an honorable one: "for often the best of men are chosen for it." He warns his son to be a "true merchant" and not a mere fraud or foisterer. The father described how merchants had to face dangers on land and sea; merchants needed to be "polite and agreeable" so as to "secure friendship of all good men." He advocated attending church services (possibly as a reminder to act becomingly), but to discern which merchants "are reputed the best and most prominent" and to follow their lead. In a sense, the father was alluding to understanding the different business mores among people. The son should carefully examine the merchandise to ascertain quality (adhering to the trust but verify notion) and enlist "a few trusty men to serve at witnesses." If the son ended up with faulty merchandise, then he should try and sell such merchandise but always revealing the defects, "then you cannot be called a deceiver." With respect to pricing, the father offered some interesting advice: "put a good price on your wares, though not too high, and yet very near what you see can be obtained; then you cannot be called a foisterer." Above all, though, the son should study the Bjarkey code (a merchant code).

The father in *The King's Mirror* also advised his son, when traveling to foreign countries, to befriend the authorities and to promptly make any required fees. The son should "seek lodgings from the innkeeper who is reputed the most discreet and the most popular among kingsmen and boroughmen." If the son succeeded and accumulated what we would call a "nest egg," his father urged investing in multiple projects (after checking out the partners involved). The father recognized that there could be losses, but by diversifying, the chance of losing all was reduced. Once the son accumulated enough, he should buy farm land, "for such property is generally thought the most secure, whether the enjoyment falls to one's self or one's kinsmen" (Larson 1972, 79–80, 83–86; see also *Bulletin of the Business Historical Society* 1935, 57–58).[2]

The Scandinavian countries' Protestantism may also have been a factor in their economic progress. In contrast, Catholic Spain was once wealthy and powerful. Spanish conquests in the New World led to enriching royalty and assorted adventurers. The adventurers were opportunistic and callous of human life. They often viewed the indigenous population as objects to fulfill a goal. The inflow of gold and silver gave Spain a glow of prosperity and may have contributed to the middle and upper classes' disdain of ordinary mercantile endeavors. The get-rich-quick mentality certainly was not conducive to inculcating the virtues of commerce and trade (Argandona 1999, 156–164). Spain's economy gradually withered.

Smuggling

Protestant and Catholic rulers alike tried to control imports. Rulers' attempts to suppress consumption created opportunities for smugglers. From an ethics point of view, one point stands out: "The inefficiency or corruptibility of underpaid customs officers and anti-smuggling squads was notorious." Smuggling became rampant (Heaton 1937, 375).

The King's and Parliament's sometimes heavy-handed edicts rankled the colonists. Many colonists were hard-headed businessmen, seeking to gain profits, even if it meant breaking laws; colonial businessmen often viewed England's laws as attempts to defraud the colonists of their rightful gains. Although historian Peter Andreas may have exaggerated in depicting the colonies and United States as "Smuggler Nation," his point is apt. The colonists found it profitable and easy to evade edicts restricting trade. Colonial North America had a lengthy, isolated coastline; the British government supplied lackadaisical administration; and custom-house officials sometimes connived with the colonists. Colonists smuggled manufactured goods and commodities into the colonies; they also exported tobacco directly to Scotland (Andreas 2004, passim; Schlesinger Jr. 1957, 39–40).

The smugglers had previously benefited colonial retail merchants and customers by providing tea at prices below the combined import price and duty, but, of course, their actions were illegal. A colonial business ethicist might have taken the long view and argued that smuggling was unethical because it might induce other illegal activities, even if it currently benefited consumers and local merchants. Shippers also resorted to bribing customs officials, who faced outrage from colonials and low or dilatorily-paid salaries.

Some business operations' lobbying efforts resulted in unanticipated outcomes. The British East India Company urged Parliament to allow them to ship tea directly between Asia to America. Parliament agreed and passed the Tea Act in 1773. Instead of English merchants purchasing tea wholesale at East India Company auctions to sell to American merchants, the East India Company could now handle the tea trade directly between Asia and America; the direct route dramatically cut tea prices for Americans. The local smugglers, who throve with the previously artificially high prices of tea charged Americans, allied with tea merchants to agitate for repeal. Naturally they alleged the East India Company was "unfair foreign competition," never mind the fact that American colonists could now drink their tea and have money left over for biscuits. Agitators raised the specters of "taxation without representation and the far-fetched threat of a British takeover of all American commerce." The allegation that the East India Company could monopolize the tea trade—and other Indian imports, including silks, calicoes, spices, and chinaware—met receptive listeners. Eventually the Americans responded with the legendary "Boston Tea Party" (Schlesinger Sr. 1917, 61–62, 67, 70–73).

Wartime Ethics

Growing international trade had other repercussions. During wartime, many governments authorized privateering ventures and issued letters of marque. Merchants and other investors found the possibility of capturing vessels laden with goods alluring. During the heyday of mercantilism, privateering had the added virtue of injuring the enemy's trade while creating an inflow of resources. Here was a case of a rather dubious activity, surely unethical, given a government imprimatur.

Merchant groups formed companies to outfit privateering vessels. Such vessels required armament and a large crew, both to handle the armament and to man captured vessels. At a port such as Bristol, there were plenty of merchants and shippers available, and many switched from transporting slaves or hauling sugar and tobacco to privateering. The owners had to supply the food and pay the fixed costs of such a voyage. They selected a captain and issued lengthy orders. Privateers differed from mere pirates in having government authorization for their predatory activities. An alternative was to apply for a letter of marque, whereby an existing cargo vessel armed itself and could capture prize vessels. Vessels carrying a letter of marque were primarily interested in carrying cargo, but their owners were not averse to picking off stray ships. In both cases, the government authorization required adhering to a set of international rules respecting the rights of neutrals and providing proof that the captured vessel was actually a legal prize (Hillmann and Gathmann 2011, 733–735, 739).

A naval historian described how "lesser merchants and tradesmen" wanted a war in 1739 (and presumably supported wars throughout the century), as such wars promised "sudden riches that privateering might bestow on the lucky share-owner or lottery-ticket holder"; he summarized the business-like attitude taken by investors: "war conceived as war for trade and profit is little more than a business enterprise" (Baugh 1965, 14–15). When the attractions of privateering and letters of marque waned and the improved overseas trading opportunities waxed, British privateering activities diminished considerably.

Pirates are very chic these days. Actor Johnny Depp's Captain Jack Sparrow in *The Pirates of the Caribbean* appears to have made pirates amusingly laid-back. Real pirates would scorn the modern depiction. Economic historians have uncovered evidence that pirate crews had rules, serious rules. After all, on a vessel teeming with cutthroats, the situation could easily exceed *The Lord of the Flies*, as those were mere British schoolboys. We are talking about desperate, rapacious men. Pirates may have pioneered worker's compensation, as they had a schedule of remuneration for various injuries. Since dividing the loot could be contentious, pirates usually drew up formal rules covering division of the spoils, *before* the spoils were in front of them. Of course, as with all rules and regulations, there was always some joker willing to break the rules. Alexander Selkirk, who was later marooned on an island off the west South American coast, found out just how duplicitous a ship's captain could be. Selkirk's privateering peers looked forward to the official division of the loot. Various parties sliced off parts of the booty for sundry expenses, including lawyers, officials, storage, and so on. Apparently the irony of businessmen cheating pirates went unremarked. The crew was shocked at how little they received (roughly one-twentieth of their estimated take). Some crew members suspected the ship's captain, Woodes Rogers, of hiding much of the loot at Batavia with the intent of going back and retrieving it (Souhami [2001] 2013, 154–156).

A Continental Scandal

On land, some businessmen were as rapacious as pirates. There were business scandals on the continent. The case of Ambrosius Hochstetter, an Augsburg businessman of the early sixteenth century, is instructive. Hochstetter was a prominent figure in Augsburg with connections to the king of Bohemia. His over-reaching violated social and moral norms. Historian Thomas Safley commented, "Underlying commercial values in Augsburg, was a merchant's '*Trauen und Glauben*, that is, his credibility and creditworthiness.'" Did the merchant pay debts promptly, deal reliably, and achieve success (Poitras 2000, 81; Safley 2009, 44–45)?

Hochstetter attempted to corner the world market in mercury. Government demand for the products of the mines stabilized prices and made investments in mining attractive. The drawback was that the prince might require mine owners to provide credit in times of need; Hochstetter and the government became intertwined. After becoming king of Bohemia, Ferdinand approved the creation of a syndicate between Hochstetter and Bohemian mines, thereby adding to Hochstetter's previous acquisitions of mines in Austria. In this way, Hochstetter attempted to monopolize mercury and cinnabar. Hochstetter's attempt to corner the market failed, when he failed to acquire mines in Almaden. His stockpiles of mercury and cinnabar failed to attain monopoly prices, and Hochstetter began to liquidate his supplies at prices below the acquisition prices. In order to salvage his operations, Hochstetter began seeking loans. Rather than limiting the damage to his associates and himself, he began to spread his insolvency among a wider circle; in essence, he "infected" his associates. He cut deals with associates and competitors—selling ore to them at sub-market prices—with the stipulation that he repurchase the ore later. These men cynically agreed, figuring that Hochstetter would never be able to repurchase the ore because of his insolvency; they repaid the loans they had extended Hochstetter from selling the ore. Eventually his scheme collapsed.

Hochstetter spent years trying to preserve his *Trauen und Glauben*, but his efforts dragged down family members and his business associates. He fought accusations of fraud and deceit. In the end, he died disgraced in prison. The opprobrium heaped upon him resulted not only because of his actions but also because many perceived his actions to be contrary to the prevailing social norms. Safley believes that Hochstetter's over-reaching appeared immoral to many of his contemporaries, although other merchants "might have seen them simply as good business." His aggressive pursuit of wealth upset the principles of a static social order and obedience to social norms. In this sense, his collapse was seen as more than just a businessman grasping for more than was prudent, his actions and subsequent fraudulent behavior in acquiring loans (when he knew he was insolvent and incapable of paying back previous loans) threatened the social order (Safley 2009, 47–54).

Financial Shenanigans, Coffee Houses, and Insurance

International trade often required larger-scale investments. Before the English Civil War, financiers were practicing merchants, who engaged in various endeavors. English monarchs frequently faced the need to borrow, and a man with capital could reap interest and concessions, such as supplying the army or other transactions. "Indeed, once a business fortune reached a certain level, political advantage and a shortage of investment outlets inevitably attracted it into state finance." Although all investments incurred risk, "the great merchant was more likely to exploit the weaknesses of the public administration and to milk the taxpayer, to take his chance or early repayment from the Exchequer, than to risk his capital in commercial ventures; at the bottom [of the pool of investors] the stock market and usurious loans were the usual method of compensating for low yields in ordinary trades" (Grassby 1970, 98–102). In sixteenth-century Antwerp, companies formed cartels, brazenly creating written agreements regarding prices, outputs, and penalties for cheaters. Although monopolies were prohibited in the Low Countries, these international cartels never ran afoul of such strictures, perhaps presaging international corporations of the future. Complaints about cartel activities were frequent, but the authorities never succeeded in breaking up a cartel by government action. Some countries, such as England, even created monopoly rights by extending exclusive franchises or patents upon particular items. Parliament passed the Statute of Monopolies that reduced royal patents, but patents for inventions continued. The Statute did not affect the East India Company and other corporations (De Roover 1951, 506–507).[3]

The English Parliament and the Crown claimed the right to grant incorporation. The Crown usually granted incorporations for exploration endeavors (e.g. East India, Hudson's Bay), while Parliament specialized in domestic requests. By defining the areas where Parliament and the Crown could grant charters, competition between the bodies was minimized. Both Parliament and the Crown expected or demanded a quid pro quo in exchange for granting a charter; the inducements included a share of the profits, loans at generous terms, or assuming some government debt. Parliament members profited directly "from bribes, gifts, and purchases of stock in the South Sea Company. Outright bribery for legislative favors was apparently the 'custom of the times'" (Patterson and Reiffen 1990, 164–166).

This was rent-seeking writ large. The tragedy was that by the seventeenth century, people devoted their ingenuity not in devising more productive processes, "but in the endeavor to manipulate the power of the state and the wealth of the community for the benefit of individuals or special interests. For, let economic historians always try to remember, the aim of enterprise is to get an income; the end matters more than the means, and if the state was the fountain of valuable monopolies or privileges, why not go there for your drink."

The [British] crown of the late 1600s "frequently regarded the companies as milch kine [milk cows]; it would blithely establish a rival company and violate an old charter if more money could thereby be obtained; it would claim a share of the capital and profit, and lean on the East India Company, the South Sea Company, and, of course, the Bank of England after 1694, for loans." This abuse of its monopoly-granting power abated in the eighteenth century, when "the state found other ways of financing itself, the sale of monopolies to corporations ceased" (Heaton 1937, 378, 387). Should sympathy be extended to those acquiring arbitrary monopoly power, when the ruler reneged?

The system of granting charters both improved the prospects of successful grantees and helped ensure Parliament and the Crown "a large share of the expected profitability of the corporation." In the case of the South Sea Company, granted a charter in 1711, the company sought an amendment to its charter allowing for raising more capital. "The 'aggressive marketing scheme' it pursued triggered a bull market, which benefited not only its own new issue of shares, but those of other incorporated and unincorporated joint-stock companies as well. Some of the unincorporated companies were in the process of seeking corporate charters; some merely claimed to be seeking charters, and some were organized for the purely fraudulent purpose of cashing in on the bull market." If investors had difficulty ascertaining between fraudulent and legitimate companies, then "Parliament's ability to raise revenue through the issuance of corporate charters was undermined" (Patterson and Reiffen 1990, 167).[4]

Although granting a monopoly privilege may seem unethical, especially given the general strictures against monopolies, the governments' policies made some sense. Before the creation of the Dutch East India Company, there was "violent and not exclusively commercial" competition among the several companies involved in the trade. The Dutch States General unified these companies into the Dutch East India Company with a 21-year charter that was renewed. Creating a monopoly, of course, did not end the difficulties. India was a long way from the Netherlands, and given the international rivalry for the trade, the Dutch company had to invest large amounts of capital into fortifications and troops. The Indian potentates expected gratuities, so the Dutch greased palms (Poitras 2000, 272–273; see also Heckscher 1935, I:356).

In some cases, rent-seeking via government-created monopolies may be productive. During early modern European history, Spain and Portugal led the way in exploiting the New World and also trade around Africa into the Indian Ocean by establishing monopolies. The Dutch, French, and English entered the contest, each establishing their own trade monopolies (such as England's East India Company). The key to this argument is that the process inspired the development of large business corporations (Bang 2012, 210–211).

In Europe, the company (VOC, based upon the Dutch translation: Verenigde Oostindische Compagnie) became a vehicle for speculation. Shares moved between traders. By 1610, it was possible to short sale shares ("in blanco"). The Dutch government banned *windhandel* ("selling the wind"), but *windhandel* proved too popular and withstood repeated legislation. The fixation on windhandel kept people from focusing on calculating the appropriate price of shares. As investors suffered through a "learning-by-doing" process, market manipulation and the natural ups and downs of the market raised cries of fraud. Some parties did attempt to use short sales and unfavorable rumors to depress the value of VOC shares. Because the Directors of the VOC were politically connected, they pushed for banning the windhandel trading; the government defined short selling as "the sale of securities not owned by the seller," both cash and forward sales. All shares sold had to be transferred within a month. To bolster its edict, the government made it possible for traders to rescind a short sale in court (Poitras 2000, 277–281).

Dutch traders began using business techniques developed by Italians and Muslims, including bookkeeping. Jan Pieterszoon Coen worked for the (Dutch) United East India Company (VOC). In addition to heralding bookkeeping techniques, he advised gaining a monopoly on the nutmeg, cloves, and mace spices and also exploiting local workers, introducing slave labor, and encouraging Dutch colonists. Coen's recommendations were adopted, and recruitment began in earnest. Similar to British recruitment of soldiers and sailors, the VOC's representatives used subterfuge and deception to enlist laborers. The Dutch used women, zielverkoopers ("soul sellers"), who plied the marks with entertainment and, presumably, liquor. The enticed young men found themselves in a hellish situation, crammed into small confines with embarrassingly high death rates. The Dutch introduced a marketable security—the *transportbrief*—which was a bet on whether a zielverkoopers' recruit lived long enough to recoup the expenses of recruitment and transportation. The longer the recruit lived and earned wages, the better for the zielverkooper; a secondary market quickly developed, whereby investors purchased *transportbriefs* at discounts, depending on how likely they thought the recruit would live or die (Bernstein 2008, 228, 235–236).

Stock Traders

Daniel Defoe depicted stockjobbers in an unflattering light. He claimed, "if you talk to them of their occupation, there is not a man will own it is a complete system of knavery; that it is a trade founded in fraud, born of deceit, and nourished by trick, cheat, wheedle, forgeries, falsehoods, and all sorts of delusions; coining false news, this way good, this way bad; whispering imaginary terrors, frights, hopes, expectations, and then preying upon the weakness of those whose imaginations they have wrought upon, whom they have either elevated or depressed." Geoffrey Poitras characterizes Defoe's description as a "polemic" instead of a "reasoned discussion of stockjobbing," but since Defoe penned this in 1719 just prior to the South Sea Bubble, his contemporaries may have found him sagacious.

Defoe described Josiah Child as an eighteenth-century market guru. "Every man's Eye when he came to the Market was upon the Brokers who acted for Sir Josiah: Does Sir Josiah Sell or Buy?" Warren Buffet may assume a similar role today. Unfortunately, Sir Josiah was not above machinations. He instructed minions to put on a pessimistic affect that started a selling spree; he might even had his people sell a few of his shares. When the price sank sufficiently, Sir Josiah instructed another group of minions to surreptitiously buy the now low-priced shares (Defoe 1719, no page numbers; Poitras 2000, 290–291, 322). One question arises, how many times could Sir Josiah pull this stunt, before investors wised up?

The English Parliament viewed stockjobbing was a skeptical eye and passed acts to suppress unlicensed brokers, misuse of options, and other allegedly unsavory aspects of the stock market. One effect of [John] Barnard's Act of 1733 was to remove legal protection for options and time bargains, "leading a loose-knit group of brokers to form the London Stock Exchange."

Brokers disagreed whether options transactions were reputable, especially since options supposedly contributed to speculative excesses. Poitras admits that options and time bargains were contributory factors in the South Sea Bubble but that John Blunt's and his associates' cash market manipulations bore greater responsibility. Since there was a lag between purchase and settlement of joint-stock purchases, time bargains arose. Much depended upon whether the selling broker did or did not have possession of the underlying stock. Brokers with securities in their possession typically were not speculating, whereas those making transactions without owning the stock were likely speculating.

After the tulip mania, Mississippi, and South Sea Bubble schemes all failed, observers and historians believed that security markets were vulnerable to "extraordinary popular delusions." More recent commentators, though, have suggested that security markets were inherently rational; bubble and similar episodes reflected basic "fundamentals" that investors use to determine security prices. The seventeenth- and eighteenth-century observers, though, attributed the bubbles to market manipulation. The general perception was that small groups of insiders made the killings in the market; other beneficiaries of the bubbles included lenders to desperate losers in the speculative bubble and a few investors with an exquisite ability to time the market (Poitras 2000, 347, 354–355, 383–384).

Some scholars attributed bubbles to "tricks" that resemble allegations made in the nineteenth and twentieth centuries, including dissemination of false news to trigger a selling spree. Sometimes the dissemination consisted of an "accidental" missive dropped at an opportune place to be found to be a credulous dupe. The dupe, thinking he now had inside information, acted upon it (sometimes letting his friends in on the secret). Another tactic was for a speculator to be seen selling at a loss; such an event lent credence to the possibility that speculators believed a bear market was imminent. On the upswing, when speculators bought, nervous and timid investors had difficulty ascertaining whether the buyers truly believed the market was stronger. "[The speculators] influence the price in this way in order to sell [short] at the higher figure and thus to gain in the end. God with one breath breathed life in Adam, whereas the bears take the life of many people by inflating the price [of the shares]." This last trick required that many traders were "influenced by observations of actual trading activity."

If Europeans had wanted, they could have discovered how a market could operate efficiently with forward contracts, options, and so on. The Osaka rice market developed in the seventeenth century. The rice traders developed a rice bill, a certificate that proved versatile. From beginning as a warehouse receipt, these bills meant that the original holder possessed rice in a warehouse. Traders eventually extended delivery dates for more than a year in the future. The traded price for a rice bill determined the current price for a commodity transaction in the future. Poitras drew comparison with the market rules for trading rice bills with modern futures exchanges, before concluding "that the Osaka rice market provides the first historical instance of a functioning future exchange. There was a built-in check upon market manipulations based on dumping or hoarding of rice. The system proved durable and lasted for centuries, until the Imperial government temporarily closed the market (it was forced to re-open the market upon the ensuing chaos)" (Poitras 2000, 365–366, 390).

If corporate charters and stock trading could be dubious ventures, more sophisticated forms of insurance proved to have flaws, too. Although insurance was a beneficial innovation, there were some people willing to abuse insurance. Gerard de Malynes described in *Lex Mercatoria* the various frauds perpetrated: over-insurance, fraudulent claims, and duplication of policies (DeRoover 1974, 346–366). In seventeenth-century England, the private insurance industry faced two difficulties: inadequate underwriting and a lack of a center to transact business. Some participants wanted to get a charter for a joint-stock company that would specialize in maritime insurance. A company devoted to maritime industry could have been an improvement over the diffuse industry; from the government's point of view, granting a charter promised to bring in revenues from selling the monopoly rights.

Defoe, in his *Essay upon Projects* (1697), lauded insurance based on mutual contributions, such as the insurance of widows. Unfortunately, many of the insurance schemes that sprouted in the decade before the South Sea Bubble proved "ill-conceived and even fraudulent." Fraudsters were attracted to the pool of funds created to pay out future claims. In addition, actuarial science was still decades away (Defoe quoted in Poitras 2000, 462; see also Price 1772, 102).[5]

Lloyd's of London and Jonathan's Coffee-House were originally coffeehouses. Coffeehouses served as meeting places for investors, brokers, and jobbers seeking news and information. Some coffeehouse proprietors realized the gains to be had by providing newspapers and other printed material. In England, the securities trading market required peer pressure. A "lame duck" was someone who defaulted on a loan or securities contract. Such characters could be banned from Jonathan's Coffee Shop, although they could remain brokers. Brokers brought together buyers and sellers; they earned income from charging commissions for their services. The broker did not take a position in the security being traded. The dealers bought and sold shares for their account. In the eighteenth-century English stock market, people sometimes acted both as brokers and dealers, with the accompanying potential for abuse. Broker/dealers faced temptations when clients sought forward deliveries and trades using options (Poitras 2000, 282, 288–290, 294–296).[6]

By the end of the seventeenth century, the Royal Exchange in London was well established. Similar to the American stock market of the Gilded Age, many Englishmen viewed the Royal Exchange as disreputable. Allegations of chicanery, though, did not stop people from engaging in the South Sea Bubble. Parliament passed a law in 1697 regulating the stock exchange; in response, stock traders moved to coffeehouses in Exchange Alley. One drawback of the coffeehouses was their public nature; the traders could not exclude riff-raff, so they moved to a permanent address (Poitras 2000, 58–59).

The South Sea Bubble (and the near-contemporaneous Bubble Act of 1720) was one of the best-known speculative bubbles in financial history. The mania followed closely on the heels of the Dutch tulip mania. When the British South Sea Company (SSC) Bubble popped, the stock lost more than fifth-sixths of its value. The ostensible purpose of the Bubble Act was to correct evils in the maritime insurance industry; Poitras characterized the preamble as "necessary in order to cloak decently the real motives that had swayed King and Parliament." The act allowed the King to grant two charters to corporations for marine insurance and to protect two incumbent insurance companies; the act, therefore, was a clear case of cronyism (Poitras 2000, 453–455; Harris 1994, 610).

Economists Margaret Patterson and David Reiffen debunked the traditional story of the bubble and the Bubble Act. Their explanation of the Act was, "As non-corporations began to assume many of the rights previously enjoyed only by chartered corporations, the ability of governmental authorities to raise revenue through the issuance of charters diminished. The Bubble Act was specifically intended to prevent non-chartered firms from using the formal market, and it succeeded in doing this."

If a company did not want to or could not get a charter, they had access to "used charters." They could buy shares of an unsuccessful corporation and use that entity's charter. Parliament had not foreseen this loophole, and the resale market siphoned off money that could have gone to legislators. Aside from the direct losses, Parliament also lost revenue because the value of charters decreased, when companies with resold charters provided greater competition for firms seeking charters. Parliament and charter holders, therefore, had a mutual desire to squelch unauthorized corporations and to limit access to the capital market. Patterson and Reiffen argued that, "the Act was designed to deny unincorporated companies access to formal capital markets and to tighten the Parliamentary control over the exercise of corporate privileges" (Patterson and Reiffen 1990, 163, 168–169).

In the case of the Bubble Act, Parliament "intended to ensure that only corporations operating within the scope of their charters had access to the formal share market…[and to] enhance the importance of charters." This would protect the government's ability to generate revenue from the right to issue charter. Researcher Henry Butler believed the Bubble Act "was a government-created entry barrier designed to put out of business all business associations which were competing with Parliament's chartering business," while others believed "the act was an attempt to hinder alternative investment opportunities and to divert more capital to South Sea shares" (Patterson and Reiffen 1990, 171; Butler 1986, 172–173; Harris 1994, 612).

The South Sea Bubble arose from a situation where investors "were heavily reliant on entrenched management's vision of the future prospects of the firm….Investors did not have sufficient information to determine whether the dividend increase was sustainable, based on actual company cash flows." Perhaps similar to Enron and modern-day accounting scandals, accounting may have played a role in such early stock market bubbles. Although double-entry accounting was well established by the early eighteenth century, many people still did not understand the concepts. The contemporary accounting techniques may not have been sophisticated enough to calculate current and future profits from prospective investments. Tied with the accounting deficiencies was an element of insider trading, as politicians wanted to profit from their positions. The South Sea Bubble involved conversion of government debt, and government officials exploited their inside information regarding, "the actual condition of the Company's account." The episode might be seen as a classic case of an intersection between government and business that led to trouble.

Banker John Blunt and his colleagues made promises of generous dividends, sought the influence of high-placed people, and used current events to paint an optimistic future for the company. In addition to promising unsustainable dividends and boosting the stock price, the Sword Blade Bank allowed investors to pay only 20% down on subscriptions. The success of such heavily leveraged and over-promised stock remains impressive even today. Blunt had succeeded in getting the majority of both the House of Lords and House of Commons to invest. Sir Robert Walpole had initially been skeptical but eventually joined up (Poitras 2000, 307–308, 403–404).

The timing of the South Sea Company's stock price collapse pretty much rebutted the idea that the Bubble Act was passed in the wake of the economic turmoil. Naturally the South Sea Company's distress translated into a market-wide bear market. One researcher comments that although the Act was assumed to be directed at bubbles and speculations, the threat of a bubble was a secondary consideration. The term "Bubble Act" was rarely found in eighteenth-century sources, and the nickname became popular only in the early nineteenth century (Harris 1994, 613).

The aftermath of the collapse of the South Sea Bubble was not catastrophic. Historian John Plumb believed the collapse coincided with "an age of political stability at home and peace abroad." Later researchers revealed that "the South Sea scheme was, after all, executed successfully, solving the pressing problems of the national debt by lowering interest payments, putting the debt on a funded basis, and attracting new public creditors. The trauma sent English public finance into a new era—more efficient, more financially sound, and less corrupted by private interest." Two economic historians stressed that the episode strengthened and improved the "links between various financial markets in Western Europe" and thus facilitated "the emergence of an integrated and efficient international financial market" (Plumb 1967, 176–177; Neal and Schubert 1990, 80; Harris 1994, 625).

Puritans

Within Protestantism there were divisions. By the seventeenth century, the Puritans played a major role in the development of the British colonies and United States. Puritans recognized the danger of too much emphasis on self-love that "shut out" God and neighbor. They argued that serving one's neighbors glorified God. They, therefore, had a relationship individualism in that the individual's vocation "was service to the community, not purely service of the self. Moral character and personal discipline were exceptionally important within this theological framework. While good character could never win salvation, good character was thought to come naturally to the elect. And one's vocation provided a channel to manifest good character. Many of the minor virtues, such as diligence, thrift, careful management, sobriety…advanced on in a calling." Their relationship morality was an obligation to obey God's moral law. "Ideally, the Puritan was motivated by duty to the will of God, not the selfish hope for reward—temporal or spiritual." They recognized, as did Benjamin Franklin, that some virtues contributed to success in business, but such consideration "was not supposed to be the motive for virtuous living. That upright character was required to glorify God and serve fellow humans was reason enough" (Frey 2009, 15).

Jean Calvin used Luke 16:2 "Render account of your stewardship" in his analysis of stewardship: "It decrees that all those things were so given to us by the kindness of God…we one day render account of them. Thus, therefore, we must so arrange it that this saying may continually resound in our ears: 'Render account of your stewardship.'" Puritan theologian Richard Baxter posed a provocative point: "If God show you a way in which you may lawfully get more than in another way, (without wrong to your soul, or to any other) if you refuse this, and choose the less gainful way, you cross one of the ends of your calling, and you refuse to be God's steward, and to accept His gifts and use them for him, when he requireth it; you may labour to be rich for God, though not for the flesh and sin" (Calvin 1960, I.x.5; Luke 16:2; Baxter 1847, I:377; Abend 2014, 334).

For Puritans, economic success was a marker of God's favor, perhaps, but so was how one used this success. One had to exercise moderation not only in pursuit of success but also with regard to using one's wealth. Puritans lauded abstemious habits, because such habits freed up resources "to serve others." One was not to be a miser who accumulated for accumulation's sake (nor, presumably, was one to be a spendthrift indulging in luxurious living). Private property was a means to an end (avoiding social disorder) and not a good in itself. Aspects of Puritan thinking aligned with individualistic economic rights: "legitimacy of wealth, modern—rather than medieval attitudes toward the poor, modern notions of contracts among individuals, acceptance of market-pricing of goods and modern attitudes toward interest on loans. In each instance, the key point was that an economic freedom or institution that could enhance the individual was never considered an absolute right. Giving a sinful human such absolute rights would invariably lead to the wrong outcome—the denial of the rightful claims of God and the neighbor on the self" (Frey 2009, 16–18).

Cotton Mather acknowledged that good works would not earn salvation, but he suggested that good works might create worldly gains, including recompense and pleasure from doing good. He even alluded to a forerunner of today's prosperity gospel, whereby tithing reaped material returns. One unique aspect of his thinking was that women might be engaged in remunerative activities, so that they could provide themselves with a comfortable subsistence, but also to answer the "grand question," "For what purpose do you live; and what is the end of the actions that employ your lives?" (Mather 1838, 41).[7]

Benjamin Franklin urged thrift and put a secular spin on the topic; his advice echoed in Phineas T. Barnum's observations in his *The Art of Money Getting*. "PRESERVE YOUR INTEGRITY—It is more precious than diamonds or rubies. The old miser said to his sons: 'Get money; get it honestly, if you can, but get money.' This advice was not only atrociously wicked, but it was the very essence of stupidity….Poor fool! Not to know that the most difficult thing in life is to make money dishonestly." He held the belief that, "none of us dare to deal with him if we suspect 'false weights and measures,'" but a man "who is known to be strictly honest, may be ever so poor, but he has the purses of all the community at his disposal;—for all know that if he promises to return what he borrows, he will never disappoint them" (Barnum 2017, 36).[8] Barnum was able to purchase the American Museum, because his reputation for honesty was supported by references and he offered collateral (Vitale 1998, 96). This belief in honesty, however, may have been more accurate in Barnum's younger years during the antebellum era, when most Americans lived in small communities, where residents knew each other. A banker would be more likely to know which poor but honest families merited loans. In the America of Barnum's later adult years, growing anonymity might have rendered his belief obsolete.

America Shakes Off Its Colonial Fetters

In the British colonies along the western Atlantic coast, dynamic economies were experiencing growing pangs. Corruption pervaded the Continental Congress and early federal government. The Continental Congress proved reticent to levy taxes upon an unruly citizenry, who, after all, had been motivated to rebel, in part, by the relatively modest tax demands of the Crown. To finance the revolution, the states and Continental Congress issued money of dubious value. Colonel William Duer and his cronies understood how to play the game of using military contracts, Continental Congress currency ("not worth a Continental"), and precious metals to enrich themselves.

Duer continued his shenanigans after the war concluded. He dabbled in government debt promoted by Alexander Hamilton. Although the

Broadway show, *Hamilton*, is currently popular, there were seamy aspects to federal government debt. Duer wrote anonymous editorials urging that the nation should encourage self-interested investors and create a good reputation for the federal government by paying off the national debt. He neglected to mention that he was one of the debt holders, nor did he mention that he traded on inside information. He saw nothing untoward in buying up land certificates knowing in advance that the committee he was serving on (as secretary of the Board of Treasury) would approve. Years later, people recalled how Duer owned a fast sloop that he used in cruising Chesapeake Bay while collecting depreciated state notes at bargain prices. One might grudgingly admire Duer's initiative, but his ethics were certainly nil.

Duer got his comeuppance, when he tried to corner the market on US bonds. He took a "bull" position on the future price of the bonds. Duer's role in the scandalous supplying of General Arthur St. Clair's bungled expedition against natives in Ohio Territory in 1792 caused him public humiliation and contributed to the unraveling of his plans in the financial markets (Nelson 2012, 8, 10–11, 26).[9]

In retrospect, Alexander Hamilton's plans for the federal government's finances were sound. To induce legislators who were dubious, however, Hamilton or his subordinates greased palms with preferred access to bank stock. Congressmen therefore acquired much of the initial public offering (shades of the aftermath of the collapse of the Soviet Union). The United States owes Hamilton and Duer credit for establishing the nation's credit in international eyes, a reputation that Thomas Jefferson, though a foe of a national bank and public debt, used to acquire the Louisiana territory (Nelson 2012, 21–22).[10]

Conclusion

Protestantism proved conductive to fostering a burgeoning capitalist economy, with England and the Low Countries leading the way. The search for wealth received a more favorable interpretation from Protestant theologians. Individual probity and honesty gained prominence as useful virtues.

These advances, though, were accompanied by episodes of brazen fraud, often intertwined with government involvement. Many investors suffered through a learning process, as new financial tools and tactics arose. Despite these reverses, the dynamism of northwestern Europe and Great Britain re-shaped the business world.

By the last third of the eighteenth century, new ideas began to displace religious strictures upon business activities. Adam Smith is renowned for his discussion of how markets work. During the eighteenth century, Smith, building up past work by his mentor, Frances Hutcheson, and other philosophers analyzed moral sentiments and economics. Smith provided secular explanations for the benefits and costs of free markets and individual self-interest. His *Theory of Moral Sentiments* and *An Inquiry into the Nature and Causes of the Wealth of Nations* formalized the idea that markets often induced self-interested agents to unintentionally act in ways that promoted social welfare. Smith certainly did not see merchants and traders as paragons of ethical behavior. His famous passage about merchants gathering and conspiring against the public revealed his suspicion about their motives (Smith 1981, 145; Smith 1982, passim).

Secular ideas regarding ethics—business and otherwise—began supplanting Catholic doctrine in Western Europe and North America. Although the idea of an all-seeing deity persisted, what was considered ethical depended less upon theological doctrines and fears of eternal damnation. The motivation for ethical behavior began shifting from fear of punishment by a vengeful deity to punishment by civil authorities. Some commentators, however, began appealing to another motivation for acting ethically: ethical behavior paid. To be sure, such beliefs inhered within monotheistic beliefs, as the worthy aspired for heavenly reward. The secular version, however, equated success in the market with ethical behavior. Business participants could hope that by doing good, they could reap profits in the earthly realm.

Immanuel Kant created a different approach to ethical behavior. He argued that people had duties. By fulfilling their duties, they acted virtuously. Kant believed that motivation mattered. Virtuous people should honor their duties simply because it was the right thing to do; motivations of self-interest, therefore, would taint the virtue in honoring duties. Kant's ideas of virtue, however, proved difficult for most, if not all, people to fulfill (Kant [1998] 2016, passim).

Notes

1. Weber cites Buckle as a predecessor (Weber [1930] 2001, 10). Buckle earlier mentioned that to the Scotch divines, "Bathing, being pleasant as well as wholesome, was a particularly grievous offence; and no man could be allowed to swim on Sunday" (Buckle, *History of Civilization in England*, 783). What a ripe crowd the Scotch churchgoers must have been at their Presbyterian churches.

2. The father's advice is modern-sounding, or perhaps more accurately, today's advice is based on ancient verities.
3. Sir Thomas Gresham complained about Antwerp merchant-bankers' machinations in the money market, even though he, himself, tried to manipulate the pound sterling (De Roover 1951, 507). People liked to complain about monopolies, but given the opportunity, they would like to be monopolists.
4. Presumably the fraudulent companies hoped to raise money from investors and then let their bogus companies crash—akin to the plot line of Mel Brooks' *The Producers*. The authors listed some of the putative purposes of dubious endeavors: "to make salt water fresh," "for fatting of hogs," "for a wheel of perpetual motion," "for importing Jackasses from Spain," and "for an undertaking which shall in due time be revealed" (Patterson and Reiffen 1990, 167).
5. The failure of many of these insurance companies may have been due more to the ignorance of actuarially sound principles instead of fraud.
6. The brokers' services resembled those of bookies in twentieth-century gambling.
7. Mather inveighed against the quest for wealth in his sermon, *Lex Mercatoria: Or, the Just Rules of Commerce Declared* (1705, 6) on the "abundance of wickedness."
8. Barnum lived up to his belief. He was an ardent supporter of his hometown of East Bridgeport, Connecticut, so he helped a clock company to relocate to the town. He signed promissory notes to assist in the move, not realizing that the company was a swindle. Barnum spent years recovering from his bankruptcy and paying off every note. The financial crisis induced him to hit the speaking trail and to write books; he proved highly successful at both endeavors (Vitale 1998, 125–126).
9. Readers may rejoice to learn that Duer eventually ended in debtor's prison.
10. Thomas Jefferson was not immune to skullduggery. He attacked the proposed bank using anonymous editorials and secret attacks on Hamilton and the proposed bank. He claimed insiders obtained bank stock using money borrowed from the bank, and that board members got favorable terms for borrowing. Jefferson's hatchet man, William Giles' attacks "shocked" many legislators (Nelson 2012, 25).

Bibliography

Abend, Gabriel. *The Moral Background: An Inquiry into the History of Business Ethics* (Princeton, NJ: Princeton University Press, 2014).

Andreas, Peter. *Smuggler Nation: How Illicit Trade Made America* (New York, NY: Oxford University Press, 2004).

Argandona, Antonio. "Business Ethics in Spain." *Journal Business Ethics* 22(3), November 1999, 155–173.

Ashley, William J. *An Introduction to English Economic History and Theory. Part 1: The Middle Ages* (New York, NY: Longmans, Green, 1913). 9th Edition.

Bang, Peter. "Predation." *The Cambridge Companion to the Roman Economy*, edited by Walter Scheidel. (Cambridge, UK: Cambridge University Press, 2012), 197–217.

Barnum, Phineas. *The Art of Money Getting* (Lexington, KY: CreateSpace Independent Publishing Platform, [1880] 2017).

Baugh, Daniel. *British Naval Administration in the Age of Walpole* (Princeton, NJ: Princeton University Press, 1965).

Baxter, Richard. *The Practical Works of Richard Baxter: With a Preface Giving Some Account of the Author, and of This Edition of His Practical Works; an Essay on His Genius, Works, and Times; and a Portrait* (London, UK: Arthur Hill, 1847). 4 vols.

Becker, Sascha and Ludger Woessmann. "The Effects of the Protestant Reformation on Human Capital." *The Oxford Handbook of the Economics of Religion* (Oxford, UK: Oxford University Press 2011), 95–110.

Bernstein, William. *A Splendid Exchange: How Trade Shaped the World* (New York: Grove Press, 2008).

Blum, Ulrich and Leonard Dudley. "Religion and Economic Growth: Was Weber Right?" *Journal of Evolutionary Economics* 11(2), 2001, 207–230.

Buckle, Henry. *Introduction to the History of Civilization in England* (London, UK: George Routledge, 1904). New and revised edition. Introduction by John Robertson.

Bulletin of the Business Historical Society. "Business Methods in Norway during the Thirteenth Century." IX(4), June 1935, 57–60. No author.

Butler, Henry. "General incorporation in nineteenth century England: Interaction of common law and legislative processes." *International Review of Law and Economics* 6(2), December 1986, 169-188.

Calvin, Jean. *Institutes of the Christian religion* (Philadelphia, PA: Westminster Press, 1960). 2 vols.

De Roover, Raymond. "Monopoly Theory Prior to Adam Smith: A Revision." *Quarterly Journal of Economics* 65(4), November 1951, 492–524.

De Roover, Raymond. "Gerard de Malynes as an Economic Writer: From Scholasticism to Mercantilism," in *Business, Banking, and Economic Thought in Late Medieval and Early Modern Europe* (Chicago, IL: University of Chicago Press, 1974), 346–66.

Defoe, Daniel. "The Anatomy of Exchange Alley." 1719. https://www.litencyc.com/php/anthology.php?UID=150, viewed June 5, 2017.

Eatwell, John, Murray Milgate, and Peter Newman. Editors. *The New Palgrave: A Dictionary of Economics* (New York, NY: Stockton Press, 1987). 4 vols.

Franklin, Benjamin. "Advice to a Young Tradesman." *Little Masterpieces*, edited by Bliss Perry. (New York, NY: Doubleday & McClure, 1902), 153–155.

Frey, Donald. *America's Economic Moralists: A History of Rival Ethics and Economics* (Albany, NY: State University of New York Press, 2009).

Friedman, Daniel and Daniel McNeill. *Morals and Markets: The Dangerous Balance* (New York, NY: Palgrave Macmillan, 2013). 2nd edition.

Grassby, Richard. "English Merchant Capitalism in the Late Seventeenth Century. The Composition of Business Fortunes." *Past & Present* 46(1), February 1970, 87–107.

Harris, Ron. "The Bubble Act: Its Passage and Its Effects on Business Organization." *Journal of Economic History* 54(3), September 1994, 610–627.

Heaton, Herbert. "Heckscher on Mercantilism." *Journal of Political Economy* 45(3), June 1937, 370–393.

Heckscher, Eli. *Mercantilism*, translated by Mendel Shapiro (London, UK: George Allen & Unwin, 1935). 2 vols.

Hillmann, Henning and Christina Gathmann. "Overseas Trade and the Decline of Privateering." *Journal of Economic History* 71(3), September 2011, 730–761.

Kant, Immanuel. *Groundwork of the Metaphysics of Morals*, edited by Mary Gregor and Jens Timmermann (Cambridge, UK: Cambridge University Press, [1998] 2016). Revised edition.

Larson, Laurence. *The King's Mirror (Speculum regale-Konungs skuggsja)* (New York, NY: Twayne, 1972).

Luther, Martin. "The Babylonian Captivity of the Church." *Luther's Works*, edited by Abdel Ross Wentz, translated by A.T.W. Steinhauser (Philadelphia, PA: Fortress Press, 1959). 55 vols. Volume 36, 5–126.

Mather, Cotton. *Lex Mercatoria: Or, the Just Rules of Commerce Declared* (Boston, MA: Timothy Green, 1705).

Mather, Cotton. *Essays to do good: Addressed to all Christians, whether in public or private capacities* (New York, NY: American Tract Society, 1838).

Muldrew, Craig. *The Economy of Obligation: The Culture of Credit and Social Relations in Early Modern England* (New York, NY: St. Martin's Press, 1998).

Neal, Larry and Eric Schubert. *The Rise of Financial Capitalism: International Capital Markets in the Age of Reason* (Cambridge, UK: Cambridge University Press, 1990).

Nelson, Scott. *A Nation of Deadbeats: An Uncommon History of America's Financial Disasters* (New York, NY: Alfred A. Knopf, 2012).

Patterson, Margaret and David Reiffen. "Effect of the Bubble Act on the Market for Joint Stock Shares." *Journal of Economic History* 50(1), March 1990, 163–171.

Plumb, John. *The Origins of Political Stability, England 1675–1725* (Boston, MA: Houghton Mifflin, 1967).

Poitras, Geoffrey. *The Early History of Financial Economics, 1478–1776* (Cheltenham, UK: Edward Elgar, 2000).

Price, Richard. *Observations on reversionary payments on schemes for providing annuities for widows, and for persons in old age; on the method of calculating the values of assurances on lives; and on the national debt* (Dublin, Ireland: James Williams, and David Hay, 1772). 3rd edition.

Safley, Thomas. "Business Failure and Civil Scandal in Early Modern Europe." *Business History Review* 83(1), Spring 2009, 35–60.

Schlesinger, Arthur Sr. "Uprising against the East India Company." *Political Science Quarterly* 32(1), March 1917, 60–79.

Schlesinger, Arthur Jr. *The Colonial Merchants and the American Revolution, 1763–1776* (New York: Frederick Ungar Publishing, 1957).

Smith, Adam. *An Inquiry into the Nature and Causes of the Wealth of Nations*, edited by R.H. Campbell and A.S. Skinner (Indianapolis, IN: Liberty*Classics*, 1981).

Smith, Adam. *The Theory of Moral Sentiments*, edited by D.D. Raphael and A.L. Macfie (Indianapolis, IN: Liberty Fund, 1982).

Souhami, Diana. *Selkirk's Island* (London, UK: Quercus, [2001] 2013).

Takenaka, Yasukazu. "Endogenous Formation and Development of Capitalism in Japan." *Journal of Economic History* 29(1), March 1969, 141–162.

Tertullian. n.d. *De Idolotria*. www.tertullian.org/works/de_idololatria.htm (viewed November 4, 2017, 10:45am).

Viner, Jacob. *The Role of Providence in the Social Order: an Essay in Intellectual History* (Philadelphia, PA: American Philosophical Society, 1972).

Viner, Jacob. *Religious Thought and Economic Society* (Durham, NC: Duke University Press, 1978).

Vitale, Joe. *There's a Customer Born Every Minute: P.T. Barnum's Secrets to Business Success* (New York, NY: AMACOM, 1998).

Weber, Max. *The Protestant Ethic and the Spirit of Capitalism*, translated by Talcott Parsons (London: Routledge-Classics, [1930] 2001).

Woodberry, Robert. "Religion and the Spread of Human Capital and Political institutions: Christian Missions as a Quasi-Natural Experiment." *The Oxford Handbook of the Economics of Religion*, edited by Rachel McCleary (Oxford, UK: Oxford University Press 2011), 111–131.

CHAPTER 12

Birth of a Consumer Society in Eighteenth-Century England

By the eighteenth century, wages were high in the Low Countries and England. These high wages reflected the high productivity of these workers. British workers enjoyed prosperity compared with most European workers (aside from workers in the Low Countries). Even as early as the fifteenth century, workers in London had incomes above a hypothetical poverty line. Workers in southern Europe fell below the poverty line and although they might have sought more work, they may have resorted to spending their income on cheaper calories, such as bread (Allen 2001, 430–432).

English workers gained a measure of prosperity beyond mere survival. To be sure, the margin was not large nor was it certain. English workers, though, could occasionally purchase a luxury item. Was it ethical for producers to cater to such consumers? At the same time, producers were improving techniques for larger-scale production of goods, often involving new forms of labor organization. Was the imposed discipline required to reap the greater productivity and accompanying higher wages ethical? Formerly independent craftsmen thought not and rebelled at the loss of their independence. Producers and merchants turned to advertising to sell off the greater amounts of goods produced.

D. G. Surdam, *Business Ethics from Antiquity to the 19th Century*,
https://doi.org/10.1007/978-3-030-37165-4_12

Today's Consumer Economy: Descendant of the Past

Compound growth rates in modern economies have succeeded in lifting almost all people's incomes, as economist Fred Hirsch pointed out: "The luxury goods of one generation became the standard items of the next and the necessities of the third; as happened with motor cars, washing machines, television sets, and foreign travel, in this century, and in slower motion, with brick houses and glass windows in earlier ones." This measure of economic welfare relies upon a "commodity fetishism." An analogy highlights the weakness of this belief: "What is neglected is that by the time the sought-after ground is reached by the rear of the column [using an analogy of a column of marching people, with the wealthiest at the front and the poorest at the rear], that ground will have been affected by the passage of the column itself." The coveted automobile of 1910 becomes the utilitarian vehicle of 1928 or later: owning an automobile no longer has the cachet it did, say, in 1910, and new owners in 1928 faced greater congestion and parking restrictions (Hirsch 1976, 166–167).[1]

The diffusion of television in the United States was a classic example. In 1946, only a few thousand Americans owned a television. Early owners invited friends over to watch the new novelty, thereby gaining some social prestige. By 1960, almost 90% of American households had televisions (Surdam 2015, 5, 189–190).[2]

John Ford's movie version of John Steinbeck's *The Grapes of Wrath* exemplifies Hirsch's thesis, when it created quite a stir in the Soviet Union. Presumably some good socialist thought the movie would demonstrate how bad things were in the decadent capitalist country. The moviegoers in the USSR were not upset with the Californians' treatment of the Joad family, but they were amazed by the fact that every American "peasant owned a car and wore shoes." Modern people forget, however, just how limited many people's budgets were in the past. Widespread rampant consumerism was impossible even in such advanced nations as eighteenth-century France (Jackson 1985, 187–188; Hufton 1974, 39, 144–145, 281–298, 330, 335–356).

Historians have identified several societies across times that may have started a revolution in consumption (McCracken 1990, 9; Mukerji 1983, 9, 12, 16–20). Not only was consumption a means for status competition but also a political tool: "The sumptuous style of life at Versailles provided little personal pleasure either for the king or for his courtiers. That was not its purpose. The ceremonies of consumption…were all part of a calculated system that had as its aim not individual gratification but enhancement of political authority. Louis XIV transformed consumption into a method of rule" (Williams 1982, 28).

Anthropologist Grant McCracken argued that, "The new prosperity of the period," especially in the Netherlands and Great Britain, "brought all of these factors, old and new, to a pitch of intensity that suggested to some contemporary observers than an 'epidemical madness' had taken hold of England." Josiah Wedgwood learned to harness these trends. "The point of entry for a fashion was the upper classes and, until Wedgwood, their choice of a new fashion was a relatively discretionary matter made according to their own pleasure and the court's direction. After Wedgwood, the upper classes became a target of marketing influence. Wedgwood sought to insinuate his goods into the lifestyle of this group in the hope that these goods would then trickle downward to the lower classes." When he succeeded, "he was able to exploit the competitive spending of the period to his own advantage. This 'domestication' of a natural market force must rank as one of the important developments in the market's growing sophistication in the manipulation of demand" (McCracken 1990, 17–18).

McKendrick's Thesis

Neil McKendrick claimed that English consumers in the late 1700s responded to increased prosperity by accelerating their purchases of consumer goods; their new propensity was a watershed. McKendrick's thesis of a consumer revolution in eighteenth-century British spurred by Josiah Wedgwood's infusing his pottery with class and status meanings has not gone unchallenged. The mark of a true seminal scholarly piece is the debate it engenders, and McKendrick was successful in that regard (McKendrick 1982, 9; Weatherill 1997, 206–227; Lancaster 1995, 162–163, Lears 1989, 74).

Historian David Eversley asserts that Wedgwood gained prestige by exporting his pottery to wealthy clients overseas, but as these were often gifts, he needed the revenues generated by selling his "seconds" to British consumers. There was another aspect to the growing prosperity of lower- and middle-income Britons during the eighteenth and nineteenth centuries. Thomas Malthus' pessimism notwithstanding, British people chose to reduce the size of their families. With smaller families, less money had to go for food, leaving a greater amount for decencies and luxuries. After 1740, "more people live in a non-catastrophic world. Food, shelter, and clothing became a certain expectation. Calamitous deaths become rarer. Opportunities for upward movement become more frequent."

Eversley concluded that the years 1750–1780 "form an essential part of the preparation for full-scale industrialization." British workers and farm laborers gained a measure of income above subsistence that was not co-opted by the government through taxation or by additional mouths. Employers were unable or unwilling to push wages down to subsistence, nor was there an influx of immigration that depressed wages (Eversley 1968, 232–234, 254–256).

Historian John Plumb agreed with McKendrick that English consumer demand rose significantly during the eighteenth century, becoming "the first society dedicated to ever-expanding consumption based on industrial production. For this to succeed required men and women to believe in growth, in change, in modernity; to believe that the future was bright... also that what was new was desirable." People yearned for "fresh experiences and novel excitements" and "aggressive consumption [was] at the heart of successful bourgeois society" (Plumb 1982, 316).

Josiah Wedgwood and the Rise of Consumer Demand

One can see examples of eighteenth-century pottery and porcelain in London's Albert and Victoria Museum. Although one can admire the craftsmanship and beauty of the objects, Neil McKendrick suggests that twenty-first-century people have difficulty understanding what the objects meant to eighteenth-century buyers: "the craving to possess [crockery] which gripped so many layers of eighteenth-century society." He likens the phenomenon to a "mania" akin to the exuberance surrounding the tulips early in the eighteenth century; underlying both manias was the participation of a wider swath of the population.

McKendrick argued that Matthew Boulton's and Wedgwood's contributions to marketing have been overshadowed by their association with the steam engine and advances in manufacturing; he made the argument that such emphasis distorts the two men—friendly rivals—and their other seminal achievements. Boulton and Wedgwood pondered how to not only exploit existing demand, but also "to release the potentiality of latent demand, and by creating new wants and provoking new needs, to create new demand." They succeeded in manipulating fashion. Both practiced what is known today as product placement; rather than place their products on the stage or other live entertainments (such as modern-day product placement in television and movies), they placed their products with royalty and, to drum up demand overseas, with ambassadors. In the 1950s, such commentators as Vance Packard and John Kenneth Galbraith would cast a doubtful eye upon the desirability of marketers "creating" demand. No doubt such commentators would question using snobbery, such as Wedgwood and Boulton had, to stoke demand.[3] In some sense, however, "creating" demand may be off-the-mark. The underlying demand to imitate one's social betters probably existed from the earliest hierarchical societies; what entrepreneurs did was to show how the low classes could do so. In any case, questions of the propriety of stoking demand remain topics of discussion in today's world.

Among their tactics to bring attention and trigger interest in their wares, Boulton and Wedgwood maintained London showrooms; used lavish, self-serving advertisements with references to royal patronage; and held "spectacular" sales. The two monitored each other's marketing activities, and one might surmise that the competition spurred them to continual improvement. Sometimes they resorted to bribing opinion makers; Boulton's agent suggested a bribe to the newspapers to get favorable publicity (puffs) (McKendrick 1982, 69–77, 100–101).

Boulton, similar to Wedgwood, knew that anticipating the public's tastes was paramount, lest his company end up with unwanted inventory. In a sense, his business plan was depended upon royal patronage as the tip and small buyers and sellers as the mass of the wedge to induce consumerism. Boulton made inroads with French buyers. He engaged in industrial espionage and bribery to gain the secret of manufacturing ormolu (gilded brass), which had been a monopoly of the French. By acting in such fashion, he provided competition in the market and benefited consumers, but, of course, the ethics of stealing industrial secrets offset the benefits. Then again, the French monopoly was an artificial barrier (Robinson 1963, 47–51, 58–59; Jones 1973, 217–218).[4]

Because of Wedgwood and Boulton's successes, their rivals, and there were some formidable ones, often made imitation the sincerest form of profitability. Rivals pirated Boulton's ideas and goods. Wedgwood, too, faced imitators, forcing him to continually seek new designs and techniques to stay ahead of his rivals. Because of Wedgwood's reputation for style and quality, he was able to charge more than his rivals; indeed, he followed a policy of "improv[ing] the quality of the articles of my manufacture, rather than to lower their price." McKendrick observes, "He did not charge his pottery at what it was worth (from the point of view of production costs) but at what the nobility would pay for it." He also worried that during business slumps, his competitors "are quite in a Pannick for their trade, & indeed I think with great reason, for *low prices* must beget a *low quality* in the manufacture, which will beget *contempt*, which will beget *neglect* [italics in original], & disuse, and there is an end of the trade" (McKendrick 1982, 104–107; see also Robinson 1963, 60).

Wedgwood's exports were successful enough that, at times, he had difficulty keeping up with demand. In some cases, he purchased products from his rivals in order to fulfill orders, passing them off as Wedgwood products—surely a dubious and risky practice. Some of his buyers realized they were being sent non-Wedgwood products, but as long as they received some actual Wedgwood products, they did not complain too vociferously. Presumably Wedgwood wanted to protect his brand name, and he may have placed the non-Wedgwood masquerading as Wedgwood pottery in "less discerning markets." Then again, Wedgwood's rivals were not unwilling to sell their products as Wedgwood products or close imitations (McKendrick 1982, 135–138).

Benefits from the Desire for Luxuries

British consumers began to indulge in such exotic fare as sugar, caffeine drinks, and tobacco. The consumption of such products raised fears that the lower classes were imitating their betters and spending profligately. Imitating their betters threatened to dilute or undermine the elite's recognizability and cachet (Shammas 1993, 178; Shammas 1990, 76).

The increase in consumption was associated with an "industrious revolution, according to economic historian Jan de Vries": "Driven by a combination of commercial incentives (changes in relative prices, reduced transaction costs) and changes in tastes, this 'industrious revolution' emanating to a substantial degree from the aspirations of the family, preceded and prepared the way for the Industrial Revolution. This industrious revolution, a change in household behavior with important demand-side features, began in advance of the Industrial Revolution, a fundamentally supply-side phenomenon." Another historian also discussed whether English workers chose to work longer hours in order to buy the enticing goods available. Jones describes an "industrious disposition," whereby family members, especially women and children, opted to work more in order for the family to enjoy some amenities.

De Vries argued that households reduced leisure, when the marginal utility of money income rose because of the availability of more desirable commodities to buy. Males might have worked longer hours or more intensively, but often women and children entered the labor force. De Vries' argument was not without detractors. There was no shortage of contemporary observers chastising workers for their lackadaisical approach to work. De Vries believes that much of these diatribes were motivated by ideology. Historian Edward (E.P.) Thompson memorably portrayed British workers as requiring a newfound discipline, replete with fines, bells, clocks, and other tactics. De Vries, though, cited contemporary observers such as Daniel Defoe and Arthur Young, who depicted industrious families working hard in order to purchase the new consumer goods (De Vries 1994, 255–258; Jones 1973, 199–201, 212–213; McKendrick 1974, 172–173, 184–199).

One economist pointed out that Thompson relied mostly upon anecdotal evidence in arguing that workers were *forced* to work longer and harder. Hans-Joachim Voth used evidence from court cases; witnesses described what they were doing on the day of the crime. Some observers during the early eighteenth century (and throughout English and American industrialization into the twentieth century) claimed paying high wages simply subsidized workers' riotous dissipation; they believed a low wage was a better disciplinarian (Voth 1998, 36; Gilboy [1934] 1969, 21).

By the 1760s and 1770s, Sir James Steuart and Adam Smith could remark with accuracy that men were working harder. Steuart pithily wrote that workers are now "slaves to their own wants," while Smith believed liberal wages induced men to "overwork themselves." Between men working harder and the entrance of women and children into the labor force, households now had greater purchasing power with which to buy consumer goods. De Vries disagreed with Neil McKendrick on the timing of the entrance of women and children into the labor force. De Vries claimed that the phenomenon began before industrialization. Both authors, though, took a more benign stance with regard to women and child labor than had many historians.

In any event, by the end of the eighteenth century, England had a large labor force accustomed to the new industrial discipline. De Vries acknowledged that this intensification of work effort was not an unalloyed good; in some cases, fathers may have exploited family members, pressing them to enter the labor force while dictating how the money would be spent (De Vries 1994, 112–114, 260).[5]

Was Consumption Beneficial?

Writers debated the desirability of widespread consumerism, but Bernard Mandeville pioneered the thesis that consumption, rather than being deleterious to a nation's interest, was actually beneficial. Mandeville's *Fable of the Bees* was both provocative and scandalous (much as Thorstein Veblen's *Theory of the Leisure Class* would be two centuries later). Mandeville stood dogma on its head, arguing that such sins as "luxury, avarice, prodigality, pride, envy, and vanity benefited society." Religious leaders, such as John Wesley, damned and politicians scoffed at Mandeville's ideas. One anonymous poet wrote lines of doggerel: "And, if GOD-MAN Vice to abolish came, Who Vice commends, MAN-DEVIL be his Name." The French hanged a copy of the book while burning Mandeville in effigy.[6]

Mandeville's idea that good wages were beneficial economically, as such wages boosted effective demand, seems tame today, but the idea infuriated his contemporaries. The specter of workers gaining a measure or more of prosperity threatened the social and political status quo. Landowners and others demanded sumptuary laws; Jonathan Swift contributed a piece inveighing against rampant consumerism. Swift and the landowners were facing a strong current of consumerism, and their ideas were repudiated. By the time Adam Smith wrote his *Wealth of Nations*, consumerism was accepted, if, in some quarters, grudgingly. Instead of using penury and want as incentives to work, the new shibboleth was that novel, exciting, and attainable consumer goods and services induced work effort.

The desire for imported goods threatened the prevailing wisdom (at least prevailing among the ruling classes) of mercantilism, with its obsession for maintaining a positive balance of payment (usually by discouraging imports and emphasizing exports). Buying luxury goods and other imports threatened the nation's balance-of-power and raised questions of whether importers were acting responsibility. The importation of cheap calico and muslins from India was an early harbinger of the new consumerism, although tobacco, sugar, tea, and coffee were also key imports (McKendrick 1982, 13–19).

Upticks in consumer spending were met by resistance. One scholar details how clergy railed against both "the love of lucre and the sin of unbridled appetite." One is hard-pressed to come up with a more adamant criticism of spending on non-essentials, than John Dennis' quote in 1711: "Luxury, the spreading Contagion of which is the greatest Corrupter of Publick Manners and the greatest Extinguisher of Publick Spirit." Spending on non-essentials was not only waste, it was dissipation and dissolution. Post-Restoration author Richard Morton detailed the inevitable fate of profligates, who indulged in lavish spending on food: "too plentiful and unseasonable gorging of meat and drink and also an imprudent choice of such meats and liquors as abound with excrementatious parts and not easy to be digested" leading to "wasting distempers" and jaundice. His contemporary, George Cheyne entitled his book, *English Malady—A Treatise of Nervous Diseases*; indulgent appetites were not only a waste of money, they wasted health. He excoriated the efforts of merchants and traders in supplying such exotics as tea, tobacco, and other goods from around the world. Modern readers would probably find his list of luxuries to be bizarre; certainly modern people would consider several of the following commodities to be necessities and not luxuries: "soft beds, late rising, later nights, artificial lighting and heating, tight-lacing and above all elaborate cuisines culled from all corners of the globe" (Porter 1994, 58–59, 62–64).

Cheyne and others used "consumption" in its dual meaning: using up a commodity and a wasting disease. They worried that the wasting disease definition was becoming widespread. The laboring poor, especially in France, hardly able to intake sufficient calories to perform light work or to beg on the streets, of course, were wasted and stunted in a literal sense.[7]

An interesting aspect of the market in early modern England was the propensity of children of wealthy families to rack up debts through lavish lifestyles. These heirs borrowed against their expected bequests. The difficulty occurred when heirs went bust; on occasion they brought ruin to their families. To Elizabethans, the specter of noble families becoming impoverished was a threat to social stability. The Chancery dealt with this problem by "developing equitable doctrines which released heirs from their debts." The rationale was to protect the social structure and to "prevent what was a growing mischief to ancient families, that of seducing an heir apparent from a dependence on his ancestor." To historian Eric Posner, "the expectant heir problem is also a possible illustration of the problem of welfare opportunism" (Posner 1995, 314–316).

Conclusion

The growing number of businessmen and tradesmen had an important ramification for the development of English society. Instead of a bourgeois made up of bureaucrats, England had a middle rank "dedicated to making money." These men did not descend from the privileged class, "Many had scrappy academic education and none paper qualifications, but they knew how to seal a deal." Some contemporaries found this an advantage, lauding the businessman of being "of liberal sentiment, a barbarous and commercial people is a contradiction." Historian Roy Porter concludes, "It was these swarms of the petty bourgeoisie who helped make the English economy special….England had a lively economy in which plenty of enterprising masters and dealers were successful, while home consumption amongst middling families proved a bellows for workshop-based manufacturing capitalism." Porter quoted Giuseppe Baretti's observation, "The English do their utmost to make money: but once they have made it, they spend it freely." Another difference was that governments employed technologists on the continent, but most of the English technologists were self-employed entrepreneurs (Porter 1982, 92–93, 97–98).[8]

A final question arises with regard to the burgeoning consumer demand of the eighteenth-century. Modern-day adherents—such as John Galbraith and Vance Packard—of the theory that marketing manipulates consumers into buying things they don't need and didn't want previously, may overstate the persuasive power of advertisers. Consumers need to translate their ability to buy into a willingness to buy; Josiah Wedgwood might have influenced this process, but, as Jan de Vries states, "it also took the willingness to shift one's tastes to acquire the ability to act on that desire" (De Vries 1993, 117; 199–201).

Without the willingness by middle- and lower-income classes to consume beyond basic necessities, the growing productive capacity of the eighteenth century on would have been for naught.

Notes

1. Friedrich Hayek claimed, "Even the poorest today owe their relative material well-being to the results of past inequality" (Hayek 1960, 44).
2. Televisions of 1960 were superior to those of 1946, but by 1960 wealthy Americans were beginning to buy the new color televisions.

3. De Beers diamond cartel practiced similar product placement, using the English royalty and American motion picture stars.
4. For Boulton's successes in selling to the Russian court, see Jones (1973, 216–217).
5. Gilboy agreed, in essence, with McKendrick (Gilboy 1932, 629–630).
6. Adam Smith was not a fan of Mandeville (Smith 1982, 308).
7. Floud et al. (2011, 11, 17–18) for caloric intake and definitions of "wasted" and "stunted."
8. Adam Smith addressed the depiction of England as a nation of shopkeepers (Smith 1981, 613; Porter 1982, 92–96).

Bibliography

Allen, Robert "The Great Divergence in European Wages and Prices from the Middle Ages to the First World War." *Explorations in Economic History* 38(4), 2001, 411-447.

De Vries, Jan. "Between Purchasing Power and the World of Goods: Understanding the Household Economy in Early Modern Europe." *Consumption and the World of Goods*, edited by John Brewer and Roy Porter (London, UK: Routledge, 1993), 85–132.

De Vries, Jan. "The Industrial Revolution and the Industrious Revolution." *Journal of Economic History* 54(2), June 1994, 249-270.

Eversley, David E.C. "The Home Market and Economic Growth in England, 1750–1780." *Land, Labour and Population in the Industrial Revolution: Essays presented to J.D. Chambers,* edited by E.L. Jones and G.E. Mingay (New York, NY: Barnes & Noble, 1968), 206–259.

Floud, Roderick, Robert W. Fogel, Bernard Harris, and Sok Chul Hong. *The Changing Body: Health, Nutrition, and Human Development in the Western World since 1700* (Cambridge: Cambridge University Press, 2011).

Gilboy, Elizabeth. "Demand as a Factor in the Industrial Revolution." *Facts and Factors in Economic History*, edited by Arthur Cole (Cambridge, MA: Harvard University Press, 1932), 620-639.

Gilboy, Elizabeth. *Wages in Eighteenth Century England* (New York, NY: Russell & Russell, [1934] 1969).

Hayek, Friedrich. *The Constitution of Liberty* (Chicago, IL: University of Chicago Press, 1960).

Hirsch, Fred. *Social Limits to Growth* (Cambridge, MA: Harvard University Press, 1976).

Hufton, Olwen. *The Poor of Eighteenth-Century France, 1750–1789* (Oxford, UK: Clarendon Press, 1974).

Jackson, Kenneth T. *Crabgrass Frontier: The Suburbanization of the United States* (New York: Oxford University Press, 1985).

Jones, Eric. "The Fashion Manipulators: Consumer Tastes and British Industries, 1660–1800." *Business Enterprise and Economic Change: Essays in Honor of Harold F. Williamson*, edited by Louis Cain and Paul Uselding (Kent, OH: Kent State University Press, 1973), 198–226.

Lancaster, William. *The Department Store: A Social History* (London, UK: Leicester University Press, 1995).

Lears, Jackson. "Beyond Veblen, Rethinking Consumer Culture in America." *Consuming Visions, Accumulation and the Display of Goods in America, 1880–1920*, edited by Simon Bronner (New York, NY: W.W. Norton, 1989), 73–97.

McCracken, Grant. *Culture and Consumption: New Approaches to the Symbolic Character of Consumer Goods and Activities* (Bloomington, IN: Indiana University Press, 1990).

McKendrick, Neil. "Home Demand and Economic Growth: A New View of the Role of Women and Children in the Industrial Revolution." *Historical Perspectives: Studies in English Thought and Society in Honour of J.H. Plumb*, edited by Neil McKendrick (London, UK: Europa Publications, 1974), 152–210.

McKendrick, Neil. "Commercialization and the Economy." *The Birth of a Consumer Society: The Commercialization of Eighteenth-Century England*, edited by Neil McKendrick, John Brewer, and John Plumb (Bloomington, IN: Indiana University Press, 1982), Vi-262.

Mukerji, Chandra. *From Graven Images: Patterns of Modern Materialism* (New York, NY: Columbia University Press, 1983).

Plumb, John. "Commercialization and Society." *The Birth of a Consumer Society: The Commercialization of Eighteenth-Century England*, edited by Neil McKendrick, John Brewer, and John Plumb (Bloomington, IN: 1982), 265–334.

Porter, Roy. *English Society in the Eighteenth Century* (Middlesex, UK: Penguin Books, 1982).

Porter, Roy. "Consumption: Disease of the Consumer Society." *Consumption and the World of Goods*, edited by John Brewer and Roy Porter (Oxon, UK: Routledge, 1994), 58–81.

Posner, Eric. "Contract Law in the Welfare State: A Defense of the Unconscionability Doctrine, Usury Laws, and Related Limitations on the Freedom to Contract." *Journal of legal Studies* 24(2), June 1995, 283–319.

Robinson, Eric. "Eighteenth-Century Commerce and Fashion: Matthew Boulton's Marketing Techniques." *Economic History Review*, New Series 16(1), 1963, 39–60.

Shammas, Carole. *The Pre-industrial Consumer in England and America* (Oxford, UK: Clarendon Press, 1990).

Shammas, Carole. "Changes in English and Anglo-American Consumption from 1550 to 1800." *Consumption and the World of Goods*, edited by John Brewer and Roy Porter (London, UK: Routledge, 1993), 177–205.

Smith, Adam. *An Inquiry into the Nature and Causes of the Wealth of Nations*, edited by R.H. Campbell and A.S. Skinner (Indianapolis, IN: Liberty*Classics*, 1981).

Smith, Adam. *The Theory of Moral Sentiments*, edited by D.D. Raphael and A.L. Macfie (Indianapolis, IN: Liberty Fund, 1982).

Surdam, David. *Century of the Leisured Masses: Entertainment and the Transformation of Twentieth-Century America* (New York, NY: Oxford University Press, 2015).

Voth, Hans-Joachim. "Time and Work in Eighteenth-Century London." *Journal of Economic History* 58(1), March 1998, 29–58.

Weatherill, Laura. "The Meaning of Consumer Behaviour in Late Seventeenth Century and Early Eighteenth Century England." *Consumption and the World of Goods*, edited by John Brewer and Roy Porter (London, UK: Routledge, 1997), 206–227.

Williams, Rosalind. *Dream Worlds: Mass Consumption in Late Nineteenth-Century France* (Berkeley, CA: University of California Press, 1982).

CHAPTER 13

Quakers and Business Ethics

Some religious groups are noted for the business successes of many of the group's members. The Quakers present a group of believers whose economic success relied upon strong ethical discipline and peer scrutiny.

Quakers also avoided producing goods and services associated with slavery and war. Since slavery and war were prevalent during the eighteenth and early nineteenth century, Quaker business owners faced chronic temptations to make profits from proscribed activities. Critics claimed Quakers were hypocritical with regard to slave labor and wage labor, but many Quakers proved more benign employers than non-Quaker employers.

Although Quakers often proved astute business operators, their children and employees often chafed at their paternalism and strict discipline. Their strict ethics contained both seeds of success and futility. The Quakers' ranks would never swell, and successful fathers might watch as sons pursued more worldly lifestyles.

The Quakers

The Quakers were dissenters; the British monarchy ruthlessly persecuted Quakers in the seventeenth century. The ruling elites had plenty of reasons to be suspicious of Quakers, since Quakers disdained privilege and rank. George Fox described the rich man as "'the greatest thief,' because he acquired his wealth 'by cozening and cheating, by lying and defrauding'"

D. G. Surdam, *Business Ethics from Antiquity to the 19th Century*,
https://doi.org/10.1007/978-3-030-37165-4_13

(Walvin 1997, 15). Even as the English rulers began to diminish their persecution, Quakers were barred from holding political office. Their persecution inspired an empathy for people facing similar injustice. The Quakers emphasized self-denial and avoidance of luxury and self-indulgence. Their tightly knit community and communal discipline created trust between members that proved useful in trade; the peer pressure aspect raised the cost of malfeasance. One difference, perhaps, between Quakers and Puritans was: "The Quaker business ethic legitimized but also tempered capitalism by defining the proper means and ends of business. It called for fair dealing and financial rectitude and encouraged the search for 'innocent trades.' The stewardship of wealth insisted on the social obligations of riches, but it did not undermine the basis of property interests." The Quakers also insisted upon philanthropy as a "test of religious purity." They conferred status upon those who did good in the world, "preferably in full public view" (Dellheim 1987, 14–15).

Because they understood what it was like to have been persecuted, Quakers opposed "outrageous penal punishments" and urged more humane treatment of prisoners, the poor, and other downtrodden people. Similar to Jesus Christ, they reached out to some of the most deprived groups. They were consistent in their call for humane treatment with regard to their own servants. Quakers were directed to obey the Golden Rule by treating their servants as they—the masters—would deign be treated.

Contemporaries recognized Quaker success in business as early as 1697: "[Quakers] Grip'd Mammon as hard as any of their neighbours; and now call Riches a Gift and a Blessing from God." By the outbreak of World War I, however, the Quakers' economic success "would have staggered their forbears" (Walvin 1997, 2, 124–125, 176–177).

Quaker Attitudes Toward Commerce and Trade

George Fox was unenthusiastic regarding commerce and trade; he held a common view that participants resorted to unethical, deceitful, and immoral practices. If a Quaker chose to engage in business, Fox urged that he not overextend his business and be unable to act with honor, meet their promises, or to maintain their reputation (Walvin 1997, 32).

Quakers' pacifism precluded military service, and their refusal to take oaths ruled out the legal profession. Their seriousness of purpose blocked entry into artistic endeavors. Fortunately for the Quakers, their mores meshed well with commerce and trade. Their financial integrity and punctuality in repaying debts made them ideal business partners. They insisted on producing goods made of high-quality ingredients. Their guarantee of absolute purity was a major factor in their products' popularity among consumers. People sometimes took advantage of the Quakers' ethos of patience and gentleness by running up large outstanding bills (Bradley [1987] 2007, 67–68).

Quaker businessmen had advantages relative to non-Quaker businessmen. The Quakers formed a network of helpful and trustworthy co-religionists. The Quakers' penchant for honest and plain-dealing differed from many of their competitors, but customers and other businessmen began to appreciate the advantages of dealing with Quakers. The Quakers' moral stance gained them business from firms looking for safe, reliable business partners and from consumers seeking quality goods and services.

Quakers traveled to London annually for a general meeting. They also traveled about Britain from meeting to meeting. They developed a dense web of friends and family, as well as conduits for information. Their stress on literacy also helped their ability to operate as merchants and traders. These trips also afforded Quaker businessmen opportunities to conclude deals in London and to take care of other business. Friends also exchanged gossip or information regarding good and not-so-good traders and manufacturers, thereby reducing the cost of searching for customers and suppliers.

The Quakers differed from other religious groups in their willingness to remove members whose "commercial dealings were less than proper." Removal was unpleasant, but historian James Walvin observes that removal was less severe than it appears. The removed person received advice and scrutiny from successful Quaker merchants. Such efforts were not altruistic, as Quakers wanted to ensure that an individual's lapses did not besmirch Quakers' "collective honest reputation" (Walvin 1997, 50, 74, 82, 208–209).

All of which is not to cast Quakers as saints. They faced temptations. Quakers struggled with the morality of selling products that they themselves disapproved, particularly luxury items. The temptation of selling such profitable items, though, sometimes overcame their scruples. Quakers also had qualms about selling goods produced with slave labor, such as tea, sugar, and tobacco.

Late in the eighteenth century, members at the Yearly Meeting of the Friends felt compelled to state its concerns regarding Friends who lapsed by participating, "in illegal dealings in the public stocks, or government securities; which is a species of gaming, and altogether inconsistent with our religious principles" (Walvin 1997, 33–35, 51–52). The Quakers condoned accumulating wealth but only under righteous conditions.

A constant worry was that members might fall into irretrievable debt (sometimes due to speculation). A floundering Friend had a responsibility to admit his troubles; experienced Quaker businessmen would then help remedy the situation, so that, again, no "public shame" or whiff of disrepute would taint the Society. Quakers scrutinized their members; someone living above their means invited comment. The member in trouble received counsel (and sometimes reprimand) from experienced members. The troubled member might also draw upon the resources from the Quaker network. When Quaker businessmen failed, their Friends analyzed the reasons for the failure. Often these Friends attributed failure to a moral lapse or to wandering "too far from the Quaker way." Quakers were vigilant toward each other, and a form of peer pressure induced good behavior or corrected errant behavior. The scrutiny, however, often paid dividends, as good ethics were often complementary with business success. Experienced Friends often offered good advice to novice entrepreneurs. Quakers in financial difficulties might also draw funds from Quaker-owned banks. Quaker-owned banks helped Quaker and non-Quaker clients alike, but Quakers seeking loans might receive preference (especially given the high level of trust among the Friends). Many banks around the world have practiced a form of "crony banking," but the Quakers probably avoided the excesses associated with such behavior. Non-Quaker bankers, too, were willing to lend to Quaker borrowers, given the Friends' reputation for prompt repayment of debts.

Quakers considered what to do with their profits. Philanthropy was one way to suppress the accumulation of wealth and to reduce the temptation to indulge in luxuries. Almost from the beginning, Quakers emphasized concern for the poor. When the Quakers were actively persecuted, they looked after one another. The Quakers, though, extended their concern to the non-Quaker poor. Edward Pease was an example of a Quaker facing conflicting feelings regarding his wealth. Pease helped create the Stockton and Darlington railway in the 1820s and 1830s; he became quite wealthy but maintained "a relatively humble existence." He devoted effort to the antislavery cause and died "as a simple Quaker."

Quakers were certainly not moral paragons, and some of them found the religious strictures onerous. Walvin acknowledged that Joseph

Rowntree and George Cadbury may have been exemplars, but some Quakers were not, as [William] Bryant and [Francis] May demonstrated. Bryant's sons were "nominally Quaker," as was their partner, Francis May. These employers apparently were not focused on employee welfare and eventually antagonized their workers, so as to incite a match-girl's strike in 1888 that led to the first women's trade union (Walvin 1997, 30–34, 55–57, 67–68, 72–77, 192–193, 208–209).[1]

Victorian-Era Quaker Businessmen

A group of Quaker businessmen achieved considerable success and acclaim during the late nineteenth century. David Davis, among other historians, highlights a characteristic of eighteenth- and nineteenth-century Quakers: "their most conspicuous characteristic, which was, quite simply, their incredible economic success." They were successful because "they brought a seriousness of purpose, a discipline of the mind, and a compelling commitment to 'useful' work. They were natural innovators, fascinated by the possibility of 'useful improvements'" (Davis 1966, 45).

Historian Ian Bradley focused on ten nineteenth-century Quaker entrepreneurs. He characterized these men as "methodical, regular and thrifty in their habits, relentless in their capacity for hard work and self-improvement, and models of self-discipline and temperance in their personal lifestyles." Some of them enjoyed "early morning plunges into cold baths," but Bradley hastens to assure readers that "they were not puritanical killjoys who sought to condemn others to a drab life deprived of all pleasures. They were...cultivated and cultured men with open-minded attitudes and interests in many artistic and political movements." He cited their "deep warmth and compassion and determination to improve the lives of their fellow men....Nonconformity may have helped to make them good businessmen but it also made them humane and concerned employers and generous philanthropists."

Most of Bradley's ten had only modest formal education, reflecting their relatively humble origins. Bradley identifies a key commonality between them: "an ability to seize on some relatively simple technique which had not been tried before and which brought spectacular results," ranging from pure chocolate, steel, forms of advertising, packaging or brand image. Bradley's ten men concentrated on producing good-quality products at reasonable prices. Andrew Carnegie was probably the chief exception to the others' concern for the welfare of their workers. On the other hand, Carnegie certainly matched the others in his giving away money. They believed they were trustees of the wealth (Bradley [1987] 2007, 10–14, 24).

Quakers were at the vanguard of various social reforms, including penal reform, abolition, and temperance. Cadburys opposed war and refused to supply troops during the Boer War with chocolates until Queen Victoria interceded. Quaker employers were encouraged to look after the welfare of their workers, but they held a range of attitudes toward their workers (Dellheim 1987, 16, 19, 35; Bradley [1987] 2007, 54–57, 59–61, 76–77; Walvin 1997, 179–182).

They often held more enlightened attitudes toward workers than most employers, but they demanded hard work. They were willing to substitute women and children for adult males in their factories. They practiced an early form of welfare capitalism by providing housing and other amenities; in several cases, they supported labor unions, although they remained opposed to giving workers a say in the operation of their factories (Bradley [1987] 2007, 10–12, 129; Walvin 1997, 166–168; Delheim, 17–21).

Bradley described the efforts Quaker capitalists exerted in providing for their workers. These entrepreneurs not only provided wages but, often, housing, health care, education, recreation, and entertainment. Bradley compared these Quakers with the prevailing ethos of Japanese employers in the late twentieth century. Sometimes the entrepreneurs did so out of paternalistic motivations, especially when they thought they knew better what was good for their workers than did the workers themselves. At other times, they fostered democratic and egalitarian attitudes among their workers. Bradley identified a key factor: "[the idea of partnership] showed itself in a refusal to be distanced from the lives of workers," especially in comparison with their own lives. The English Quaker entrepreneurs generally lived in modest homes near their factories.[2]

Joseph Rowntree's son, Seebohm, became a dedicated researcher on poverty. The Rowntrees were at the forefront of improving conditions for their workers. The family understood the need to pay a "living wage." Seebohm argued that employers who paid "starvation wages" should "abandon their role," as such meager wages were no longer tolerable (Walvin 1997, 204–205).

George Cadbury consistently supported trade unions. He encouraged his workers to join trade unions. Cadburys presaged labor agitation for shorter hours; the company was already heading toward a 40-hour work-week for their workers by 1919; the company was the first firm in

Birmingham to give workers Saturday afternoons off. The company also provided medical and dental care. Charles Dellheim made the amusing remark, "The dental care being especially useful in a chocolate factory" (Dellheim 1987, 27–29; Bradley [1987] 2007, 128).[3]

The Cadburys believed it their responsibility to promote their company town, as "the advancement of the social, moral, and physical well-being of all connected with Bournville." Unlike many employers, the Cadburys believed that "business efficiency and the welfare of the employees are but different sides of the same problem." They saw a virtuous circle whereby improved employee benefits would bolster efficiency, which would afford the means of additional welfare scheme. In essence, "The directors rejected the pervasive, self-serving notion that morality and profit were mutually exclusive" (Dellheim 1987, 26).

These men, aside from Carnegie, maintained modest lifestyles, despite their wealth. George Cadbury limited his spending to ten shillings a week. He once stated that he kept his expenditures, outside of housing and food, to £25 a year. "It is just the money that I saved by living so sparely that carried us over the crisis." In addition to living modestly, the Cadbury brothers remained close to their workers, interacting with them. This closeness probably precluded them from viewing labor as a commodity or a means to an end. "They also tended to shun social engagements and conspicuous expenditure, preferring to spend their money on others rather than on themselves." Carnegie, again, might have been the exception, as he spent large sums upon his family and himself, in addition to giving away fabulous sums (Bradley [1987] 2007, 11–12, 128). Carnegie, moreover, distanced himself from his workers more than the others, which may have contributed to his ill-fated relationship with the workers at Homestead.[4]

Quakers worried about advertising. They were often content to rest upon their reputations, and, as Walvin reflected, many of these Quaker businessmen failed to see the usefulness of advertising. They associated advertising with sleazy quacks and manufacturers with adulterated products whose advertisements were "more important than the product itself." However, Cadbury and [Joseph Storrs] Fry realized that their pure chocolate, which they considered a healthy beverage, gave them something to emphasize, if not boast about.

The Cadburys were successful, because they insisted on producing high-quality goods at good value. Although the company maintained a good reputation with the public, there were occasional controversies. One revolved around the company buying raw cocoa grown on islands off

Portuguese West Africa. The plantation owners used quasi-slaves. A newspaper reporter snidely wrote, "Mr. Cadbury might have been expected to take some interest in the owners of those same grimed African hands, whose toil also is so essential to the beneficent and lucrative operations at Bournville." Cadburys sued for libel and won, but the jury awarded just one farthing. Cadburys then attempted to ameliorate labor conditions for the cocoa growers but to no avail. They then stopped buying cocoa from these plantations. Dellheim observes that, "although their will was good, their judgment was dubious and their actions were slow. They relied on the advice of the Foreign Office—rarely a wise idea—but even when we take this into account, it is difficult to avoid the conclusion that commercial interests constrained their actions."

Henry Isaac Rowntree lagged his peers George Cadbury and Joseph Storrs Fry II in using to the Dutch press to make better-taking, pure chocolate. His company was, therefore, at a disadvantage. He resorted to what is now called industrial espionage. He was always trying to pry secrets about his rivals' manufacturing processes. Even so, Henry was in a bad way financially, and his brother, Joseph, agreed to join the company, possibly to avert family shame resulting from a bankruptcy. Joseph improved the family fortunes with bookkeeping skills and sales instincts, although he hesitated to resort to advertising. On the other hand, Joseph continued Henry's dubious industrial piracy and espionage. Joseph interviewed job applicants regarding their former or current employers' practices. Sometimes he paid for production recipes that they had absconded with from their employers. Walvin wryly commented, "Not surprisingly he [Joseph Rowntree] was alert to any such misdemeanours among his own workers…but it is curious that those commentators on the man and the company have simply overlooked this remarkable episode" (Walvin 1997, 161–165, 168–170; Dellheim 1987, 36).

The Rowntrees believed that maintaining a healthy workplace was a necessary condition for a successful business. Their belief did contain a kernel of pragmatism: "In keen competition the vigour and intelligence of the workmen are likely to be a determining factor." Despite this benign attitude, Rowntree, Cadbury, and some of the other Victorian Quaker employers dismissed women upon their marriage and tried to employ mostly young workers, even children. Men who sired children out of wedlock before marriage forfeited the three-day honeymoon holiday. Rowntree also disqualified workers absent due to venereal disease. These moralistic edicts created friction between Rowntree and his workers, but such friction was probably inevitable in the wake of World War I and altered moral standards (Walvin 1997, 184–185).

Joseph Rowntree left a legacy to his children, sharing his wisdom regarding wealth. "[A]ny considerable amount of wealth more often proves a curse than a blessing....I know how easy it is to acquire expensive habits which, so far from increasing the real richness and fullness of life, add to its burden. One of the mischievous ways in which these expensive habits tell is by increasing the barrier between wealthy people and their fellows. It lessens that realizing sense of human brotherhood." He encouraged his children to live simply (Bradley [1987] 2007, 155). If wealth was so burdensome, it is a fair question to ask why Rowntree didn't simply quit. Presumably he, as with many wealthy people, found fulfillment in creating and maintaining a profitable business; he may have also believed that to be idle was sinful.

A contemporary of these ten Victorian Age Quaker businessmen was Hetty Green, the American investor and well-known tightwad. Green inherited money from her father, and she enlarged her wealth by astute investments. Rumors abounded that she may have forged a will that gained her an inheritance from a relative and that she refused to pay for an operation for her son, who ended up lame for life. Green did not pamper herself, however, as she chose to live a life of penury (wearing old clothes, being unkempt, and living in run-down rental units). She was litigious but often did not bother to pay her attorneys, triggering added rounds of litigation. Green was nominally raised a Quaker, but she certainly took the Quaker virtue of thrift and plain living to extremes (Lewis 1963 is a biography of Green).

Troublesome Issues

Quakers took stands against two of the prevalent institutions of their times: slavery and war. From the inception of their society, Quakers eschewed violence and war. Such activities—being involved in war or slavery-related trade—though, raised the ire of other Quakers and could lead to "separation," the Quaker variation of Catholic excommunication (Greaves 1992, 250; Price 1996, 65; Walvin 1997, 76–77).

Quakers disliked war, but they liked profits. They lived in a country that was frequently at war, and the temptations to make money from war created tensions within Quaker communities. Some Quakers thought that arming vessels or even taking out letters of marque for defensive purposes was permissible. Others leased their ships or used their ships to convey war materiel for handsome rewards. The British government put out lucrative contracts for war supplies and equipment. Quakers debated whether they could fill such orders. Firearms, cannon, and other obvious weapons of war were off limits, but what about food, clothing, medicine, and other goods that could be used peacefully or belligerently? Did it matter to what use the goods were put (Price 1996, 68–69)?

Abraham Darby and other Quakers tried to adhere to Quaker ethical expectations, sometimes refusing to profit from wartime booms, even to the extent of moderating their prices for products in the face of heightened demand. Darby did not realize that his kitchenware was destined for the slave trade, although one wonders just how oblivious he must have been. Darby eventually began manufacturing firearms (Walvin 1997, 109–111).

During 1744, Bristol Quakers sorrowfully voted to separate from members who had engaged in privateering. Separation was not imposed lightly nor was it an empty threat. Quaker meetings wrestled with difficult issues that often caused disruption among the community. To be separated meant losing many of the ties and access to a reliable source of loans and business assistance. After the war ended, the Bristol community recognized the inconsistency of separating privateers but not members who had armed their vessels for defensive purpose. The meeting voted to restore the privateering members. Similar questions arose in 1778, when George Champion owned a vessel that he armed with 32 guns, as well as receiving letters of marque. The local meeting voted to disown him; one of Champion's associates, when threatened with separation, decided to opt out of the agreement with Champion (Price 1996, 69–71).

Some Quakers could not resist the profits to be made from manufacturing guns. Three generations of Samuel Galtons were in the gun-manufacturing business. "The conflict between business (or cupidity) and conscience affected them all, though it only drew an indignant defence from the second of the trio [Samuel 'John' Galton, or Samuel Galton, Junior]." To further create consternation among Quakers, the Galtons' cheap muzzleloaders were often sold to African slave traders; the Galtons apparently never sold guns directly to Africans in exchange for trade. Some of the weapons allegedly burst the first time they were fired. That gun manufacturers could sell such poor weapons to hard-headed African slave traders seems dubious; perhaps the Europeans might have initially been able to foist such weapons, but presumably the Africans would insist on testing the weapons before purchase.

Eventually the Society of Friends looked in askance at the Galton's gun selling business. At the 1790 yearly meeting, with Revolutionary France threatening the continental peace, the Society sent a written missive reminding members that "none amongst us, whose principle is peace, be employed to prepare the means" of war. The Birmingham monthly meeting did not adopt this epistle, but members were fully aware of the Galtons' activities. Only two years later, when the Birmingham meeting was considering enlarging their meeting house, did one member object to the Galtons' "making of guns, their poor quality and to their sale in Africa, where they were conducive to tribal wars (and slaving) and he thought it undesirable that the Meeting House even in part should be built from the profits of such dealings."

Samuel Galton the elder decided the controversy was proving a good time to quit the business. His son, Samuel Galton the younger (and there would be one more Samuel Galton), however, proved more resistant. He was a gun manufacturer and seller, true, and he sold guns for military purposes. He cited the fact that the Society had not objected to his family business (going on 70 years) in the past. He inherited the trade, and he would be unable to divest himself without loss; therefore he was engaged in the trade not out of choice but from necessity. This argument must have struck the fellow Friends as disingenuous at best, since during the French Revolutionary Wars, the gun trade surely was robust and potential buyers plentiful. He also argued, "that the manufacture of arms implies no approbation of offensive war" nor did it "promote war, or increase its calamities." His arguments may have seemed pretty weak to his fellows. His next argument compared gun-making and selling to being a brewer; he was not responsible for how people used his products, and, indeed, guns were often used to maintain the peace or to prevent war. Then he made two arguments that must have discomfited some members: one minister had put his son into an apprenticeship with a gun maker without censure, and all of the Quakers contributed to war by their payment of taxes or by purchase of East India Stock.

With regard to the aspect of selling guns to African slavers, Galton made the modern-sounding argument that Quakers used and profited from slave-produced products. He denied that guns were the cause but rather the consequence of slavery and warfare. These arguments failed to persuade his peers. The Birmingham meeting voted to disown him, but he was free to attend Quaker worship. He was simply not allowed to attend business meetings (Smith 1967, 132–134, 137–139, 143–146).

Slavery was another troubling issue for Quakers. Quakers probably had a natural animus for the institution of slavery, having been persecuted by the English government. At the same time, Quakers struggled with the slavery problem. Some of their goods were used to trade for slaves or to supply slaves with clothing or food. Slaves grew foodstuffs, tea, cotton, tobacco, and a wide array of commodities; should Quakers shun such trades? Quakers were antislavery, but they faced a conundrum regarding efforts to stop the trans-Atlantic slave trade. The British (and American) navies were authorized to use violence to stop the trade; Quakers abhorred violence (Walvin 1997, 89, 149).

Quakers realized that slave-owning endangered both the slave and the master; the latter was tempted by selfishness and a potential for denying "human kinship." John Woolman, in particular, highlighted the imbalance of power between slave and master that could lead to the master's demoralization (Frey 2009, 21–22).

Some Quakers had owned slaves during the mid-eighteenth century, but the Friends began to repudiate slavery. British Quakers tried to divest ownership of slaves and of commercial endeavors that were tainted by slavery. Relatively few English Quakers owned slaves in England, but some owned slaves in Jamaica or other colonies. Quaker David Barclay found out that his brother and he had gained Jamaican slaves in payment of a debt, and he found it difficult to emancipate the slaves (because doing so was unpopular on the island). Instead he had an agent transport the blacks to Philadelphia, where they were apprenticed. The British Quakers proved adept at using publicity to influence political leaders, even though the Quakers themselves had limited political power. The American Quakers were more familiar with slavery, as some northerners owned slaves. Because of their familiarity, American Quakers were more cognizant of the ingrained racial prejudices and the difficulties of transforming slaves into freedmen. The American Quakers wanted to stop the importation of slaves, to remove legal barriers to private manumission, to stop re-enslaving of free blacks, and to prepare blacks for living as free men (including education, apprenticeship, and old-age assistance). The American Quakers, especially before 1775, relied upon their English cousins to take the lead in stopping the Atlantic slave trade (Davis 1966, 37–38; Midgley 1992, 14). The Quakers took the lead in the abolition movement.

Conclusion

Many modern Americans know of Quakers, perhaps, only from the iconic Quaker on oatmeal containers. This is a pity, as Quakers offer much regarding business ethics. Quakers relied on a shared, ingrown ethos and secondarily upon punishment (such as separation) or reward. They maintained their ethics when dealing with non-believers.

Quaker business influence has waned. The Quakers struggled with a dilemma. Their standards were rigorous, and many younger Quakers opted out. The remainder "comprised in effect an elite of preselected personal and social qualities....[who] proved themselves incapable of maintaining popular support. A wider base to the Society might have undermined that success....the Friends needed to add to their numbers and to revitalize their collective tone." Otherwise the Society was destined to dwindle in numbers and influence (Walvin 1997, 132–133).

In the twenty-first century, Cadburys transferred some of its production to Poland, where labor was cheaper. Workers at the Somerdale Factory in Keynsham found out on October 3, 2007 that their factory and jobs were ending. The management feared worker violence and imposed a lockout with security guards. There was no violence, although the workers took the news hard. One worker stated, "They [the workers] would have worked to the death for the factory, but the directors didn't know that." The generations of Cadburys after George and Richard had begun to distance themselves from Quakerism and the company. The company went public and the company was "no longer a Quaker venture" (Meek 2017, 4). Over time the non-Quaker ownership began to see labor less as a familial relationship and more as an input. Management did offer terms of settlement with the workforce, many of whom were nearing retirement, and the workers voted to accept it.

Notes

1. Some of the workers developed "phossy jaw" from contact with the matches.
2. Cadbury once explained to a visitor why the art work on the walls of his home was so poor: "Why should I hang fortunes on my walls while there is so much misery in the world?" (Bradley [1987] 2007, 142).
3. One wonders whether the workers might have tired of chocolate and therefore consumed little of what they produced.

4. Dellheim discussed whether the Cadburys were paternalistic or exerted "social control" with regard to their workers. He concluded, "Indeed, it is more accurate to say that the firm empowered workers by establishing works councils, supporting trade unions, and providing education. Cadburys practiced the ethics of social contract, not the ethics of social control" (Dellheim 1987, 41–42).

Bibliography

Bradley, Ian. *Enlightened Entrepreneurs: Business Ethics in Victorian Britain* (Oxford: Lion Hudson, [1987] 2007).

Davis, David. *The Problem of Slavery in Western Culture* (Ithaca, NY: Cornell University Press, 1966).

Dellheim, Charles. "The Creation of a Company Culture: Cadburys, 1861–1931." *American Historical Review* 92(1), February 1987, 13–44.

Frey, Donald. *America's Economic Moralists: A History of Rival Ethics and Economics* (Albany, NY: State University of New York Press, 2009).

Greaves, Richard. "Shattered Expectations? George Fox, the Quakers, and the Restoration State, 1660–1685." *Quarterly Journal Concerned with British Studies* 24(2), July 1992, 237–259.

Lewis, Arthur. *The Day They Shook the Plum Tree* (New York, NY: Harcourt, Brace & World, 1963).

Meek, James. "Somerdale to Skarbimierz." *London Review of Books* 39(8), April 20, 2017, 3–15. https://www.lrb.co.uk/v39/n08/james-meek/somedale-to-skarbimierz, viewed April 20, 2017.

Midgley, Clare. *Women against Slavery: The British Campaigns, 1780–1870* (London, UK: Routledge, 1992).

Price, Jacob. "English Quaker Merchants and War at Sea, 1689–1783." *West Indies Accounts: Essays on the History of the British Caribbean and the Atlantic Economy in Honour of Richard Sheridan* (Kingston, Jamaica: Press University of the West Indies, 1996), 64–86.

Smith, Barbara. "The Galtons of Birmingham: Quaker Gun Merchants and Bankers, 1702–1831." *Business History* 9(2), 1967, 132–150.

Walvin, James. *The Quakers: Money and Morals* (London, UK: John Murray, 1997).

CHAPTER 14

Labor Relations Through the Ages

Modern people take it for granted that they have a property right to their own labor. Throughout most of human history, however, such a property right was uncertain to be recognized or honored.

People have labored under the jurisdiction of other people throughout recorded history and probably earlier. Sometimes the relationship was voluntary; often the relationship was coercive in some fashion. Work relationships could mimic family relationships, whereby the worker served as a member of the family; at the other extreme, a worker might toil as part of a mass of workers with no direct contact with the employer. Employer/employee relationships were rife with ethical considerations, especially as workers and employers pursued their own self-interests. What were ethical ways to determine wages or to elicit effort? The coercive aspects of many labor relationships led to unethical behavior, mostly on the part of employers, but, on occasion, also by employees.

There was a continuum from slavery to independent, worker-owners with intermediate forms, such as indentured servitude, serfdom, corveé labor, and military drafts. A person working their land clearly exercised their property right to their labor; if, however, governmental or church authorities claimed the land in some abstract or not-so-abstract way, they could demand labor service from the putative owner.

Economic historian Stanley Engerman delineated the distinctions between legally free people, who worked for others and who worked for themselves. If you worked for others, you "lacked full property" in yourself

D. G. Surdam, *Business Ethics from Antiquity to the 19th Century*,
https://doi.org/10.1007/978-3-030-37165-4_14

and were "'free' only in a restricted self. The development of the 'free labor ideology' emphasized the importance of working for oneself as a central part of the definition of self-ownership." This ideology gradually evolved so that people who worked for another might still be considered to have property in oneself if such employment was temporary and "merely a step in the reclaiming of the use of one's own labor" (Engerman 1992, 3). Economists, too, may have contributed to the idea of labor as a "means to an end," when they denoted labor as a "factor of production."

Basic Moral Problem of Labor Relations

Much of the ethical considerations revolved around whether labor was considered simply an object to use in attaining an end. Owners of slaves and employers of coerced workers might view their workers as chattel, not fully human with inherent rights. Such attitudes affected issues of compensation, working conditions, arbitrary treatment, and so on. The employer-employee relationship was not always seen as one requiring reciprocity.

According to some religions, a strong element of reciprocity should exist between workers and employers. Jewish traditions did not rely upon employer generosity and, instead, supported employee rights, such as organizing into unions or collectives. Jewish artisans formed associations to train apprentices and set up rules governing working hours and conditions as far back as the Talmud and possibly even to the Temple times. Although rabbinical thought recognized the rights of competent adults to formulate their own agreements, it insisted that certain ethical values were not negotiable, such as employers delaying payment of wages. Employers should also provide sickness and accident pay. To reciprocate, employees must do a fair day's work for a fair day's pay. On a practical level, employees should not moonlight, if doing so would affect their productivity on their original job.

The Confucian take on this is that "Managers are supposed to exhibit a benevolent concern for the welfare of their subordinates, and subordinates are supposed to show a corresponding loyalty, obedience, and trust in relation to their managers." Chinese, Japanese, and Korean businesses, although often family-based, often consider their non-related employees as members of an extended family. Westerners might find such hierarchical relationships awkward or unnatural. In modern times, westerners claim that Asian business firms' emphasis upon providing security for their employees made such firms less nimble in responding to changing business conditions. Buddha also discussed the employer-employee relationship. Employers should not only consider what they wanted from the worker but also what the employee's abilities and capacities were. Employers should pay a specified and "adequate" wage and disburse part of their profits to their workers in the form of periodic bonuses. Buddha stated that employers should also cover their workers' medical needs. Employees were to respond by being hard-working, honest, and obedient. Workers were not to cheat their employers (Zinbarg 2001, 120–124, 216–217).

These religious arguments did not resonate with all employers. Some employers displayed a callous attitude toward worker morale: "If a man is dissatisfied, it is his privilege to quit" (Brody 1960, 78).[1]

Economists discuss how people can sell their time in labor markets. They characterize such choice as "freedom," but some critics disagree. Theologian Douglas Meeks argues, "When people have nothing to offer in their pursuit of livelihood except their labor, they must depend on jobs alone to protect their freedom in the market." Meeks does not ask why workers don't save some of their wages and become investors, or, heaven forbid, capitalists. In any event, workers without savings or a steady income from non-job sources may be vulnerable to coercion in a weak labor market. He agrees with a political scientist, who wrote, "Only in a market system in which all persons are provided, through money income, with a generous basic livelihood whether they work or not would these coercive possibilities in exchange vanish." Meeks uses this argument to conclude, "unemployment compensation and other security and welfare programs are, according to the logic, necessary to freedom in the market" (Meeks 1989, 63; Lindblom 1977, 48). Both duck the issue of who pays for these programs and what is the justification of taking from some to give to others.[2]

Labor Contracts

Workers and employers create formal or informal contracts. A difficulty in creating contracts between employers and labor is that much is left unstated in the contracts, creating potential for workers or employers to act opportunistically. In addition, since monitoring worker performance is often imperfect and costly, workers have potential to shirk. On the other hand, employers have opportunities for deceit. The importance of norms and moral dispositions can be encapsulated in the slogan, "a fair day's work for a fair day's pay," creating, in essence, an exchange of gifts—a gift of work effort above what can be enforced and a gift of pay above what the market demands. A related issue is creating trust in long-term work relationships, especially when the rewards for reliable service lies in the distant future. Japanese lifetime employment is an example of cultural norms creating cooperation and work effort (Hausman and McPherson 1993, 685).[3]

Philosopher Daniel Hausman and economist Michael McPherson delineate some possible principles that employees use in determining whether a given wage structure is fair: "(1) More difficult, unpleasant, or dangerous work should be better paid. (2) Jobs that carry a great deal of responsibility should be better paid. (3) Hard work should be rewarded. (4) Seniority is fair; those who have worked for a given employer for a long time should be better paid. (5) Wages should not depend on race, sex, or arbitrary whim. These are only a few of many such principles, and there are other principles establishing priorities in case of conflict among these." Some philosophers and economists dispute some of these principles, arguing that although the first principle seems fair on an intuitive level, attention should be directed more to reducing inequalities in wealth and income (Hausman and McPherson 1993, 700).

Large Landowners' Need for Labor

Land ownership remained paramount in most economies; the landowners sought to acquire a stable, controlled workforce. If large landowners and manufacturers could keep the mass of people from owning land, then the landless people would have to enter the labor force. Having an ample supply of labor presumably benefited landowners and manufacturers. Serfdom and reduced ownership of land did not always create a sufficient labor force, and societies often resorted to other repressive means, such as laws against vagrancy, taxes requiring payment in cash, and debt peonage. The latter institution, widespread in Spanish America and the postbellum American South, had two diverse effects. "First, as a form of monopolistic discrimination by merchants, it could be used to force workers (and/or landowners) to a subsistence income. A second purpose of debt peonage would thus be to create continued negative wealth in order to force a higher labor input" (Engerman 1992, 15–18).

As an example of using taxes to generate a labor force, British imperialist Cecil Rhodes needed workers in the Cape Colony in southern Africa. He decided that a "hut tax" payable in cash was a dandy way to force the natives to hire on with white employers. Perhaps he even believed his self-serving and patronizing defense of such legislation: "You will remove them [the natives] from that life of sloth and laziness, you will teach them the dignity of labour and make them contribute to the prosperity of the state" (Harrison 1981, 69). Rhodes probably knew enough British history to realize that he was simply replaying an old game from the 1700s in coercing people to work for an employer.

Alternatives to Slavery

If one thinks of forms of labor comprising a continuum between slave and free labor (ignoring self-employment), what are the intermediate forms of labor? Richard Hellie, an expert on Russian serfdom, pointed out that serfs differed from slaves in that serfs were "the subject of the law" and had some rights; slaves were the "object of the law" and had minimal rights. Serfs were bound to the land, which they cultivated with their personal means of production. Slaves typically owned nothing. On the other hand, serfs were subject to taxes, corvée labor (unpaid, sporadic labor at the behest of a landlord or government authority), and military service. In both cases, these people often had a harsh life. By the eighth century, serfdom "meant the protection of a feudal lord." The contract had mutually beneficial aspect in that the serf exchanged labor and loyalty for sustenance. One scholar argued that serfdom failed to benefit the peasants, and some serfs sought to "buy back their liberty." Historian Bronislaw Geremek observed that peasants in distress sometimes voluntarily entered serfdom. The free man turned serf, however, was not always driven by misery but by the mutually beneficial relationship of becoming a serf: "to the lord, hereditary labour; to the serf a mixture of advantages, from a simple money payment or an additional holding of land to the benefits of religious fraternity." Over the centuries, though, the serfs' position deteriorated (Hellie 2010, 27:289; Geremek 1994, 54–55; Southern [1953] 1976, 102–103).

Modern people consider the prospects of being a serf to be dreary, but, "Men of some consequence…made themselves and their children serfs for one reason or another; but except for the small annual payment which symbolized their servitude their property was not affected." Why did these men give up their status as free men? Usually they gained a payment of money or land from the landholder. Landowners, including monks administrating large estates, were willing to make such payments, "as a way of establishing a new claim to a man's loyalty and aid. Land was plentiful: labourers were comparatively few....The condition of serfdom, though it did not take away a man's property, prevented him from moving elsewhere." Historian Richard Southern compared this practice to modern situations when an employee of an industrial firm accepts a sum of money incumbent upon not moving elsewhere. One big difference is that the modern-day firm is not interested in the employee's children, since there is no guarantee such children would be useful to the firm, whereas eleventh-century landlords knew that children were usually capable of serving on the estate. The securing of a serf's children was a key attraction to the transaction. A serf had to make payment to his lord on the marriage of his daughter (the *merchet*); the lord had to grant his consent. "This control was not a senseless humiliation. If the serf's daughter married away from the lordship, she and her children were lost to the lord. It was otherwise with the man (son): the woman came to live with him, the labour of the children were secure" (Southern [1953] 1976, 100–102).

Indentured Servitude

In a precursor of sorts to English indentured servitude, some craftsmen in fifth- and sixth-century Iran sold themselves into slavery in order to finance their passage to areas paying higher wages (Silver 1985, 92). Before the large-scale importation of slaves from Africa, English colonial landowners seeking labor resorted to indentured servitude. Movies such as Cecil B. DeMille's *Unconquered*, depicted a rather distorted view of indentured servitude, with Amy (played by Paulette Goddard) being condemned to death or indentured servitude. Although a kindly military man (Gary Cooper) buys her contract and sets her free, another character, sleazy and lustful, kidnaps Amy and forces her to honor the indentured contract (this being a DeMille production, naturally there is more than a hint of salaciousness involved). Audiences of the 1940s could be excused for thinking poorly of indentured servitude.

Modern-day Americans, reading cursory descriptions of indentured servitude, are apt to take a dim view of the institution. Yet traces of indentured servitude exist today, in moderated form, of course. College students can have much of their educational costs covered by the military in exchange for serving a specified number of years. Some businesses may help employees with their college tuition, usually with stipulations that the employee work for a mandated period of time afterward.

One history text concedes that indentured servitude gave poor people an opportunity to reach America and to obtain some land and capital, but the text points out that many servants were overworked. Worst of all, "the program had unfortunate results in accustoming Americans to non-free labor." But apprenticeship was similar to indentured servitude, and it is difficult to see why the latter seems to rate lower with these authors (Curti [1953] 1969, 31–32).[4]

Radical historian Howard Zinn chose to focus on the negative aspects of indentured servitude; undoubtedly some servants were abused. Some died en route or shortly thereafter, so did plenty of wealthier settlers. Zinn, however, emphasized "Beatings and whippings. Servant women were raped….The master tried to control completely the sexual lives of the servants" (Zinn 1980, 44). Zinn admitted that the earliest indentured servants had opportunities to move up the economic ladder, but he fails to answer the question, "If indentured servitude was so terrible, why did people continue to voluntarily contract to become indentured?" Certainly these people were facing unenviable opportunities, and one might argue that they really didn't have any attractive choices.

Another historian painted a subtler portrait, while acknowledging that conditions varied, depending upon the crop, location, and master, some indentured servants became tenants and, in some cases, landowners. Indentured servitude was voluntary and temporary, unlike slavery. Two historians provided a brief description of servitude; they, too, mentioned the "harsh" conditions and the runaways, but they provided a more optimistic picture of servants' subsequent experiences: "Indentured servants… were given or otherwise secured land, and the more enterprising souls often became prosperous. Nor did any serious social stigma attach to them. Some even broke into the upper crust of aristocracy, and two became signers of the Declaration of Independence. The indentured-servant system admittedly inflicted much hardship, but it did give tens of thousands of impoverished people a chance to start anew in the Land of Opportunity" (Ginger 1975, I:34; Bailey and Kennedy 1983, 64–65).

Some historians believe that a majority of white immigrants to British America came as indentured servants. Given the longstanding English tradition of hiring out youngsters for farm work in rural Britain, hiring out as indentured servants was not as drastic a step as it would appear. Many of these young workers faced the choice of working for landowners in England or moving to North America, where long-term prospects might be better.

Crossing the Atlantic, even under the meager accommodations of the 1600s, required a fairly large sum of money. Most young people did not have such capital. The English capital market was ill-equipped to lend money to prospective immigrants. The immigrants, of course, had no collateral and collecting debts when the debtor was across the ocean was unlikely. Even in the modern world, banks are hesitant to lend money for college expenses, and governments often get involved. Governments typically have better ability in tracking debtors and are better able to coerce repayment or to impose binding punishment. When facing a borrowing constraint, what could an ambitious youngster to do?

Indentured servitude proved remarkably sophisticated. For instance, since the cost of passage was roughly the same for all of the indentured servants, the length of the indentured contract depended on several factors. Those young people who could read and write or had skills typically received contracts with the shortest indenture. Unskilled laborers, of course, received longer lengths of servitude. The prospective English indentures often had some inkling of conditions in the New World. They recognized that the West Indies were an undesirable destination. They also understood that working on rice, sugar, and tobacco plantations was more onerous than other farm work. Indeed, African slavery arose because of the need to use gang labor and to impress workers to perform these arduous and dangerous tasks. In addition, when wages in England rose, new indentured servant contracts became shorter (Galenson 1984, 1–3, 10–11).

Because escape was possible, indentured servants had some leverage with respect to their masters. The masters might have found that positive incentives worked better than negative ones. Unlike a slave owner, though, the master, especially as the contract was nearing its conclusion, might have had an incentive to dangerously overwork the servant. Masters and servants, then, faced various ethical issues: maltreatment, reneging on the contract by running away, and so on.

Sharecropping

Sharecropping, whereby landless tenants agreed to share part of the crop with the landowner, has been a widespread practice throughout history. From the American South to European countries, sharecropping proved to be a mutually beneficial institution, although certainly one with potential exploitation.

In France, sharecropping became prevalent as the Middle Ages waned until 1700. Peasants became indebted and lost their land, and the transfer was "the most decisive event of French social history," hurling peasants from landowning to tenancy or sharecropping on land they formerly owned. The ramifications of this land transfer, according to many historians, were all bad: social stratification, stagnation of the French rural economy, and lack of incentives by sharecropper or landowner to improve the land. A fundamental question, though, is why sharecropping? Why not some other method of getting landless peasants to work the land? (Bloch 1966, 125, 146–148; see also Hoffman 1984, 309).

Southern planters in the Spring of 1865 had plenty to worry about. Those who were Civil War veterans undoubtedly returned to farms and plantations in dilapidated conditions. The planters who formerly owned slaves, of course, faced an additional problem of obtaining sufficient labor to plant and harvest crops. The growers, of course, hoped to replace slavery with a close facsimile of the peculiar institution. They hired freedmen but drew up contracts that proved so odious to the former slaves, including work-gang conditions that many freedmen refused to hire on. White Southerners described the freedmen as lazy and indolent, unwilling to work as hard as before. Of course, that was precisely the point of being free: The white planters failed to admit to the obvious fact that the former slaves undoubtedly wanted to work less and under less arduous conditions now that they were free. Southerners also doubted whether former slaves had the wherewithal to manage planting and harvesting. Undoubtedly there was a learning process for the former freedmen, just as there would be for European immigrant farmers. Since a reversion to the status quo ante bellum failed, planters and laborers sought new forms of crop-making arrangements. Renting involved a fixed crop payment, whereas sharecropping specified a fixed proportional share to the landowner. A successful labor contract had to apportion the risk and to create the proper incentives; such a contract was often difficult to create (Reid 1974, 107–112).

Industrialization and Labor

The movement of labor off the land and into factories provoked controversy. Many critics accused the burgeoning factories as being hellish, but these critics may have glossed over the lousy existing working conditions in agriculture. There was another facet to industrialization; some of the factory owners attempted to ameliorate working and living conditions for their workers, as we shall see. The workers on the land were the losers, as large landowners enclosed greater proportions of arable land (Porter 1982, 109).

Labor historians Ivy Pinchbeck and Margaret Hewitt rebut John Ruskin's romanticized view of domestic weavers and pride in their work. "Doubtless some did—pride in work, mercifully, is not uncommon—but it seems unlikely that the average weaver, toiling hour after hour, throwing the shuttle backwards and forwards on work which was monotonous and exhausting, had the reactions which would satisfy a modern enthusiast for peasant arts" (Pinchbeck and Hewitt 1973, II:398–399).

Upper-class Victorian observers may have had a skewed perception regarding industrialization. Certainly the ubiquitous coal smoke appeared to mark a decline in living standards. The "London fog" became a standard nuisance, but coal smoke implied that a greater proportion of Londoners could *afford* coal to cook, to keep warm, and to keep clean. "The issue appears to be one of environmental ugliness in the eyes of the Victorian upper-class beholder versus improved living standards for the urban poor. In the standard-of-living debate, it's the latter who matter in the real wage versus city beautification trade-off." An economist concluded that the evidence fails to support the "Dark Satanic Mills" depiction that it "simply will not wash." Not only that but the urban disamenities were not so large as to "account for much of the measured rise in wages" (Williamson 1981, 82–83).

Free Labor and Factory Discipline

The early British steam-powered factories required a steady, reliable labor to keep the machinery operating at efficient levels. Although the capital required to set up factories had not soared to levels beyond individuals or partnerships' resources, the requirements were enough that the investors did not want a workforce putting forth sporadic effort. Today's workers give little thought to their employers' insistence upon punctuality and regular work habits. A few centuries ago, such acceptance was novel.

There were opposing schools of thought regarding factory discipline, as shown by economist Gregory Clark. Under early factory conditions, employers hired workers, who labored in workshops or manufactories; the working conditions, however, remained similar to the workers' former independence. Workers retained a considerable amount of discretion over conditions. It was the second change, one denoted as factory discipline that created much animosity. Under factory discipline, the employer began establishing work rules and forcing workers to alter their habits. There was much to criticize regarding the factory discipline, especially looking backward from our vantage point (and, to be honest, some working conditions, in contemporary America and Europe, are harsh).

Economist Stephen Marglin argued that factory discipline was a means to force workers to exert more effort than they would freely choose encapsulated much of the critics' view, although critics also bemoaned the sometimes inhumane working conditions and loss of autonomy. Clark classified these arguments as the *coercion* theory. In contrast, defenders of factory discipline, although admitting it could be unattractive and onerous, suggested that accepting such discipline meant, in return, eventually receiving a higher standard of living. Similar to a military unit, each worker must do their job when it is needed; slackers or absentees could derail the work of many. In addition, laxity was dangerous in a world of whirling machinery. Clark dubbed this the *coordination* theory. The coordination adherents claimed that where labor markets were competitive, coercion was not possible. Workers were often aware of conditions offered by various employers; any employer whose conditions and demeanor were aberrant would have difficulty attracting workers and may have had to raise wages to compensate. The competition would then lead to an efficient outcome. Under this theory, workers chose discipline and, therefore, lowered manufacturers' costs and received higher wages. "Workers, in this view, preferred discipline and higher wages to freedom and lower wages. Their protection was and is the market." Clark performed regression analysis to see what the data revealed. He concluded that the empirical tests "support the coercion theory and suggest that the demands of coordination on Industrial Revolution technologies were generally unimportant. These findings indicate that, contrary to appearances, the labor markets of the Industrial Revolution were not competitive, because…coercion is not possible in a competitive market" (Clark 1994, 128–130).

The evidence, though, also suggested that discipline *was* associated with higher wages. Factory workers received more per week than handworkers in homes or in undisciplined shops. An experiment in Britain during the early twentieth century found that for a given set of workers, "the imposition of tighter discipline increased weekly production, even for workers on piece rates." Clark concludes that factory discipline was coercive in altering worker behavior, but "the worker was in no sense exploited by the introduction of discipline. The workers voluntarily entered into the temporary servitude of the factory and were appropriately rewarded for its disamenities with higher wages. Had they been able to exercise more self-control, factory discipline could have been avoided for most technologies in the nineteen century" (Clark 1994, 144, 148, 161). His conclusion makes it unclear whether factory owners were behaving unethically with respect to their workers.

Creating Disciplined Workforces

Richard Arkwright and other pioneers struggled to create factory discipline. The existing weavers and textile workers were used to dictating the pace and timing of work effort. Mondays and Fridays were often days of relaxed work effort, clearly undesirable in the new factories. Workers wanted to earn just enough to maintain their current standard of living; they did not seem inclined to improve their standard of living if it meant giving up control of their work pace and leisure. Even enlightened factory owners, who foresaw that the improved productivity possible under the factory system could raise living standards and improve their workers lives, were frustrated by their workers' sloth; these owners resorted to strict discipline with punishment for infractions. Factory owners found they had to start with very young workers and then train them for the necessary discipline involved in factory work. Andrew Ure, an observer of Arkwright's factory, described Arkwright as "a man of a Napoleon nerve and ambition, to subdue the refractory tempers of work-people accustomed to irregular paroxysms of diligence…such was Arkwright" (Ure 1835, 16; Marglin 1974, 84–85, 91–92).[5]

Historian Edward (E.P.) Thompson asserted that British workers had to be trained and disciplined to become adequate workers in the pioneering mills. Time now took an importance it had lacked before, and owning an accurate time piece became de rigueur. Manipulation of time pieces became a simple ruse to elicit more or less work. A Dundee factory boy recalled that "masters and managers did with us as they liked. The clocks at the factories were often put forward in the morning and back at night, and instead of being instruments for the measurement of time, they were used as cloaks for cheating and oppression." Clock tampering was a game workers and employers could both play. A factory owner complained that his clerks "have been so unjust as to reckon by clocks going the fastest and the bell ringing before the hour for their going from business, and clocks going too slow and the bell ringing after the hour for their coming to business, and those two black traitors Fowell and Skellerne have knowingly allowed the same." He literally took time into his hands by locking up the clock (Thompson 1967, 81–82, 86; Gutman 1976, 37–38).

Josiah Wedgwood organized his pottery factory to increase efficiency. He used conveyor belts between the shops, so that the clay moved in a circle en route to becoming a finished product. Workers were trained to do a single task; the rules were so strict that workmen could not "wander at will from one task to another as the workmen did in the pre-Wedgwood potteries." Training workers to do one task meant better quality that led to higher wages and more regular employment. Although his workers each completed a specific task, the assumption that the workers' skill was eroded was misplaced. His workers were trained to do their task at a higher level of execution, although such training, in his own words, served to "make such *machines* of the *Men* as cannot err." There is no doubting the quality of Wedgwood's products, but commentators then and now question whether it was necessary or ethical to make "machines" out of men. Wedgwood's tactics resembled nothing less than molding men to be soldiers in a planned campaign. Wedgwood himself told his partner that, "It is hard, but then it is glorious to conquer so great an Empire with raw, undisciplin'd recruits. What merit must the General have who achieves such wonders under such disadvantageous circumstances" (McKendrick 1961, 32–35).

Wedgwood was not alone in training a new breed of workers; his contemporaries, James Brindley, James Watt, Richard Arkwright, and George Stephenson also had to train or re-train their workers. That they succeeded in creating workforces suited to the new industrialization greatly contributed to the success of the new production processes. Training often included inculcating such basic traits as punctual attendance, diligence during the routinized work days, cleanliness, and avoidance of waste (McKendrick 1961, 74).[6]

One controversial change was the general prohibition on consumption of alcohol; drinking on Saint Monday and other days had long been an attraction (and curse) of skilled crafts. For the next 150 years or so, employers had no compunction against banning alcohol at work (and, often, during off-hours). Many workers chafed at and resented the new strictures. The debate over employer scrutiny and control over employees' lives remains alive today.

Wedgwood's strictures do not appear to have been arbitrarily imposed; he posted very detailed and clear rules for his employees. Some of his rules were intended to protect his workers from industrial hazards, such as lead poisoning. He also understood that it was necessary to be "one who…has not only full command over the workmen, but is likewise possessed of their goodwill and cordial assistance." In the end, he transformed his "dilatory drunken, idle worthless workmen" into "a very good sett of hands." Historian Neil McKendrick notes that John Wesley's influence in getting people to lead more orderly lives may have helped Wedgwood and his contemporaries build a reliable workforce (McKendrick 1982, 37–46, 54, 104).

Wedgwood's success in training a motivated, skilled workforce had its drawbacks. Other employers tried to lure his workers to their factories, both for their productivity and for their knowledge. Wedgwood, as with other industrialists, were jealous of their industrial secrets, although many were not so scrupulous as to forego industrial espionage of their own. One of the purposes behind hiring abstemious workers was that hard drinkers were often easily plied with alcohol in an attempt to pry trade secrets. Another problem was immigration of skilled workers, some of whom desired to start their own businesses. Free movement of workers, of course, was a priceless right, but hiring workers to get secrets was a form of intellectual property theft. So irritating was industrial skullduggery that an editorial suggested imposing a "painful death" for one found guilty of such perfidy, but nothing came of this suggestion. Wedgwood's attitude toward sharing his ideas hardened as the years passed. With regard to losing his workers, he acknowledged that his workers' civil liberties limited any potential law restricting their movement. Fortunately for Wedgwood, most of his workers came to accept the regimentation (McKendrick 1961, 46–47, 50).[7]

Wedgwood took a paternalistic view toward his workers. For a person fixated on quality and efficiency, he had an imagination. He saw his early workers perhaps as similar to the clay he used to produce beautiful pottery. The workers were unruly, dissipated, and slovenly in their work habits. Wedgwood and other industrialists believed they could improve their workers' lives, both by higher wages and by moral instruction. The industrialists themselves would gain by having a more reliable workforce, so the motives underlying their paternalism may have been mixed. Wedgwood, however, foresaw a world where "there was little place for brothels, alehouses, cock-fighting and bull-baiting of the ease and amusement of his workmen. In their place there would be schools for their children, hospitals for their sick, homes for their orphans, and societies, libraries and institutions for themselves. For all there would be better food, better clothes, better houses, better roads and better transport. Their streets would be lit, their roads paved, and their towns drained." Such gains would not magically appear: "To achieve these ends, [Wedgwood] demanded complete obedience, and complete submission. He also expected hard work. Accustomed to long hours and unremitting labour himself, he expected an effort of a similar nature from his workmen." Other draconian employers may have only wanted hard work and obedience, without offering a better life in return. Wedgwood succeeded in raising his workers' standard of living. He recalled that he wanted to elevate his workers from their "miserable huts" and poverty; to a large degree, he succeeded, and his workers moved into comfortable houses. One can imagine Wedgwood's pride, as he looked about his factories and the surrounding area. Wedgwood's achievements were worthy of pride. He built better houses for his workers, and the factory working conditions at Etruria were not William Blake's "dark Satanic mills"; in fact, contemporaries, including John Wesley, lauded them. Wesley noted how much improved the residents' dispositions were (McKendrick 1961, 51–54). The world Wedgwood and his peers created was not perfect and contained its elements of harshness, but, nevertheless, it was a better world with promise of more improvements to come. There would be setbacks amidst the gains, but English workers were not retreating.

In the end, English workers gave up much autonomy and other charms of the old crafts trade. A historian reflected, "If the workers of the eighteenth century had refused to conform to some code of conduct when at work, there could have been no factory system, and no such rise in output, and hence of the standard of life as was, in fact, attained in the nineteenth century." Well into the twentieth century, however many workers chafed at the mind-numbing aspect of working on an assembly line. Two researchers interviewed workers after World War II and found that workers cited a lack of alternatives for taking jobs and remaining on a General Motors assembly line (Ashton 1955, 212; see also Walker 1952, 85–87).

Factory Working Conditions

Factories allowed bosses to impose discipline and to supervise workers. Economist Stuart Marglin wrote that discipline and supervision meant, "the thought[s] of employers turned to workshops where the men would be brought together to labor under watchful overseers, and to machines that would solve the shortage of manpower while curbing the insolence and dishonesty of the men." Such would promote the direction or and coordination of labor (Marglin 1974, 157; see also Landes 1969, 60; Landes 1966, 14).

Bosses and foremen or forewomen were frequently petty tyrants, although in fairness to them, they often worked alongside their employees. Employers tacitly or explicitly created lengthy sets of rules for supervisors to enforce. Factory rules often prohibited laughing, singing, talking, eating, or, in the case of shopgirls, sitting down. A corset factory's rules stressed that workers coming in late would be fined or even refused admittance; workers required an "excuse ticket" in order to leave the workroom (Cox and Alm 2001, 16).[8] Lunch breaks were often brief and there were no coffee breaks.

The Crowley Iron Works took rules and regulations to an extreme: "[the owner] found it necessary to design an entire civil and penal code, running to more than 100,000 words, to govern and regulate his refractory labor force." The owner defended his policy, claiming that he had been cheated, "by sundry people working by the day with the connivance of the clerks…and paid for much more time than in good conscience I ought and such hath been the baseness & treachery of sundry clerks that they have concealed the sloath & negligence of those paid by the day." Even jobs in light manufacturing, such as Sister Carrie's first day working at a shoe-making factory could become soul numbing.[9] Charlie Chaplin's *Modern Times* and Fritz Lang's *Metropolis* depicted the alienating aspects of mass production, but Adam Smith had identified the changing nature of work decades before Marx (Thompson 1967, 81; Dreisler [1900] 2006, 26–29; Smith 1981, 13–24).

Sometimes industrialists made stunning admissions regarding their attitudes toward workers. Charles Harrah, President of Midvale Steel, testified before the United States House Committee on Labor: "We have the most improved type of machinery now; but we make it a rule to run a machine to break." When asked whether the firm was operating at full capacity, Harrah responded, "Absolutely; yes sir—we have *absolutely no regard for machinery or for men* [italics added]" (Kolker 1928, 89).

Karl Marx understood the simplification of tasks to allow manufacturers to match tasks "to the exclusively special functions of each detail labor." Marx disliked specialization's stripping of a worker's independence that converted the worker "into a crippled monstrosity, by forcing his detail dexterity at the expense of a world of productive capabilities and instinct." Managers in Soviet Russia wanted to put the factory workers under a single roof to enable surveillance of the workers' general discipline and effort but failed to consider the supervision of quality. The Soviets never quite understood standardization of quality products. The well-known Soviet penchant for poor quality ensued (Marx 1961, I:341, 360; Landes 1986, 58; Seabright 2004, 160).

Stuart Marglin disputes the standard story that the division of labor associated with putting-out work and the centralized organization endemic of the factory system arose because of the technical superiority of such process; he, instead, argues that "these innovations in work organizations were introduced so that the capitalist got himself a larger share of the pie at the expense of the worker" and that economic growth camouflaged the capitalist class interest: "the origin and success of the factory lay not in technological superiority, but in the substitution of the capitalist's for the worker's control of the work process and the quantity of output" (Marglin 1974, 62).[10]

Conclusion

Employers with some coercive power over workers all too often treated workers as objects, as means to an end. Such behavior violated Immanuel Kant's ethical precepts, as well reciprocity. Employer-employee relationships evolved across the seventeenth and eighteenth centuries. Employers of the late nineteenth century gradually began ameliorating working conditions but remained loath to relinquish control of decision making.

Employers' attempts to control workers, even when sheathed in a velvet glove, did not placate workers during the late nineteenth century and early twentieth century. All too often the employers' self-interest or ignorance of their workers' sentiments torpedoed well-meaning (or sometimes devious) intentions. Workers began issuing persistent calls for greater autonomy and an end to perceived employer abuses. The relationship between workers and employers was destined to become embroiled in strife and violence. Workers began to organize; the nineteenth and twentieth centuries would see a crescendo of union activity before a marked retreat after World War II.

Notes

1. Arthur C. Allyn, Jr., owner of the Chicago White Sox, said, "The players, it is true, either have to sign a contract with us or not at all, but they do have the privilege of not at all" (U.S. Congress, Senate 1965, 144).

2. Finland recently has announced to implement a basic income for *all* citizens (Worstall 2015, no page numbers).
3. Paul Seabright described an experiment where "workers" and "employers" demonstrated reciprocity. The workers who were employed by generous employers were more likely to invest in learning to do their jobs better (Seabright 2004, 55–56).
4. See Porter for a description of English apprenticeship relationships, good and bad (1982, 100–106).
5. The ghosts of St. Monday persists; a Google search of "buying cars made on Mondays" reveals a range of opinions but precious few facts.
6. Japanese textile manufacturers and Indian employers faced similar struggles (Saxonhouse 1974, 164; Wolcott 1994, 307–308, 315–316).
7. *The New York Times* reported that fast food franchisees sign agreements prohibiting them from poaching workers from other franchises within the same chain (Abrams, September 28, 2017, B1 and B3).
8. "Regulations to Be Observed in the Lewiston Mills," circa 1867, posted at http://invention.smithsonian.org/centerpieces/whole_cloth/u2ei/u2images/act9/New_rules.html, viewed May 8, 2013, 1:50pm). Readers may recall their school days, when hall passes were required to use the restrooms.
9. Sister Carrie discovered that the shoe-making factory was a dirty, comfortless place, replete with "disagreeable, crude, if not foul," washrooms (Dreisler [1900] 2006, 29).
10. Marglin believed owners made themselves indispensable by assigning tasks to workmen, although workmen might have done so themselves (Marglin 1974, 594–595). David Landes argued that Marglin downplayed costs in his condemnation of owners. Marglin did not emphasize the critical role of entrepreneurs in finding ways to mix the factors of production in order to reduce costs.

Bibliography

Abrams, Rachel. "Trapped in Fast Food's Slow Lane." *New York Times*, September 28, 2017, B1.

Ashton, Thomas. *An Economic History of England: The 18th Century* (New York, NY: Barnes & Noble, 1955).

Bailey, Thomas and David Kennedy. *The American Pageant: A history of the Republic* (Lexington, MA: Heath, 1983).

Bloch, March. *French Rural History: An Essay on Its Basic Characteristics* (Berkeley, CA: University of California Press, 1966).

Brody, David. *Steelworkers in America: The Nonunion Era* (Cambridge, MA: Harvard University Press, 1960).

Clark, Gregory. "Factory Discipline." *Journal of Economic History* 54(1), March 1994, 128–163.

Cox, W. Michael and Richard Alm. "Have a Nice! The American Journey to Better Working Conditions." *Federal Reserve Bank of Dallas Reprint from Annual Report 2000* (Dallas, TX: Federal Reserve Bank of Dallas, 2001).

Curti, Merle. *History of American Civilization* (Freeport, NY: Books for Libraries Press, [1953], 1969).

Dreiser, Theodore. *Sister Carrie* (New York, NY: W.W. Norton, [1900] 2006), Norton Critical Edition, Third Edition.

Engerman, Stanley. "Coerced and free labor: Property rights and the development of the labor force." *Explorations in Economic History* 29(1), 1992, 1–29.

Galenson, David. "Rise and Fall of Indentured Servitude in the Americas: An Economic Analysis." *Journal of Economic History* 44(1), March 1984, 1–26.

Geremek, Bronislaw. *Poverty: A History* (Oxford, UK: Blackwell, 1994).

Ginger, Ray. *People on the Move: A United States History* (Boston, MA: Allyn and Bacon, 1975). 2 vols.

Gutman, Herbert. "Work, Culture, and Society in Industrializing America, 1815–1919." In *Work, Culture, and Society in Industrializing America; Essays in American Working-Class and Social History* (New York: Alfred A. Knopf, 1976), 3–78.

Harrison, David. *The White Tribe of Africa: South Africa in Perspective* (Berkeley: University of California Press, 1981).

Hausman, Daniel and Michael McPherson. "Taking Ethics Seriously: Economics and Contemporary Moral Philosophy." *Journal of Economic Literature* 31(2), June 1993, 671–731.

Hellie, Richard. "Slavery." *The New Encyclopaedia Britannica* (Chicago, IL: Encyclopaedia Britannica, Inc., 2010). vol. 27. 288–300.

Hoffman, Phillip. "The Economic Theory of Sharecropping in Early Modern France." *Journal of Economic History* 44(2), June 1984, 309–319.

Kolker, Kenneth. "The Changing Status of the Foreman." *Bulletin of the Business Historical Society* 22(3), June 1928, 84–105.

Landes, David. "Structure of Enterprises." *The Rise of Capitalism* (New York, NY: Macmillan, 1966). 99–111.

Landes, David. *The Unbound Prometheus: Technological Change and Industrial Development in Western Europe from 1750 to the Present* (London, UK: Cambridge University Press, 1969).

Landes, David. "What Do Bosses Really Do?" *Journal of Economic History* 46(3), September 1986. 585–623. Landes. What Do Bosses Really Do?

Lindblom, Charles. *Politics and Markets: The World's Political-Economic Systems* (New York, NY: Basic Books, 1977).

Marglin, Stephen. "What Do Bosses Do? The Origins and Functions of Hierarchy in Capitalist Production." *Review of Radical Political Economics* 6(2), July 1974, 60–112.

Marx, Karl. *Capital: A Critical Analysis of Capitalist Production* (Moscow, USSR: Foreign Languages Publishing House, 1961). 3 vols.

McKendrick, Neil. "Josiah Wedgwood and Factory Discipline." *Historical Journal* 4(1), 1961, 30–55.

McKendrick, Neil. "Commercialization and the Economy." *The Birth of a Consumer Society: The Commercialization of Eighteenth-Century England*, edited by Neil McKendrick, John Brewer, and John Plumb (Bloomington, IN: Indiana University Press, 1982), Vi–262.

Meeks, M. Douglas. *God the Economist: The Doctrine of God and Political Economy* (Minneapolis, MN: Fortress Press, 1989).

Pinchbeck, Ivy and Margaret Hewitt. *Children in English Society. Vol. II: From the Eighteenth Century to the Children Act 1948* (London, UK: Routledge & Kegan Paul, 1973).

Porter, Roy. *English Society in the Eighteenth Century* (Middlesex, UK: Penguin Books, 1982).

Reid, Joseph. *Sharecropping as an Understandable Market Response* (Chicago, IL: University of Chicago Press, 1974).

Saxonhouse, Gary "A Tale of Japanese Technological Diffusion in the Meiji Period." *Journal of Economic History* 34(1), March 1974, 149-165.

Seabright, Paul. *The Company of Strangers: A Natural History of Economic Life* (Princeton, NJ: Princeton University Press, 2004).

Silver, Morris. *Economic Structures of the Ancient Near East* (Totowa, NJ: Barnes & Noble Books, 1985).

Smith, Adam. *An Inquiry into the Nature and Causes of the Wealth of Nations*, edited by R.H. Campbell and A.S. Skinner (Indianapolis, IN: Liberty*Classics*, 1981).

Southern, Richard.W. *The Making of the Middle Ages* (New Haven, CT: Yale University Press, [1953] 1976).

Thompson, Edward P. "Time, Work-Discipline, and Industrial Capitalism." *Past & Present* 38(4), December 1967, 56–97.

Ure, Andrew. *The Philosophy of Manufacturers: Or, An Exposition of the Scientific, Moral, and Commercial Economy of the Factory System of Great Britain* (London, UK: Charles Knight, 1835).

U.S. Congress. Senate. *Professional Sports Antitrust Bill—1965: Hearings before the Subcommittee on Antitrust and Monopoly of the Committee on the Judiciary*, 89th Cong., 1st sess. (Washington, DC: Government Printing Office, 1965).

Walker, Charles. *The Man on the Assembly Line* (Cambridge, MA: Harvard University Press, 1952).

Williamson, Jeffrey. "Urban Disamenities, Dark Satanic Mills, and the British Standard of Living Debate." *Journal of Economic History* 41(1), March 1981, 75–83.

Wolcott, Susan. "Perils of Lifetime Employment. Systems: Productivity Advance in the Indian and Japanese Textile Industries, 1920–1938." *Journal of Economic History* 54(2), June 1994, 307–324.

Worstall, Tim. "Finally, Someone Does Something Sensible: Finland to Bring in a Universal Basic Income." Forbes. December 6, 2015. https://www.forbes.com/sites/timworstall/2015/12/06/finally-someone-does-something-sensible-finland-to-bring-in-a-universal-basic-income#7704773a, viewed September 23, 2017, 12:45pm.

Zinbarg, Edward. *Faith, Morals, and Money: What the World's Religions Tell Us about Money in the Marketplace* (New York, NY: Continuum, 2001).

Zinn, Howard. *A People's History of the United States* (New York, NY: Harper & Row, 1980).

CHAPTER 15

Slavery Throughout History

Slavery was a kaleidoscopic institution that varied across societies and times. Although perhaps not ubiquitous, slavery was certainly prevalent. Attitudes toward slavery changed over time, and the institution was an example of changes in ethical beliefs.

Some of the key ethical issues inherent in slavery revolved around the authority to apply corporal punishment, the economic and moral exploitation, and the potential for abuse inherent within the relationship. The severe imbalance of power within the relationship resulted from or triggered viewing slaves as sub- or non-human or as objects, making unethical behavior almost inevitable. Even kindly slave owners still subscribed to the hierarchical arrangement and often resented slaves who attempted to transcend their role. Some people asserted that slave owners owed duties to their slaves.

Of course, the world has long featured imbalanced relationships between and among people, most fraught with ethical quandaries. What aspects made slavery especially obnoxious to the slaves and, eventually, the abolitionists? Why did an economically viable labor institution largely disappear?

Slavery Around the World

Many slave owners desired slaves to gain status. The household, patriarchal, or domestic slavery was common throughout history. Sometimes the household slaves became, in effect or in reality, members of the

D. G. Surdam, *Business Ethics from Antiquity to the 19th Century*,
https://doi.org/10.1007/978-3-030-37165-4_15

family. Slave owners adopted males and had sex with females (and, quite likely, males, too) (Hellie 2010, 288).

People around the world used slaves. A few examples suffice. After 1727, Dahomey became a major exporter of slaves through its captured port of Whydah. Slaves were usually war captives or criminals, so transporting slaves through Dahomey was a matter of security. On the other hands, slaves were elite goods, so the Dahoman kings exercised control of the trade (Arnold 1957, 171). Amalfitans traded slaves with North Africa, although Amalfi (along the southern Italian coast) "was not in direct contact with the great supply market of Central Europe; slaves, in short, were more an occasional than a regular item of trade" (Citarella 1968, 538). In the Aztec world, slavery was widespread. Men could sell themselves or their children into slavery; slaves were allowed to buy slaves. Slavery existed along the northern Pacific coast region of present-day British Columbia. The slaves, taken in raids, produced wealth and status for their owners. Slavery persisted in Saudi Arabia into the twentieth century. King Ibn Sa'ud's 1936 law "restated the teachings of the *Qur'an*...[and] required owners to register slaves with the government and licensed slave traders" (Chapman 1957, 124; Carlson 1994, 348; Hellie 2010, 294).

Concubinage was a common form of slavery, as slave owners sought female slaves to satisfy sexual and power urges but also to perpetuate family lineages. Many societies stipulated that children born from such relationships were free (and sometimes the concubine, too), but the American South and Rome were exceptions; these societies maintained that mother and child remain slaves. The insider/outsider concept found in Islam might have ameliorated the plight of African slaves in North America, but American slave owners often could not or would not view their slaves as potential insiders. Northern European slave masters and their slaves were separated, and the slave owners proclaimed that Africans were incapable of operating as free individuals (Hellie 2010, 296–298).

Slavery in the Ancient World

Slavery differed across ancient societies, as shown in previous chapters. Deuteronomy 15:12–15 placed a limit on the duration of bondage. "If your brother, a Hebrew man, or a Hebrew woman, is sold to you, he shall serve you six years, and in the seventh year you shall let him go free from you. And when you let him go free from you, you shall not let him go empty-handed; you shall furnish him liberally out of your flock, out of your threshing floor, and out of your wine press; as the Lord your God has blessed you, you shall give to him."[1]

Paul in the New Testament took a different stance. He advised Philemon to take back Onesimus, Philemon's runaway slave, "without suggesting any change in his status. But [Paul] exhorts Philemon to treat Onesimus as a 'dear brother,' which scarcely suggests the continuation of a master-slave relationship" (Philemon 1:16; Hay [1989] 2004, 85). Millenniums later, this passage and Deuteronomy 23:15–16 would appear to repudiate the infamous Fugitive Slave Act of antebellum America, the Dred Scott case notwithstanding.

Jewish rabbis observed that the Torah acknowledged slavery but recognized an inherent contradiction: "a slave was in many ways treated as a chattel, a 'thing,' yet he was also a human being." The writers of the Torah were unable to resolve the conundrum but depicted slavery as both "inherently evil" and recommended "humanizing" the institution. There were some individuals who repudiated slavery.

People fell into slavery in various ways, including birth, debt, or as prisoners of war. "The *eved ivri* was likely a person who paid off a debt by serving his master….If *eved ivri* meant a man from an Israelite tribe (rather than a person belonging to a particular class of civil servants) then it is clear that the Torah aimed at wiping out slavery from the Israelite people and considered such bondage, if voluntarily perpetuated, an affront to the dignity of God's people." Deuteronomy 23:16 stressed that, "It should further be noted that an escaped slave was not to be returned to his master—another clear indication that the Torah's acceptance of slavery showed ultimate reservations about the institutions as such." Slavery persisted, however, and the Rabbis came to accept it as part of life; they urged redeeming or contributing to ransoming Jewish slaves. Such activity became a common "and all too often necessary adjunct of Jewish life in Talmudic and medieval days, and the Psalmist exalts God as the one 'who sets the prisoners free (146:7).'" All this meant that, Jewish memories of being enslaved in Egypt permeated their attitudes toward slavery (see Job 31:15) (Plaut 1981, 570–571).

Did Hebrew slave owners follow the edicts cited in Deuteronomy and Exodus? Apparently not, as the prophet Jeremiah excoriated slave owners for violating the edicts. In a scolding manner—he refers to the Lord's past admonitions (although one can easily imagine that Jeremiah implicitly meant *his* own admonitions) that were ignored—he groused, "You recently repented and did what was right in my eyes…but then you turned around and profaned my name when each of you took back his male and female slaves, whom you had set free according to their desire, and you brought them into subjection to be your slaves." Jeremiah 34:15–20 proclaimed that big trouble was ahead for such recalcitrant slave owners by describing, perhaps with too much relish, the unpleasant fate awaiting, concluding, "I will make like the calf which they cut in two and passed between its parts...and I will give them into the hands of their enemies and into the hands of those who seek their lives. Their dead bodies shall be food for the birds of the air and the beasts of the earth."

Moses Finley describes the variability in slave experiences in the Greco-Roman world. "The swineherd Eumaeus, the favourite slave of Odysseus, was property; so was Pasion, the manager of the largest banking enterprise in fourth-century B.C. Athens, who soon enough was freed and eventually was honoured with Athenian citizenship; so was any slave working in the notorious Spanish mines...so was Epictetus, the Stoic philosopher...originally the slave of one of Nero's freedman-secretaries." As Finley points out, slaves were punished, they resisted, and sometimes they escaped, as did animals. Owners of slaves were liable for their slaves' negligence in causing bodily harm and property damage, just as owners of animals. He identifies two key elements that differentiated slaves from animals: masters could force slaves to have sex and possibly beget children and the murder of a slave "required some form of purification." Slaves, however, sometimes gained freedom and rose to economic prosperity, if not full citizenship (Finley 1973, 62–63).

In the eastern Mediterranean and Near East, contractual slavery or bondage and the credit market were intertwined. A prospective borrower could pledge himself or a family member as collateral for a loan. If the borrower defaulted, then the creditor could seize the borrower, as related in 2 Kings 4:1, when a widow implored the prophet Eli'sha to help her: "the creditor has come to take my two children to be his slaves." Selling oneself into bondage occurred in the third millennium in Mesopotamia and in first millennium Assyria. The Assyrians inserted a clause guaranteeing the buyer against the incapacitation of a slave from disease for 100 days and for other misfortunes. Such contractual bondage for debts was either written into the loan contract or was statutorily imposed. Hammurabi's Code stipulated three years. Slaves could be transferred between owners (Silver 1983, 68–69).

Selling oneself or a family member into bondage was not necessarily the result of destitution. For some people, debt bondage was a way to accumulate some capital for economic self-improvement. To be certain, contractual slavery held benefits for the lender: tighter control over the slave's services and consumption level and the ability to transfer slaves to other owners, affording the original owner liquidity from owning the slave. The Greeks, though, began to disapprove of self-bondage. Aristotle lauded Solon for prohibiting such actions at the close of the seventh century BCE. The Romans recognized the right to sell oneself into bondage, with Trimalchio's guest in Petronius' *Satyricon* stating that although he was the son of a king, he put himself into slavery in order to end up a Roman citizen. Although Morris Silver questioned Dio Chrysostom's claims that "tens of thousands of men sold themselves into slavery," the practice was known; the practice, however, may have been tied to the Roman practice of peculium, whereby slaves borrowed working capital from their masters. Trimalchio was a fictitious character, but many commentators view the character to have been representative of a type of Roman character (Silver 1983, 70–71).[2]

Slavery, Roman Style

Slavery in Rome was often harsh and cruel, reflecting Roman life in general. Slaves in Rome, though, possessed a level of discretion denied slaves in the colonies that later became the United States. Slaves in Rome, although under the aegis of their masters, could seek occupations that used their particular skills. Slaves could acquire wealth and responsibility, and owners preferred an educated, smart slave with initiative to a more brutish slave. Part of the difference between Roman and American slavery was that many Roman slaves were victims of military defeats and included highly educated Greeks and other people from around the Mediterranean basin. "Roman slavery was at the opposite extreme from slavery in the southern United States; many Roman slaves—like free workers—responded to market incentives" (Temin 2013, 121).

There were two ways that labor becomes an item for trade: being sold (slavery) or being hired (wage labor). Economist John R. Hicks singled out Rome as an example (surprisingly enough, given Rome's reputation for cruelty) of slavery that was mitigated to some degree. For some members of the early Roman Empire, slavery was preferable to being free; slaves often had more opportunities for advancement than did free labor. The funerary inscriptions in various Italian cities reflected the disproportionate number of freedmen (former slaves) among those honored (Hicks 1969, 123; Temin 2013, 132–133, 138).

Peter Temin observed, "The sharp separation between slave and free characteristic of modern slavery was not observed in ancient Rome, and some ambitious poor people sold themselves into slavery as a long-term employment contract that promised, however uncertainly, more advancement than the life of the free poor. This action, however rare in the early Roman Empire, was more like the process of apprenticeship in early modern Europe than American slavery; it revealed the integration of Roman slavery with the overall labor market." A slave with business talents was a highly-prized possession, if one was to refer to a human as a possession. Owners used positive incentives with talented slaves, encouraging their slaves to gain education and to obtain attractive jobs. In addition, by endowing slaves with a peculium and freedom, masters gained a valuable ally (Temin 2013, 121–122, 129, 199–200).[3]

The laws of manumission were, according to Richard Hellie, "the litmus test of a particular society's views of the slave." Islamic societies, resting upon Hebrew prescriptions, generally mandated manumission after a number of years, roughly the time it took for an "outsider" to transform into an "insider." Other societies gave masters carte blanche to manumit slaves; in some cases, masters had to manumit their slaves, when the slave converted to the owner's religion. Proximity between the slave and master was a key factor in whether a slave received manumission. Household or domestic slavery quickly "converted the outsider into an insider." Many slave societies mandated manumission after three generations. The *Qur'an* recommended manumission of children born to slaves, as did the Aztecs (unless the child's parent or parents were traitors). In Thailand, many owners freed their slaves in their wills (Hellie 2010, 296).[4]

One historian observed that in ancient and modern slave societies, "gift exchange affected not only the relationship of masters and slaves but also the manumissions by which masters might give slaves freedom." In many slave societies, the master maintained a relationship with the emancipated slave, usually a subservient client relationship. Such relationships did not exist in the American South. "The gift conferred a dishonor, aggravated by racist fears that consigned them to a lower status than their counterparts in other slave societies." Since slaves could not give gifts to their masters, "'an emancipation that assumed the form of a gift paradoxically reconfirmed the master-slave relationship.' Consequently the 'images of Abraham Lincoln and Northern soldiers as great emancipators—as bringers of the gift of freedom to the downtrodden—actually worked both to liberate and to degrade newly freed slaves'" (Morgan 2004, 129).[5]

Christian Attitudes

Catholic Fathers considered slavery as a "respectable private-property institution." They accepted slavery as part of the world (indeed, some saw it as both punishment and remedy for sin), and what doubts they had were no more than their concerns about private property itself. The early Church owned slaves. The Church did not advocate mass enfranchisement of slaves, although it considered owners who liberated their own slaves as meritorious, but especially when the owners were pagan. In fact, some pagan philosophers, excepting Plato and Aristotle, condemned slavery. The early Fathers, though, did insist on more humane treatment of slaves, because, unlike many other people, the Fathers viewed slaves as equals to their masters in the eyes of God: "the Fathers insisted that slavery was a merely material condition not affecting the spiritual quality of the slave….The only real slavery was the slavery to sin and subjection to the evil passions; the virtuous slave had more true freedom than the sinful master" (Viner 1978, 26).

St. Ambrose did not advocate an end to slavery nor did he encourage slave revolts. He propounded reasons why slavery might have been beneficial. The first was that "he who cannot govern and control himself ought to serve and be in subjection to one who is more prudent, that he may be governed by his counsel, and not stumble and fall through his own rashness and folly." In a similar vein, he suggested that "wild people" might benefit from the discipline of a strong and wise ruler. Slavery only affected the body, but "the mind is free." Slavery is also an opportunity for a person to display humility, forgiveness, obedience, and other virtues. Of course, he made the obligatory admonition that masters should treat their slaves as human beings (Dudden 1935, 544–545).

Thomas Aquinas, for instance, affirmed that slavery was not in accord to the highest intent of nature, but it conformed to the second intent of nature that took into account man's limited capacities. He could even find support for the Roman rule stipulating that the offspring of a free man and bond woman was a slave (apparently the possibility of a child born to a free woman and bond man was not considered). Luther and Calvin also did not repudiate slavery. There were, however, some non-conformists. The controversial perfectionist and millennialist sects, who tried to live sin-free lives, emphasized mutual love and recognition; their beliefs precluded them from treating people "as objects, even as objects with souls" (Davis 1992a, 21). The proscription against treating people as objects or as means to an end, of course, was a basic tenet in most business ethicists' belief systems.

Treatment of Slaves

The treatment of slaves would shock twenty-first-century ethical sensibilities. Slave owners did not always have complete property rights over their slaves, although some Neolithic and Bronze Age societies denied slaves even a right to life. Ancient Egypt was an example where slaves were killed to accompany their masters; other societies practiced similar burial traditions. On the northwest coast of America, the Tlingit might kill slaves to show off their disdain for property and wealth; the Tlingit also sometimes killed economically valueless slaves—old or unwanted. In many societies, an owner could kill his or her slave without legal repercussion, but the Hebrews, Athenians, and Romans often restricted the right of slave owners to kill their slaves. The Code of Justinian made it punishable (by death) for an owner to kill his slave using torture, poison, or fire (which still left a myriad of other nasty ways to kill a slave). The Ch'ing Chinese law held a master accountable for killing his slave, and the punishment increased if the slave had done the owner no wrong. The Aztecs sometimes executed slave owners, who killed their slaves.

More recent slave societies proscribed brutal and sadistic murder of slaves by their owners, because such actions upset other slaves and might instigate rebellion. Although codes in the American South suggested forced sale to another owner or even emancipation for mistreated slaves, such instances were probably rare. Laws, though, were uniformly harsh with regard to a slave who killed his or her master. Possibly as a deterrent, Roman law stipulated that all the slaves living in a household be killed, if a fellow slave killed their master.

Richard Hellie pointed out that, "Homicide of a slave by a stranger was a revealing test of a society's attitude toward the slave." In some cases—Mesopotamia and Islamic states—the killer simply paid the owner for "the loss of his property." Roman Law eventually recognized that a slave was a person, so killing a slave was a crime under the Code of Justinian. Even in North America between 1770 and 1830, "the killing of a slave was equated in common law with the murder of a white person." Of course, "Laws were uniformly harsh when a slave killed a stranger who was a freeman." Roman law decreed that masters could not kill their slaves, because the state "had no intention of surrendering to the masters and mistresses of slaves its monopoly of cruel and unusual punishments….[The Roman system] was calculated to keep humanitarian sentiments in deep freeze" (Hellie 2010, 294–295; Brown 2012, 60–61).

Many owners would probably assert that slaves were "lying, lazy, dull brute[s] who had to be kicked or whipped." Sea captains might have said similar about their crews and responded with negative incentives (although calling whipping, branding, or any of the other brutal punishments available to both slave owners and sea captains "negative incentives" would be too much of an euphemism). Beating and whipping ran the risk of further demoralizing or physically injuring their slave property. Slave owners used regimentation, such as the notorious gang system, for particular crops (Hellie 2010, 298). Other owners resorted to more positive inducements.

Being a free laborer was no guarantee of good treatment. Service in the British Navy up to the times of the Napoleonic Wars was deemed worse than being in prison. Samuel Johnson remarked, "no man will be a sailor who has contrivance enough to get himself into jail; for being in a ship is being in [gaol] jail, with the chance of being drowned." The War of 1812, of course, hinged, in part, to American irritation at British impressments of sailors from American vessels. American sailors went to undue lengths to avoid serving, including maiming themselves (Boswell 1953, I:151; Berton [1980] 2012, 37). Even British citizens swept into the British Navy had reason for complaint. Food was poor, and discipline was draconian. Floggings and harsh treatment were trademarks of most navies. The ship's captain held power of life and death over the crew. Aside from Johnson's gibe about drowning, being on a warship during battle was a truly terrifying experience.[6]

Slaves Versus Free Labor

Although modern people own the right to their labor, being a free labor in the past was often harsh. There were unethical behaviors in the relationship between employers and employees. Slavery differed across societies and often was similar to free labor with respect to conditions and remuneration:

> The Marxian term, wage slavery, emphasizes how hard it is to represent labor conditions by a simple binary comparison, since the term, slavery, was used to express the limitations of choice by 'free' workers: 'The worker *appears* to be free because he is not bought and sold outright. He is sold piecemeal by the day, the week, or the year. Moreover he is not sold by one owner to another, but he is forced to sell himself in this fashion. He is not the slave of a single individual, but of the whole capitalist class. As far as the worker is concerned, however, there can be no doubt as to his servile status (Engels 1958, 93).'

A longstanding controversy revolved around the relative status of free labor and slaves. The Greeks unfavorably compared free labor with slavery. Apollo and Poseidon, gods no less, recalled working for Laomedon for a "stated hire," but after building walls for the Trojans and herding cattle, they were bilked: "headstrong Laomedon violated and made void all our hire, and sent us away, and sent threats after us. For he threatened to hobble our feet and to bind our arms, to carry us away for slaves in the far-lying islands" (Homer [1951] 1974, 430).

Being landless was a despised situation. Moses Finley points out that *thetes*, although free men, held a precarious perch in Greek society. Slaves were attached to an *oikos*; landless free men were susceptible to crop failures, compulsory army services, and the vagaries of civil and foreign turmoil. Landless free men often ended up in debt bondage in both Athens and Rome; these men pressed for a prohibition of such bondage. Such debtors often found themselves trapped in bondage for years, even beyond their tenure if they were still in arrears. The plight of men enmeshed in debt bondage, then, seems not too unlike that of many slaves. Greek and Roman casual laborers led even more precarious lives, as they depended upon meager earnings from seasonal harvesting and or acting as porters or construction workers. Few, if any, employers hired semi-permanent workers (Finley 1973, 66–73, 108). American southerners boasted that their slaves were treated better than free labor toiling in northern factories.

Slavery, American Style

Although slavery in the American South was, in many ways, harsher than in other societies, one factor stood out. Because the Constitution prohibited the importation of slaves after 1808, the huge increase in the number of slaves between 1790 and 1860 was a result of natural growth. As Richard Hellie observed, "the slave population of the South expanded enormously (almost six-fold)…one of the fastest rates of population growth ever recorded prior to the advent of modern medicine. Paradoxically, although the Southern slave regime was one of the most dehumanizing ever recorded, it was one of the most favourable on record demographically, because the nutritional and general living environments were highly conducive to explosive population growth" (Hellie 2010, 298). To say this is not to condone slavery, of course, but to remark on one of the paradoxical aspects of the institution in the United States.

Jefferson Davis, president of the Confederate States of America, and his elder brother Joseph, for instance, maintained unique relationships with their slaves. Joseph Davis retrieved Ben Montgomery, after the young man ran away. Davis realized Montgomery's abilities and, in violation of the law, educated him. Montgomery became a trusted slave, who eventually became the manager of Joseph Davis' plantation and an entrepreneur. Montgomery eventually came to oversee Jefferson Davis' plantation. Jefferson Davis, who treated people subordinate to him in social or military status with kindness and consideration (or condescension), but who had difficulty with equals or superiors, emulated his brother's treatment of slaves. For the younger Davis, James Pemberton assumed the role of Ben Montgomery and had responsibility for running Jefferson's Brierfield plantation. Davis refrained from corporal punishment and allowed his slaves some self-governance. When Davis left for Montgomery, Alabama, to assume the presidency of the Confederate States of America, he entrusted Ben Montgomery with running the plantation. After the war, Davis sold the plantation to Montgomery. All of which does not deny the underlying element of coercion involved (Davis 1992b, 79, 661). One of the inconsistencies of nineteenth-century Anglo-Americans was their attitudes toward Asians and freedmen. According to many white Americans during the postbellum decades, Asians worked too hard and freedmen worked too little. The white Americans were difficult to please.

Slavery, Brazilian Style

Brazil was the last country to officially outlaw slavery (1888). The experiences of Portuguese mine operators in the Rio das Velhas region organized as the Minas Gerais demonstrated the varying nature of slavery throughout the western hemisphere. The Portuguese enslaved some of the natives, a few Chinese and Europeans, but mostly Africans from Benin and Angola. The mixture of Angolan and Benin slaves, though, had a side benefit for owners: slaves from the different regions had difficulty fomenting revolts, since each group did not want to follow a leader from the other group. Mining gold was hard work. Slaves stood in cold water during the hot summer months: The mortality rate was ferocious. Estimates of a slaves' expected working life ranged from 10 to 12 years. In addition, the operators seemed rather callous in supplying food, skimping on both quantity and quality.

On the other hand, slaves were given Sundays to work on their own plots of land or to mine for gold; slaves could lawfully own gold. Some slaves became goldsmiths; Portuguese masters taught goldsmith slaves the art of adulterating their products to make it appear more valuable; they did this in the hopes of defrauding English and Dutch rivals, but the corruption disrupted government attempts to mint coins. Gold dust was easy to conceal, so many slaves, through their efforts on their own behalf or through embezzlement, purchased their manumission. Slave owners who took slave women as concubines granted a *carta de alforria* [a letter of manumission] to the woman and her offspring. As many mine owners found gold mining unprofitable, they sometimes found it cheaper to manumit their slaves. Slaves who wanted immediate freedom found it relatively easy to flee, as the backlands beckoned. The permission to carry gold dust facilitated escapes, as did the lack of patrols and security to stymie escape attempts. Another factor helped slaves: tavern and store owners were often willing to accept gold in return for abetting slave escapes.

These factors created a different relationship between masters and slaves. "[T]he relationship between master and slave was likely to be more personal than on the plantations. Moreover, the dependence of a miner on his slave was so great that by his behavior a slave could literally make or break his master." The law made masters responsible for the misdemeanors and criminal acts of their slaves. Slaves sometimes purposely broke the law, knowing that their master could not pay the fine. In such cases, the slave was auctioned to a new master. Slaves could also gain their freedom by accusing their masters of not remitting the quinto gold tax to the government. Because of these factors, "masters in the mining areas were unusually tolerant of slaves' misdemeanors." One observer wrote, "these Americans [Portuguese miners] regard their blacks as demigods" (Russell-Wood 1977, 66–68, 73–74, 78–79, 81–82).[7]

Slavery in Africa

Who were the enslaved? A few were people who chose slavery over starvation during famines; others were criminals or "persons with poor political judgment, who would otherwise have been exiled or executed by their own societies." Many were captured in wars. Africa was a bustling slave trade region. Islamists, Christians, and Africans participated in various ways. Slavery under Islam varied considerably. In many cases, Islamic slavery supplanted pre-existing slavery. Africans exported slaves from sub-

Sahara to the Islamic world and around the Indian Ocean. The trade to the New World occurred late in the history of African slavery (roughly 1500 with European exploration of the west African coast en route to India), so the trade from Africa to Islam involved many more slaves (but over a longer period) than the cross-Atlantic trade. According to Richard Hellie, the New World trade proved "highly complementary." African slave owners wanted women and children for lineage and status and usually killed male captives because of the security risk. The New World, on the other hand, preferred male slaves of prime age. The ironic outcome was that, "The transatlantic trade…saved from certain death many adult males who otherwise would have been slaughtered outright by their African captors." When the trans-Atlantic trade ended in the early nineteenth century, a few African societies started using captured males in productive work (Hellie 2010, 290).

Because much of Africa featured abundant land versus a relative scarcity of labor, slavery was longstanding in sub-Sahara Africa, although it was less brutal than American-style slavery. Historians Robert Thomas and Richard Bean compared it to manorial Europe; at times slaves were expected to help defend their masters' land, so masters had reason to tread lightly with their slaves. Some of the slaves were already slaves, whose former owners found it more lucrative to sell rather than to retain them as slaves; in other words, a proportion of the slaves simply exchanged masters. Local rulers might have been tempted to enslave their own people, but two constraints operated to curtail such impulses: civil unrest and the potential weakening of the ruler's ability to defend his territory if too many males were enslaved.

Thomas and Bean pointed out that for slaves whose fate would have been immediate death, had there been no American outlet: "It is difficult to see how these particular slaves were made worse off by the Atlantic slave trade.…If this had been the only source of slaves there could be no doubt that Africa gained from the slave trade. However, persons under sentence of death [or male war captives] composed only a small part of the slaves exported" (Thomas and Bean 1974, 905–907).

The Trans-Atlantic Voyage

The trans-Atlantic slave traffic was notorious for the high mortality rate among slaves. Some historians claimed that ship captains, trying to maximize profits, skimped on food and health measures, but these writers sometimes neglected that fact that dead slaves brought no profit. Although the captains were not solicitous toward the humanity in their charge, they did have an interest in conveying as many slaves alive as possible within the constraints they faced. The question arises, "why slave mortality was so high on average and what factors led to normal variations in the rates?" Ship captains decided how many slaves to cram into the holds of their vessel and how much provisions to load; these decisions "could affect the number of slaves delivered alive in the Americas (on average)." Economic historians Raymond Cohn and Richard Jensen noted that non-slave ships had fairly low mortality rates. The vessels transporting convicts to Australia had death rates of about 10% in the 1790s but only 1% decades later. They attributed this to "paying captains a fixed amount per convict delivered alive rather than per convict boarded." After England emancipated the slaves on the British Caribbean Islands, planters sought labor from India. The mortality rates on these voyages were similar to those experienced on the slave trade, but the really striking fact was that the mortality rate of Indians was higher on the return than on the outbound trip. "Obviously, the Indian servants were more valuable economically before they had fulfilled their contract than afterward. This idea was implemented in at least one case by increasing crowding and lowering provisioning on the return voyages relative to the outward voyages" (Cohn and Jensen 1982, 270–272).[8]

As an example of changing business ethics over time, slave trading was considered "just another business" until the early 1800s. Then again, some captains of slave ships later refused to engage in further slave voyages. Ethics aside, the ship captains considered the prices of slaves and provisions in making decisions, including where and how many slaves to buy at each port, how much provisions to load, and which destinations to sail for. Ship captains had a general idea of the average duration of a voyage between different ports, and they undoubtedly factored in additional supplies in case conditions proved unfavorable. However, stocking an inordinate amount of supplies to ensure that the ship would never run out was uneconomical (Cohn and Jensen 1982, 273–274). Even if the ship captain's plans were rational, exceptionally bad conditions could turn a profitable voyage into a losing endeavor, as mortality rates rose and the number of live slaves delivered fell, thereby cutting into anticipated profits. Although the slave trade had risks, ship captains appeared to have acted rationally (but not morally) in making decisions.

One of the first steps in ameliorating the conditions of the Atlantic crossing was the British Parliament's enactment of Dolben's Act in 1788; the act limited the number of slaves that could be carried in a vessel, depending upon the vessel's size. In addition, slave vessels were now required to carry a surgeon to care for the Africans (and, presumably, the crew) and to keep a detailed journal listing deaths and the causes. Finally, the act created "a system of bonuses to ship captains and surgeons." Parliament passed the act after lengthy hearings regarding conditions on slave vessels. Anti-slave advocates, as with many advocates, sometimes exaggerated the severity of the conditions or made erroneous assumptions and conclusions. Of course, the conditions were often so deplorable that no exaggeration was needed. "Critics of the trade emphasized conditions on board ships, especially tight packing and inadequate provisions. Defenders of the trade pointed to large differences in the share of slaves who died by region of embarkation in western Africa, which suggested that adverse conditions in Africa were largely responsible."

The evidence was mixed on the causes of the high mortality among both Africans and crew members. Some researchers found evidence against the argument that overcrowding was a key element in the mortality; other researchers concluded that insufficient provisions contributed to high mortality, when a voyage proved unexpectedly long. The period when traders accumulated Africans for loading onboard also proved deadly, with gastro-intestinal and fevers claiming many victims both among slaves and crew. Indeed, the rate of death for crew members greatly exceeded that of the Africans during loading and during the trans-Atlantic crossing. Economists Richard Steckel and Richard Jensen's findings suggested the "claim that adverse conditions in Africa were paramount is not supported by our finding that slave death rates were relatively low during loading and the early part of the voyage. Slaves destined for the West Indies were not driven to the point of poor health in Africa, only to die in large numbers shortly after loading."

Steckel and Jensen confirmed the argument that African conditions were important to slave health, as slave mortality varied considerably by region of embarkation. "Yet most slaves died after the voyage was well underway but before cuts in provisions were likely….A poor diet in Africa and on ships made the slaves vulnerable to [bacillary dysentery]." Slaves, too, undoubtedly suffered from demoralization and stress. They noted that the medical personnel attempted to reduce mortality by screening slaves before embarkation, cleaning the slave quarters on the ships, isolating sick slaves during the voyage, and other palliatives. Given the scanty medical knowledge of the time (especially the ignorance of the germ theory), some of these actions succeeded despite not being grounded in medical knowledge.

Dolben's Act may have alleviated some of the worst ramifications of overcrowding. Given that the data used by Steckel and Jensen date to the 1790s, after over a century of experience in transporting African slaves, the mortality rates may have fallen regardless of the Parliamentary debates of the 1780s. The terrible conditions onboard slave ships were no secret. Crew members were aware of the risks and, just as economic theory would predict, they demanded and were paid a premium for assuming the risks (Steckel and Jensen 1986, 57–64, 73–75). The Africans, of course, had no recourse to payment for "assuming" the risks; nor, unlike indentured servants, could slaves exercise any choice as to their destinations, which, of course, varied greatly as to mortality and arduousness of the work.

The Shocking Demise of Slavery

Modern Americans take it for granted today that slavery is a moral evil. We cannot fathom how people throughout history even considered slavery a positive good. Yet a small number of activists, primarily in Great Britain and the United States, were the people who succeeded in largely eradicating slavery in North America between the mid-1700s and 1865 in the face of strenuous opposition or passive indifference. People rarely reflect (or even know) that primarily Anglo-Americans decided that slavery was a moral evil and worked to eradicate the institution. Certainly African slaves themselves sporadically struggled to regain freedom or at least a release from the horrors of slavery—from jumping off slave ships, to trying to overcome slave ship crews, to running away from plantations and masters, and, on several occasions, erupting in rebellion. During the Civil War, a large number of former slaves and freedmen actively fought to defeat the Confederate States of America and to end slavery in America.

The abolitionists were moral pioneers in many ways, although to modern sensibilities, they had moral blind spots. Economist Robert Fogel observed, "The alternative to slavery generally embraced by the abolitionists, while morally better than slavery, is to the modern mind still brutal and exploitative." The abolitionists, who held varying opinions regarding race relations and the correct tactics with which to combat slavery, all too often made compromises and skirted ethical bounds by exaggerating the effects of or employing specious arguments regarding slavery. In this, these pioneering social activists were not too different from later activists—the rightness of the cause imbued many with over-exuberance, leading to questionable tactics. The reality in the eighteenth and nineteenth centuries was that building a plurality or majority of voters in favor of antislavery policies meant jettisoning any "pure" antislavery position in favor of a compromise solution. "It is easy to invent an antislavery policy that would be far more congenial to the predominant moral standards of our own age than the policies actually put forward by any of the major historical players. To censure the abolitionists for not full anticipating our values, however, would be foolish. A policy congenial to us could not have built the political coalition needed to destroy slavery. Even policies that now seem conservative were too radical to succeed in 1860" (Fogel 1989, 388).

Why Abolitionism Arose

Why were Quakers, who were noted for their business acumen, as well as to probity and integrity, in the forefront of the abolitionist movement? Were their religious beliefs the sole source, or did their participation in the market inculcate ethical beliefs that made them sensitive to the plight of slaves?

Historian Thomas Haskell suggests that the market induced people to keep their promises and to consider the "remote consequences" of their actions; such people coalesced and began agitating for moral changes. These moral pioneers found themselves in a "new moral universe" in which they recognized not only the immorality of slavery but also their ability and responsibility to relieve the suffering of slaves (Haskell 1992, 141).

Haskell points out that promise keeping appears to be a trait separating man from other creatures, citing Friedrich Nietzsche, who wrote that promise keeping required a "memory of the will" and also a realization of likely chains of events extending into the future. Haskell believes that prior to the eighteenth century in Western Europe, England, and North America, promise keeping was not widespread; by the 1750s, promise keeping became a social norm. The rise of contract law mirrored the rise of promise keeping, as the willingness to enter into a contract required the intention and ability to deliver on a promise in the future. From there, once business participants adhered to the norm of keeping promises and accepting legal penalties for failure to do so, it was a short step to reflect upon one's covenant with God. The Golden Rule assumed greater relevance (Nietzsche [1967] 1989, 58; Haskell 1992, 143–145).

Since conscience and promise keeping pre-dated eighteenth- and nineteenth-century capitalism, Haskell emphasized the importance of the novelty of economic systems that relied upon the expectation (and reality) that people would be conscience-ridden enough to keep their promises. At this juncture promise keeping became a "general social norm" and decision makers could rely upon mutual promises and contractual relations instead of "status, custom, or traditional authority [which] comes very close to the heart of what we mean by 'the rise of capitalism.'" Coincident with the growing prevalence of promise keeping was another lesson taught by the market: "to attend to the remote consequences of one's acts." Successful business owners needed to accurately forecast how their decisions would play out. In a world fraught with uncertainty, investors sought information and clear-headed thinking about business conditions. Promise keeping and considering consequences of actions went hand-in-hand. The "Age of Contract" coincided with an "Age of Principle," according to Patrick Atiyah; out of these coinciding tendencies arose "Men of Principle," whose defining characteristic was the willingness to adhere to "highly generalized maxims of conduct" predicated not on short-term but on long-term consequences.

By the 1800s, Victorian Britons assumed that successful business operators combined foresight with self-restraint. This was a person, who, in the terminology of economists, had a low rate of time preference; in other words, this was a person who was willing to be patient, to forego immediate gratification today for a greater gratification in the future. Although such people have long existed, the growing dominance of the market altered the equation: "Scrupulous attention to remote consequences brings little advantage when life is either fixed by tradition or so lacking in fixity that it defies prediction." Haskell concludes that capitalism was a necessary "precondition" for the rise of abolitionism, as it expanded the "conventional limits of causal perception and moral responsibility that compelled some exceptionally scrupulous individuals to attack slavery and prepared others to listen and comprehend….The argument…is not that markets breed humane action but that in the particular historical circumstances of late eighteenth-century Anglo-American culture the market happens to have been the force that pushed causal perception across the threshold that had hitherto made the slaves' misery seem a necessary evil." He recognized that under mature capitalism, the market might have presented a face "far less supportive of the humanitarian sensibility."

But scrupulosity was a necessary but not a sufficient condition to induce people to act on behalf of slaves. Another necessary condition was that the scrupulous people believed they had the ability to affect the slaves' condition and that the ability (or "relevant recipes" to use Haskell's phrase) was "so familiar that not to use them would stand out as an abnormality." Ways to ameliorate or even to end the slaves' miseries began to appear practical. "The combination of changeability and foreseeability created powerful incentives for the development of a manipulative, problem-solving sort of intelligence." Haskell added, "The abolitionists were notoriously men and women of principle, and…they bear more than a passing resemblance in this regard to Nietzsche's 'sovereign individual.'" People had to learn to "think causally" and to contemplate the "remote consequences of his (or her) actions" (Haskell 1992, 143–144, 147–149, 151–156).

The abilities to foresee distant consequences of one's actions combined with the willingness to delay gratification did not exist in all people. Although the burgeoning British middle class was beginning to develop such abilities, many, if not most, among them smugly (and perhaps accurately) believed that many other people lacked such self-control. By the nineteenth century, such beliefs were ingrained. Herbert Spencer advocated severe prison discipline for inmates who considered only present and not long-term consequences of their action. Recent economic studies of prison inmates suggest that many inmates have a "high rate of time preference," in other words, they prefer things now rather than to wait. Haskell cited Spencer's and Nietzsche's agreement that "people who 'dwell only in the present' live in a world that cannot sustain 'bad consciences' or acute sensations of moral responsibility" (Haskell 1992, 153–155; Spencer 1888, 216–217).[9]

An Exemplar

Quaker abolitionist John Woolman provides an example of Haskell's argument. Woolman lived near Philadelphia and became a successful businessman, but he became dissatisfied with his life (modern-day people might say he had a "mid-life crisis"). He sold off his business and became an itinerant Quaker minister with a unique ability for challenging "the morality of slaveholding without offending slaveholders." His beliefs certainly would not pass muster with modern-day American activists, who all too often antagonize others with their self-rectitude. Woolman advocated abolition not social equality; he conceded that God may have intended

Anglo-Americans to rule over Africans, but that made no difference with regard to God's love for all people, a love that all people were called to imitate. He invoked the Golden Rule; what if Anglo-Americans were slaves (and, indeed, some Europeans were enslaved at this point in time) (Leviticus 19:34; Haskell 1992, 156–157)? He argued, "Had these people come voluntarily and dwelt amongst us, to have called them strangers would be proper. And their being brought by force, with regret and a languishing mind, may well raise compassion in a heart rightly disposed. But there is nothing in such treatment which upon a wise and judicious consideration will any ways lessen their right of being treated as strangers."

Woolman also addressed the slave owners' plaint that they had invested large sums into their slave "property." He conceded that "in a practice just and reasonable such objections may have weight; but if the work be wrong from the beginning, there's little or no force in them. If I purchase a man who hath never forfeited his liberty, the natural right of freedom is in him….How should I approve of this conduct were I in his circumstances and he is mine? (Woolman 1971, 203–204; Haskell 1992, 157).

Woolman exhibited graciousness in conceding that some people simply "were virtually incapable of perceiving their acts or omission as significant contributory causes of the slave's plight." His graciousness likely arose from his reliance upon "the mercies of the Almighty," that reshaped his, to use a modern term, lifestyle. He chose a simpler way of living that freed up much time for pondering Truth. As a businessman, he was troubled, when he sold items that appealed to his customers' vanity; he felt this was contrary to his Christian beliefs. He found that, all too often, merchants sold goods that enticed poor people to incur debt: "Having often observed occurrence of this kind, I found it *good for me* to advise poor people to take such goods as were most useful and not costly." He also noted that "spirituous liquors" and ostentatious clothing got people into financial difficulties. In recounting his awakened concern for the plight of slaves, he recognized a change in his life: "The increase of business became my burden, for though my natural inclination was toward merchandise, yet I believed Truth required me to live more free from outward cumbers, and there was now a strife in my mind between the two." He decided to reduce his business activities and notified his customers of his intent; he began to live a simpler life as a tailor and orchardist (Woolman 1971, 53–54, italics mine).

Woolman spent time touring among slave owners and listening to their defense of slavery. He civilly and with sympathy tried to demonstrate the error of their denial of responsibility for, say, the miseries inflicted upon slaves by the initial enslaver (Woolman 1971, 211, Haskell 1992, 158).

Owners often argued that they were caring for the slaves and that they were not around during the initial enslavement. Woolman debunked this argument; he conceded that Africans fought among and often enslaved each other, but he argued that European involvement intensified the trading in slaves, thereby becoming accessories with slave traders in oppressing Africans who had not injured Europeans. Woolman demonstrated the moral equivalence of kidnapping and selling the slave with purchasing the slave. "[I]t is clear and plain to an upright mind that such distinction is in words, not in substance; for the parties are concerned in the same work and have a necessary connection with and dependence on each other. For were there none to purchase slaves, they who live by stealing and selling them would of consequence do less at it."

Woolman excoriated justifications for buying and selling children of slaves, noting the falsity of such arguments. Claiming the right to own children of slaves piled another wrong upon the original wrong and meant that, "of necessity we must either justify the trade or relinquish our right to them as being children of slaves." Non-slave owners, who adhered to such arguments out of self-interest, were therefore guilty of perpetuating the wrong, too (Woolman 1971, 233–235; Haskell 1992, 158).

Haskell emphasizes that it was natural for Woolman to conclude that he had a responsibility to inveigh against slavery. He notes that Woolman anticipated Adam Smith's *Wealth of Nations* and the growing recognition of the importance of supply and demand considerations. He lauds Woolman's tolerance for people who did not recognize these connections: "Woolman…was ahead of his time and knew better than to be angry when his contemporaries failed to perceive the 'dependence' and 'necessary connection' that seemed so obvious to him." Haskell then sums up his thesis by noting the stunning triumph of the abolitionist movement, against well-entrenched political interests and widespread support for the sanctity of private property, even property rights in human beings. Abolitionists succeeded in eradicating a labor institution that might have resolved employers' need for disciplined labor forces and was still both economically and technically viable. The abolitionists' success was never assured and was contingent upon a concatenation of factors. He concludes, "What it shows instead is the force of the conventions that govern causal perception and moral responsibility, without which we would not know what our interests are or what it means to be responsible" (Haskell 1992, 159–160).

Quaker Agitation Against Slavery

John Woolman was not the only Quaker advocating abolition. Historian Darnold Wax comments that, "There is at least some suggestion that moral objections voiced by the Quakers were supplemented and strengthened by economic considerations." A few Quakers bought and sold slaves as late as the mid-1700s. In the late seventeenth century, Quakers had not yet developed their antislavery stance, but by 1696, Philadelphia Quakers began expressing concern "about Friends who sold slaves 'at the publick Markett place & Outcry.'" The slaves brought little, if any profitability, as the West Indian slaves consigned to the Quakers were "of poor quality." Essentially the West Indians relinquished only worn-out or debilitated slaves; these poor souls fared poorly in the Pennsylvania climate (Wax 1962, 147, 151).

Quakers were not alone in questioning the ethical basis for slavery. Thomas Hobbes suggested that bondage could be so absolute that masters could kill their slaves without legal sanction; by reducing the slave-master relationship to fear, power, and self-interest, "Hobbes removed any ethical basis for condemning a successful revolt." He also eliminated such distinctions as natural merit and assigned status, thereby knocking out the classical and Christian rationales for "unquestioned dominion." John Locke's theory of natural liberty meant that he "had to place slavery outside the social compact." These philosophical ideas began to trouble English and French writers in the 1730s. Montesquieu "put the subject of Negro slavery on the agenda of the European Enlightenment, weighing the institution against the general laws or principles that promoted human happiness, and encouraging the imaginative experiment of a reversal of roles in a world turned upside down" (Davis 1992a, 22). Europeans should not have had much difficulty imaging a world where they were enslaved. Even in the eighteenth century, Europeans falling into the hands of Barbary Coast pirates, for instance, were enslaved. Europeans colonizing the New World also faced the risk of being enslaved, if captured by indigenous people.

Some contemporaries questioned the Quaker's seeming fixation on the plight of slaves, when English free labor was suffering. These critics argued that the Quakers were diverting attention from English workers, in part because Quakers employed free labor in their factories and other businesses. "A Journeyman Cotton Spinner," addressed a crowd of Manchester workers in 1818: "The negro [sic] slave in the West Indies, if he works under a scorching sun, has probably a little breeze of air sometimes to fan him: he has a space of ground, and a time allowed to cultivate it. The English spinner slave has no enjoyment of the open atmosphere and breezes of heaven. Locked up in factories eight stories high, he has no relaxation till the ponderous engine stops, and then he goes home to get refreshed for the next day; no time for sweet association with his family; they are all alike fatigued and exhausted." Other critics accused the Quakers of touting emancipation, because they stood to profit from the abolition of slavery. In reality, such arguments were inaccurate, although Quakers were involved at least indirectly in slavery-tainted industries, especially in their role as merchants (Davis 1966, 54–55, 61–62; see also Thompson 1964, 201).[10]

Quaker concern for the slaves dovetailed with their attitudes toward labor in general. Quakers believed people should engage in honest productive labor requiring discipline. Their vision of labor infused their activities on behalf of prisons and the factory floor. They advocated rehabilitation of prisoners to transform them into productive members of society. For immigrants and indigenous poor, they advocated for policies including freeing immigrants of disease and disorder that could disrupt the established society. Quakers hoped to instill sobriety and self-discipline among the slaves and freedmen. Some of the Quaker efforts were viewed with skepticism, as critics believed the Quakers wanted to free slaves in order to suppress the wages of free labor (Davis 1966, 52–53).[11]

Thomas Haskell took exception to some of historian David Davis' description of the Quakers' abolitionism. He acknowledged that Davis avoided the pitfalls of portraying the Quakers as solely motivated by economic self-interest or that their quest to "improve" labor by inculcating discipline and habits of sobriety did not mean they ignored the struggles of their own labor force. And yet, Quakers were businessmen with experience in dealing with "an 'unruly labor force' prone to 'uninhibited violence' and not yet 'disciplined to the factory system,' late eighteenth-century reformers had strong incentives to formulate an ideology that would 'isolate specific forms of human misery, allowing issues of freedom and discipline to be faced in a relatively simplified model.'" For Haskell, Davis appears vexed that the Quakers seemingly took so long to recognize the comparability of chattel slavery to wage slavery, as did other thinkers. Haskell lists Robert Owen, Charles Fourier, Karl Marx, and Friedrich Engels, who did make the comparison, although these thinkers wrote during the 1800s. The argument that the Quakers could have exerted more concern regarding free labor does not necessarily imply that they did not do so because they deceived themselves.

Haskell asks why slavery suddenly emerged as someone's responsibility, which was the revolution in moral sensibility. Why did Quakers "perceive themselves to be causally involved, either by commission or omission" and why did they feel they had the "recipe for intervention that they and the people around them habitually use[d]" leading to them to "potentially feel [themselves] to be the cause of an evil?"

Haskell associates the rise of capitalism with humanitarianism: "The idea that humanitarianism arose from or depended in any way on the marketplace, with its notoriously lax ethical standards, will seem perversely counterintuitive." Haskell argues that a belief in *caveat emptor* and the law of contract could create "a license for callousness" based on the assumption "that the individual is not only the sole proper judge of his own needs and interests but also their sole proper guarantor." Many people believe that laissez faire capitalism exacerbates the instinct to be greedy, but "greed is not the distinguishing feature of the capitalist," as the desire to acquire occurs in a wide spectrum of societies. "Unlimited greed for gain is not in the least identical with capitalism, and is still less its spirit. Capitalism may even be identical with the restraint, or at least a rational tempering, of this irrational impulse." The capitalist marketplace is a churning maelstrom, and today's winner can become tomorrow's loser. Entrepreneurs struggle to meet changing preferences of customers while all the time trying to minimize costs, but the marketplace features restraint, as "many holds are barred." Frank Knight demonstrated that "the social system of liberalism embodies a genuine ethical ideal and to make clear what the ideal is."[12]

The abolitionists and others of their times viewed the market as inculcating social discipline and "character modification." The marketplace's impersonality represented a new form of social discipline and educational force. "The market altered character by heaping tangible rewards on people who displayed a certain calculating, moderately assertive style of conduct, while humbling others whose manner was more unbuttoned or who pitched their affairs at a level of aggressiveness either higher or lower than the prevailing standard" (Haskell 1992, 115–116, 124–125, 133–134, 137–140; Weber [1930] 2001, xxxi).

Why Abolitionism Prevailed

After decades of studying the economics of slavery, Robert Fogel summarized the moral aspects that made North American and West Indies slavery anathema to many (but, in all likelihood, still only a minority). Fogel was troubled by his co-author Stanley Engerman's and his discovery that slave plantations were economically more efficient than farms in the North. The idea that oppressed slaves could somehow be transformed into an efficient labor force seemed paradoxical. Slave owners, to be sure, relied on the omnipresent threat of draconian physical punishment, even onto death, and sexual exploitation, but they also employed positive incentives to induce productivity. Fogel and Engerman's research confirmed the southern slave owners' boasts that their slaves were better fed and clothed than many free labors in the burgeoning northern factories.

In reflecting upon the antislavery movement's political success, which he noted differed from "the more radical and more frankly ethical position" held by more ardent abolitionists, Fogel thought a *modern* indictment of slavery consisted of four main points revolving around the issues of dominance, denial of economic opportunity, denial of citizenship, and denial of cultural self-identification (Fogel 1989, 301–302, 393–398).

First, allowing individuals of one group to "exercise unrestrained personal domination over another group of people" was the original moral basis for the earliest abolitionists, because, according to historian David Davis, slavery violated the idea that "all men were equal before God." Slaves became, in essence, "the mere extension of his master's physical nature" (Davis 1966, 306; Fogel 1989, 394; Davis 1975, 561). Inherent in this dominance was the potential for cruelty and abuse.

Some commentators observed a paradox regarding slavery. Aristotle believed, "the slave could affirm his consciousness…by partaking of his master's consciousness and by becoming one with his master's desires.… the perfect slave…would be the automatic agent of his creator's will (not an autonomous Adam free to disobey)." This led to the "problem" of slavery: "The more perfect the slave, as Hegel later observed, the more enslaved becomes the master. For the master's identity depends on having a slave who recognizes him as master: the truth of the master's independent consciousness lies in the dependent and supposedly unessential consciousness of the bondsman." Greek philosophers recognized that slaves were tools of their master's wills, but that the slave remained a free soul who could surmount the physical reality and attain true virtue. The master, again, might be the true slave, especially in the eyes of his slave. Christian theology accepted this "transvaluation." "No human master could usurp God's role and demand absolute and unconditional submission from another man. The only slavery that mattered was slavery to sin, from which no man was exempt" (Davis 1992a, 17–18, 20).

But Christianity's view of masters and slaves being enchained by slavery and of the heavenly rewards for the virtuous also contained a conundrum. Concentration upon the heavenly realm meant acceptance of this world's injustices; Ephesians 6:5 stated, "Slaves, be obedient to those who are your earthly masters, with fear and trembling, in singleness of heart, as to Christ." The passage continued by exhorting slaves to render "service with a good will as to the Lord and not to men, knowing that whatever good any one does, he will receive the same again from the Lord, whether he is a slave or free." There was an admonition to masters to treat slaves with goodness, but the passage certainly was amenable for those wishing to maintain the status quo. In any event, New Testament passages provided some succor for slaves, and abolitionists could use other passages to support their arguments.

Although owners occasionally granted favors to slaves, including some incentives to exercise initiative to improve their material condition, such favors remained at the behest of the owner. Slaves usually could not independently seek to improve their material well-being, unlike free labor. Certainly many free workers found it difficult to improve their well-being, but they were not denied the opportunity to try. Although slaves in America may have had better material sustenance than free workers, they were not free to organize through unions or worker cooperatives in order to improve their lot. Certainly many abolitionists and employers in general distrusted associations of free workers; slave owners, too, feared collective action on the part of their slaves, whether it be demands for better conditions or out-and-out uprisings. Slave owners proved ruthless in suppressing organizations and collective actions by slaves. Free labor often experienced improvement in their material prosperity due to individuals improving their own skills, through technological improvements that raised their productivity, or through collective bargaining. Slaves rarely enjoyed such improvement, as the owner kept the gains from productivity improvements.

While most free labor, including freed descendants of Africa, in Great Britain and in America did not have full citizenship rights, such as the right to vote, they were recognized as having various rights to protection of their person, family, and property. Free males could at least aspire to influence government actions. Slaves, to a large degree, lacked even these elementary protections. Fogel notes the "curious anomaly" in slave regimes; slaves under the American or British systems might have better material conditions than slaves in Latin America under the French or Spanish, but the latter colonies had a modicum of civil rights, often—but not always—overseen and moderated by the Catholic Church. Certainly the enslaved indigenous and, later, African populations of South America might have viewed Spanish oppression as differing little from that of the British colonies in the seventeenth and eighteenth centuries.

With regard to the denial of cultural self-identification, slaves often originated from various tribes and regions in Africa, partly by design, as owners hoped to prevent slaves from organizing. Slave owners hoped to mold slaves into "a new kind of worker, well suited to serve as a cog in the large-scale systems of production that they were building." Such cultural memories and remnants that slaves possessed might be tolerated, as long as these artifacts did not interfere with the labor system. To some degree, employers of immigrant and rural workers held similar aspirations for their workforce, but the slave owners went much further in suppressing cultural expression than did employers of free labor. Free labor, especially various immigrant groups, often created vibrant, wide-ranging cultures, unlike the slaves.

Fogel suggested that this new list of indictments against slavery fits the facts better than the abolitionists' arguments; the earlier indictments sometimes rested upon shaky foundations, especially with regard to economic aspects. He believed that the majority of antislavery supporters would have accepted his first proposed indictment but not the other three. He noted that most eighteenth- and nineteenth-century employers, whether antislavery or not, would not have embraced the indictment of denying economic opportunities for slaves. Many of the British employers would have viewed touting economic opportunities for their workforce as tantamount to demagoguery and radicalization. British employers were imbued with the Malthusian idea of a fixed, subsistence wage; attempts to raise the mass of workers significantly above this subsistence was worse than quixotic, it was dangerous. American employers could see that the Malthusian fears were not applicable to conditions in their country, so they boasted about opportunities for common citizens to exercise initiative, work hard, and honesty in attempting to gain prosperity. Northern employers worried that southerners coveted the newly opened western lands; northern factions intended to keep the western lands for free and white labor. Even among ardent abolitionists, there was scant support for full brotherhood and interaction with free or enslaved blacks, so Fogel's third and fourth suggested indictments probably would have been opposed by many antebellum Americans; antislavery candidates had to rebut charges of being "lovers" of African-Americans. Few viewed African-

Americans as social equals; those few, such as abolitionist James Birney, who decried the rampant prejudice argued that "If the professed friends of the colored people avoid social intercourse, *only because they are colored* [italics in original] disregarding their individual intelligence and moral worth—their professions will be suspected—their sincerity will not be trusted in, and all hold on their confidence for good will be lost."

Political reality forced many antislavery radicals to accept compromises in agitating for civil rights for blacks. Many Americans, especially of the dominant Protestant, Anglo-Saxon ethnicities, disavowed cultural self-identification for Irish Catholics, native Americans, freed blacks, slaves, and the growing number of mainland European immigrants. The battle over cultures, of course, remains a reality in twenty-first-century America. Many of the abolitionists, whether explicitly or in the deepest recesses of their being, subscribed to the idea that the Anglo-Saxon culture represented the pinnacle of human development. To some degree, many leading Americans and Englishmen believed that they had a responsibility to inculcate their reigning cultural norms among slaves and free labor (Fogel 1989, 395–405).

Some abolitionists resorted to illegal and immoral actions. New England abolitionists transplanted to "bleeding Kansas" were manipulated by Boston bankers. "The so-called Boston Associates, previously investors in textile mills who supported slave-produced cotton, now arrived on the scene as liberators promising 'practical' antislavery." Men such as John Murray Forbes and Nathaniel and Eli Thayer were interested in a Hannibal and St. Joseph railroad. Because the federal government offered land grant bonds, railroad men and bankers were interested in building the railroad. Forbes clandestinely acquired land-grant railroads, as he coveted the land; he did so illegally, as state charters forbade railroads to have interests in other railroads. The Boston group used chicanery to gain control of the Hannibal and St. Joseph. They also used an emigration aid society to further their scheme. Thayer transformed the society into an antislavery society, in order to coax New Englanders to invest in the aid society. Forbes and the Thayers concocted the "free soil" term to market their railroad ambitions. Historian Scott Nelson observed, "By 1855 abolitionists who had formed the Free-Soil Party were willing to accept the financial, political, and even military help of Boston capitalists. Within a year the aid society began sending rifles to Kansas" (Nelson 2012, 135–139, 142–143).

The American abolitionists ultimately achieved a remarkable if only partial triumph. The election of Abraham Lincoln in 1860 had not signaled the end of slavery; Lincoln, himself, avowed only a determination to contain slavery to its contemporary boundaries. By late 1862, emancipation became an explicit aspect of the war, joining mending and preserving the Union as war aims.

Even to achieve the election of an antislavery candidate, though, antislavery adherents faced what Fogel described as a dilemma and a paradox. The dilemma emanated from political reality: "that led leaders of a just cause to compromise principles, join arms with opportunists, accept immoral propositions, misrepresent their ideas, disguise their real goals, and deliberately mislead, not for careerist advancement or financial gain… but to strike down an exceedingly evil foe." Deception arose when economic conditions demonstrated that abolition of slavery in the West Indies was deleterious to production, just as pro-slavery forces predicted. The antislavery adherents had frequently argued that forced labor was inefficient labor, so the revelation of reduced sugar production was highly embarrassing. Antislavery proponents resorted to new arguments—denying that output had actually fallen or suggesting that former slave owners had failed to make the adjustment to free labor. In order to attract sufficient votes to win elections, the radical abolitionists often downplayed their ultimate goals in favor of publicizing more palatable (at least, to the general electorate) goals, such as merely preventing the extension of slavery to the territories. Such compromises antagonized some of the most radical abolitionists, but these individuals faced the choice of maintaining their principles or failing to achieve any amelioration of slavery.

The paradox revolved around the abolitionists' oft-repeated claims that slavery was inefficient relative to free labor. They often argued that ending slavery would prove an economic boon. Slave owners, of course, rebutted these claims, although sometimes they played along by portraying themselves as "philanthropists" who were helping the Africans, who were really, in their eyes, just children. The abolitionists' refusal to concede the economic realities often exposed them to serious attacks on their credibility and integrity. Pro-slavery supporters, too, manipulated public opinion by appealing to economic self-interest, as many northerners relied on slave-grown cotton and other products for their livelihoods. Any threat to a reliable crop of cotton incited fears among New England and British textile employers and workers in the important cotton textile industry. All too many government investigations demonstrated that freedmen worked fewer hours and less intensively than did their slave brethren, which was, after all, the appeal of forced labor—owners could induce forced labor to do things they would not do voluntarily.

Fogel concludes that the demise of slavery in the United States was not a triumph of good over an inefficient and evil system, but a triumph of good over an efficient and evil system. It was, to use his term, "an act of 'econocide,' a political execution of an immoral system at its peak of economic success" (Fogel 1989, 406–410).

Conclusion

Slavery stands as an example of changing beliefs on what is or is not ethical in business. The abolitionists' triumph presaged changes in attitudes and working conditions for women and children in the decades to follow. The abolitionists succeeded in first putting slave owners on the defensive and then persuading a sizable bloc of voters to elect legislators willing to halt the expansion of slavery. The compromise of the contested 1876 presidential election threw blacks in the South back upon the often-merciless white populace. The abolitionists' triumph, even with lingering racial inequalities, still remains impressive 150 years later.

Despite these advances in human morality, conditions of free workers were not pristine, as shown in the previous chapters. Rising living standards and better working conditions were largely due to increased productivity, often harnessed by a set of sometimes ruthless and unethical industrialists.

Notes

1. Exodus 21:2 simply states the limit of six years and release in the seventh.
2. Michael Rostovtzeff and John D'Arms disagreed about Trimalchio's meaning to Romans (D'Arms 1981, 98–99 and 102–104).
3. Cato temporarily operated a school of slaves, teaching them business skills before selling them (Temin 2013, 129–131).
4. Given the bloodthirsty reputation of the Aztecs, their manumission upon birth is surprising.
5. Perhaps Frederick Douglass and others understood this and urged freedmen to join the Union army and navy to *fight* for their freedom and for slaves to run away to *gain* their freedom. Douglass wrote, "Once let the black man get upon his person the brass letter, U.S., let him get an eagle

on his button, and a musket on his shoulder and bullets in his pocket, there is no power on earth that can deny that he has earned the right to citizenship" (https://www.americancivilwar.com/colored/frederick_douglass.html, 3, viewed November 6, 2017, 10:35am).

6. John Keegan's *Price of Admiralty* (1990) provided many examples of harsh treatment in His/Her Majesty's navy.
7. Although this amelioration of their situation existed, the owners skimping on rations argue otherwise.
8. Shaw (1966, 116, 363 ff) for convict death rates; Tinker (1974, 79–80, 145, 162–163, 175) for Indian workers death rates.
9. An example of research relating criminal behavior and time preference is Akerlund, Golsteyn, Gronqvist, and Lindahl (2014, 11–12).
10. Adam Smith and others thought the Quakers in Pennsylvania didn't own many slaves and, therefore, weren't sacrificing much with their abolitionist stance (Smith 1981, 387–389; see also Viner 1972, 83–83).
11. The Quakers were not advocating the African slaves as social equals, but their racial attitudes were still well beyond those of most of their fellow Britons. Davis remarked that Quakers "quietly dissuaded" their freed slaves from joining the Society of Friends. Quakers hoped the freedmen would "become a diligent, sober, dependable worker who gratefully accepted his position in society." They remained paternalistic toward Africans. To twenty-first-century readers, the Quakers seemed hopelessly chauvinistic, but one must not forget how progressive the Quakers were relative to their contemporaries (Davis 1966, 64).
12. For Knight, the essential social-ethical principle of liberalism was that: "all relations between [people] ought ideally to rest on mutual free consent, and not on coercion, either on the part of other individuals or on the part of 'society' as politically organized in the state." Such a definition left only one legitimate function for the state, which was "to use coercion negatively, to prevent the use of coercion by individuals or groups against other individuals or groups" (Knight 1939, I, 5).

Bibliography

Akerlund, David, Bart Golsteyn, Hans Gronqvist, and Lena Lindahl. "Time Preferences and Criminal Behavior." *IZA Discussion Paper Series*. No. 8168. May 2014.

Arnold, Rosemary, "A Port of Trade: Whydah on the Guinea Coast." *Trade and Market in the Early Empires: Economies in History and Theory*, edited by Karl Polanyi, Conrad Arensberg, and Harry Pearson (Glencoe, IL: Free Press 1957), 154–176.

Berton, Pierre. *The American Invasion of Canada: The War of 1812's First Year* (New York, NY: [1980] 2012).
Boswell, James. *Life of Johnson* (Oxford, UK: Oxford University Press, 1953).
Brown, Peter. *Through the Eye of a Needle: Wealth, the Fall of Rome, and the Making of Christianity in the West, 350–550 AD* (Princeton, NJ: Princeton University Press, 2012).
Carlson, Roy. "Trade and Exchange in Prehistoric British Columbia." *Prehistoric Exchange Systems in North America*, edited by Timothy Baugh and Jonathon Ericson (New York, NY: Plenum Press, 1994), 307–361.
Chapman, Anne. "Port of Trade Enclaves in Aztec and Maya Civilizations." *Trade and Market in the Early Empires: Economies in History and Theory*, edited by Karl Polanyi, Conrad Arensberg, and Harry Pearson (Glencoe, IL: Free Press 1957), 114–153.
Citarella, Armand. "Patterns in Medieval Trade: The Commerce of Amalfi Before the Crusades." *Journal of Economic History* 28(4), December 1968, 531–555.
Cohn, Raymond and Richard Jensen. "The Determinants of Slave Mortality Rates on the Middle Passage." *Explorations in Economic History* 19(3), July 1982, 269–282.
D'Arms, John. *Commerce and Social Standing in Ancient Rome* (Cambridge, MA: Harvard University Press, 1981).
Davis, David. *The Problem of Slavery in Western Culture* (Ithaca, NY: Cornell University Press, 1966).
Davis, David. *The Problem of Slavery in the Age of Revolution, 1770–1823* (Ithaca, NY: Cornell University Press, 1975).
Davis, David. "What the Abolitionists Were Up Against." *The Antislavery Debate: Capitalism and Abolitionism as a Problem in Historical Interpretation*, edited by Thomas Bender (Berkeley, CA: University of California Press, 1992a), 17–26.
Davis, William. *Jefferson Davis: The Man and His Hour* (New York, NY: HarperCollins, 1992b).
Dudden, F. Holmes. *The Life and Times of St. Ambrose* (Oxford: Clarendon Press, 1935). Vol. II.
Engels, Friedrich. *The Condition of the Working Class in England*, translated and edited by W.O. Henderson and W.H. Chaloner (New York, NY: Macmillan Company, 1958).
Finley, Moses. *The Ancient Economy* (Berkeley, CA: University of California Press, 1973).
Fogel, Robert. *Without Consent or Contract: The Rise and Fall of American Slavery* (New York, NY: Norton, 1989).
Haskell, Thomas. "Capitalism and the Origins of the Humanitarian Sensibility, Part 2." *The Antislavery Debate: Capitalism and Abolitionism as a Problem in Historical Interpretation*, edited by Thomas Bender (Berkeley, CA: University of California Press, 1992), 136–160.

Hay, Donald. *Economics Today: A Christian Critique* (Vancouver, BC: Regent College Publishing, [1989] 2004).

Hellie, Richard. "Slavery." *The New Encyclopaedia Britannica* (Chicago, IL: Encyclopaedia Britannica, Inc., 2010). vol. 27. 288–300.

Hicks, John. *Theory of Economic History* (Oxford, UK: Clarendon Press, 1969).

Homer. *The Iliad of Homer*, translated by Richmond Lattimore. (Chicago, IL: University of Chicago Press, [1951] 1974).

Keegan, John. *The Price of Admiralty: The Evolution of Naval Warfare from Trafalgar to Midway* (New York, Penguin, 1990).

Knight, Frank. "Ethics and Economic Reform. I. The Ethics of Liberalism." *Economica* 6(21), February 1939, 1–29.

Morgan, Edmund. *The Genuine Article: A Historian Looks at Early America* (New York, NY: W.W. Norton, 2004).

Nelson, Scott. *A Nation of Deadbeats: An Uncommon History of America's Financial Disasters* (New York, NY: Alfred A. Knopf, 2012).

Nietzsche, Friedrich. *On the Genealogy of Morals and Ecce Homo*, translated by Walter Kaufmann and R.J. Hollingdale (New York, NY: Vintage Books, [1967] 1989).

Plaut, W. Gunther. *The Torah: A Modern Commentary* (New York, NY: Union of American Hebrew Congregations, 1981).

Russell-Wood, A.J.R. "Technology and Society: The Impact of Gold Mining on the Institution of Slavery in Portuguese America." *Journal of Economic History* 37(1), March 1977, 59–83.

Shaw, Alan. *Convicts and the Colonies: A Study of Penal Transportation from Great Britain and Ireland to Australia and other parts of the British Empire* (London, UK: Faber and Faber, 1966).

Silver, Morris. *Prophets and Markets: The Political Economy of Ancient Israel* (Boston, MA: Kluwer-Nijhoff, 1983).

Smith, Adam. *An Inquiry into the Nature and Causes of the Wealth of Nations*, edited by R.H. Campbell and A.S. Skinner (Indianapolis, IN: Liberty*Classics*, 1981).

Spencer, Herbert. "Prison Ethics," *Essays Moral, Political, and Aesthetic* (New York, NY: D. Appleton, 1888), 210–250.

Steckel, Richard and Richard Jensen. "New Evidence on the Causes of Slave and Crew Mortality in the Atlantic Slave Trade." *Journal of Economic History* 46(1), March 1986, 57–77.

Temin, Peter. *The Roman Market Economy* (Princeton, NJ: Princeton University Press, 2013).

Thomas, Robert and Richard Bean. "The Fishers of Men: The Profits of the Slave Trade." *Journal of Economic History* 34(4), December 1974, 885–914.

Thompson, Edward P. *The Making of the English Working Class* (New York, NY: Pantheon Books, 1964).

Tinker, Hugh. *A New System of Slavery: The Export of Indian Labour Overseas, 1830–1920* (London, UK: Oxford University Press, 1974).
Viner, Jacob. *The Role of Providence in the Social Order: an Essay in Intellectual History* (Philadelphia, PA: American Philosophical Society, 1972).
Viner, Jacob. *Religious Thought and Economic Society* (Durham, NC: Duke University Press, 1978).
Wax, Darnold. "Quaker Merchants and the Slave Trade in Colonial Pennsylvania." *The Pennsylvania Magazine of History and Biography* 86(2), April 1962, 143–159.
Weber, Max. *The Protestant Ethic and the Spirit of Capitalism*, translated by Talcott Parsons (London: Routledge-Classics, [1930] 2001).
Woolman, John. *The Journal and Major Essays of John Woolman*, edited by Phillips Moulton (New York, NY: Oxford University Press, 1971).

CHAPTER 16

Conclusion

From primitive people to the end of the eighteenth century, people had learned the benefits emanating from peaceful trade. Although the temptation to lie, cheat, and steal persisted, most people had enough self-control to resist such temptation. Reinforcing such behavior, rulers and theologians promulgated laws governing behavior in business, adding an element promoting ethical behavior: fear of punishment. Philosophers and theologians often gave only grudging approval of merchants' and traders' activities. Of course, not all trade in goods was mutually satisfactory or desirable.

By the end of the eighteenth century, Western Europeans were developing the rudiments of modern economies. The so-called Age of Discovery vastly expanded the scale and extent of international trade. Englishmen now sipped tea imported from the Far East. The transfer of economic power and prestige from nobility and clergy to businesspeople, often of humble origins, proved disruptive, and opponents of such change often appealed to ethical considerations. Was it ethical to incite desire for consumer goods among the masses? The new technologies, such as the steam engine, threatened to displace longstanding forms of production. Was technological change ethical?

Another area of business ethics—relations between employers and workers—remained unsettled (the slave trade being an obvious example). A determined group of abolitionists decided that slavery was morally wrong. Their qualms became one of the fiercest debates regarding ethics,

D. G. Surdam, *Business Ethics from Antiquity to the 19th Century*,
https://doi.org/10.1007/978-3-030-37165-4_16

business and otherwise, of the nineteenth century, culminating in a bloody Civil War. The abolitionists, always a minority in the United States, succeeded in toppling an institution that was well-nigh ubiquitous throughout history, an exemplar of changes in what was considered ethical.

Index[1]

[1] Note: Page numbers followed by 'n' refer to notes.

D. G. Surdam, *Business Ethics from Antiquity to the 19th Century*,
https://doi.org/10.1007/978-3-030-37165-4

C

CPSIA information can be obtained
at www.ICGtesting.com
Printed in the USA
LVHW022236020220
645584LV00008B/181

9 783030 371647